Reading the Early Church Fathers

From the Didache to Nicaea

James L. Papandrea

Paulist Press
New York / Mahwah, NJ

Note to the Reader: For a list of the primary sources Internet links, select the Online Resources tab at www.paulistpress.com and then select the book's title, *Reading the Early Church Fathers*.

Cover Image: Chrysostom and Athanasius, Ridley Hall Chapel, Cambridge, from a photograph by Stephen Day.
Cover design by Cynthia Dunne, www.bluefarmdesign.com
Book design by Lynn Else

Library of Congress Cataloging-in-Publication Data

Papandrea, James Leonard.
Reading the early church fathers : from the Didache to Nicaea / James L. Papandrea.
    p. cm.
Includes bibliographical references and index.
ISBN 978-0-8091-4751-9 (alk. paper)—ISBN 978-1-61643-091-7
    1. Fathers of the church. 2. Christian literature, Early—History and criticism.
I. Title.
BR67.P365 2011
270—dc23

                                                                2011036793

Published by Paulist Press
997 Macarthur Boulevard
Mahwah, New Jersey 07430

www.paulistpress.com

Printed and bound in the
United States of America

Contents

Contents

Contents

For Susie, my soul mate, who brings out the best in me

What kind of yoke is that of two believers,
of one hope, one desire, one discipline, one and the same service?
…Both are equal in the Church of God,
equal at the banquet of God….
Between the two echo psalms and hymns,
and they mutually challenge each other
which shall better chant to their Lord.
When Christ sees and hears such things, he rejoices.
To these he sends his own peace.
Where these two are, he is there himself.
—Tertullian, *To His Wife*

Acknowledgments

I would like to thank those who went before me in the study of early Christianity; although the reader may notice that the endnotes for this volume emphasize the primary sources (and this is intentional, since I believe the primary sources are the place to begin), nevertheless I recognize that I stand on the shoulders of my predecessors in the field. I especially want to thank those who taught me to love the early Church and to appreciate the importance of historical theology: my professors at Fuller Theological Seminary, including James E. Bradley, Marianne Meye Thompson, Ralph Martin, and Colin Brown; my dissertation advisors, Dennis E. Groh and Robert Jewett, and Northwestern professors James Packer and John Wright; my students, including the Holy Family Bible Journey group and the students at Garrett-Evangelical Theological Seminary. Last but far from least, I want to thank those colleagues, friends, and conversation partners who have always supported me, encouraged me, challenged me, debated with me, and taught me so much about the grace of God, including Rich and Karin Vetrano, George Kalantzis, Stephanie Perdew VanSlyke, Glenn Murray, Paul Jarzembowski, Graziano Marcheschi, and my bandmates in *Remember Rome*. Getting to this point would not have been possible without each of you, and I have valued our conversations immeasurably. Finally, to my friends at Paulist Press, thank you for your confidence in me and in this project. May God bless those who read it, and may it draw them closer to God through Christ, in the spirit of James 4:8, *Draw near to God, and he will draw near to you.*

Introduction

The period of the Church fathers (usually defined as the first five centuries of the Christian era) is known as the *patristic* period. Therefore, the study of *patristics* refers to the study of the history and theology of the early Christian Church. We will begin our study with the *subapostolic* age, which, as the name suggests, begins where the apostolic age ends, with the leadership of those whom the apostles had chosen to succeed them. However, we can already see the second generation of Church leaders in the pages of the New Testament, in people like Mark, Luke, Timothy, and John the Elder, to name just a few. Therefore, the subapostolic age overlaps somewhat with the New Testament, and in fact there is no well-defined line of division between the age of the apostles and the next phase of Church history. At the very least, we have to acknowledge that some apostles lived longer than others; thus, the second generation of leadership begins earlier in some places than in others.

Therefore, our exploration begins in the late first century, and though we will not focus on any of the documents that would come to be included in the New Testament, a few of the documents we will examine were written before the latest of the New Testament writings. One must keep in mind that the "New Testament" as we know it was not yet a standardized collection in the second century, and while the formation of the New Testament canon is a subject for a later chapter, we will begin to ask the question why some of the earliest Christian writings were not included in the Christian Bible.

The subapostolic age encompasses two phases of the history of the Church. The first phase is often referred to as the age of the *apostolic fathers*. The second is the age of the *apologists*. Each will be explained as we come to it. For now, however, it is important to note that just as there is overlap between the apostolic (New Testament) age and the subapostolic age, there is also an overlap and no clear dividing line between the time of the apostolic fathers and the apologists within the subapostolic age. Therefore we will not concern ourselves with attempting to define these stages of Church history by a strict time frame. In general, chapters 2 through 4 will cover about a century, from the last decades of the first century to the last decades of the second century, or about 80 CE to 180 CE. This date is a turning point because the first true theologians emerge at the end of the second century, beginning a new era in the history of the Church. After that, the next four chapters will examine the Church up to the early fourth century, leading to the Council of Nicaea in 325 CE. This time is taken as a watershed in Christian history, for reasons that will become evident below. The final chapter will look at the major themes that emerge from the early Church and track their trajectories in the fourth and fifth centuries and beyond.

HOW TO READ EARLY CHRISTIAN TEXTS

Before we can examine the various writers and documents of the subapostolic age, we need to pause for a moment to address the differences between the writings of the early Church and modern literature. It is tempting to read early Christian documents as though they always give us just the facts; often, however, the authors are presenting more of a wish list than a news report. We must keep in mind that most of the early Christian writers were not consciously writing history for our benefit today; they were writing for the people of their own time, to convince them of something. Therefore, the following caveats will be helpful to keep in mind while reading the patristic documents.

Don't assume uniformity across the Roman Empire, or uniformity of development.

Just because a certain document includes evidence of a particular belief or practice, one cannot generalize that belief or practice as if it were universally held by the whole Church. As long as the Church was not legally recognized, communication was limited between cities and especially between the eastern and western halves of the Roman Empire. Even where communication was easy, Christians in different areas did not necessarily agree. Proof of this is in the New Testament itself, where many of the earliest Christian documents (the letters of Paul) would not exist if it were not for conflict and disagreement. Therefore, one must take the origin of a document into consideration when one is trying to determine what the Church believed and practiced. In reality, the old impression of the early Church (based on Acts 2:44), that it was characterized by a uniformity that was eventually lost and never regained, is probably far from the truth. In fact, as it happened, it was most likely quite the opposite. There was certainly a significant amount of diversity within the early Church that over time went through a kind of standardization as the boundaries of acceptable belief and practice were drawn.[1]

In addition to diversity across the empire, we also have to acknowledge a diversity across time. In other words, we cannot assume that traditions developed at the same rate from one place to another. For example, if we can determine that the limitation of one bishop per city had developed in Antioch, that does not necessarily mean that it had also developed in Rome by the same time. The end result is the same: just because a document provides evidence of a belief or practice at a particular place and time in history (assuming that the document can even be dated with accuracy), that does not necessarily mean that the same belief or practice was held in other places at the same time, or in other times at the same place.

Don't assume that something is new the first time it is mentioned.

Unfortunately, there are many early Christian documents that we no longer possess. Some were lost to the decay of time, others were deliberately destroyed. In fact, there may be more documents that we *don't* have than that we do. The documents available to us are called *extant*, in that they thankfully still exist. But the fact that there are many missing pieces of the early Christian puzzle means that we cannot assume that a lack of mention of something in the extant sources is definitive proof that it did not exist. An argument from silence is not evidence of absence. What is more, we cannot assume that the early Christian writers told us everything, or even tried to. Often the beliefs and practices most universally agreed upon in the early Church are the very ones that no one bothered to write about. Why take up precious parchment or vellum writing down what everyone already agrees about? For the most part, issues are discussed precisely because they are not agreed upon.

Therefore, if something shows up for the first time in a certain document written at a certain time, we cannot assume that it did not exist in the Church before then. In fact, it is safer to assume that it was not new, since, as we will see, the early Christians were often skeptical of anything new, and to be accepted, an idea had to have at least an air of age to it.[2] On the other hand, it is also possible that an author will exaggerate the length of time a particular practice has been around in order to enhance its credibility.

Don't assume that a tone of certainty is evidence of agreement.

Since the main reason for writing was often to enter into debate and convince someone of a particular point of view, the authors of early Christian documents will naturally write as though what they are saying is the only reasonable point of view. Here we need to read between the lines, however, and recognize that if, for example, Ignatius says that everyone knows there should be only one bishop in each city, there is obviously some disagreement on that point or he wouldn't bother to write it. If everyone really did know it, they would not need Ignatius to tell them. Therefore, if an early Christian writer takes the attitude that "everyone knows this is how it's always been done everywhere...," you can be sure that someone was out there doing it differently.

When reading patristic texts, always ask yourself why the text was written. Who is the opponent? What is the agenda? In order to properly interpret a document, we must keep these things clear in our minds, especially when the authors resort to ridicule and name-calling (and they do).

Don't assume that the content of early Christian documents is raw information.

Remember that reading patristic texts is not like reading a contemporary history. The aim of early Christian authors was never just to report the facts, but to convince and convert. We must assume that even when they are reporting historical events, the documents already contained at least one layer of interpretation. This is because the ultimate goal of early Christian authors was to promote a Christ-centered view of history, and while it is certainly the case that they believed Christ to be Truth incarnate, this conviction did not lead them to create unbiased accounts. On the contrary, their accounts are biased because they are first and foremost statements of faith. Therefore, early Christian texts of the sub-apostolic period and beyond are not to be treated as divinely inspired. They are the product of sincere but evangelistically motivated Christians attempting to interpret the inspired texts and the events of history, both of which they believed to be a product of God's providence. But, to put it bluntly, they could be wrong at times. A case in point is Irenaeus, who was a brilliant theologian and a pioneer in the interpretation of scripture, but nevertheless had his Roman history wrong and thought that Jesus had lived in the time of Claudius (reigned 41–54 CE).[3] Eusebius of Caesarea, the first Christian historian, combined oral and written records to create his *Ecclesiastical History*, but at times he contradicts himself when reporting competing traditions.

For our purposes, we will still focus on the primary sources as the best record of the history of the early Church, and we will take them as reliable in the absence of contradictory evidence. Eusebius is an especially valuable source, and often he is our only source of information about the Church fathers and their writings, sometimes preserving documents (or fragments of documents) that are otherwise not extant. We simply have to keep in mind that he was a fourth-century writer, in the East, who seemed to have as his agenda a desire to promote the glory of the Constantinian dynasty.

Therefore, we take his word with a grain of salt when he is transmitting traditions from the first centuries of the Church, or from the West, or from sources hostile to his cause. At one point, this bishop of Caesarea was even questioned as to the orthodoxy of his faith (that he might have leaned toward Arianism), and so this, too, must be kept in mind.

CHAPTER 1

The Church in the Roman Empire

WHAT DO WE MEAN BY *CHURCH*?

First of all, we have to ask, What do we mean by *church*? There were no cathedrals, in fact no church buildings of any kind.[1] One could not walk down the street and see "*a* church." Christians met in homes, in groups small enough to fit into one room of a house or apartment. As the group of Christians in any given city grew to the point where they all could no longer fit into one house, the group divided between two or more houses.[2] Therefore, *the Church* was not yet a tangible entity, but more of a concept.[3] It was the body of Christ, understood to be the extension of the kingdom of God on earth, and it existed wherever people gathered in the name of Christ (Matt 18:20).

Initiation into the Church was, of course, by baptism, and thus baptism formed the boundary of the Church. In other words, the Church was the worldwide community of the baptized, and the local expression of the Church was a group of the baptized in a particular city. Baptism required catechesis, so the local communities of Christians quickly devised methods for training initiates and preparing them for baptism. This would eventually evolve into the catechetical "school," which could be very informal or, in the larger cities, a more formal program, something like the philosophical schools of the time. Early Christian catechesis focused more on ethical concerns than theology, and from the very beginning it was extremely important to draw the lines of distinction between Christian morals and the morals of the rest of Greco-Roman culture and society.[4] In the second and third centuries (and beyond), the Church was literally struggling to define Christianity itself. It did so first ethically, then theologically.

Since the Church was understood to be the extension of God's reign on earth, and since the conflict between Church and culture would soon force the Church into an "us versus them" position, the boundary lines of the Church became tied not only to the initiation of baptism, but also to the culmination of that initiation, the table of the Eucharist. In other words, what baptism initiated one into was the mystery of the incarnation of Christ, celebrated—but also participated in—at the eucharistic table. The table of the Lord *was* the kingdom of God on earth, the down payment of the Christian's heavenly inheritance. Therefore, salvation itself, as participation in Christ, was embodied in the Eucharist, and so the Church came to be defined by the table. And since salvation was found at the table of the Eucharist, and the Eucharist was found in the assembly of the Church, the early Christians believed that there was no salvation outside the Church.[5]

RELATIONS WITH JUDAISM

When one reads the New Testament, it is relatively easy to see that the movement Christ started was in conflict with Judaism from the beginning. At first, that conflict was an internal struggle between two competing ways of understanding God's revelation. Both sides were forced to face their irreconcilable differences when the Temple in Jerusalem was destroyed in 70 CE. After that point, the sacrifices ended and the priesthood eventually died out, and Judaism itself had to figure out how to continue as a religion without the sacrificial system that was once central to its faith.

The vast majority of Jewish faithful followed the Pharisees, the experts in the Jewish law who became the Rabbis. They made the written word of God, the *Torah*, the new center of their faith. A minority of Jewish believers went a different way, however. They followed the disciples of a man called Jesus of Nazareth, and these disciples taught that Jesus was himself the *living* Word of God. Those who took this path, of course, would eventually be called Christians, but we have to keep in mind that the concept of "Christianity," as a separate religion, did not exist in the beginning. In the first century, the movement Jesus started was known simply as "the way" (Acts 9:2, cf. John 14:6), and it was only after the destruction of the Temple that Christianity would finally become a separate religion.

All this is to say that Christianity and Rabbinic Judaism are twins from the same parent (Temple Judaism). As such, there was a lot of sibling rivalry, especially at the beginning when Christianity was still seen as a sect within Judaism. During that time, Christians continued to worship in the synagogues with their Jewish family and neighbors, but they also met at dawn on Sunday mornings to do something that would horrify their fellow Jews: they worshiped Jesus. This became the greatest bone of contention between the more traditional Jews and the earliest followers of Jesus. A traditional Jew would wonder how one could worship Jesus and still say one is a good Jew—for Judaism must be monotheistic (Deut 6:4). For the followers of Christ, their liturgical practice would put them on the defensive theologically, forcing them to try to figure out a way to justify the apparent oxymoron of Christian monotheism. The result was the development of doctrine in the early Church, and the answer to the question of Christian monotheism was the doctrine of the Trinity.

Therefore, much of the dialogue between Christians and Jews in the early decades centered around the Christian conviction that Jesus fulfilled the prophecies of the Hebrew Scriptures. Some Jews were convinced by these arguments and converted to Christianity. Many were not convinced and continued to believe that what the Christians were doing was a form of polytheism, and blasphemy against God. Some even felt justified in following in the footsteps of the preconversion Paul as they participated in persecution against their Christian neighbors (Acts 17:5ff). But the persecution of the Church by Jews would give way to persecution by the Roman Empire when the Romans began to take notice of the Church as something separate from Judaism. Ironically, as long as Christianity was seen as a sect within Judaism, the Romans left it alone, either reasoning that it was part of an ancient religion and was probably not a threat, or failing to notice that it even existed. Once Christianity was out from under the umbrella of Judaism, it became perceived as something new and therefore potentially dangerous.

RELATIONS WITH THE ROMANS AND THE BEGINNING OF PERSECUTION

Somewhere around the year 52 CE, the Roman emperor Claudius heard that there was some sort of conflict in the Jewish quarter of Rome. What was probably a conflict between Christian Jews and non-Christian Jews was perceived by the Romans as an internal dispute among the Jews—and in a way, it was. To prevent any possible unrest, Claudius expelled all Jews from the city of Rome, including, of course, Jewish Christians.[6] This is why the apostle Paul encountered Priscilla and Aquila outside of Rome— they had been forced to leave with all the rest (Acts 18:2). But this left the Christian community in the city of Rome in the hands of newly converted Gentiles. Those who had been Christian the longest, who knew the stories of Jesus, and who understood the tradition and roots in Judaism were now gone. This may have been the occasion for the writing of the Gospel of Mark, since the Gentile Christians who remained would need to know the stories. In any case, the fact that the Jews had left Rome, but some Christians remained, demonstrated that Christianity was not simply a Jewish sect. Therefore, even before the final split between Judaism and Christianity that took place after 70 CE, the Romans began to notice the existence of the Church.

The first impressions of the Church on its Roman neighbors were not good, mainly because of misunderstandings. Hearing that Christians ate the body of Christ and drank his blood, some believed they were cannibals. Hearing married Christians call each other "brother" and "sister" led to rumors about incest. The fact that the Christians met at dawn left some thinking they were another mystery cult, like the ones that already existed in Roman society, yet with the distasteful additions of cannibalism and incestuous orgies.[7] Roman writers thought that Christianity was bad for society, and called it a "destructive superstition."[8] The Roman historian Suetonius would call the Church "a new and mischievous superstition."[9]

In general, therefore, the Roman attitude toward the Church, once the Romans realized it existed, was unfavorable. Those in the

Roman government feared that it might be subversive, like the movement of the Zealots in Judea. The Zealots, born out of the annexation of Judea to Syria as a Roman province in 6 CE, would eventually provoke the Romans into the war that led to the fall of Jerusalem and the destruction of the Temple in 70 CE.[10] So one can see how the Romans would view any new "movement" as suspicious. In addition, the average Roman would have worried that people who refused to worship the gods of Rome would anger those gods, causing them to remove their protection from the empire. Ironically, the Christians, who worshiped only one God as opposed to many, were called "atheists."

At the same time, the Roman emperors were enjoying their ability to be treated as gods themselves. Julius Caesar, who was assassinated to prevent him from becoming emperor, was still proclaimed a god by the senate after his death. When his nephew and heir, Octavian, became the first emperor, it was natural that he be considered the "son" of a "god." So when Jesus came into the world during the reign of Octavian (who had come to be called Augustus), and the Christians said that Jesus was *the* Son of God, this was in direct competition to the emperor, who was called a son of a god. The next emperor, Tiberius, apparently reasoned, Why wait until you're dead to be deified? A son of a god is a god, right? Therefore, he demanded to be called *dominus*, or "lord." So when Jesus was conducting his ministry during the reign of Tiberius, and his followers called him Lord, this was in direct competition to the lordship of the emperor. By the time the emperor Domitian reigned at the end of the first century, he demanded to be called *dominus et deus*, or "lord and god." So when the Fourth Gospel recorded that Thomas called Jesus "My Lord and my God" (John 20:28), the Church held this up as their way to say, *Jesus* is Lord and God, *not* that one in Rome who claims to be lord and god! In the minds of many, this pitted the kingdom (or empire) of God against the empire of the Romans. As we will see, the emperors will eventually try to force their Christian subjects to choose between Christ and Caesar (cf. Luke 23:2, John 19:12, 15).

On July 18 in the year 64 CE, a fire broke out in the city of Rome. It leveled a major part of the center of the city. Coincidentally (or not), the emperor Nero had plans on his desk

11

for a new palace to be built on that spot. Naturally, rumors began to circulate that he had started the fire to make room for his new "Golden House." Nero needed a scapegoat to divert attention away from himself. He blamed the fire on the Christians, and most people were happy to vent their frustration on the Church, though many did not believe its members were guilty.[11] Thus the first persecution of Christians at the hands of the Romans began. Anyone admitting to being a Christian was charged with the crime of arson and could be executed. Many people died in the circus of Nero, which is now in the Vatican, at the site of St. Peter's Basilica.[12] The apostles Paul and Peter were martyred at about this time; Peter himself was crucified in Nero's circus.[13] The important thing to note is that the persecution set a precedent for the future attitude of the Romans toward the Church. Though this persecution was limited to Rome and was temporary, the official position of the Roman government was that Christians were to be seen as enemies of the state.

In the year 81 CE, the emperor Domitian came to the throne, and in 95 CE he began persecuting the Church.[14] According to tradition, Domitian had his own cousin, Flavius Clemens, executed for "atheism." It is likely (but not certain) that this refers to Christianity, though the actual motivation for the execution might have been anything. As the story goes, Clemens's wife, Flavia Domitilla, was subsequently exiled, leaving land to the Roman Christians that would eventually be used for the catacombs named after her.[15] It was also at this time that the apostle John was exiled to the island of Patmos, where he would write the Book of Revelation.[16] But even at this time, persecution was sporadic and regional. Christians continued to worship, though at some times and places they had to meet in secret. The early Christians, however, never hid in the Roman catacombs, as some legends (not to mention movies) suggest. The catacombs were legally registered burial grounds, so the Romans knew exactly where they were. They may have had funeral services at a burial site, and there are some chapels in the catacombs that attest to this, but the cramped quarters, the lack of light and fresh air, not to mention the possible smell of decaying bodies, would make regular worship (let alone hiding out for any length of time) impossible.

In the early second century, a Roman governor named Pliny wrote from his province in the east to ask the emperor Trajan for advice on what to do about the Christians. Trajan, who was emperor from 98 to 117 CE, wrote back and confirmed that although Christians deserved to be executed, Pliny should not try to seek them out. If any were accused, he should interview them and ask them whether they were Christians. He should not take the accuser's word for it, since anyone might accuse someone to avoid paying a debt or to settle a conflict. Therefore, the accused were given a chance to speak for themselves, and if anyone denied being a Christian, proving it was as simple as swearing an oath to the emperor and making some act of worship of the traditional gods, perhaps as little as throwing a pinch of incense on a pagan altar.[17] If there was still some question about a person's sincerity, they could be required to curse Christ, since even Pliny believed that a true Christian would never do that.[18] If anyone was willing to do this, they were to go free. If they were not willing, they could be tortured, or sent into exile, having all their property confiscated, or possibly sent to the mines, which was essentially a slow death sentence. If they were Roman citizens, they were sent to Rome for trial and execution, as Ignatius of Antioch was in the year 110 CE. Otherwise, they were sentenced to death, which could come by beheading (if the governor wanted to be merciful), crucifixion, burning at the stake, or being thrown to the wild beasts in the arena. According to Eusebius, no distinction was made for age or sex.[19] The important thing to note here is that, by the second century, we have two important milestones in the history of persecution. First, we have gone from requiring a crime, like arson, to accuse someone, to simply the name of Christian being a capital offense.[20] Second, we see the use of pagan sacrifice as a test of loyalty to the state.

The irony, which Tertullian would later point out, is that the Romans were torturing prisoners to try to make them *deny* the accusation they were charged with, not admit it.[21] A denial of the charge would result in acquittal, and a Christian would only be punished if he or she refused to deny the faith.

In the middle of the second century, Antoninus Pius (ruled 138–61 CE) made conversion to Judaism illegal, which would set a precedent for similar laws against Christian evangelism.[22] It was during his reign that Polycarp would be burned at the stake, shortly after a dream in which he saw his pillow on fire. Justin Martyr wrote his first *Apology* as an open letter to Antoninus. It is impossible to know whether Antoninus was personally invested in the persecution, but it is clear that it continued during his reign.[23]

Marcus Aurelius (who reigned from 161 to 180) issued an edict in 167 CE ordering pagan sacrifice in the emperor's honor as a test of loyalty.[24] Refusing to make such a sacrifice was an act of treason.[25] Though he did not specifically target Christians (he didn't understand that Christians could not just add Jesus to the league of gods in the pantheon), pagan sacrifice became tied to patriotism. Justin Martyr wrote his second *Apology* to Marcus Aurelius and was subsequently beheaded. Also during Marcus Aurelius's reign, the martyrs of Lyons and Viennes met their end at the hands of an angry mob in Gaul in 177 CE, and the Scillitan martyrs were the victims of a massacre in North Africa in 180.

After Septimius Severus became emperor in 193, he travelled to the East to survey his empire. There he saw the famous Christian school in Alexandria, which was attracting so many people to Christianity that Severus saw it as a threat to traditional religion and to the stability of the empire. Persecution began in earnest in Alexandria in about 201.[26] It would be Septimius Severus, in 202 CE, who would issue the first imperial edict that specifically mentioned Christians, that they should be sought out, arrested, and executed.[27] He made conversion to Christianity illegal (based on the precedent of Antoninus's edict) and tried to close down the catechetical schools. Many people took this as fulfillment of predictions of a "tribulation" in the Book of Revelation.[28] Another significant milestone in the history of persecution had been reached, since now Christians could be sought out and rounded up.[29] This is exactly what happened to Perpetua and her catechism classmates.[30] Even though there would not be a systematic, empire-wide persecution of the Church until the middle of the third century, it was nevertheless the case that the Christian leaders and writers of the early Church were conducting their ministry in a world that wanted them dead (Matt 10:22).

14

THE MARTYR DOCUMENTS

The word *martyr* is simply the Greek word for "witness." In the Church, it became the technical term for one who dies as a witness to the faith. One of the types of literature we encounter in the subapostolic age is the *martyr document* or *martyr acts*. They chronicle the experience of the martyrs as they faced their accusers and executioners.

When a Christian was brought before a Roman official and asked whether he or she was a Christian, they knew this was a moment of truth and a matter of life or death. Christians could save their lives by denying the faith, but they knew the words of Jesus in Matthew 10:33, "[B]ut whoever denies me before others, I will also deny before my Father in heaven." So to save one's life was to lose eternal life (Matt 16:25). But to lose one's life for Jesus' sake was seen as a guarantee of eternal life. Therefore, martyrdom was believed to make up for any sin, including previous apostasy.[31] Even before there was a sacrament of reconciliation, martyrdom was the ultimate penance.[32]

The Church also remembered the words of Jesus in Matthew 10:19–20, "When they hand you over, do not worry about how you are to speak or what you are to say; for what you are to say will be given to you at that time; for it is not you who speak, but the Spirit of your Father speaking through you." Christians took Jesus at his word, believing that anyone who admitted to being a Christian at the risk of physical life was therefore filled with the Holy Spirit. Christians who confessed their faith to the Romans were called *confessors*. These confessors sometimes lived to tell of their experience, but even if they were eventually martyred, during the time they were in prison awaiting execution, they were treated as though they were prophets. They were invested with a certain kind of authority, which we will call *charismatic authority*. People would come to visit them in prison to get advice, and they became, in effect, the first spiritual directors. Eventually, people started asking them for reassurance that their sins were forgiven, so the concept of confessor became expanded to mean someone to whom one might go to confess one's sins. The point is that confessors and martyrs were treated almost as though they were a new set of apostles, and the stories of their heroic confessions and deaths became beloved devotional material in the early Church.[33]

The martyr documents have two main parts. Some of them contain both parts, but some contain only one part or the other. The first part is a record of the interrogation and confession. These tend to be very matter-of-fact, straightforward dialogue between the accused and the Roman magistrate. These may very well be based on actual court proceedings, and are probably quite historical. The second part is the account of the martyr's death. These include details of the imprisonment, torture, and execution, and often a public death in the arena. Some of these are embellished with legendary material, and the later ones become somewhat apocalyptic. Included are such elements as miracles of protection (the first attempt to kill the martyr rarely works), out-of-body experiences complete with the smell of incense, and even painless death.[34] The martyr is depicted as a hero, like an athlete winning a contest, or a soldier victorious in battle.[35] In the end, however, they do die, so the victory is not in cheating death. The victory is in the refusal to deny the faith, and it is seen as a victory over the devil.

Martyrdom was understood as a birth to new life; therefore, the date of a person's martyrdom was celebrated as his or her "birthday."[36] The martyr documents were used in these celebrations, along with the reading of scripture. Often a martyr was celebrated with a feast, or what amounted to a picnic that was held as close to the burial site as possible. Being close to the martyr's remains was like being close to the martyr, and (since one could be certain that the martyr was in heaven with God) being close to the martyr was like being closer to God.[37] Later, when it was more difficult to be physically close to one's favorite martyr, parts of their remains could be taken to other places so that the people there could feel closer to God. These *relics*, from the Latin word *relicta*, meaning "remainder" or "something left behind," could be body parts such as bones, or personal effects such as a piece of clothing or even a lock of hair.

Since martyrdom was believed to guarantee salvation, one could be absolutely certain that anyone who died for the faith was in fact in heaven with Christ, and even though the word *saint* ("holy one") originally meant any Christian, many people came to believe that the only way one could be sure that someone made it to heaven was if they had died a martyr's death.[38] Therefore, it became a tradition to call someone a saint only when you could be sure. These people, the "saints for sure," were in heaven with God and had the Lord's ear, and therefore they could be called on to intercede for those on earth as their confessors in heaven.

We will look at several of the martyr documents as they come up in our exploration of the subapostolic age. Many of the important writers of this time period were in fact martyred, sometimes because their writings made them more visible to the Romans. But they recognized that the danger of martyrdom was part and parcel of a Christianity that stood against the culture. As Ignatius of Antioch said on his way to Rome to be executed, "Christianity is greatest when it is hated by the world."[39]

CHAPTER 2

The Apostolic Fathers

THE DIDACHE

The word *didache* means "teaching." It is actually a short form of the full Greek title, which is translated, *The Teaching of the Twelve Apostles*. Although the authorship of this document is unknown, the Didache gained widespread acceptance in the early Church. It claims to be directly from the apostles, but was almost certainly not written by an apostle. Since we do not know who wrote it, we cannot be sure when it was written, although it may have been written as early as the second half of the first century; thus it is possible that some of the content does go back to apostolic teaching. It may be contemporaneous with the Gospel of Matthew and may have formed a companion volume to the gospel(s).

The Didache is a manual for the Church. It consists of two main parts, one for instructing those preparing for baptism and one for church leaders. The first part is based on a Jewish teaching called the "Two Ways" (Deut 30:15, 19). As indicated above, early Christian catechesis was not so much concerned with teaching theology as it was with teaching morality. Since the ethical expectations of the Church were often much stricter than the expectations of the culture, a convert needed to know before initiation how to behave as a Christian. The Church could not afford to have its members hindering its evangelization efforts with embarrassing conduct, but more importantly, since it was understood that one could "undo" one's baptism through sin, it was imperative to instruct converts in proper behavior before their baptism.[1] Therefore, the initiate is instructed in the "Two Ways" of life and death and encouraged to choose the way of life. The motivation for, and urgency of, this teaching is explained at the end of the book. Jesus would return soon, and the believer must be ready.[2]

The other part of the Didache is a manual for church practice, and it is a gold mine of information about the early Church. The details of the contents will enter into our discussion about early Church worship and practice below. One thing, however, is worth highlighting at this point: the Didache shows that from the very beginning of its existence the Church has opposed abortion and the exposure of infants.[3] In the Roman Empire, it was acceptable to abort a preborn child or even to "expose" a newborn, to leave her outside to die, if she was unwanted.[4] Consistent with its counter-cultural morality, the Church taught that Christians were not to engage in these practices and that abortion, no less than exposure, constituted a form of infanticide.[5] In fact, some Christian writers pointed out that in spite of the false accusation of incest directed at Christians, Romans ran the risk of unintentional incest when they exposed their daughters who could then be taken by slave traders and raised to be prostitutes.[6]

No doubt, the lack of identifiable apostolic authorship led to the Didache being given a status of "worthwhile, but not inspired" in the Church. Most early Church leaders encouraged Christians to read it, but said that it did not belong in the canon. A few did consider it scripture, but not enough to sway the majority.

CLEMENT OF ROME

Clement was probably born around 30 CE and was the bishop of Rome from 88 to 97 CE. According to tradition, he was a disciple of the apostle Peter. Paul mentions a Clement in Philippians 4:3, though there is no way to be certain whether it is the same Clement. He may have been a freed slave from the household of Domitian's cousin, Flavius Clemens. According to tradition, Domitian had his cousin killed for his faith, and it is reasonable to believe that upon his death the will of this Clemens, or Clement, provided for the release of his slaves. If this is the case, a newly freed slave could take his master's name, and as a Christian freed-man could have become a leader in the church of Rome. It is important to note that the office of bishop as it existed then was nothing like the office of bishop today. The details of this will be discussed below, but for now it is enough to note that at the time of Clement, the bishop of Rome functioned as the chair of the council of priests in the city, and in that role he was charged with corresponding by letter with the Christians in other cities. As we will see, one of the earliest noncanonical Christian documents is one of those letters.

According to tradition, Clement was eventually banished from Rome by the emperor Trajan. He went east, where he converted many to the Christian faith; however, this led to increased visibility, which in turn led to his martyrdom. He was thrown into the Black Sea, tied to an anchor. Legend says that in the ninth century, St. Cyril found his body and brought it back to Rome, where it is buried in the church that bears Clement's name. Visitors to the church of San Clemente in Rome can still see remains of what may have been a house where Christians met for worship in Clement's time.

First Clement

This document, called First Clement (1 Clement), is a letter written by Clement on behalf of the church in Rome to the Christians in the Greek city of Corinth, the same city to which the apostle Paul wrote the Corinthian letters in the New Testament, but now forty years later. First Clement was probably written in the early 90s of the first century, shortly before the Book of Revelation. In the letter, Domitian does not seem to have begun persecution yet, since Clement advocates praying for government leaders, implying that they are appointed by God.[7]

The letter is written in the form of an ancient epistle of negotiation. Just as the church in Corinth experienced division in Paul's time, so now there is still division, and Clement writes in an attempt to reconcile the factions. Therefore, the letter is much more practical in tone than its apocalyptic cousin, the Book of Revelation. Apparently, there was conflict in Corinth over the authority of some priests.[8] We can't be sure what the real issue was, though it may have been a dispute over the election of a bishop (or council chair).[9] If a bishop's election was being challenged, this might be evidence of a transition in the office of bishop from one who represents the priests (but is essentially an equal) to one who has real authority over the other priests. The factions seem to be along generational lines, with tension between older and younger members of the church.[10] This would be consistent with an evolution in the office of bishop, since older members might want to reject any new authority that was being given to the bishop. In any case, Clement does not give the details of the dispute because he says he is sending negotiators to do the real work of reconciliation, and the letter is simply to set the stage.[11] Clement writes with urgency, though, because the threat of schism is causing some to doubt the faith,[12] and it is an embarrassment to the cause of evangelization.[13]

Historically, the most important thing about 1 Clement is the tone of authority with which Clement writes. He assumes that the Christians in Corinth, who have their own leaders, should listen to the bishop of Rome and accept his advice. The reason that this is so is based on the belief that the church of Rome was founded by the apostle Peter, and that his authority as Jesus' right-hand man and leader of the apostles (Matt 16:18–19, John 21:15–17) is transferred to his successors in the city.[14] This concept of the transfer of authority from apostles to bishops is known as *apostolic succession*. The assumption is that the first bishops of the Church were consecrated by the apostles, who handed down the mantle of authority, and conferred the anointing of the Holy Spirit, in an unbroken line going back to Jesus himself. Subsequent generations of bishops would in turn be ordained and consecrated by their predecessors in the succession, keeping the line of authority intact. In addition, whatever a bishop teaches is assumed to have been learned from his predecessor in the same city. Therefore, any bishop should be able to trace his line of succession—both the content and the authority of the teaching office—like a pedigree, back to the founder of the church in the city where he is bishop. If one wants to rest assured that a bishop's teaching will not lead the faithful astray, simply ask whether that bishop's teaching (and hence his authority) can be traced back to an apostle. If so, one can be confident that the bishop in question is on the same page, so to speak, with the other bishops, the apostles, and, ultimately, Jesus himself.[15]

What happens, however, when two bishops disagree? The bishop with the higher authority (both theologically and ecclesiastically) will be the one who can trace his succession back to one of the original apostles. If both of them can, then the one with the greater authority will be the one who can trace his succession back to one of the inner circle of Jesus' closest disciples: Peter, James, and John. Ultimately, though, since Peter was made the leader of the disciples, Peter trumps all others, even Paul. Therefore, since the church of Rome claimed an unbroken chain of succession going back to Jesus through Peter, it eventually just became easier to ask whether any church was in agreement with Rome. The important point to note is that even before the office of bishop in general evolved into the authoritative role that it would eventually become, the church of Rome was already coming to be seen as the church with which anyone had to agree if they wanted to be considered part of the universal Church.

One has to understand that the worldview of the early Church was not like today. We live in such a technology-driven culture that we are conditioned to believe that whatever is newer is automatically better. This was not the belief of people in the ancient world. To them, whatever is older is better, because it's established and has stood the test of time.[16] If something new comes along to challenge what already exists, the new thing is suspect. So in Clement's world, the tradition is always more trustworthy than the innovation. Therefore, since the oldest teaching is always the most reliable, and since the authority of the church of Rome was seen as going back to the original leader of the apostles, the church of Rome, and whoever is in leadership there, assumes an authority, even over the bishops of other cities.

Of course, this doesn't mean that everyone accepted this unconditionally. But it is remarkable that we can see that as early as the late first century a bishop of Rome is writing to other churches with a tone of authority as though he speaks for Peter. In fact, Clement believed the Corinthian Christians should listen to him as though he were Peter, even implying that this letter might be taken as inspired.[17] Therefore, 1 Clement is our earliest witness to the claim of apostolic succession.[18]

So why wasn't this letter included in the New Testament?

Clement, as a possible disciple of Peter, could have been seen as a secondary apostle, much like Mark or Luke. In fact, some did treat this letter as scripture and advocated including it in the Christian canon. But in the end it did not stand the test of time. The letter is quite long compared to the New Testament letters and has little theological content. Indeed, when Clement wanted to talk about the resurrection, instead of mentioning the empty tomb, he compared Jesus to a phoenix, the mythical bird that rises from its own funeral ashes every five hundred years.[19] Finally, the fact that Clement sees the Roman government as ordained by God must have worked against acceptance of his letter in times of persecution.[20] While it is true that the Letter of Philemon is also a personal letter without a lot of theology and yet was included in the New Testament, Clement is not Paul, and he was just not close enough to Jesus to merit this letter being included in spite of its difficulties.

SECOND CLEMENT

The document known as Second Clement (2 Clement) was almost certainly not written by Clement of Rome. In fact, we have no idea who wrote it (or when it was written), but since it was found in manuscript collections with 1 Clement, tradition associated them. Second Clement is not really a letter, but more of a homily. The primary concern is to warn the reader against false teachers, specifically those who deny the reality of Christ's humanity (cf. 1 John 4:1–3). These false teachers are said to be leading Christians astray, putting their salvation at risk.[21] It also warns about the persecution and serves as a reminder to resist apostasy.[22] The author states that to deny Christ is to "undo" one's baptism.[23] It is clear from this and other similar writings that the early Christians were aware of the possibility of the loss of salvation after baptism, which could happen because of continuing in sin, following a heresy, or, in times of persecution, by denial of the faith.[24]

The author of 2 Clement knew Matthew's Gospel and probably Luke's. He quotes Matthew 9:13 and calls it scripture.[25] He also quotes a few sayings of Jesus that are not found in the New Testament gospels. For example, Jesus is quoted as saying, "Even if you were gathered together with me in my very bosom, yet if you did not keep my commandments, I would cast you off, and say to you, 'Depart from me! I don't know where you come from, you who do evil.'"[26]

After quoting Matthew 10:16, in which Jesus says, "You shall be as lambs in the midst of wolves…," 2 Clement continues, "And Peter answered and said to Him, 'But what if the wolves should tear the lambs to pieces?' Jesus said to Peter, 'After they are dead, the lambs need not fear the wolves; and in the same way, do not fear those who kill you, but can do nothing more to you; but fear the one who, after you are dead, has power over both soul and body to cast them into hell.'"[27] Thus the author connects these sayings of Jesus to the context of persecution. However, we do not know where these additional quotations come from.

There are also some supposed words of Jesus that seem to come from sources on the fringe of the Church, ironically possibly even sources connected to the very false teachers this author is writing against.[28] It was probably for this reason, and due to the unknown authorship, that this document was not considered for inclusion in the New Testament. In addition, depending on how one dates this document, it could come from later in the Church's history, too late to be considered apostolic or be included in the canon.

IGNATIUS OF ANTIOCH

Ignatius, bishop of Antioch in Syria, was born around 50 CE. According to tradition, he was a disciple of the apostle John. Since John is said to have lived to the end of the first century, this is certainly possible. Ignatius had been arrested for spreading the faith, at about the same time that Pliny was corresponding with Trajan. However, the governor of Syria was sending him to Rome for trial and execution. On his way to Rome, his guards allowed him to meet with other Christians, and he even stayed briefly in Smyrna with his friend Polycarp. Ignatius wrote seven letters during that time, mostly to the Christians in cities along the way. One of the letters mentions a bishop of Ephesus named Onesimus, who, according to tradition, is the same Onesimus mentioned in Paul's

Letter to Philemon (Phlm 1:10, Col 4:9).[29] He would have been about seventy years old, so it is certainly possible. Ignatius's letters were written about 108 to 110 CE, and he was martyred shortly after writing them, in about 110. The letters of Ignatius are as follows:

Letter to the Ephesians
Letter to the Magnesians
Letter to the Trallians
Letter to the Romans
Letter to the Philadelphians
Letter to the Smyrnaeans
Letter to Polycarp

Ignatius wrote with authority, but did not claim apostolic authority like Clement of Rome. Ignatius wrote with the charismatic authority of a confessor. In fact, on several occasions he makes a point to take a position of humility with regard to his audience: "I am not commanding you, as though I were someone important...."[30] "I do not think myself qualified... as though I were an apostle...."[31] "I do not give you orders like Peter and Paul...."[32] While it has been argued that this shows that Ignatius had no concept of apostolic succession, two things must be kept in mind. Ignatius was not the bishop *of Rome*, and he did not need apostolic succession, since he was a confessor.

On the other hand, Ignatius was a bishop, and he was a strong advocate for the newly emerging office of bishop and its authority. This authority was primarily meant to maintain the unity of the Church. For Ignatius, to oppose the bishop was to threaten to split the Church.[33] In fact, he wrote that to disobey a bishop was to disobey God,[34] and that Christians must listen to the bishop as though it were the Lord himself.[35] Calling himself "a man set on unity," he believed that the unity of the Church required a limit of one bishop per city, since more than one bishop in a city could lead to disputes, and inevitably to division.[36] Of course, Ignatius is preaching what he thought was the ideal, and the very fact that he feels he has to say it with such urgency means that it is not always happening that way. The truth is, many cities at the time may have had more than one bishop, perhaps even with more than one catechetical school. It is easy to see, however, that Ignatius feared such a situation would lead to schism.

Ignatius is the first person we know of to use the Christian application of the word *catholic*.[37] Originally the word meant "universal." The *catholic* Church was the universal Church, but its unity was already threatened by teachers of alternative interpretations of the person of Christ. Therefore, the word *catholic* would come to take on the connotation of the *true* Church as opposed to any alternative expressions. The concept of the "universal" Church would be used to exclude those who were considered outside the Church, as the word was employed in the attempt to set the boundaries of what was correct Christian teaching. In other words, the teaching of the *catholic* Church would not lead one astray. The same could not be said for the teachings of those who separated themselves from the universal Church—and that included anyone who was not in unity with the bishops, the successors of the apostles.[38]

The primary threat to unity in Ignatius's letters seems to be the same false teachers mentioned in 2 Clement. They were teaching that Jesus was not really human, but was pure spirit (cf. 1 John 4:1–3). The implications of this teaching will be discussed below; however, the problem for Ignatius was that these "false teachers" were holding their own meetings, separate from the rest of the Church, and without the sanction of the local bishops (cf. 1 John 2:19).[39] Although in a Jewish context any ten men could form a synagogue, Ignatius was arguing against a Christian version of this system. As long as the Church was still defining itself, meetings, worship, and especially the teaching of the Church must be more controlled in order to prevent the propagation of incorrect interpretations that would lead the innocent astray. In this sense, the "false teachers" are *heretics*, in the truest sense of the word. *Heresy* comes from a Greek word meaning "to separate," so for Ignatius there is no difference between (theological) heresy and schism. Ignatius says that no group can call itself a church without the bishop, priests, and deacons.[40] Therefore, whoever does not meet with the authorized assembly has separated himself from the Church,[41] so there should be no gatherings without the consent of the bishop.[42]

Since the Church was defined in terms of the Eucharist, it is not surprising that Ignatius connects the Eucharist to the office of the bishop, saying that the only true Eucharist is that which is presided over by the bishop.[43] There can be only one Eucharist, and to divide the table is to divide the Church.[44]

Finally, in Ignatius's letter to the Romans, he anticipates his arrival in Rome and his own death. He begs his Roman brothers and sisters not to try to interfere with his martyrdom.[45] In humility, he says he is only beginning to be a disciple of Jesus, a process that will be completed in his martyrdom. There is a more practical reason why he cannot afford to be rescued, however. Though he does not say it in the letter, he knows that if he were to appear alive after his scheduled execution, many people might assume that he had denied the faith to save his life, and this would be discouraging to the faithful. There was nothing to do but see it through, believing that those who follow Christ in death will follow him in resurrection.

We know from Polycarp's letter (below) that soon after Ignatius's death his letters were copied and circulated as a collection, much like the letters of Paul and the four gospels were.[46] So why weren't Ignatius's letters included in the New Testament? They have a reliable authorship (though this has been debated at times) and no objectionable content, yet for various reasons the later writers, especially the theologians, did not quote them as authoritative. In other words, they did not come to be treated as scripture, in the sense of inspired, and so they did not stand the test of time. By the time the New Testament canon was being standardized, they had gone by the wayside.

POLYCARP OF SMYRNA

According to tradition, Polycarp was also a disciple of the apostle John, along with Ignatius. Not much is known about his early life, but as bishop of Smyrna he was the mentor and teacher of Irenaeus of Lyons. Polycarp seems to be the last bishop to have known any of the apostles personally, and he represents that generation called "elders" who are the link between the apostles and successive generations of leaders (cf. 2 John 1, 3 John 1).[47] Polycarp had traveled to Rome to meet with the bishop there to discuss the proper way to calculate the date for the celebration of Easter. They agreed to disagree, but parted amicably.[48] Shortly after that, Polycarp was martyred, in about 156 CE.

Letter to the Philippians

This is the only writing we have from Polycarp, written shortly after Ignatius died, in about 110 CE. Polycarp assumed that Ignatius had been martyred, but wondered if the Christians in Philippi had heard any of the details of his death. Following his friend Ignatius, Polycarp warns of the heretics who are denying the reality of Christ's humanity. He quotes 1 John 4:2–3, that those who deny that Christ came with real flesh are "antichrists." These also denied the resurrection, claiming that spiritually they were already living the resurrection life (a concept known as *realized eschatology*, cf. 2 Tim 2:17–18).

The letter includes a message of hope in the midst of persecution, much like we find in the Book of Revelation, though without the apocalyptic symbolism. The point is that those who follow Jesus in death will follow him in resurrection.[49] This is the promise that should give Christians the strength to resist the temptation to deny the faith to save their lives. Finally, Polycarp encourages his audience to pray for those who persecute them.[50] He would soon have the opportunity to practice what he preached.

THE MARTYRDOM OF POLYCARP

This is the oldest of the martyr documents that we have. It is actually a letter from the church of Smyrna telling the story of Polycarp's martyrdom. It is probably also the most historical of all the martyr documents, possibly based on the actual proceedings, and having been embellished with fewer legendary elements than the later stories. Still, this embellishment meant that the martyr documents in general would not be seriously considered for inclusion in the New Testament.

According to the story, Polycarp had a vision or a dream in which he saw his pillow on fire. By this he knew he was to be burned at the stake. At first he tried to avoid arrest, but when the soldiers came for him, he did not resist, he only asked to be allowed to pray. At his interrogation, he was of course given the chance to deny his faith to save his life. To go free, he would have had to curse Christ and swear an oath to the emperor, saying, "Caesar is lord." When he refused, the Roman official tried to provoke him, yelling at him to denounce his Christian community by saying, "Away with the atheists." Polycarp turned to the crowd of pagan accusers that had gathered, pointed to *them* and said, "Away with the atheists!" And so his fate was sealed. After his death, his bones were kept as relics.

PAPIAS OF HIERAPOLIS

Papias was a contemporary and a colleague of Polycarp. It was said that he knew the daughters of the apostle Philip.[51] Some later writers said he knew John the apostle, though he does not seem to have claimed this himself. Probably he knew John the Elder, the author of the New Testament letters 2 John and 3 John. He is also said to have personally known some people whom Jesus had healed, who were still alive when he was young. These stories of secondhand connections to Jesus must, of course, be taken with a grain of salt, since they may have been invented by people who were devoted to Polycarp in order to increase the credibility of his teachings.

Exposition on the Sayings of the Lord

This is the only document we have from Papias, and it does not exist in its entirety. In it, Papias interprets the so-called millennium of the Book of Revelation as a literal one-thousand-year reign of Christ on the earth. Using 2 Peter 3:8 ("with the Lord one day is like a thousand years, and a thousand years are like one day," cf. Ps 90:4) as his interpretive key, he reasoned that the seven days of creation in Genesis are a metaphor for the whole of human history.[52] He taught that there would be four thousand years from the time of creation until the coming of Christ, then another two thousand years between the advent of Christ and his return. This makes six thousand years, with the seventh thousand years as a millennial "sabbath."[53] As it was, the majority of the Church did not accept this interpretation, and thus this document was not accepted as authoritative by the early Church. A similar view was shared, however, by a fringe group known as the Montanists (see below), and Papias's interpretation influenced the theologians Irenaeus and Tertullian.[54] Not only was Papias's writing rejected by the majority of the Church, but his interpretation almost got the Book of Revelation itself excluded from the canon.

THE EPISTLE OF BARNABAS

If this document was written by someone named Barnabas, it was not the Barnabas of the New Testament. The authorship is unknown, but we can date the writing to shortly after the last rebellion in Judea, about 135 CE.[55] The "epistle" is really an ethical treatise, possibly for catechesis, and somewhat like the ethical section of the Didache. It has a heavy emphasis on good works as evidence of devotion to God. The questionable authorship was probably enough to disqualify this document from the New Testament, though there is some questionable theology in it as well.[56]

THE SHEPHERD OF HERMAS

The actual title of this document is simply *The Shepherd*, but it is traditionally attributed to Hermas, the brother of Bishop Pius I of Rome (bishop from 140 to 155 CE). The premise of the writing is that Hermas was given a vision, much like the vision of the Book of Revelation. The "shepherd" is not Jesus but a guardian angel who brings the message of the vision to Hermas.[57]

The majority of the book is an allegory of a tower, which represents the Church. The tower is still being built, and as stones are added to the structure, Hermas realizes that the stones are people.

Some are ready to be built into the tower, but others are not ready, and are set aside. This is not a problem, as long as these stones become ready before the tower is finished, because after that time it will be too late to be added to the tower.[58] The end of the age of the Church will come when the tower is finished. Then Jesus will return. Jesus does stop by a few times in the vision, though, to see how the building is coming along. He is described as a man who is taller than the tower.[59] It is all very vague, however, and Jesus is never actually identified by name. Jesus is called the "angel of justification,"[60] while the shepherd is referred to as the "angel of repentance."[61] There is also a confusing cast of characters reminiscent of some of Jesus' parables, such as the parable of the ten bridesmaids (Matt 25:1–13).

Hermas seems to be using the allegorical vision to critique what he perceives as hypocritical behavior in the Church. The problems include doubt (or not practicing what one preaches, in some translations called "double-mindedness"),[62] anger,[63] and wealth, which leads one to postpone one's baptism for worldly reasons.[64] Also criticized is fear, which leads to apostasy in times of persecution.[65] Hermas warns that while those who denied their faith in a previous persecution might be forgiven,[66] presumably because they did not understand the implications, those who deny the faith in any future persecution could not be forgiven.[67] Clearly, Hermas was concerned that the reconciliation of some who had denied the faith to save their lives would lead others to take the same path in the future.

According to Hermas, the remedy for these problems is faith,[68] self-control,[69] and charity. He believes it is God's will for the rich and the poor to live in a kind of symbiotic relationship, whereby the rich help the poor by giving them resources, and the poor help the rich by giving them a ministry (that is, almsgiving).[70] He probably saw it as a Christian version of the patron-client relationship that existed in Roman society. By that system, wealthy patrons offered favors to their clients, who in turn could be asked to do anything from providing an entourage to voting for whomever the patron supported. In this way, someone of a lower economic status who might not otherwise have friends in high places could, if he got into trouble, hope to rely on the influence of an aristocratic patron. In return, the patron had someone to do his dirty work for him. Hermas apparently saw a divinely appointed patron-client system at work between the rich and poor. If you are wealthy, Hermas says, God made you rich specifically to help the poor.[71]

There are many reasons why this document is not included in our New Testament. In general, there seems to be a consensus that by now we are just too far from the apostolic period to ascribe any kind of inspiration to a text. In spite of that, several of the early theologians, including Irenaeus, did quote from *The Shepherd*. Even if they didn't see it as inspired, it remained popular devotional reading for centuries. But on the whole, it is simply too long and too obscure to have stood the test of time, let alone gain a tradition of reading in liturgy. In addition, it never mentions Jesus by name, so it was probably seen as insufficiently christocentric. In fact, the theology of *The Shepherd* may tend toward another early heresy, the opposite of the one we have already seen. While 2 Clement, Ignatius of Antioch, and Polycarp all seem to be opposing a heresy that denied the real humanity of Jesus, *The Shepherd* seems to lean in the other direction, denying or diminishing the divinity of Christ, as if he were only an angel (that is, a created being). Jesus is never called Lord, nor is he presented as a savior per se, and it seems to be possible to earn salvation by good works alone.[72] In fact, for Hermas good works are everything, and salvation comes through self-control. He basically says that if you enjoy something, it must be a sin.[73]

The Shepherd enjoyed a resurgence of popularity in the fourth century, though this was because it emerged in an edited version that was corrected to make it more acceptable. Specifically, the term *Logos*, referring to Christ, was inserted where the original had used the word *spirit*.

CHAPTER 3

The Apologists

The apologists are a group of early writers who wrote *apologies*, or a justification of the faith to those outside the Church. An *apology* is not to express regret for something, but to give a rationale for it, in the spirit of 1 Peter 3:15. Most of the apologists were philosophers who had converted to Christianity and then taught Christianity as a philosophy. Their writings were meant to try to explain Christianity and its value to the very people who persecuted the Church, but because they were writing to non-Christians, they preferred to make their case from philosophical arguments rather than from scripture. It is not that they never referred to scripture; rather, they recognized that scripture was not authoritative for their primary audience, so an appeal to scripture would not be convincing.[1] In addition, there was still no universal consensus about which of the early documents should be included in the Christian Bible. On the other hand, the apologists did quote extensively from the Old Testament when they were writing for a Jewish audience.

For the sake of clarity, the writings of the apologists can be contrasted with the writings of the theologians, who will be the subject of a later chapter. The audience of the apologists is non-Christians, those outside the Church. Since the apologists are converts from philosophy and still consider themselves philosophers, they believe in the value of philosophy for demonstrating the truth of the Christian faith. This is partly based on an assumed optimism about the capacity for human reason to grasp ultimate truth. In contrast, the theologians will be skeptical of philosophy, believing human reason to be so flawed as only to lead one down the wrong path. For them, philosophy is the root of all heresy. What is needed is revelation, and human reason must be subject to it. Also, the focus of the theologians will shift from an external audience to an internal audience. The theologians were writing for fellow Christians, to warn them of the dangers of heresy and to teach correct doctrine. Therefore, they will claim that they do not rely on philosophy, although to a certain extent they still do; rather, they will intentionally support every argument with scripture. The last of the apologists was Clement of Alexandria, and the first of the theologians was Irenaeus of Lyons, so even though they were contemporaries, we will have to wait until later to meet Irenaeus.

The writings of the apologists have much in common with one another, as they used many of the same arguments to try to convince their readers of the validity of the Christian faith. These arguments fall into two types, or themes, based on philosophical categories: Christianity is *truth*, and Christianity is *virtue*.

To show that Christianity is *truth*, the apologists often denigrate Greco-Roman religion by comparison. To the modern sensibility, it doesn't seem like a good idea to try to convince someone of the truth of your religion by telling them that their religion is ridiculous, and yet this is what they did. The apologists write extensively about how the traditional mythologies of Greece and Rome are silly superstition. They argued that the idols the Romans worship could not be real gods for three reasons: (1) The idols were made by humans, while the real God made humans; (2) the idols require sacrifices from humans, while the real God gives to humans what they need;[2] and (3) the idols made of gold and silver need to be guarded by humans, to prevent them from being stolen, but the real God guards (protects) humans.[3] The apologists would also point out that if you were to climb Mt. Olympus, you would find it deserted.[4] Therefore, the gods of Rome are not gods at all, but are either completely fictitious or are mere humans who have been proclaimed to be gods after their death.[5]

Another tactic the apologists used to show that Christianity is truth was to argue that Christianity was older than Greek philosophy. In a world where the more ancient teaching is often assumed to be the better one, the apologists showed that the Hebrew prophets predate the philosophers, and then demonstrated the continuity between the prophets and the Church.[6] In fact, they claimed that anything good that the philosophers said was actually plagiarized from the prophets.[7] Therefore, the apologists reasoned that

Christianity is the best philosophy, the most rational, and the logical conclusion of all good philosophy. It is superior to Greek philosophy because it combines the best of both worlds, revelation from God and human reason.

To show that Christianity is *virtue*, the apologists argued that Christian morality is a higher standard than that of Roman society, and is in fact the best way to achieve the good life. In spite of the rumors, Christians do not practice incest and cannibalism.[8] In fact, they do not even practice the immoralities that the Romans indulge in. As I have indicated, the Church saw itself as countercultural in its morality, especially since in times of persecution it could not afford to give its neighbors any more reasons to be suspicious of it. This may have worked against the Church, however, since the claim of superior morality was of course a critique of Roman society, and the refusal to participate in accepted Roman activities (including entertainment) could be seen as antisocial.[9] For example, the patron-client system was used by wealthy men to entice boys into sexual relationships. In his list of the Ten Commandments, Clement of Alexandria actually has eleven, because he inserted the phrase, "Thou shalt not seduce boys" into the Decalogue.[10] We have also already noted how the Church criticized the culture for allowing abortion and child exposure. The apologists went on to argue that even the stories of the gods recount how they committed acts of murder and adultery, so not only do the Christians behave better than the Romans, they even behave better than the gods of the Romans!

Finally, sometimes the apologists felt the need to claim superiority to Judaism as well. In 135 CE, the last of the Jewish rebellions resulted in the expulsion of all Jews from Jerusalem, which left some Romans believing that Jews were rebellious and violent by nature. The apologists wanted to assure their Roman rulers that the Church was not a threat to the empire. To do that, they made a point to show that Christianity was separate from Judaism. Unfortunately, in the attempt to distance Christianity from Judaism and show that the Church was not treasonous, some of the apologists laid the foundation for later anti-Semitism. Wanting to make the case that Romans and Christians were on the same "peace-loving" page, the apologists downplayed the role of the

Romans in Jesus' death and laid all the blame at the feet of his Jewish enemies.

The point that the apologists wanted to emphasize to the Romans was that Christianity, far from being a danger to the empire, was actually good for it. Christians do not kill, they do not steal, they are faithful to their marriages, and they pray for the empire and its leaders.

THE APOLOGY OF ARISTIDES

Aristides was an Athenian philosopher who converted to Christianity. He wrote an apology to be given to the emperor Hadrian, who was traveling in Greece in 125 or 126 CE.[11] Aristides argues that Christianity is better than the traditional Roman religion because it is historical, while Greco-Roman religion is mythological. He also has an interesting version of an "intelligent design" argument, saying that creation implies a Creator.[12] According to tradition, he actually received a response from the emperor. A letter from Hadrian is preserved in Eusebius's *Ecclesiastical History*; however, the letter may not be authentic.[13]

THE *EPISTLE TO DIOGNETUS*

The author of this letter is unknown.[14] It is written to a Roman official named Diognetus, who had apparently asked for more information about the Christian faith. The reply is the standard apologetic fare, including pointing out how ridiculous the mythological gods are, as well as an assurance that the Christians are not like the Jews. Unlike the Jews, who have a different diet from the Romans, the only thing that sets Christians apart from Roman society is better morals. If the need to show the difference between Christians and Jews comes from a context of recent Jewish rebellion, that could place the writing of the document shortly after 135 CE. The atonement of Christ is explained as a "sweet exchange," in which he took the punishment of humanity, and humanity in turn received his immortality (Gal 13:13–14).[15] The author concludes that the truth (and divine origin) of Christianity should be sufficiently demonstrated by the fact that the martyrs are willing to die for it.[16]

JUSTIN MARTYR

Born somewhere between 110 and 114 CE, Justin was a Greek philosopher from Samaria, living in Ephesus. As one might guess, "Martyr" was not his last name; it describes his fate. At a time when philosophers were becoming more and more accepting of various forms of monotheism, he began a personal quest of exploring different philosophical systems to determine which one was the best. He was impressed with the way Christians interpreted Christ as the fulfillment of Hebrew prophecy, and with the high moral standards of the Church. His conversion to Christianity, however, came by the testimony of the martyrs.[17]

Some time between 130 and 132 CE, Justin joined the Church and became its greatest advocate since the apostles. Like the other apologists, he understood Christ according to the philosophical concept of the *Logos*, the Word of God (following John 1:1). He moved to Rome, where he taught Christian philosophy. The teachers of other systems of philosophy in Rome were envious of his abilities and his success, however, and they conspired against him. He was martyred in 165 CE.

First Apology

Justin's *First Apology* (*1 Apology*) was written in the 150s CE and addressed to the emperor Antoninus Pius.[18] Interestingly, Justin takes an antagonistic attitude with the emperor, saying in effect, You can kill us, but you can't hurt us (cf. Matt 10:28).[19] He even threatens the emperor with eternal punishment if he should continue harassing the Church.[20] In contrast, Justin says a good emperor would not persecute the Church, since that's what the Jews did in the early days, so the Romans should not do such a "Jewish" thing as persecute Christians.[21] A good emperor would recognize that the Church is good for the empire, and would want more people to be like the Christians.[22] A good emperor would recognize the truth in what people are willing to die for, since no one would die for a myth.[23]

Probably the most interesting aspect of Justin's *First Apology* is toward the end, where he explains to the emperor what Christians do in their meetings.[24] Here, from little more than a century after Christ, we have an order of worship that looks remarkably similar to liturgy today. All the major liturgical elements are there, including the reading of the gospels, a homily, prayers of intercession, the eucharistic prayer, the sacrament of the Eucharist (with the elements taken out to those who could not be there), and an offering, all of which shows that the basic structure of Christian worship has not changed much in almost two thousand years.[25]

Second Apology

The *Second Apology* (*2 Apology*) was written to Marcus Aurelius, the son of Antoninus Pius and the emperor who would have Justin executed. It is relatively short and even sounds a bit desperate, with its claims that no man should be honored above the truth[26] and that anyone who persecutes Christians must be possessed by demons.[27]

Dialogue with Trypho

Trypho is probably a fictional character invented for the purpose of the *Dialogue*. He is presented as a sincere but misguided Jew who meets the philosopher Justin and enters into a debate over the proper interpretation of the Old Testament. The *Dialogue* is apparently meant as an apology for a Jewish audience, hoping to convince them that Jesus was in fact their Messiah. Most of its readers, however, were probably actually Christians who either hoped to use the contents as ammunition in debate with Jews, or who simply read it for the encouragement of their own faith. It is full of quotations from the Old Testament, as one would expect, and also, as one would expect, the philosopher wins the debate by producing the more convincing arguments. It can be a bit confusing, however, since it actually begins with a narrative about another dialogue that led to the philosopher's own conversion to Christianity.

On the Resurrection

Though this document no longer exists in its entirety, there is enough available to get the sense of Justin's teaching on the resurrection of the body. Justin is arguing for the Pauline understanding of the future resurrection (1 Cor 15), as opposed to a Greek philosophical view of the afterlife. Against such a view, Justin argues that we are not destined to be disembodied spirits, but that at the resurrection our bodies will be reunited with our spirits.[28] Salvation, he says, is for the whole human, not the spirit only. Since Jesus was raised and ascended in the flesh, so will we be.

It is clear from the text that Justin had encountered the objection that human bodies will have decayed. Yet he argues from the principle of the conservation of matter that even when decayed all the elements of the body remain, though they may be scattered. Therefore, like an artist who creates a mosaic from individual tiles, God can put the body back together again, since he is the one who made the body in the first place. While we might not be used to thinking in terms of this much continuity between the present body and the resurrection body, the important concept here is that for Justin the body is part of our humanity, and to be saved into the kingdom without it would be to lose part of our humanity.

THE MARTYRDOM OF JUSTIN

Since this martyr document describes the martyrdom of Justin and others in Rome, it was not written by Justin himself, but was written after his death. Like most of the martyr acts, the confessors' dilemma is presented as a choice between following human laws and following the law of God. When Justin was interrogated, the Roman officer tried to find out where the Christians were meeting, but Justin simply said, We meet wherever we can, since there are too many Christians in Rome to meet all in one place.[29] Justin and his companions refused to make the required sacrifice, and so they were led outside the city walls and beheaded. Some of the Christians were able to take Justin's body and bury it.

TATIAN

Tatian lived from about 110 to 172 CE and was a student of Justin Martyr in Rome. He is often accused of heresy by later writers, though there is not enough of his writings left for us to know with any certainty whether the accusations are true.[30] He did leave Rome after the death of Justin and seems to have gone back to his hometown in Syria, where he taught an extreme asceticism that advocated celibacy for all Christians.

Address to the Greeks

In this apology, Tatian attempted to explain Christ as *Logos* to a philosophical audience. His explanation is problematic, however, because he imagined that the preincarnate Word of God existed in two phases, the first phase of which made the Logos nothing more than the wisdom of the Father.[31] The Logos then went from being the wisdom of the Father to being the Word of the Father, at which point, as he describes it, the Logos became "a work of the Father." Tatian used the same language to describe this "work of the Father" that he used to describe creation. In doing so, he made it sound like the Logos was created. For this reason, it can be said that he probably had more influence on future heresy than on future orthodoxy.[32]

Diatessaron

Tatian is most famous for his *Diatessaron*, a harmonization of the four gospels, written about 170 CE. Only fragments remain, but we can tell from the fragments that he used the four canonical gospels and based the structure on the chronology of John's Gospel. Other writers also attempted to write one gospel that collated the information from all four, but the practice didn't catch on, probably because Irenaeus would soon sing the praises of the fourfold canonical gospels.[33] The importance of the *Diatessaron* is in the fact that it demonstrates that only the four canonical gospels were considered authoritative.

MELITO OF SARDIS

Melito was another student of Justin Martyr who became bishop of Sardis in Asia Minor. Like his teacher, he wrote an apology addressed to the emperor Marcus Aurelius, though only a fragment of it survives.[34] In it, he argued that the empire should not persecute the Church since both empire and Church were "born" at about the same time.

Homily on the Passover

Melito is best known for his *Homily on the Passover*, sometimes known simply as *On the Passover*. It is actually an Easter homily, preached around 176 CE, which connects the passion of Jesus to the Exodus in the Old Testament. Unfortunately, this is probably the most anti-Semitic of the subapostolic documents. Following the *Epistle of Barnabas*, Melito believed that the covenant in the Old Testament was no longer valid.[35] He says that the scriptures and traditions of the Jews now belong to the Church, implying that the Jews no longer deserve them. In his interpretation, the bitter herbs of the Passover represent the bitterness of the Jews who rejected their Messiah, and he claims that Jerusalem fell and the Temple was destroyed because the Jews killed Jesus.

ATHENAGORAS

Athenagoras was an Athenian philosopher who converted to Christianity. His conversion to the faith is said to be the indirect result of the apostle Paul's preaching in Athens (Acts 17). According to the story, Athenagoras had set out to disprove Christianity. He was especially interested in refuting the Christian understanding of the resurrection of the body, in favor of the philosophical belief in the immortality of disembodied souls. When he read the apostle Paul's letters, however, he was convinced of the truth of Christianity and joined the Church.

On the Resurrection of the Dead

Athenagoras's attempt to find a way to discredit Christianity had failed, and in the process it had changed him. The result was a treatise that defends the very belief he set out to disprove. It appears to be heavily influenced by Justin Martyr's writing on the same subject.

A Plea for the Christians

Sometimes translated as *A Supplication for the Christians*, this apology was written about 177 CE and addressed to the emperor Marcus Aurelius and his son (the next emperor) Commodus. Athenagoras tried to explain the relationship between God the Father and Christ the Son as similar to the relationship between the emperor and his heir. They rule jointly, and the son carries the father's authority, yet the father is the source of that authority, and in that sense has authority over the son. While the analogy ultimately falls short of adequately describing the Trinity, it was ahead of its time as a way to try to explain both the unity of the Father and Son and the distinction between the persons.

THEOPHILUS OF ANTIOCH

Born around 115 CE, Theophilus was bishop of Antioch in Syria from about 168 or 169 CE until his death, though accounts differ as to whether he died in 181 or 188 CE. Antioch was emerging as one of the most influential centers of Christian thought, and Theophilus (as a successor of Ignatius in the same see) contributed to that. Antioch had been the headquarters of the original mission to the Gentiles and was the place where followers of Jesus were first called "Christians." At first it was a derogatory term used by the enemies of the Church to try to insult them, as if to say they were the slaves of an executed man. But Christians liked thinking of Jesus as their master, and so the name stuck. Theophilus refers to this in his writings, saying that the name *Christian* means more than just a follower of Christ—it means one who is also anointed like Christ.[36]

To Autolycus

Theophilus's only remaining work, this document is a compilation of a series of letters written to a pagan friend named Autolycus. We can date the correspondence to the early 180s CE, since by this time Marcus Aurelius was dead, yet Commodus had not been emperor long enough to escalate persecution. Therefore, we seem to be in a short lull in the persecution, when Theophilus, like Clement of Rome, can say that the emperor rules by God's will. In trying to convince Autolycus of the truth of Christianity, Theophilus argued that just because the blind cannot see does not mean the sun doesn't shine.[37] He also followed Aristides in arguing for a Creator based on a version of an argument from intelligent design. Since a ship sailing on the sea implies a captain, therefore the universe must also have its pilot, who is God the Creator.[38]

While the Church has always conceived of God in the divine relationship that is Father, Son, and Holy Spirit (Matt 28:19), the *doctrine* of the Trinity was only in its infancy at this time. In fact, Theophilus was the first to attempt to put a name on the Trinity, calling God a "Triad," or *Triados* in Greek. A generation later, Tertullian would be the first to use the word *Trinity* in Latin (*Trinitas*). Theophilus's theology has its problems, however, since he seems to follow Tatian in dividing the preincarnate existence of the Logos into two phases, based on the analogy of the Word of God with a spoken word. In the first phase, the Word was *in* the Father (like a thought in the Father's mind), and in the second phase the Word was *emitted*, or "spoken forth." This is connected to the concept of God creating by speaking, as in Genesis chapter 1. Thus the Logos goes from being *in* the Father to being *with* the Father. The problem with this is that even though both phases exist before the creation of the universe, in the first phase the Son of God does not seem to have his own distinct existence, but only exists as the wisdom of the Father. This implies a change in the very being of the Logos (going from internal to external relative to the Father), which would contradict the universally held assumption that divinity is *immutable*—that is, it cannot change (Heb 13:8). Therefore, Theophilus's way of dividing the preincarnate existence of the Word into two phases did not survive in later theology.

Theophilus should probably not be called a heretic, however, since it would be unfair to hold him to later standards of orthodoxy, but it is likely that his thoughts about the preexistent Logos influenced later heresies, including Arianism (see chapter 8 below).[39]

One interesting feature of Theophilus is a distinction he made between *worship*, which is reserved for God alone, and *reverence*, which can be legitimately directed toward the emperor. In making this distinction, he was attempting to clarify why Christians cannot participate in the imperial cult, but he also anticipated the conclusions of a later debate over the proper use of religious icons. Later councils would conclude that it is acceptable to show reverence to icons, but not to worship them.

CLEMENT OF ALEXANDRIA

With Clement, we come to the last of the apologists. In some ways he is a transitional figure, because he wrote for Christians as well as for non-Christians and he did use scripture to support his arguments. He was a priest but not a bishop, yet we call him Clement "of Alexandria" to distinguish him from Clement of Rome.[40] Born approximately between 150 and 160 CE, Clement is yet another example of the philosopher who set out to find the best philosophy and ended up a Christian. When he sought out someone who could teach him about Christianity, he found one Pantaenus, who was the leader of the church's catechetical school in Alexandria, Egypt. Clement followed Pantaenus to Alexandria, joined the church there, and eventually succeeded Pantaenus as the head of the school in about 190 CE. As leader of the school in Alexandria, he would be the teacher and predecessor of Origen, whom we will meet later. When persecution came to Alexandria at the beginning of the third century, Clement left and went to Jerusalem, then Antioch, and eventually Cappadocia in Asia Minor. He died there in about 215 CE.

Exhortation to the Greeks

Sometimes known as *Exhortation to the Heathen*, or by its Greek name, *Protreptikos*, this is an apologetic defense of Christianity as a philosophy. Clement says that the philosophers were right to reject the old pagan mythology, but that they were wrong to trade it for atheism. For Clement, superstition is one extreme and atheism is the other. True religion is found in the middle between the extremes.[41] He said that Socrates believed in one God, and his disciples would have proclaimed the same if they had not been afraid to share his fate.[42] Clement's explanation of Christian monotheism is in many ways a summary of the Logos Christology of the apologists. While he does not add much to the development of doctrine per se, his *Exhortation to the Greeks* is an excellent epitome of the state of Christian theology in the age of the apologists.

Finally, in this document, there is an interesting quote of an early Christian hymn. The same hymn (based on Isaiah 52:1–2) is quoted in Ephesians 5:14, though Paul only gives us the first stanza. Clement provides the second verse:[43]

Verse 1	Awake, Oh sleeper
	Arise from the dead
	And Christ will give you light
Verse 2	Christ, the sun [*sic*] of resurrection
	Who existed before the morning star
	With his light he gives life

The Instructor

This is a catechetical manual, often known by its Greek name, *Paidagogos*. It must have been written for use in the catechetical school at Alexandria to prepare initiates for baptism. True to the times, catechesis was instruction not in theology but in morality. Church leaders of the subapostolic age must have assumed the faithful would get their theology in the liturgy after their baptism. What they needed before joining the Church was to learn how to live as a follower of Jesus. In other words, Christ is our Instructor, and we are his students, though "students" here is meant more in the sense of a young apprentice who learns much more than simply information but, rather, follows the instructor as a disciple, and is formed into a lifestyle. Therefore, catechism had to do with behavior, not belief. It is important to keep in mind that conversion to

Christianity could mean a drastic change from the lifestyle that people were used to, especially for the wealthy.

Clement goes to the extreme, however, and it is difficult to imagine that everything he preached was actually followed. To his credit, he advocates living simply and caring for the poor. But for him, as for Hermas, every luxury is a sin, including gourmet food, imported wine, and colorful clothing. In truth, the very fact that he urges so strongly and goes to such extremes probably tells a story of much more conformity to culture among the Christians than he would like.

We can also see in Clement of Alexandria a very strict approach to sexuality. He strongly promoted the idea that sex, even within marriage, is only for procreation, and here we are already seeing an association of all sexuality with sin.[44] This will lead to a doctrine of original sin that claimed that human sin and guilt are transmitted through sexual intercourse, and to the belief that celibacy is a higher calling than marriage.[45] Clement's own student Origen would demonstrate the unhealthy consequences of his attitudes toward sex, as we will see. But in the second century, the affirmation of apologists like Justin and Athenagoras that the body is part of the whole human, that it is part of God's good creation, and that it will be redeemed along with the soul in the resurrection is at odds with the negative attitudes toward sexuality of writers like Clement. We can probably blame the extreme hedonism and pedophilia within Roman culture for the fact that the Church would choose to distance itself from society by following Clement's lead.

The Miscellanies

As the name suggests, this is not a unified work so much as a collection of thoughts on various subjects, most of which have to do with comparisons of Christianity to the various systems of philosophy and heresies that existed on the fringe of the Church. It is sometimes referred to by its Greek name, *Stromateis* or *Stromata*. The approach is what we might call *internal apology*, since it was written with an apologetic tone, yet it was intended for a Christian audience. Here Clement famously says that philosophy is to the

46

Greeks what the Old Testament is to the Jews, a "schoolmaster" (think headmaster, or even truant officer) to bring them to Christ.[46]

Note that older editions of *The Instructor* and *The Miscellanies* have some sections that are not translated into English. Nineteenth-century editors apparently felt that the sections having to do with sexuality were not for the eyes of the layperson, so those sections are only given in Latin. The *Fathers of the Church* series, however, does have the full English translation.

Who Is the Rich Man That Shall Be Saved?

This is a homily on Jesus' words in Matthew 19:24, "...it is easier for a camel to go through the eye of a needle than for someone who is rich to enter the kingdom of God." Clement's interpretation is that spiritual wealth is different from worldly wealth. A person can be poor in the eyes of the world, yet rich in the things of God. In the same way, a person can be rich in the eyes of the world, yet poor in relation to God. In fact, material wealth has the potential to distract one from focusing on God. Yet, it is not the case that no wealthy person can be saved, since if everyone were poor, who would give to the poor? Clement is clearly influenced by Hermas's *The Shepherd* and its concept of the symbiotic relationship of rich and poor. Therefore, the rich man who will be saved is the one who gives to the poor.

CHAPTER 4

The Church in the Subapostolic Age

THE DEVELOPMENT OF
THE HIERARCHY

As we have already seen, two kinds of authority existed side by side in the subapostolic age: *apostolic authority*, which was based on the concept of apostolic succession and which came to be centered in the bishops, and *charismatic authority*, which was invested by the grassroots of the laity in certain people such as the confessors. In the second century, a movement emerged that forced the Church's hand in favoring the former type over the latter. The movement was known at the time as the "New Prophecy" but is now generally referred to as Montanism. It is named after its founder, a Phrygian named Montanus, who with his daughters claimed to be prophets speaking with the voice of the Holy Spirit.

The Montanists were an ascetic faction within the Church who practiced charismatic gifts and believed that the return of Christ was imminent. They found some influential supporters, including at least one bishop of Rome (temporarily) as well as Irenaeus and Tertullian. As we will see, Tertullian would eventually associate with the Montanists in North Africa. But their rising popularity would prove to be their downfall, since anyone who claims to have a direct connection to God and to speak with the voice of the Holy Spirit presents a problem for the unity of the Church. How does the Church prevent a person or group who claims charismatic authority from preaching something different from the bishops—something that would divide the Church? Also, the Montanists followed Papias's interpretation of the Book of Revelation, which included a literal interpretation of the so-called millennium, and which the majority of the Church would reject. The result was an uncertainty about the usefulness of the Book of Revelation and, significantly, a growing suspicion of prophecy as a challenge to both the authority and the unity of the Church.

Consequently, two things happened in the subapostolic age. First, prophecy as a gift of the Spirit was edged out of the Church. As it turned out, preaching replaced prophecy as the proclamation and interpretation of revealed truth.[1] The other thing that happened was the separation of clergy from the laity (preserving the teaching authority in the clergy) and the evolution of church leadership as a vocation. These two things are, of course, interrelated.

As we look at the development of the hierarchy in the subapostolic age, we can see two distinct phases. The first phase is consistent with what we already see emerging in the New Testament as the apostles chose and commissioned their successors. In that context, the Greek terms that we translate as "bishop" and "priest" are basically synonymous. Therefore, the first phase is a four-tiered structure that we can still see in the Didache, which looks like this:

- Apostle/prophet—Itinerant missionaries
- Bishop/priest—Resident pastors
- Deacon—Assistant to the pastors
- Laity

The apostles were considered to be inspired, on the level of the Old Testament prophets (Rev 18:20), and of course we know that their writings would come to be called scripture (2 Pet 3:15–16).[2] Their immediate successors, called "elders," were also given a certain status and authority, and some of them are also New Testament authors.[3] The apostles were itinerant, moving around as they established and supported various local Christian groups. They had authority over those local churches and over the resident leaders there, primarily because they had appointed and commissioned these second-generation church leaders (often to be leaders over churches they themselves had founded), but for many of the apostles they also had authority because they knew Jesus—they had been his disciples.

The resident pastors are referred to in the New Testament and Didache as either *episcopos* (bishop, overseer) or *presbyteros* (priest, elder), implying that the two words are used more or less synonymously.[4] In Justin Martyr, the leader is called a presider (*proestos*, sometimes translated "president"). These pastors preside over the church meetings, but this may be simply because the meeting is in their homes. They are also called teachers, since they are the ones who read and explain the letters from the apostles and passages from the gospels, and generally encourage the faith of the group.[5]

When the church in any city grew to the point where all the Christians there could no longer fit into one house, or when multiple house-churches arose in different parts of the city or among different ethnic (language) groups, the house-church presiders must have met together periodically to compare notes, share letters, and support one another.[6] When it became necessary to correspond with the Christians in another city, one member of the group was chosen to write the letter on behalf of the rest.[7] As this practice grew, at some point the word for "bishop," which literally means "overseer," came to be used exclusively for the one priest chosen to be the chair of the council. This development probably happened sooner in the larger cities like Rome; however, even there it is probably the case that at first the bishop functioned only as chair of the council and was directed in his official duties by the rest of the priests.[8]

By the time of Clement of Rome, in the last decade of the first century, we can see that Rome has one priest who has been designated as "bishop," who is probably still advised by the council of the rest of the priests, but has the authority to write on behalf of the Christians of Rome. As we have already seen, Clement wrote 1 Clement with an air of authority even over the Christians in Corinth, based on Rome's association with Peter. What this demonstrates is that by the time of Clement, the role of bishop is understood to be an *office* of the Church, and that office in Rome is already associated with the apostle Peter as the first "overseer" there. It is important to note, however, that at this point in history, even when church leadership becomes an "office," it is still not a "job." Church leaders do not make a living leading the Church, and laypeople are understood to be in ministry as much as the leaders.[9] Clement of Rome is therefore a transitional figure in whom we can see the title "bishop" separated from the general priesthood and used for one priest who is chosen to represent the rest. It is probably still the case, however, that the authority of the bishop is limited to that given him by the council.

Although it happened at different paces in different places, by the time of Ignatius of Antioch we can see the second phase in the evolution of the Church's hierarchy. Two important things have happened to move the process along. First, the apostles died. With the death of John after the turn of the century there were no more apostles left, and only a few remained who had known them personally. Even these so-called elders were not given the same status as prophets, and with the controversy over Montanism, prophecy never became a leadership position within the Church. The second thing that happened was the growth of the Church to the point where there were multiple house-churches in each city. This meant that the leaders of the individual house-churches within each city had to keep in touch, and the leadership of each city had to try to keep in touch with the leadership in other cities, in order to make sure that the Church stayed unified.

Staying unified, however, requires maintaining a unified body of teaching. If different pastors are teaching conflicting interpretations of Christ and the scriptures, the Church will split. Therefore, as Ignatius knew, it is not enough to have a council of priests; there must also be a centralized authority to resolve disputes that arise. The office of bishop emerged as that authority. The bishop was still one of the priests, but the bishops took the place of the apostles as "overseers," in the sense of having an authority over the other priests. The primary difference between the first phase and the second phase is that in the first phase, even when there is a bishop functioning as the chair of the council, the priests tell the bishop what to do. In the second phase, the bishop tells the priests what to do.[10] In the first phase, the bishop is a representative of the council; in the second phase, the bishop is the authority over the council.

In this second phase we still have a four-tiered hierarchy; however, now it looks like this:

- Bishop—Overseer/teaching authority
- Priest—Pastor/teacher
- Deacon—Assistant to the bishop
- Laity

The bishop has replaced the apostle as overseer but is not itinerant; he is local to his *see*, which is his city and the sphere of his influence. The bishop may be one of the resident pastors (especially early on), and he is the chair of the council.[11] Ignatius argues for the ideal of one bishop per city,[12] but that is not necessarily the reality, especially in the bigger cities. In a place like Rome, it is entirely possible that when the church got large enough there could have been more than one intracity council (perhaps based on language), each with its own chair, and possibly each with its own catechetical school.[13]

The priests were still the pastors of the individual house-churches; however, the bishops reserved the authority to preside over the sacraments, or the "mysteries" of the Church. It is unclear how one bishop could preside over the Eucharist in multiple house-churches on Sunday mornings. In some places, it is possible that individual house-churches may have met on Sunday mornings for a liturgy without the Eucharist. Then Christians from across the city would gather in a larger place in the evening for a eucharistic meal presided over by the bishop.[14] It was also inevitable that in the larger cities the priests were eventually granted the authority to preside over the Eucharist in their individual meetings, as long as they were in agreement with the bishop. This seems to be the case in Rome in the middle of the second century, based on the liturgy of Justin Martyr.[15]

Baptisms generally took place once a year at Easter, when the bishop would initiate all the candidates of the city, with the assistance of the deacons. The bishops may have also held some authority over burials; at least we know this was so by the third century. Once the church of a city could acquire and control land for burials, the bishop or his appointee would manage the cemetery and (we assume) the bishop would conduct the burials. Marriage at this time was not a ritual of the Church but a legal contract. A tradition of going to the bishop for a blessing emerged, however, and Ignatius advised that all Christian couples should get the bishop's permission to marry.[16]

The priests were considered the teachers of their house-churches, but now the bishops became the authority over the content of the teaching, so that they are the ones who would ultimately settle questions of interpretation. In other words, the priests must teach what is consistent with, and acceptable to, the bishops, since the bishops are the successors to the apostles. Based on the concept of apostolic succession, the unity of the Church is guaranteed by the consistency of its teaching, which in turn is guaranteed by the integrity of the teaching office. The responsibility for this integrity rested with the bishops.

In this second phase of the development of the hierarchy, the deacons appear to have gone from assisting the priests in general to assisting the bishops specifically, especially in the sacraments. The deacon's role was always associated with the sacraments, however, and now that the office of bishop is distinct from the rest of the priests, the sacraments are centralized in the bishop, so the deacons become the assistants to the bishops. Eventually, the deacons would distribute the eucharistic elements.[17] In some places, the deacons also functioned as ushers, or "doorkeepers," with the responsibility of questioning visitors before they were allowed into the assembly where they would receive the Eucharist.[18] In general, the deacons represented the bishop, and part of the deacons' responsibilities included visiting the sick and keeping the bishop informed of the needs of the people in his see.[19] We learn from Justin Martyr that the deacons are also charged with taking the eucharistic elements to shut-ins and prisoners.[20] Therefore, there must be enough deacons, "in proportion to the number of the congregation of the people of the church."[21] While in one sense church leadership came to be defined as the three "orders" of bishop, priest, and deacon, however, the deacons were not considered clergy since their role in liturgy was limited and they did not have the authority to preside over the sacraments.[22]

As I have noted, the controversy over the Montanists and other factors led to a separation between clergy and laity, and though church leadership was still not a "day job," there was less and less talk of the laity having a part in ministry. In some places, laymen continued to be teachers, and there are hints of laypeople involved in ministries of healing.[23] Nevertheless, in some ways we have gone from seeing the Church as Christians witnessing and ministering to the world to seeing the Church as clergy ministering to the laity. In fact, it has been remarked that the clergy would become like the patrons of the laity.[24] No doubt the persecution of the Church by the empire contributed to this inward shift of focus.

WORSHIP AND THE SACRAMENTS

Much could be said about worship in the early Church, and it should go without saying that many whole books have been written on the subject.[25] Since we are focused on reading the documents of the early Church, we will only briefly survey worship as it relates to the early texts. For instance, there are some extant examples of early Christian hymns, such as are contained in the New Testament itself (Col 1:15–20, Phil 2:6–11, Eph 5:14, to name a few). We have already looked at the verse included in Clement of Alexandria's *Exhortation to the Greeks*. In addition, there are two documents from the subapostolic age that appear to include Christian songs, or at least poems. It should be noted that the early Church did not know our modern distinction between singing, chanting, and reciting.[26] Hymn singing probably meant something like chanting in unison, with a melody of a limited range.[27] There is evidence that the hymns were accompanied by the lyre, which was a sort of cross between a guitar and a harp.[28]

The *Sibylline Oracles*

The Sibyl was a Greco-Roman female medium. She supposedly had mystical visions inspired by the gods and pronounced oracles, or prophecies, based on those visions. These oracles were then written down and consulted later after significant events, something like the way the writings of Nostradamus are supposed to have predicted certain disasters. Jewish apologists wrote their own versions of these oracles, presenting them as older prophecies of current events. Following their lead, some Christians modified the Jewish versions, rewriting them to appear to be pre-Christian predictions of Christ. They seem to be intended to resemble the Book of Revelation, except the predictions of the life of Christ are not even subtle, let alone symbolic. While the majority of the Church did not accept these as real prophecy, they do seem to have been used as devotional poetry. Books 1, 6, and 8 of the *Sibylline Oracles* may have been used in Christian worship. Book 6 especially may be an early Christian hymn and includes a reference to the Eucharist, comparing the advent of Christ to the nourishment of bread.[29]

The *Odes of Solomon*

Sometimes called an early Christian hymnal, the *Odes* are written like a Christian version of the Psalms. They are allegorical to the point of being mystical, and they even use some surprising feminine images for God, including presenting God as a nursing mother who provides life-giving milk for her children.[30] The Virgin Mary has a somewhat prominent role in Ode 33.[31] We also get an interesting glimpse of prayer in the *Odes*, which suggests that at least on some occasions Christians prayed in a cruciform position, standing with arms outstretched to the sides, in imitation of Christ on the cross.[32]

The Sacraments

The early Church did not have a set list of seven sacraments such as the Catholic Church has now. All the rituals existed in the subapostolic age in one form or another, however, with the possible exception of marriage, although how elaborate or ritualized the bishop's blessing may have been is not known. A rite of ordination must have emerged as the hierarchy moved from phase one into phase two, and there was a need to formally consecrate new church leaders.[33] At first, new priests were probably chosen by the existing priests and laity; however, in phase two of the hierarchy the new priests and deacons were chosen and ordained by the bishops. The bishops were elected by the council of priests (in some places, with the ratification of the laity).[34] A newly elected bishop would be consecrated by other bishops from the region.[35] Eventually, however, the election of bishops came to be reserved for fellow bishops, as the elevation of a bishop shifted from the priests choosing one of their own to lead them to the bishops choosing one from the lower rank to join them.[36]

Baptism and confirmation were originally one ritual. The baptism itself was the sign of the acceptance of the faith by a new convert, while the confirmation was the Church's response to it and a consecration of the new Christian. This consecration was done by an imposition (laying on) of hands, and possibly anointing with oil. Baptism was preceded by a time of catechesis in which the convert learned the expectations of the church community with regard to morality and behavior. Also, while theology per se was not a priority, the initiate was taught a statement of faith. The earliest examples of baptismal statements of faith are preserved in the New Testament and could be as simple as saying, "Jesus is Lord" (1 Cor 12:13). These statements of faith were the Church's first creeds (from the Latin word *credo*, meaning "I believe"). Examples of creeds in the subapostolic age can be found in Ignatius of Antioch and Aristides.[37] At the time of baptism the new believer would show his or her sincerity of faith before the congregation, by either reciting the statement of faith or responding affirmatively to it in question-and-answer form. As infant baptism became the norm, the rites of baptism and confirmation became separated, and the affirmation of faith was postponed with the confirmation until the individual could claim the faith for him- or herself.

Baptisms, originally done once a year at Easter, were preceded by fasting. Both the initiate and the presider were expected to fast.[38] In fact, the original time of *Lent* commemorated the forty hours between Jesus' death and resurrection. Candidates fasted during that time and celebrated Jesus' resurrection with a symbolic resurrection of their own—coming up from the water of baptism.[39] Full immersion under water was the norm, since going under the water and coming back up symbolized dying and rising with Christ. If a body of water was not available, however, pouring water over the initiate's head was acceptable.[40]

In obedience to Christ (Matt 28:19), baptism was always done in the name of the Father, Son, and Holy Spirit.[41] The baptism was described as the "seal" of eternal life.[42] There seems to have been widespread agreement in the early Church, however, that baptism only washes away the sins one committed prior to the baptism.[43] Postbaptismal sin was a problem, and many people believed that the sins Christians committed after baptism would be held against them.[44] As we have already noted, it was assumed that one could lose one's salvation, especially by committing a serious sin after baptism.[45] "Serious sins" included apostasy, idolatry, murder, and adultery. Eventually, that category would be expanded to include any sin that broke one of the Ten Commandments. Some writers would talk of the possibility of forgiveness for *one* postbaptismal sin,[46] especially for new converts, but the strict application of Hebrews 6:4–6 and 10:26–29 led to the very real expectation that a Christian, once baptized, was not supposed to sin. Not surprisingly, this led to the practice of postponing baptism until all wild oats were sowed. The men of the aristocracy, especially, who knew that joining the Church would conflict with their careers, often waited until retirement to join their wives as baptized members. Eventually, the reality that human beings cannot stop sinning simply because they are baptized would contribute to the development of the sacrament of penance and reconciliation.

The Eucharist was called *the* "Mystery of the Church."[47] The word *Eucharist* means "thanksgiving," and from the very beginning of the Church it was seen as a ritual act of thanks for the sacrifice of Christ, based on both the Jewish Passover meal and the Last Supper of Jesus. At first it was part of an actual meal called the *agape*, or love feast (cf. 1 Cor 11:18–22), but by the time of Ignatius, it was already a liturgical rite, separate from the meal.[48] Probably in most places the Eucharist became part of the Sunday morning meeting, while the meal was a "potluck" relegated to Sunday evening.[49]

Although the writers of the subapostolic age did not have a highly developed eucharistic theology, there was a general consensus that what happens in the Eucharist is much more than a mere symbol or a memorial.[50] The Eucharist was seen as a reenactment of the passion of Christ (1 Cor 11:26), much like the Jewish Passover meal, in which a past event is mystically made present. The Eucharist was associated with the incarnation of Christ, so that the Eucharist becomes in a way a new incarnation.[51] Just as the Word became flesh, the eucharistic bread and wine become the flesh and blood of Christ. Irenaeus specifically said that the eucharistic elements *become* the body and blood of Christ.[52] Therefore, the Eucharist was never thought of as a symbol or memorial only, but a mystery, and the early Christians knew that whatever was happening in the ritual, it was a miracle of incarnation in which Christ was present as the Word made flesh.

Just as baptism included confirmation, the Eucharist included confession.[53] Confession of (smaller) sins was expected of everyone before receiving the Eucharist, though this probably took the form of the congregational recitation of a prayer of confession. Later, those who committed serious sins would be expected to confess publicly in front of the congregation before reconciliation. As we have already seen, the table of the Eucharist was believed to be the earthly expression of the kingdom of God, and so was connected to salvation. Therefore, to be excluded from the Eucharist was to be excluded from the kingdom, and excommunication emerged very early as a form of discipline within the Church (1 Cor 5).[54] Excommunication meant being *excluded* from *communion*. Reconciliation meant being readmitted to the table, but since the bishop held the authority over the sacrament, reconciliation meant returning to the bishop.[55] This is another reason why it became important to limit the number of bishops to one per city. When there was more than one bishop in a city, a person who was excommunicated by one bishop could try to receive the Eucharist from the other bishop. If bishops did not enforce each other's excommunication, then the unity of the Church was threatened. For most people, however, every Eucharist was also a reconciliation service in which daily sins were confessed and access to God through Christ was granted.

We have already noted the detailed order of liturgy preserved for us in Justin Martyr's *1 Apology*. We can now see that the Church conducted weekly Eucharist/reconciliation services, annual baptism/confirmation services, and ordinations and burials as needed. Marriage at this time was probably not a ritual, although the bishops would bless couples and perhaps give their permission for Christians to marry.

CHRISTOLOGY AND THEOLOGY IN THE SUBAPOSTOLIC AGE

Clement of Alexandria was on to something when he said that true religion can be found in the middle between the extremes.[56] As the Church read the Hebrew Scriptures and the writings of the apostles, it was inevitable that diverging interpretations would emerge, some of which were mutually exclusive. As it turned out, these diverging interpretations (or "heresies") can be described as two extremes, existing on the fringes of what, for lack of a better term, might be called the "mainstream" Church in the middle.[57] Simply put, some denied the humanity of Christ and said that he was pure spirit, while others denied the divinity of Christ as said that he was only a man. The mainstream church affirmed both the humanity and the divinity of Christ and defended the middle against the extremes.

Docetics, Marcionites, and Gnostics

In the church at Corinth, the apostle Paul had had to deal with a problem of division between two groups of people, whom we will call the philosophical and the charismatic (1 Cor 1:10—4:20).[58] The philosophical group was the minority in the Corinthian church. They were wealthy and prided themselves on their education and their reading of Greek philosophy. Therefore, they considered themselves wise—that is, more enlightened—than the others. They reasoned that since idols are not really gods, there is no moral problem with eating meat from an animal that had been sacrificed to an idol. Since they were wealthy and moved in aristocratic circles, they were still getting invited to the pagan feasts held by their non-Christian friends (1 Cor 8:10).

The other group was the majority, but from the lower economic classes and so probably could not even afford meat on a regular basis.[59] Eating or not eating idol meat was not a choice they had to make very often, since they were not as likely to get invited to pagan banquets at which meat that had been sacrificed to idols would be served. They are probably the charismatics Paul addressed in 1 Corinthians 14.[60] They were disturbed by the fact that the wealthy among them were going to pagan banquets and would eat meat that had been part of a pagan sacrifice. This became a practical problem when the philosophical group treated the Christian fellowship meal (the *agape* meal) like one of their pagan banquets. Since they did not really have to work for a living, they could gather in the afternoon, eat all the best food that was brought, and help themselves to extra servings of wine. When the working class finished their day at sundown, they would arrive at the Christian gathering to find all the best food eaten and their wealthier (and supposedly wiser) brothers and sisters drunk (1 Cor 11:17–22). In this early version of the potluck meal, those who came without a pot were out of luck. In fact, situations like this may have been the reason that the sacrament of the Lord's Supper became separated from the fellowship meal.

In any case, those who considered themselves wise thought the charismatics were superstitious and therefore foolish for worrying about whether meat had been sacrificed to an idol. Paul responded to this by turning the concepts of wisdom and foolishness upside down: human wisdom is foolishness to God and the wisdom of the cross seems like foolishness to Jews and Gentiles alike. Paul admits that those who call themselves wise have a strong faith and that in a way the faith of the others is weaker; however, he also turns this distinction on its head by saying that even he (Paul) is weak, but God has chosen the weak to shame the strong. By responding in this way, Paul was calling into question the value of philosophical wisdom or indeed of anything that would allow some Christians to see themselves as above the others and above responsibility to others.

The important thing for our observations on Christology and theology in the subapostolic age is that the philosophical group was made up of Gentile Christians, converts from paganism, who did not feel the need to distance themselves completely from their pagan roots. They may have seen themselves as disciples of Apollos rather than Paul, and may have valued the eloquent philosophical style of speech of Apollos over the down-to-earth approach of the former Pharisee (Acts 18, 1 Cor 1:12, 3:4–6). In Greek culture, it could easily be assumed that the more eloquent the speech, the truer the content, and so Paul himself might have been looked down upon by this group.

All of this was typical of some early Christian converts from paganism, who apparently were not concerned to shed all the elements of their former religion. This included a certain philosophical concept called *dualism*, which, when brought into the Church, directly affected a person's understanding of Christ. Philosophical dualism goes back to the teachings of Plato and assumes that whatever exists in the material world is somehow not as real as that which exists in the spiritual realm.[61] The things of the physical realm were considered to be mere shadows of the true realities that exist in the spiritual realm. An extreme version of this assumed that whatever is of the spiritual realm is good, but whatever is of the physical world is inherently evil.[62] If one applies this extreme dualism to Christ, one would have to conclude that Christ could not really become human, since pure spirit (the divine *Logos*) cannot touch evil matter (flesh). Therefore, there were some within the early Church who came to believe that Christ only *seemed* to be human but was really some kind of phantom, or just a vision (cf. Mt 14:26, Mk 6:49). The Greek verb *dokein*, meaning "to seem" or "to appear," gives us the word *docetism*. Docetism was the belief that spirit is "light" and flesh is "darkness," and therefore Jesus was not really flesh and blood, but only appeared to be.[63]

Docetics reasoned that if Christ was not really human and his body was only an illusion, then the resurrection was not a real bodily resurrection but simply another vision of Christ, although perhaps without the illusion of human appearance. They further reasoned that since Christ was, in effect, always in a "resurrected" state, those who follow him are also already living the resurrection life, and therefore they denied any future resurrection. In the letters of Ignatius of Antioch we have already encountered this *realized eschatology*, the conviction that true believers are already somehow living in a postresurrection state and have achieved the transcendence that Christ promised. Two people who taught this idea are mentioned by name in 2 Timothy 2:16–18. Therefore, since Hymenaeus and Philetus taught that "the resurrection has already taken place," they apparently denied the future resurrection based on a rejection of the flesh and so are probably the earliest Docetics we know of by name.[64]

Since Docetics taught a strict separation between the spiritual and the physical, many saw themselves as primarily spiritual beings untouchable by the corruption of the flesh. This made them believe they were immune to evil and therefore what they did with their bodies could not affect their spirits. This would have allowed the "wise" of Corinth to eat meat sacrificed to idols, but it also allowed some Docetics to justify all kinds of immorality based on the assumption that their spirits were exempt from moral responsibility or accountability (cf. 1 Cor 6:12). Therefore, docetism could lead to a hedonistic lifestyle, and this may be part of what Paul was referring to when he said that they did not correctly understand the body (1 Cor 11:29).[65] Paul obviously believed that what one does with one's body *does* affect one's spirit, but even if idol meat does not directly affect the one who eats it, it does affect others who are part of the same body of Christ, the Church (1 Cor 6:12–20). Ironically, a docetic philosophy led some others to attempt to deny the flesh and live an ascetic lifestyle that punishes the body and rejects physical pleasure (1 Cor 7:1, Col 2:20–23). Not surprisingly, Paul advocates the middle way, that is, to respect the body as the temple of the Holy Spirit: do not punish it, but also do not indulge it.

Pagan converts to Christianity were also susceptible to what Paul calls superstition. Since they were used to the idea of worshiping multiple deities, it was easy for them to accept the worship of angels and other supposed heavenly "authorities and powers" as well as the practice of certain aspects of the occult, including magic and astrology. We can see Paul dealing with this in his Letter to the Colossians. Some of the Christians in Colossae were apparently being led to incorporate elements of paganism with their (docetic) version of Christianity (Col 2:8–19). This merging of elements from different religious systems is called *syncretism* and might be thought of as the "salad bar" approach to spirituality. It allows one to choose which parts of each system to accept based on preformed assumptions or simply on what feels most comfortable, and of course it allows the person to reject aspects of one tradition or another based on the authority of one's own preference.[66] Sometimes evidence of syncretism in the New Testament is called *proto-gnosticism*, because it is the precursor to the development of gnosticism in the second century.[67] While we can definitely see the seeds of gnosticism in the Docetics of the New Testament, it is too early to call this real gnosticism. We can, however, understand this progression as an equation. Gnosticism is the result of the combination of docetism and syncretism; that is, docetism plus syncretism equals gnosticism.[68]

Docetic Christology did not have a problem with the idea of worshiping Christ. Since Docetics came from a background of polytheism, limiting worship to one God was not necessarily a priority for them. Therefore, they were perfectly comfortable with the concept of the divinity of Christ. Their docetism led them to deny the real humanity of Christ, however. In their way of thinking, he could not become human because he could not become flesh. Therefore, in response to the Docetics, Paul had emphasized the true humanity of Christ and his real flesh and blood (Col 1:22). He did that by talking about the cross. Paul wrote that our sins were nailed to the cross along with Jesus' body, and so if he had no body, we are still dead in our sins (Col 2:12–14). In addition, Paul implies that since Christ is the new Adam, he must be human as Adam was human (1 Cor 15:44–49).[69] If Christ is to be the savior of humanity, he must be truly human. If he is to be the mediator between God and humanity, he cannot represent humanity unless he is really one of us (1 Tim 2:5–6). So Paul connects our very salvation with the humanity of Christ: if he was not human, he could not save humans. This was the basis for later arguments against docetism (*what is not assumed is not saved*).[70]

Pauline texts that affirm the humanity of Christ are, of course, numerous; however, one stands out as a direct confrontation of docetism. In Colossians 2:9, Paul expands on a point made in the hymn quoted earlier in the letter, specifically Colossians 1:19. There it says that all the "fullness" dwelt within Christ. In Colossians 2:9, Paul explains that it is the fullness of Deity, or divinity itself, that dwells within the person of Christ. Of course, the Docetics would not have a problem with this idea. But the other shoe drops when Paul finishes the sentence, "All the fullness of deity dwells within him...*bodily*." In other words, in this one verse Paul affirms both the divinity and the humanity of Christ. He was divine, but he also had a real human body, with real flesh and blood. Therefore, his incarnation was an act of solidarity with us, and in his death he died as a representative of humanity, dying our death so that we could live his life (2 Cor 5:21).

The legacy of the Docetics of the first century emerges in the second century in the Marcionites and Gnostics.[71] As we saw in the New Testament documents (cf. 1 John 4:3) and in the letters of Ignatius of Antioch, there were those who taught that Christ was human in appearance only, that he did not have real flesh and blood.[72] Thus they denied the reality of Jesus' human nature. Second-century Docetics apparently argued from Romans 8:3 and Philippians 2:7–8 that Jesus only appeared in the "likeness" of flesh, not in real flesh.[73] They further argued from 1 Corinthians 15:50 that flesh and blood cannot be redeemed.[74] They apparently applied to Jesus what the angel Raphael says about himself in Tobit 12:6–22: "Even though you watched me eat and drink, I did not really do so. You were seeing a vision" (v. 19). Therefore, their dualism led them to reject the concepts of physical incarnation and bodily resurrection in Christ. Also, since they were primarily converts from paganism, they were willing to accept the possibility of multiple deities without feeling the need to preserve the oneness of God.

The most famous Docetic was Marcion. Marcion, however, was apparently the disciple of one Cerdo (also known as Cerdon), who was later called the "founder of the Marcionite error."[75] We know very little about Cerdo other than the fact that he was teaching in Rome in the 130s CE.[76] According to his opponents, he taught that the God of the Old Testament was actually a different God from the Father of Jesus revealed in the gospels.[77] He said that the Old Testament God was a God of justice and punishment, but that the God and Father of the Lord Jesus Christ was a higher God, a God of love and mercy. In fact, Old Testament claims that the God of the Hebrews is the only God were presented as the prideful and ignorant boastings of a less than omniscient deity.[78] Based on a literal interpretation of anthropomorphisms of God in the Old Testament, Cerdo had reasoned that the God described there could not be the true Supreme Being, but must be an inferior deity, or *demiurge*.[79] This demiurge was the creator of the world, but that was precisely the problem. The material world was evil, or at least it included evil, which meant that this creator god was also the creator of evil (using Isaiah 45:7 as a proof text).[80] It was said that Marcion embraced Cerdo's teaching because he was obsessed with the problem of evil, and Cerdo's theology provided a solution that made the God of the Old Testament responsible for evil while exonerating the "real" God whom Jesus revealed.[81] Part of Marcion's motivation for rejecting the Old Testament may also have been a desire to distance himself from Judaism, following the second Jewish revolt and the fall of Jerusalem in 135 CE.[82]

After a time of study with Cerdo, Marcion became a teacher in his own right, gaining followers and teaching his own brand of docetism. According to early tradition Polycarp, the bishop of Smyrna, once met Marcion and called him to his face "the firstborn of Satan."[83] None of Marcion's writings are extant; however, some fragments of his teaching are preserved in Tertullian's *Against Marcion*, which is our primary source for understanding his thought.[84] Consistent with his teacher, Marcion taught that it was a mistake to associate Jesus with the messiah promised in the Old Testament prophets. In reality (he taught), Jesus did not come as a representative of the God of the Old Testament, but came to rescue humanity from that God. The God who had created the world was keeping humanity imprisoned in the material realm (and in physical bodies) and Jesus came to free humans from this prison. Jesus was not born as a baby nor did he grow up, but he appeared on earth as an adult shortly before his baptism.[85] He was not human, but was a spirit who never actually suffered on a cross.[86]

By about 140 CE, Marcion had published a list of the documents he thought should be included in the Christian canon. Marcion's canon included only one gospel, the Gospel of Luke, but with significant edits. He removed all references to Jesus' birth (his version of Luke began with Luke 3:1) and also any references to Jesus' Father as Creator, or to Jesus as the fulfillment of Old Testament prophecy. He included some portions of Paul's letters that did not make Jesus sound too human.[87] The Old Testament itself, not surprisingly, was excluded completely. Because his canon was unacceptable to the majority of the bishops, it forced the Church to step up its efforts at coming to a consensus about which documents would be included in the Christian Bible, a topic that will be addressed in chapter 6 below.

Marcion was excommunicated from the church of Rome in 144 CE by Bishop Pius I (bishop of Rome 140–55 CE), at which point he seems to have separated from the Christian community and started a schismatic movement, in which his followers (the "Marcionites") continued his teaching until we lose track of them.[88] Since Marcion's dualism led him to advocate a strict asceticism, including a requirement of celibacy for all members, their inability to pass their beliefs on to second-generation members may have contributed to their eventual extinction.

Apparently, Marcion allowed up to three baptisms for believers, the result of a strict asceticism that was unrealistic in actual practice. If one could not live up to the expectations of the group after the first baptism, up to two more baptisms were allowed. Also, because Marcion's asceticism probably prohibited the drinking of wine, but more importantly because his docetism meant he did not believe Jesus had any real blood, the Marcionites rejected the use of wine in their Eucharist. If they practiced a Eucharist at all, they used water only.[89] Their docetism also led the Marcionites to believe that their members had transcended their sexuality (cf. Gal 3:28), so that it appears they allowed women to administer the sacraments, something that would have distinguished them from their mainstream counterparts. Finally, they seem to have followed a Platonic view of the afterlife that included reincarnation rather than resurrection.[90] This is, of course, consistent with the docetic rejection of the physical in favor of the spiritual. For the Marcionite, the goal of a blessed afterlife would be the freedom of the spirit from the body, like a snake shedding its skin. Whoever did not achieve this transcendence would be reincarnated into another body.

As I suggested above, docetism plus syncretism results in gnosticism; and the Gnostics created a blend of polytheism and Christianity that would take docetism even further than Marcion, eventually turning it into a whole new religion, complete with various systems of mythology and cosmology.[91] Like earlier versions of docetism, Gnostics had no problem with the idea of multiple deities, but their dualism prevented them from believing that Christ could really be human. While all gnosticism was basically docetic, the hallmark of gnosticism (and the main difference from pre-gnostic versions of docetism) was a belief in secret *knowledge* (in Greek: *gnosis*).[92]

True gnosticism seems to begin with Menander (see Chart 1, *The Gnostic Family Tree*), who taught that salvation required learning secret knowledge, which was supposedly brought to earth by Jesus.[93] This knowledge included the revelation that the world was created by a lower order of deity, angelic beings known as *aeons*, and that the God of the Old Testament was simply one of these *aeons*.[94]

Carpocrates, who is sometimes called the "father of the Gnostics," also taught that the world was created by angels and that salvation would entail an escape from this world.[95] Therefore, the way to realize one's potential was to despise the material world and even flaunt a disregard for its values and its taboos. In fact, the Carpocratians were said to end their meetings with orgies.[96] They believed that the only way to end the cycle of reincarnation was to try everything that the physical world had to offer (and they did mean everything).[97] In this way one could disregard the material realm by "getting it out of one's system." Only when a person had had every possible earthly experience could he or she hope finally to transcend the material world.

Within gnosticism there were two main approaches to Christology. The first was a truly docetic Christology that envisioned Christ as purely spiritual, with no tangible body. Just as the Docetics of the first century had taught, the Marcionites and those Gnostics who held this belief assumed a dualism that could not accept any real contact between the spiritual (pure good) and the material (inherently evil). Those who believed in a docetic Christ tended to advocate an ascetic lifestyle, probably because their extreme dualism led them to believe that the only valid response to the material world was to reject it completely. Gnostics who taught a docetic Christology included Menander, Saturninus, and some followers of Valentinus.

Saturninus, from Antioch in Syria, was the founder of a sect whose members were called Encratites.[98] The name *Encratites* comes from the word for "self-restraint" and referred to their ascetic lifestyle, which was influenced by Marcion.[99] They were vegetarians and advocated celibacy for all members.[100] Like the Marcionites, they only used water without wine in the Eucharist and they may have only used oil without water for baptism.[101] But unlike Marcion, they completely rejected Paul's letters as well as the Book of Acts, apparently believing that not enough in these documents was useful for promoting a docetic Christology.[102] They were also called Severiani, after one of the disciples of Saturninus named Severus.[103]

The other gnostic approach to Christology was, for lack of a better term, a "hybrid Christology," still based on an extreme dualism but allowing for some kind of tangible body of Jesus.[104]

According to these Gnostics, Jesus was still not really human and his body was not really "material"; rather, it was described as an ethereal or "luminous" body. This seems to be a concession to account for elements in the gospel story that show Jesus as tangible. For some Gnostics, this allowed them to admit that Jesus was born, grew up, and even appeared to die, though they did not all agree on whether his birth was a virginal birth or whether his death was something more than an illusion.[105] Proponents of this hybrid Christology made a distinction between Jesus and "the Christ," allowing some aspects of a "bodily" existence for Jesus but not for "the Christ." In this way, they preserved "the Christ" as entirely docetic while avoiding having to explain away references to his body in the text of the gospels. Specifically, "the Christ" was immutable and impassible, but Jesus was subject to change.[106] Still, Jesus' "death" was not a passion, in the sense of a sacrifice that included real suffering, but was only meant to reveal his true, nonhuman self as he shed his body. This would have been understood as a lesson on the true nature of all humans, who were really spiritual beings trapped in material bodies.

A teacher named Cerinthus seems to have added the idea that it was the immutable Christ who descended on Jesus at his baptism but left him just before his death on the cross.[107] Cerinthus's Christology would influence later Gnostics, including Basilides and Valentinus. Other Gnostics who also taught a hybrid Christology included Carpocrates and Apelles.

Basilides was from Alexandria, the ancient world's incubator of philosophy and gnosticism.[108] Like the Carpocratians, Basilides taught that the only way to inner peace was by indulging all the desires of the flesh and leaving nothing unfulfilled. He seems to have expanded the early forms of gnosticism into a more complex cosmology that would in turn influence others to expand it even further. Basilides's system included the personification and deification of biblical and philosophical concepts or virtues, such as wisdom (*Sophia*) and mind (*Nous*).[109] In fact, "the Christ" was understood as simply another name for the divine *Nous*. Basilides's followers celebrated the feast of Jesus' baptism, emphasizing this as the point at which the divine *Nous*, or "the Christ," descended to earth and entered into Jesus.[110]

In addition to the concept that the world was created by

angels, Basilides taught that there were 365 levels in the heavens, each one created by a different angel. The last angel was the God of the Old Testament, who created the lowest level of the universe, or the world as we know it. Salvation is an escape from the physical world (and from the prison of the body) and an ascent through the levels of the universe to the highest heaven.[111] At each level of heaven, the angelic creator of that level would have to be appeased in order to pass and ascend to the next level. Basilides taught that "the Christ" (*Nous*) had come from the highest heaven to teach the secret knowledge (*gnosis*) that would allow the Gnostic to ascend past the angels and through the levels of heaven to reach the highest heaven.[112] The secret knowledge was supposedly handed down from Christ through Matthias (cf. Acts 1:21–26), which was meant to explain why none of the mainstream Christian bishops knew about it.[113] Their sect was organized like the mystery cults of the Roman Empire—secret societies with secret initiation rituals and protection of the essentials of the group from outsiders.[114]

Basilides also taught that Christ had magically switched forms with Simon of Cyrene when Simon was conscripted to carry the cross, and that Christ stood by laughing while Simon was crucified in his place.[115] This is apparently meant to protect Christ from the passion (and therefore from mutability); however, it is not entirely clear why Christ would laugh at Simon. It was probably a way of ridiculing the Pauline concept of atonement, which required a human body of Jesus on the cross. Since gnostic salvation was understood as an escape from the physical world, Gnostics rejected the concept of atonement as suffering or sacrifice. Jesus did not come to die for our sins, he came to bring the secret knowledge that would allow humanity to ascend to the highest heaven and transcend the physical realm. Unfortunately, the extant gnostic documents never actually say what the secret knowledge is, although immortality is promised to those to whom it is revealed.

Gnostic documents such as the *Infancy Gospel of Thomas* portray Jesus as a magician, not motivated by compassion for humanity (as in the canonical gospels) but with an arrogance and an attitude that only the illuminated elite were worthy of him. The good news is not heard as a public proclamation for all, but a secret revelation for the select few.[116] This elitism contributed to the eventual separation of the Gnostics from the mainstream Church, as they rejected and ridiculed the authority of those who led the Church (cf. 1 John 2:19).[117] Gnostics in general believed that martyrdom was foolish, and the followers of Basilides would have said that this was because the martyrs were really only following in the footsteps of Simon of Cyrene and not those of Jesus.

Sethian gnosticism is the name given to a sect of Gnostics who believed that the real hero in the human story is Seth, the third son of Adam and Eve.[118] With some influence from Hebrew wisdom tradition, Sethian Gnostics accepted certain aspects of the Old Testament as the story of a struggle between good and evil, with humanity caught in the middle as helpless hostages. To them the God of the Old Testament is not just inferior; he is evil and antagonistic toward his creation, including humanity. Good angels, the *aeons*, fight on behalf of the true Supreme Being (the God and Father of Jesus) against the demiurge's demons, or *archons* (cf. "principalities," Rom 8:38). In their fall from grace in the Garden of Eden, Adam and Eve lost the original knowledge (*gnosis*). But the *aeons* restored this knowledge to Seth, who began the tradition of passing it down through the generations. The story of the flood is then interpreted as an attempt by the God of the Old Testament to wipe out humanity, except that a few are saved by the true Father God and his *aeons*. Thus Seth is seen as the ancestor of the true Gnostics and Jesus was believed to be either a descendant or a reincarnation of Seth. Jesus' descent to earth is seen as a mission to rescue humanity from its Creator, and since the earth is the realm of evil, this descent is interpreted as a descent into Hades.[119]

The most famous gnostic teacher is Valentinus. Probably from Alexandria, born around the turn of the second century (ca. 100 CE), he came to Rome in about 137 or 138. The height of his activity as a gnostic teacher was during the time that Pius I was bishop (140–55 CE).[120] Valentinus taught a hybrid Christology and lived a libertine lifestyle, as did most of his followers. He seems to have left Rome for Cyprus in about 160 CE and probably died there around 175.

The followers of Valentinus did not call themselves Valentinians, they called themselves Spirituals.[121] Following an earlier trend, they believed that the true *gnosis* was meant only for a spiritual elite. Valentinus taught that there were three kinds of people: spiritual, soulish, and physical.[122] The Spirituals believed that they were actually a higher order of being than the rest of humanity, each one a divine spark, but fallen and trapped in a body.[123] The *gnosis*, and therefore salvation, was meant for them. The soulish were an intermediate level. There may be a lower form of salvation available to the soulish, but not the full ascent to the highest heaven, perhaps a version of reincarnation. The physical people had no hope of salvation. Their fate was to remain in the physical realm forever, probably on a never-ending cycle of reincarnation. This combination of fatalistic predestination and elitism meant that the Valentinian Gnostics saw themselves as the Spirituals, the non-gnostic Christians as the soulish, and the Jews and pagans as the purely physical people.

Valentinus expanded the gnostic cosmology to its furthest extent. He taught of a primordial heavenly realm, called the *pleroma* (the "fullness"). Within this *pleroma* there were many *aeons*, one of whom was *Sophia*, who was the mother of the God of the Old Testament.[124] For Valentinus, the God of the Old Testament was at least incompetent and probably evil. Though there are multiple versions of the myth, the world was created either by mistake or as the result of an ill-fated attempt by Sophia to become a creator without the help of a divine male consort. The result of this premundane debacle was the creation of the physical world with all its imperfections. Another *aeon*, also a son of Sophia, was Christ, who came down into the physical realm to unite with Jesus and pass along the secret knowledge so that the Spirituals could ascend back to the *pleroma*. This was based on the assumption that the Spirituals were originally sparks of the divine who had cooled and fallen from the *pleroma*, like cinders from a bonfire, and so salvation for them meant getting back to the highest heavenly realm from which they had come. The so-called *Gospel of Truth* may have been written by Valentinus himself.[125] This "gospel" tells us that salvation is knowledge and the only real sin is ignorance.[126] In fact, the true goal of the Gnostic is to know *oneself* (that is, that one is a divine spark), as if to say that knowledge of self is what liberates, or saves, one from ignorance.[127] The implication is that Christ is not unique in his divinity and that all Spirituals equally come from the *pleroma* and are des-

71

tined to return to it. The "good news" for them was that they are divine. Whatever relationship Jesus has with the true supreme God that he calls his Father, the Gnostic believed that he or she shared that same relationship and the same divine nature.[128]

Valentinian gnosticism eventually split into two factions. The Western group (probably the majority) followed Valentinus's disciples Heracleon, Ptolemy (leader of the Ptolemaeans), and Apelles.[129] They remained true to Valentinus's hybrid Christology, teaching that there was a distinction to be made between "the Christ" and Jesus.[130] Christ is pure divine spirit, impassible and intangible. Jesus had a body, though it was a "luminous" body and not truly human. Because of this, he could eat and drink but did not need to relieve himself. The Christ spirit united with Jesus at his baptism but left him before the crucifixion, so the connection between Christ and Jesus is only temporary and only for the purpose of his mission of passing on the secret knowledge.[131] Apelles explained that Christ had a cosmic body that was crucified, and thus he was able to show his wounds during his postresurrection appearances. However, his body dissolved back into the cosmic elements from which it was made before the ascension, since it could not ascend into heaven.[132] The Eastern faction, on the other hand, followed Valentinus's disciples Theodotus, Marcus, Axionicus and Bardesanes, who moved toward a purely docetic Christology.

The two types of gnostic Christology, docetic and hybrid, led to two very different lifestyle responses. Those who taught a purely docetic Christ responded with an ascetic lifestyle. For them Christ had no real contact with the material world, and the believer's response should be to distance oneself from the physical as much as possible. Therefore, they tended to be ascetic, celibate, and even vegetarian. On the other hand, those who believed in a hybrid Christ tended to go to the opposite extreme from the ascetics and adopt a hedonistic approach to life and morality.[133] They apparently believed that Jesus could have some contact with the material world and still transcend it. They further believed that they were already living a resurrected life and reasoned that since they transcended the physical realm, what they did with their bodies could not affect their souls, so they allowed themselves every indulgence.

Following is a summary of general gnostic beliefs by the time that the Gnostics were separating from the mainstream Church:[134]

- Belief in many deities, including various biblical and philosophical names, concepts, and virtues personified. These deities were often expressed as male-female pairs who procreated, resulting in the creation of more deities. Angels are also considered divine beings and are worshiped by some Gnostics.
- Evil is not the consequence of human sin, but is part of creation.
- The God of the Old Testament is not the Father that Christ preached.
- Salvation is not from sin, but from ignorance and from the material world.
- There is no atonement as the mainstream Church understood it; Christ did not come to offer forgiveness, but enlightenment.
- Salvation is an ascent back through the many levels of the universe to the highest heaven.
- Salvation is not a redemption of creation, but rescue from it.[135]
- Jesus' death (for those who believed he had "died") was not a substitution or a sacrifice, but simply a way of revealing his true, nonhuman self.
- Jesus' resurrection does not foreshadow the bodily resurrection of humans, but shows that the "spiritual" person, or Gnostic, is already resurrected.
- A predestinarian caste system meant that only the spiritual person had a divine origin and could transcend this world and ascend to the highest heaven.
  - The soulish people were predestined to some lower order of salvation, the physical to eternal reincarnation.
  - The Spirituals are actually a divine spark (albeit fallen and embodied) and as such, they are no different in essence from Christ himself.[136]

- Gnostic Christology falls into two main types:
  - Docetic
    - Christ is pure spirit, a phantom who only seemed to be human but was in no way tangible.
    - Those who held to this type of Christology tended to follow an ascetic lifestyle.
  - Hybrid
    - There is a distinction made between Jesus and "the Christ."
    - "The Christ" is pure spirit, but Jesus had a "luminous," "ethereal," or "cosmic" body (somewhat tangible, though not really human).
    - "The Christ" united with Jesus at his baptism, but left him before his death on the cross.
    - Those who held to this type of Christology tended to follow a hedonistic, or libertine, lifestyle.

To the outsider, perhaps the most obvious difference between mainstream Christianity and emerging gnosticism was that the Christians would tell you their good news and then invite you to join. The Gnostics would require you to join before telling you their secrets. As gnosticism separated from the Church, different gnostic groups wrote their own gospels to distinguish themselves from Christianity and to remove any mention of Jesus' humanity, or any connection with the Old Testament. In these gnostic writings Jesus does not suffer, and if he appears to die, it is all an illusion meant to teach us that our ultimate goal is to escape from this body, this world, and the one who created them. There are a wide variety of gnostic writings available today, and it is not our purpose to survey them all, but a sample of the best-known ones will suffice. It is important to point out that these gnostic documents were never considered for inclusion in the New Testament. In spite of some popular accounts that wish to sensationalize the fringe and claim that the Catholic Church is hiding something from us, these are not "lost books of the Bible." They were written precisely because the communities that produced them were separating from the Church, so the last thing the Church would have ever done would be to include these documents in its canon. Thus it is clear that the ones that claim apostolic origin or authorship are pseudonymous.[137] Finally, when one reads these documents one has to keep in mind that often the version we have is from as late as the fourth century, and so it has gone through extensive revisions, and there is no way to know what was actually in these documents in their original versions in the subapostolic age.

The *Infancy Gospel of Thomas*

The document is meant to supply the story of Jesus that is not in the New Testament gospels: it is the story of Jesus as a child. This is, however, a story of a wizard child who does magic tricks to confound the adults in his life and who strikes other children dead when they do anything that bothers him. Yes, you read that right—Jesus kills children in this story. This is a Jesus who is disrespectful of his teachers and even his parents. Some commentators charge the author(s) with anti-Semitism, since Jesus seems to have a disdain for Jewish teaching and tradition. This would be consistent with the docetic view of the Old Testament, and in fact, the Docetics and Gnostics tended to be more anti-Semitic than the mainstream writers.

There is a famous story in this document in which Jesus makes birds out of clay on the Sabbath. When he is confronted with the fact that he is doing work on the Sabbath, he tells the birds to come to life and fly away, and of course they do. On the surface, it may seem like a harmless, precious story of Jesus as a child; but the scene is part of the greater attitude of disrespect that Jesus shows toward elders in the document. Even more important, it is a picture of a docetic Jesus, who is not really human and in fact looks down on humans and treats them with disgust. It is far cry from the New Testament gospels that show how Jesus' miracles were motivated by compassion, and that they were all *signs* that taught an important lesson or pointed people to God.

The *Gospel of Thomas*

The *Gospel of Thomas* is simply a list of supposed sayings of Jesus. There is no story to speak of, and not surprisingly it doesn't tell us anything about Jesus' life, especially that he was Jewish.

Since Gnostics did not believe in Jesus' humanity, the story of his life (if they thought he had one) is not important. Jesus is not presented as the fulfillment of Old Testament prophecy, as he is in the New Testament gospels. There are some sayings similar to those we find in the New Testament, however, but often they are changed or twisted in ways that distort the meaning.

Like many Gnostics, the writer(s) of the *Gospel of Thomas* believed that the secret knowledge was for a select few. This only served to exacerbate the growing rift between the Gnostics and their non-gnostic coparishioners. It may be that the Gnostics separated themselves from the mainstream Church before they were asked to leave, but in any case, by the time this document was written there was already some division and rivalry between the mainstream bishops and the leaders of the gnostic factions. In fact, in the *Gospel of Thomas* Jesus makes a disdainful remark about "those who lead you." The apostles Peter and Matthew are presented in a negative light, but Thomas (the doubter) is held up as *the* apostle. In short, we can see that this is a document originally written during the time of separation from the Church.

In none of the gnostic writings are we ever actually told what the secret knowledge is. It has something to do with the realization of each person's divinity. It probably also has something to do with knowing the names of all the gods and angels in their elaborate mythology. There seems to be a sense in which the ascent to the pleroma would require appeasing the angelic gatekeepers at each of the levels of heaven. Perhaps knowing their names would function as a kind of password to get through the heavenly tollbooth. We will never know, because in the *Gospel of Thomas*, when the apostles ask Thomas to tell them what secrets Jesus told him, he responds with the second-century equivalent of, "I could tell you, but then I'd have to kill you."[138]

The *Gospel of Philip*

It seems that the Gnostics claimed to have their own version of apostolic succession. Just as the *Gospel of Thomas* was supposed to have come from the apostle Thomas, the *Gospel of Philip* was supposed to come from a tradition that goes back to Philip. Of course, the bishops of the Church knew that these documents had no connection to the apostles whatsoever, and in fact that is what sets them apart from the New Testament documents.[139] Still, it is curious how in our own time some people have chosen to give more historical credence to the gnostic gospels than they do the canonical gospels. The *Gospel of Philip* is one such document that has gained popularity in recent years.

True to its gnostic agenda, the *Gospel of Philip* upholds four virtues: faith, hope, love, and knowledge. There is also a disturbing account of how Joseph the carpenter made the cross on which Jesus was hung. But this is all part of the gnostic attitude that the crucifixion is just a big joke. As mentioned above, in one version of the gnostic story Jesus dupes Simon of Cyrene into getting crucified in his place and stands by laughing.

The *Gospel of Philip* is the source of speculation about a relationship between Jesus and Mary Magdalene. In the story it says that Jesus "kissed her on her..." and then there is a gap in the text. How one fills in the blank will determine the extent of the relationship. Of course, even if it said something scandalous, there is no historical validity to this document.

There is one redeeming feature in the *Gospel of Philip*, an analogy that is used to encourage its readers to practice what they preach. The works of one's life are compared to the child of a woman who had an affair. Though she may proclaim to the world that she loves her husband, her baby will look like her lover. In the same way, we may proclaim our love for God, but if we secretly love anything other than God, our works will bear the resemblance of our true love.

Judaizers and Ebionites

At the other extreme from the Docetics was a group known to us as the Judaizers. Just as the Docetics were Gentile (formerly pagan) Christians who were apparently comfortable retaining elements of paganism, the Judaizers were Jewish Christians who wanted to retain much of their Judaism. We can see them most clearly in Paul's Letter to the Galatians. The Judaizers advocated following the whole law and requiring Gentiles effectively to become Jews in order to become Christians. They are famous for demanding circumcision of men who wanted to enter the Church. Knowing that this would restrict his mission, Paul opposed this faction. He called them "certain men from James" (Gal 2:12). This does not imply that they had the approval of James, who was the leader of the church in Jerusalem; it only means that they came from Jerusalem. They may have been Pharisees, like Paul, who were converted to Christianity, but who did not see the law in a new light as Paul did (Acts 15:5). Paul calls them "false brothers" (Gal 2:4) and said that they preached a different gospel, which was antithetical to the true gospel and which would not lead to salvation (Gal 1:6–9). Eventually, in about the year 50, a council was held in Jerusalem, the first council of the Church, in which it was decided that Gentile men would not be required to be circumcised in order to be baptized, nor would Christians have to follow the Jewish dietary laws (Acts 15:1–21).

While there is no direct evidence in the New Testament that the Judaizers denied Jesus' divinity or rejected the worship of Christ,[140] they would probably have understood Jesus as Messiah strictly in Old Testament terms. Since there is little or no hint of the divinity of Christ in the Old Testament messianic prophesies,[141] the Judaizers would have understood him as an anointed man but still a mere human, much like the judges, kings, and prophets of the Old Testament. Therefore, they would most likely have rejected the idea of a divine nature in Christ. Jesus would be seen as a messenger of God but not really the incarnation of God. Paul's response to this was to argue that believing in a Christ who was human only would be to put one's trust in the flesh, rather than in the spirit (Gal 3:1–5). In other words, the Judaizers (and possibly the Galatian Christians) were putting their trust for their salvation in the law (human effort) rather than in God's grace (divine intervention).

Paul's response to the Judaizers is similar to his response to the Docetics, in that he goes right to the cross. Paul is adamant that if one adds any requirements for salvation (such as following the law), one makes the cross insufficient and ineffective, and if that is the case then Christ died for nothing (Gal 2:21). Either the cross is enough for salvation, or it isn't. And if one needs to be circumcised, or follow dietary restrictions, then the cross is not enough. In fact, Paul went further, saying that if you advocate following the whole law (circumcision), you are cutting yourself off from Christ (Gal 5:2–4, note the play on words with the concept of "cutting off").

What is most important for our purposes is that Paul emphasized the divinity of Christ against those who might diminish or deny it.[142] We have already seen Colossians 2:9 in which we are told that the fullness of Deity dwells within him (cf. Heb 1:3–8). In addition to this, he affirms that Christ was present in the days of the Old Testament and therefore preexisted his incarnation (1 Cor 10:4, cf. 1 Cor 8:6, John 1:1).[143] This preexistence demonstrates that he is more than a mere human. His incarnation is then understood in terms of a descent from an exalted state to a state of humility (Gal 4:4, 2 Cor 8:9). Furthermore, his death was the ultimate humiliation, a sacrifice for our sin (Rom 8:3, 1 Cor 5:7–8, Phil 2:6–8).[144] However, Jesus was raised from death (restored to his rightful place, Phil 2:9–11) and in fact his resurrection will lead to our own (Rom 6:5–14, 1 Cor 15:16–28). All this strongly suggests that, at the very least, Jesus is not a mere human and that the birth, life, death, and resurrection of Jesus were the result of divine intervention.

In the second century, the theological descendants of the Judaizers were the Ebionites.[145] According to tradition, the Ebionites were born out of the Jerusalem church after the fall of Jerusalem in 70 CE, when the Temple was destroyed and the sacrifices discontinued.[146] They called themselves "Ebionites" (which means the "poor ones") to emphasize the supposed poverty of Jesus and their belief that they were following in his footsteps.[147] Just as the Judaizers were Jewish Christians who wanted to maintain a strictly Jewish understanding of Jesus as prophet-messiah, the Ebionites were also predominantly Jewish Christians who emphasized the law and who saw Jesus as an anointed human whose mission it was to show the way to perfect obedience. Philosophically, the Ebionites were also concerned to safeguard the immutability of God by rejecting the divinity of Christ.[148] In other words, the Ebionites could not reconcile the obvious human changes that Jesus experienced (Luke 2:40) with their assumption of divine immutability, so they reasoned that there could be no divine nature in Jesus.

The earliest teacher on record who was an Ebionite is known to us as Theodotus the Elder (also known as Theodotus the Tanner or Theodotus the Cobbler/Shoemaker).[149] He was excommunicated from the church at Rome by Bishop Victor (bishop of Rome from 189 to 199 CE), on the charge that he was teaching that Christ was a mere human.[150] A disciple of Theodotus the Elder was another Theodotus, called the Younger (or Theodotus the Banker),[151] and his disciples called themselves Melchizedekians, teaching that Christ was subject to a higher priest, the Melchizedek of Genesis 14 (cf. Heb 5—7).[152]

In the primary sources written by their opponents, the term *Ebionite* eventually came to be used as a catchall for any Christology that emphasized the humanity of Christ to the exclusion of the divine nature. There were apparently two main forms of this Christology: *spirit Christology*, which emphasized the role of the Holy Spirit as empowering the man Jesus, and which seems to have been the point of view of the majority of Ebionites; and *angel Christology*, which speculated that it was an angel, or archangel, that indwelt Jesus.[153]

The Ebionites used a version of Matthew's Gospel, possibly in Hebrew or Aramaic but edited to exclude any reference to the divinity of Jesus and probably also without the story of his miraculous birth.[154] Although some (angel Christology) did seem to accept a version of the virgin birth, most Ebionites believed that Jesus was born naturally from Mary and Joseph.[155] They may have had their own versions of the birth narrative, but interpreted the "virgin" of Isaiah 7:14 to mean simply "young woman."[156] They may also have had their own written gospels that no longer exist, but which would have presented Jesus as a prophet and emphasized following the Jewish law.[157]

For the Ebionites, Jesus was an ordinary man who achieved extraordinary status through personal discipline and righteousness.[158] Because he was perfectly obedient to God and fulfilled the whole law, he was rewarded with God's anointing at his baptism and with a spiritual indwelling.[159] The baptism of Christ was seen as the moment of his adoption by God, probably based on the way Jewish proselyte baptism was understood as effecting an adoption into the family of Abraham.[160] When he is called God's "beloved son" at his baptism, that is actually the moment at which Jesus *became* a son of God. Therefore, to the Ebionites, Jesus is not *the* Son of God, but *a* son of God by adoption. What is more, he is not *the* Christ, but rather *a* christ, having earned the anointing and the title by perfectly obeying the law. This is another reason why most Ebionites were not normally interested in the gospel accounts of Jesus' birth. It was not until his baptism that he arrives at his (adopted) sonship.[161] Therefore, the Ebionite view of Christ, along with successive versions in the third and fourth centuries, is generally called *adoptionism*.

Ebionites believed that at Jesus' adoption he received the Holy Spirit, implying that he did not have the Holy Spirit before that time.[162] In general, the Ebionites envisioned a Jesus who was anointed and indwelt by a preexistent Holy Spirit (or by the Logos, or by "the Christ," or by an angel, in the case of angel Christology).[163] The indwelling Spirit was understood to be a created being, however, and this indwelling was only temporary. The Spirit indwelt Jesus from the time of his baptism (or conception, as in the case of angel Christology) until the cross, when Jesus was left alone (their interpretation of Matthew 27:46).

Since Jesus was seen as an ordinary human who earned divine adoption by achieving righteousness, the Ebionites reasoned that any human could follow his example and achieve the same status—in fact, salvation would require it.[164] The mainstream critique of this Christology was that, in essence, Jesus required adoption in order to receive salvation himself, and if we want to receive salvation, we would have to follow his example and earn our adoption through perfect righteousness.[165] Rather than saying, as the Catholic Church did, that we are adopted sons and daughters of God, but that Jesus is the "natural" Son of God (the Son of God by nature), the Ebionites' claim was that Christ is not ontologically different from the rest of humanity. This places Christ on the receiving end of grace, just as created humanity. He was adopted, just as we might be, so therefore his uniqueness among humanity is only as a pioneer, not as a divine giver of grace.[166] He received the Holy Spirit; he does not give the Holy Spirit. He was elevated by his indwelling; he did not descend to an incarnation. It should come as no surprise then, that the Ebionites rejected the letters of

Paul, who emphasized grace over the law against their predecessors the Judaizers.[167] They preferred to hold up as the true apostles those who were considered to be Jesus' blood relatives. This was probably due to the Judaizers' connection with the Jerusalem church where James, the "brother of the Lord," was a leader. In any case, it began a tradition of speculation about the descendants of Jesus' family that sometimes continues to this day.

Because Jesus was considered to be a mere human, the Ebionites tended to see resurrection as simply a metaphor for eternal life. Jesus was "raised" only in the sense that he transcended this earthly life after his physical death. Since the Ebionites also did not believe that the blood of Jesus held any saving significance, they (ironically, just like the Docetics) rejected the use of wine in the Eucharist, using water only.[168] This practice would come to be called *aquarianism*.

Apart from a few possible fragments, we have no documents that we can identify with certainty as the products of the Ebionites; however, there are some that seem to have been favored by them. These include the later *Clementine Homilies* and possibly *The Shepherd* by Hermas. There is also a group of documents called the *apocryphal acts* that seem to have been used by heretics on both extremes, but they fit well within the context of the Ebionites' legalism.[169]

Apocryphal Acts

The apocryphal acts claim to be the stories of certain apostles and their missions after the ascension of Jesus. They combine traditional material about the lives of the apostles with legend and outright fiction. In reality, they tend to be documents of propaganda, promoting an agenda of extreme asceticism. Like Tatian, these authors believed that all sin ultimately comes from lust, and therefore many of the apocryphal acts advocated celibacy for all Christians, even going to the extreme of supposing that conversion to Christianity must mean a rejection of marriage.

A common theme in the apocryphal acts is the conversion of a wealthy woman by the apostle's preaching. But the problem is that the woman is either married or engaged. In converting to Christianity she rejects her husband or fiancé, who (understandably) becomes upset. The husband or fiancé conspires with local authorities to persecute the apostle, who flees, leaving the newly converted noblewoman to endure humiliation, risking torture and even execution. Therefore, the real heroes of these stories are not the apostles, but the women. The stories were probably popular with women at the time because they were stories of women who found a way to have some personal power and reject the lordship of a man. So even though the woman in the story suffers, she is portrayed as having preserved her nobility and her integrity by rejecting the advances of men.

The apocryphal acts present the world as a battleground. Spiritual warfare rages all around, and the pagan idols, far from being benign blocks of wood and stone, are actually demons. These demons will attack if opposed, and the only way to gain power over them is through self-control, which means a rejection of lust and the suppression of sexual desire. If one is chaste, then the sign of the cross will overcome the demons. This worldview leads the authors of the apocryphal acts to present a radical separation from society as the only valid form of Christianity. As is the case with the gnostic writings, there are many apocryphal acts; however, a few of the more well known will suffice as examples.

The *Acts of Paul and Thecla*

The *Acts of Paul and Thecla* is probably the most famous of the apocryphal acts. It is originally part of a larger document called the *Acts of Paul*. In the story, however, the real hero is not Paul, but Thecla, a woman who is converted when Paul preaches "the word of God about self-control." This is the good news that Paul preaches, a salvation by asceticism. In the story, Paul has his own version of the Beatitudes: "Blessed are they that have wives as not having them." Therefore, baptism is only for those who are ready to be celibate, and the resurrection is only for those who can keep themselves chaste. At first, Paul does not think Thecla is ready for baptism, so when she becomes separated from Paul, she baptizes herself (though not with the correct formula).

There were apparently some in the early Church who used this document as evidence in favor of allowing women to be priests, since Thecla performed a baptism (her own). Tertullian argued against this interpretation by discrediting the document's authorship, saying that it was written by an Eastern priest who was removed from his office for having forged the document.[170] The end result was that the use of this document backfired on the proponents of female priesthood, since it would ultimately be argued that only heretics allowed women to baptize.

As the story continues, Thecla is persecuted but survives the attempts on her life. She becomes a hermit and lives out her years in a cave, and when she dies, her body is taken to Rome to be buried near Paul. In one version of the story, some men come to her cave to try to rape her, but she escapes, leaving behind her veil. This veil then becomes a relic. There is also an interesting hint at an early expression of the belief in purgatory, when a woman who befriends Thecla asks her to pray for her dead daughter.[171] Devotion to Thecla as a saint grew, including pilgrimages to the supposed site of her cave. Today, some still consider her a saint.

The *Acts of Thomas*

In this story, Thomas does not want to go to India, so the risen Jesus appears and sells Thomas as a slave to someone who happens to be going to India. Thomas then preaches the message that Jesus has sent him to preach, which amounts to the conviction that following Jesus means leaving one's spouse. Marriage is described as "filthy intercourse" and the opposite of holiness. In one scene we find out that sexual intercourse prevents one from receiving the Eucharist, as a certain man's "lust" causes his hands to wither when he touches the consecrated bread. The man's hands were then healed with what appears to be one of the earliest references to holy water.[172] The point of the story seems to be that all sex is sinful, and as such, it corrupts the Eucharist and must be kept apart from it. This is interesting because one of the earliest justifications for a celibate clergy in the Western church was the belief that one had to abstain from sexual intercourse for twenty-four hours before receiving the Eucharist. Since a priest says Mass every day, he must be on a permanent fast from sex and therefore cannot be married.

Even within marriage, sexual intercourse is presented as unacceptable for Christians, and while the mainstream Church said that procreation was a legitimate reason to have sex, the *Acts of Thomas* describes children as a nuisance and not worth the trouble, as if to try to talk its readers out of wanting to have children. Perhaps in a world where infant mortality was high and death in childbirth significantly lowered the average life expectancy of women, this was meant as a justification for choosing not to have children. Still, it is not the procreation but the sexual intercourse that is the problem. In one scene there is an interesting vision of hell, one of the earliest to include all the traditional elements, such as caverns, fire, sulfur, smoke, and stench—and yet there is a special place in hell for people who had a physical marriage.

The story includes the martyrdom of Thomas, who is taken up to a mountaintop and killed with a spear. Later, the king who had him killed goes up to the mountain to try to find Thomas's bones, hoping to use them to cure his son who is ill. Thomas appears to the king and rebukes him for not believing him while he was alive. In any case, the bones are not there; they had been taken to the West by Thomas's disciples. Today, pilgrims to the church of Santa Croce in Gerusalemme in Rome can see the relic of Thomas's finger bone, presumably the very finger that touched the wounds of Jesus.

The *Acts of Peter*

The *Acts of Peter* is worth reading for one story, made famous by the classic film, *Quo Vadis* (1951). In this account, Peter has been talked into leaving Rome to avoid the persecution of the emperor Nero. He is walking out of Rome along the Appian Way when he sees the risen Jesus coming toward him, heading into Rome. As Jesus approaches, Peter asks, *Quo vadis, Domine?* (Where are you going, Lord?). Jesus replies that he is going to Rome to be crucified again. By this, Peter knew that it was his destiny to return to Rome where he would be martyred by crucifixion. To this day, there is a small church on the Appian Way at the site where Peter's vision of Jesus is supposed to have taken place. The place where Jesus stood is marked by marble footprints.

The Orthodox Middle

Against the two extremes of Docetics and Gnostics on the one hand, and Ebionites on the other, the mainstream writers of the subapostolic age argued for both the humanity and the divinity of Christ.[173] One could not emphasize one and diminish the other; one had to accept both (see Table 1, *Christology and Theology in the Subapostolic Age*). They believed that anything else would not be a faithful witness to the teaching of the apostles. As I have indicated, the writers of the second century, many of them philosophers, explained the person of Christ in terms of the Logos, the Word of God, and therefore their understanding of Christ is generally called Logos Christology.

While the two natures of Christ presented something of a paradox for the Church, the apologists were convinced that both extremes of Docetic/Gnostic and Ebionite were each in their own way an unfaithful interpretation of the person of Christ. Against the Docetics and Gnostics, they emphasized the humanity of Jesus. They argued that his real humanity was proven by his birth as a baby and especially by his suffering and death.[174] And while we might expect them to claim that the resurrection of Jesus proves his divinity, they actually used it as a proof of his humanity, since he was raised with a body that could eat and be touched.[175] There was an assumption, though not yet articulated well, that in order to be the savior of humanity, Christ had to be human. Clement of Alexandria called him the *champion* of humanity, reminiscent of the ancient practice of representative warfare, by which one person could fight for the whole army (as in the story of David and Goliath). In this case, Christ is the champion who fights for the human race. He achieves victory through death and in the end wins our salvation. Therefore, to deny the flesh (humanity) of Christ is to deny Christ.[176]

Against the Ebionites, the apologists emphasized the divinity of Christ. They believed he must be divine; otherwise he could not be a savior, since salvation required divine intervention.[177] They maintained that the person of Jesus is the preexistent Logos of God and the agent of creation.[178] When God said, "Let there be light…" that was the Father creating by his Word. When God said, "Let *us* make humanity in *our* image," that was the Father speaking to his Logos.[179] Christ can be seen in the Old Testament, whenever God is said to be visible.[180] The Logos was the inspiration of the prophets.[181] His miraculous virgin birth also demonstrates his divinity.[182] In fact, the Son is equal in divinity to the Father.[183]

The apologists of the second century established the orthodoxy of the two natures of Christ, which of course was consistent with the apostolic documents that would become the New Testament. Melito of Sardis summed it up: "He was buried as a human, he rose from the dead as God."[184] But the apologists did not yet have a well-defined concept of the Holy Spirit, and in fact often confused the Holy Spirit with the preincarnate Christ.[185] Therefore, a fully developed doctrine of the Trinity would have to wait until the third century. In fact, there are two documents that seem to represent mainstream responses to the extremes but that demonstrate how the state of theological debate was in flux. Since these documents work so hard to refute one extreme, they waffle back and forth, sometimes making concessions to the position they argue against, sometimes leaning a bit toward the opposite extreme.

The *Letter of the Apostles*

More often known by its Latin name, *Epistula Apostolorum*, this is not a letter from any of the original apostles but a second-century response against gnosticism. It was written some time after 135 CE but before the 180s, since in it Jesus tells the apostles he is returning in 150 years. It contains numerous historical errors, including mistaking Cephas (the Aramaic version of Peter's name) for another apostle beside Peter. Interestingly, though, the document locates the place of the Skull (Golgotha) as the place of Jesus' burial. The gospels say only that Golgotha was the place of the crucifixion, but this document corresponds with the tradition that locates Golgotha as the general area of both the crucifixion and the tomb of Christ. This location is now the site of the Church of the Holy Sepulcher in Jerusalem.

The *Epistula* was clearly written to emphasize Jesus' humanity against gnostic docetism. Jesus is born as a baby and is raised in the flesh. After the resurrection, his feet make footprints and the disciples touch his body. In this account, Peter, not Thomas, touches his wounds. On the other hand, at times Jesus sounds more like the Jesus of the *Gospel of Thomas* than the Jesus of the New Testament gospels.

The *Protevangelion of James*

The word *protevangelion* is like saying the "pregospel." This is the story before the story, and it details not only the birth of Jesus but the birth of Mary as well. It claims to be by James, the half brother of Jesus, but was probably actually written in the second century to emphasize the divinity of Jesus against the Ebionites. In the process, however, it makes Jesus' birth sound so divine that he ends up seeming almost docetic.

In this document we find a precursor to the doctrine of the immaculate conception of Mary. Probably to highlight Jesus' own divinity, his mother Mary is also born under miraculous circumstances. We are also told that the brothers and sisters of Jesus in the gospels are actually the children of Joseph from a previous marriage. Mary remains a virgin after the birth of Jesus, not only because she remains celibate but because Jesus' miraculous birth left her physically as though she had never been pregnant. Thus the document takes the mainstream belief in a miraculous *conception* of Jesus and expands it to include his actual birth.

Finally, there is another interesting connection to the tradition of Christian holy sites. To the Western mind, when we read in the New Testament that Jesus was laid in a manger because there was no room in the inn, we usually picture a freestanding wooden stable or similar structure. According to the *Protevangelion*, however, Jesus was born in a cave. The Church of the Nativity in Bethlehem is built over a cave, where early tradition tells us our Savior came into the world.[186]

FROM APOLOGY TO THEOLOGY

With the last decades of the second century we come to the end of an era. We leave the subapostolic age and make the transition from Christian apology to Christian theology. Another way to look at it is that apologetics have shifted from an external focus (trying to convince non-Christians of the validity of Christianity) to an internal focus (warning Christians against heresy). This internal apologetic blossoms into real theology as the emergence of heresies on the fringes of the Church force the mainstream bishops and theologians to define more clearly what correct belief is. In doing so, the theologians turn away from philosophy and turn to the scriptures as the source of authority for supporting their interpretations.

In addition, persecution also forced the Church to turn inward. Throughout the second century the world became increasingly hostile to the Church, which caused it to "circle the wagons." Three documents remain to be mentioned before we turn to the theologians. They are martyr documents that chronicle the deaths of three groups of Christians in the last decades of the second century and at the turn of the third century, and they highlight just how precarious the situation had become.

The Martyrs of Lyons and Viennes

During the persecution under the reign of Marcus Aurelius, public sentiment against the Christians in Gaul (modern France) led to violence. The year was 177 CE. Polycarp had sent the priest Irenaeus to Lyons to assist Bishop Pothinus. While Irenaeus was away in Rome speaking on behalf of the Montanists, an angry mob, fearing the loss of their religion if too many people should convert to Christianity, took up arms and killed a group of Christians, desecrating their bodies and then refusing them burial (cf. Rev 11:8–10). By this time everything from failed crops to natural disasters could be blamed on the Christians, who were now a fair target for public rage. In some places it could be dangerous for Christians even to go about in public. Church leaders were, of course, a target, and Bishop Pothinus was murdered. When Irenaeus returned to Lyons, he found that his bishop was dead and that he had been elected the new bishop. It is possible that Irenaeus himself wrote the account of the martyrs of Lyons and Viennes. It is certain that the event must have affected him, contributing to his skepticism of Roman virtue, reason, and philosophy.

In this martyr document we meet the heroic Blandina. She is typical of many of the female martyrs in that she meets her death with courage and dignity. She becomes the very image of Christian virtue, shaming the so-called virtue of the Romans. The interesting thing about this is that in both Greek and Latin, some words for virtue are based on the same roots as words for "strength" and "man," which betrays the Roman bias that to be truly "virtuous," one must be a man.[187] Yet in these martyr documents we see Christian women who exhibit a strength that puts Roman men to shame.[188] It almost seems as though these women are granted a charismatic gift of "manliness" to meet death with courage; however, there is more to it than that. On one hand, the point is to hint again at the apologists' argument that Christians are more virtuous than non-Christian Romans, as if to say, "Our women are stronger than your men." On the other hand, as the apostle Paul said, "...there is no longer male and female; for all of you are one in Christ Jesus" (Gal 3:28). Therefore, it is not that these heroic women are turned into men, but that when it comes time to face death, men and women are equal as Christians. At first glance, some of this might seem similar to the stories of heroic women in the apocryphal acts. In the more mainstream martyr documents, however, their power to face death comes not from celibacy or self-control, but from their faith and, ultimately, from Christ himself.

The Scillitan Martyrs

This document tells the story of the martyrdom of a group of Christians from North Africa who died in Carthage on July 17, 180 CE. This was not long after the death of Marcus Aurelius, so their deaths would still be seen as justified under his edict. For our purposes it is enough to note just how far the persecution has come, and how bold the pagan mob could be in disposing of their Christian neighbors.

The Diary of Perpetua

Carthage in North Africa would also be the scene of the famous martyrdoms of Perpetua and Felicitas, which took place on March 7, 203 CE. Vibia Perpetua was a young aristocratic woman who was in catechesis preparing for Christian baptism when she, along with her servant Felicitas (sometimes translated "Felicity") and other members of her catechetical class were arrested. By this time, the right of a Roman citizen to a trial in Rome was gone. While in prison awaiting her execution, Perpetua kept a diary, which was later finished to include the account of her death and published, perhaps by Tertullian.[189] The diary is a very personal and poignant account of Perpetua's faith and her own father's attempts to convince her to denounce the faith for the sake of her newborn baby.[190] Like Blandina, Perpetua is given strength and courage from Christ to meet her death in the arena.

The account of Perpetua's martyrdom, which includes her dreams and her experience in the arena, is interesting for several reasons. In some ways, it uses apocalyptic imagery, much like the Book of Revelation, to reinforce the idea that martyrdom is a victory over Satan. At one point, in a vision, in order to climb the ladder to heaven, Perpetua must step on the head of a dragon (cf. Gen 3:15, Rev 12:1–6). The fact that Perpetua is a new mother symbolizes that martyrdom is both a birth, in the sense that the martyr is born to eternal life, and it is also a mother, in the sense that the Church is born through martyrdom.[191]

We look back on Polycarp, who followed in the footsteps of Jesus himself, and of Stephen, when he prayed for the forgiveness of his killers. But when we come to the beginning of the third century, one of Perpetua's classmates will gesture to the crowd in the arena, as if to say, *What you do to us, God will do to you!* It is no wonder, then, that the stance of the Church shifted from Christians ministering to the world to clergy ministering to laity, and that its focus would shift from outward to inward. The Church was wounded, and it had barely even begun the task of defining its own identity.

CHAPTER 5

The Theologians

IRENAEUS OF LYONS

We have already met Irenaeus in the context of the incident of the martyrs of Lyons and Viennes. Born in the 120s in Asia Minor, he probably came from Smyrna. He was a student of Polycarp, and possibly also of Justin Martyr, which makes him a third-generation bishop, only two steps away from the apostles themselves. Polycarp sent him to Gaul to be a priest under Bishop Pothinus. He probably only escaped martyrdom because he had gone to Rome to speak to the bishop there on behalf of the Montanists, the charismatic group also from his home region of Asia Minor. As we have seen, when Irenaeus returned from Rome in 177, he found his bishop dead, and he had already been elected the successor.

As bishop, Irenaeus wrote several works, of which only two are extant; however, they mark a turning point in the history of the Church. Before Irenaeus, the writers were catechists, ethicists, apologists, and philosophers. Although his work is heavily influenced by Justin Martyr and to some extent by Theophilus of Antioch, he surpasses them in the explanation of Christology and in theology in general. Irenaeus was the first real theologian since the apostles, because he is intentional about supporting every argument from scripture rather than philosophy. He believed that reliance on human reason (philosophy) results in heresy, so for him the Christian faith must be founded on divine revelation as opposed to human reason. With the transition from apology to theology, the primary audience for the documents in question is now Christian, so the goal of writing is no longer simply apology or even conversion but orthodoxy.[1] Correct belief matters, since to believe in the *wrong* Christ is to believe in no Christ at all.

Most of Irenaeus's quotations and references to scripture are from the Old Testament, for two reasons. First, Irenaeus was arguing primarily against gnosticism, which rejected the Old Testament and its connection to Jesus Christ. Therefore, Irenaeus meant to show how the Old Testament pointed to Christ and how the two testaments were connected. Second, the New Testament was still in its early stages of development, a development to which Irenaeus himself will contribute, as we will see in the next chapter. According to tradition, Irenaeus died a martyr in the year 202 CE. He leaves us two of the most important early Church documents.

Against Heresies

Written about 185 CE, the actual title of this document is *The Detection and Refutation of Knowledge Falsely So-Called.* The "so-called knowledge" is a reference to gnosticism, named from the Greek word *gnosis*, which means "knowledge." As indicated above, gnosticism was actually a vast array of philosophical systems, based on an extreme docetism but only loosely connected to each other by a similarity of concepts. While there were many different gnostic teachers on the fringes of the Church in the second century, Irenaeus attempts to explain and refute them all one by one, often going into great detail about the gnostic systems, which (while it can be tedious for the reader) is invaluable for the historian.[2]

The various forms of gnosticism incorporated complicated and elaborate cosmological myths, which Irenaeus attacks and sometimes mocks. The most important problem with gnosticism, however, was that it tended to deny, or at least diminish, the real humanity of Christ. For the Gnostics, Christ was either a phantom who only appeared to be human, or a spirit who "possessed," or temporarily indwelt, a semitangible Jesus. For them, Christ had no connection to the Old Testament and his Father was not the God of the Hebrews. In fact, as we have seen, some taught that the creation of the material world was a cosmic blunder, and Christ came to save humanity from the inept (or evil) Creator God of the Old Testament. He would do this by bringing secret knowledge (*gnosis*), which would allow the enlightened to ascend to the highest levels of heaven at the point of death.

Irenaeus countered the Gnostics' claim to secret knowledge with the concept of apostolic succession. He reasoned that if Jesus had indeed brought secret knowledge, he would have told the apostles, who would in turn have told their successors, the bishops.[3] Since Irenaeus himself was a bishop, he argued that if any secret knowledge had been handed on by Jesus, he would know it. He further criticized the Gnostics for claiming to know the secrets of God while ignoring divine revelation.[4] To counteract the gnostic rejection of the Old Testament, Irenaeus showed the continuity between the Old and New Testaments. Creation was not a mistake, and in fact Christ was the agent of creation. The God of the Old Testament is the God and Father of the Lord Jesus Christ, and creation is good. Irenaeus connected the Old Testament to the New by the use of typology. Old Testament types foreshadow parallel events in the life and ministry of Jesus and the early Church. For example, Adam was created from the virgin earth and was the first man; Christ was born of the Virgin and was the second Adam (1 Cor 15:44–47). Eve disobeyed God and brought death into the world; Mary obeyed God and brought life by becoming the mother of Christ.[5] The tree of the knowledge of good and evil in the Garden of Eden was the occasion for sin; the tree of Golgotha, the cross, was the remedy for sin. Thus Christ can be seen in the Old Testament, which prepared the world for his arrival. In his zeal to defend the Old Testament from a Christian perspective, Irenaeus went even further and attempted to show the continuity between the Old and New Testaments with an early form of dispensationalism that followed Papias's interpretation of the Book of Revelation.[6]

The Ebionites had reasoned that since Christ suffered, he could not be divine. The Docetics and Gnostics said that since he was divine, he could not have suffered. Ironically, both extremes were trying to safeguard the impassibility and immutability of divinity. The Docetics and Gnostics went so far as to reject the Old Testament because its anthropomorphisms seemed to describe a God who changes. Irenaeus, as a proponent of Logos Christology, affirmed both the human and divine natures of Christ against these two extremes. For Irenaeus, the key is the incarnation. The divine Logos became human, so the impassible became passible, by becoming human. Technically, the divine nature of Christ remains impassible, while the human nature can suffer and die for the sake of humanity's reconciliation with God. This does not imply that Jesus is the name for the human nature and Christ is the name for the divine nature (as some had speculated), but that Jesus Christ is one person who has both a human and a divine nature. For Irenaeus and the other writers of the late second through the early third centuries, the humanity of Christ is the Son of Man, or Son of David; the divinity of Christ is the Son of God. The Son of Man can suffer his passion, while the Son of God remains impassible.

Demonstration of the Apostolic Preaching

Also called *Proof of the Apostolic Preaching*, this much shorter document is a good recommendation for the student of early Christianity who wants a firsthand introduction to Irenaeus. It was probably written in the late 180s, after *Against Heresies*. It is addressed to a priest named Marcianus, who may have been Irenaeus's brother, and it amounts to a combination of internal apology and catechesis, written for a Christian audience. The literary form is that of a public letter, which means it was probably meant to be read to an assembly.

Irenaeus's *Demonstration of the Apostolic Preaching* is in many ways a summary of orthodox Christian theology up to the end of the second century. Thus it is very valuable for the study of the early Church, in spite of the fact that Irenaeus gets some of his history wrong and even confuses the sequence of emperors in the first century. The document represents Logos Christology, in which the preexistent Word of God can be seen in the theophanies of the Old Testament. This is because God the Father cannot be localized in time and space (or *circumscribed*), so any appearance of God in the days before Jesus must be an appearance of the preincarnate Christ.[7] Therefore, it was God the Son, the preincarnate Logos, who walked in the Garden of Eden and talked with Adam, not God the Father.[8] It was also the Son, rather than the Father or the Holy Spirit, who inspired and spoke through the prophets.[9] Typical of Logos Christology, there is no clear distinction made between the preincarnate (or for that matter, postascension) Christ and the

Holy Spirit, so that there is some confusion of God's Word and God's wisdom.[10]

A milestone of early Christian doctrine is apparent in this document, where Irenaeus becomes the first to say explicitly that the Father and Son are one and the same essence.[11] The principle behind this assertion is that the one who is begotten (or *generated*) from God must also be God (that is, divine). In other words, the Father and the Son share the same divine essence, or the same divinity. Therefore, because of the generation of the Son from the Father, the Father and Son are one in power and one in being (or *consubstantial*). Yet there is a distinction between the Father and Son, and an order, or hierarchy, within the Trinity.[12] The distinction between the Father and Son is described in terms of relative approachability. The Father is utterly transcendent and invisible, and therefore is not directly approachable. The Son, on the other hand, can be visible and circumscribed, and therefore can appear in time and space, primarily in his incarnation but also in the pre-incarnation theophanies. This implies that the Son is somehow less transcendent, or more immanent, than the Father and consequently he is approachable. So one cannot approach the Father directly, but only through the Son (John 14:6). Put another way, the Spirit brings us to the Son, and the Son brings us to the Father.[13]

Furthermore, there is a hierarchy of authority in the Trinity, in which the Son obeys the Father.[14] The Son is the Father's messenger, the agent of the Father who comes with the Father's authority but who nevertheless does the Father's will, not his own (John 6:38). This means that as the Sender, the Father has a level of authority above that of the Son, the Messenger.[15] In describing the Trinity, Irenaeus used an analogy of anointing. The Father is the one who anoints, the Son is the anointed one, and the Holy Spirit is the ointment. Thus Irenaeus has set the stage for the third- and fourth-century descriptions of the Trinity.

For Irenaeus, the Father, Son, and Holy Spirit are the "three articles of our seal," a reference to baptism in the triune name.[16] A correct understanding of the Trinity is important because it has implications for the sacraments, especially for baptism, which makes one a Christian. Baptism was seen as spiritual rebirth, "the seal of eternal life."[17] It was analogous to Jewish circumcision, which was also understood as a seal or mark of membership in the community.[18] In baptism one received the Holy Spirit, but for Irenaeus it was correct belief and morality that kept the Holy Spirit from leaving the individual after baptism.[19] So baptism is one's entrance into the family of God, but orthodoxy was required to maintain that membership. In other words, baptism may be a rebirth and a sealing for eternal life, but one could lose one's salvation if one accepted a heretical view of Christ.

TERTULLIAN

Septimius Tertullianus was born about 145–50 CE in North Africa, probably in Carthage.[20] As far as we can tell, he lived into the 220s. Since his writings come from at or after the turn of the century, he is considered the first theologian of the third century. He was also the first Christian theologian to write in Latin, and he coined the Latin term *Trinitas* for the Trinity. For these reasons, he is called the father of Latin theology.

Tertullian was raised in a pagan home and given the standard classical education.[21] It has traditionally been assumed that he was a lawyer or at least had studied law, though this is far from certain. Eusebius tells us that Tertullian was "skilled in Roman law."[22] It is true that he is famous for having used Roman legal terminology to describe the Trinity, and his apologetics do contain some legal argumentation, but it is probably the case that any educated Roman would have known enough legal jargon and rhetoric to apply them to theology as he did.[23] Tertullian's genius was not in the world of law, but his talent emerged when he became a Christian in about 185 CE. Apparently Tertullian got married shortly after his baptism, so his wife may have had something to do with his conversion. In any case, he took to the Church and became one of its most important proponents, even helping to define Christianity itself by way of its doctrines.

It is not clear whether Tertullian was ever ordained. There is a tradition that he was a priest in Rome around the turn of the century; however, in some of his writings he seems to consider himself a layperson.[24] On the other hand, the documents in question were probably written after he left Rome, and other documents appear to be homilies. If he was a priest, he was never a bishop. Around the turn of the third century, he apparently had a falling out with the leadership in Rome, probably over their rejection of the Montanists, whom Irenaeus had supported and with whom Tertullian had begun to associate.[25] It is possible that Tertullian had been a priest in Rome but left the priesthood when he left Rome and afterward considered himself a lay teacher.[26] This would be consistent with the Montanist movement, since they operated outside the developing hierarchy.

Tertullian was apparently drawn to the Montanists for their stricter morality, their emphasis on continuing charismatic inspiration, and their millennialism. Their belief in ongoing prophecy combined with a conviction of the immanent return of Christ led to their ethical rigorism and dispensational interpretation of the Book of Revelation. For Tertullian, who was both a strict moralist and a devoted student of the writings of Irenaeus, the Montanists had it right, and they made the mainstream Church and its Roman leadership look morally lax. Tertullian criticized the Roman bishops for allowing second marriages, which he said was the same as forgiving the sin of adultery (Matt 19:9).[27] The Montanists, on the other hand, did not want to allow second marriages.[28] Because Tertullian came to disagree with the Roman bishops over matters of discipline, he concluded that authority was not necessarily in the bishops but wherever the Holy Spirit is.[29] Thus in practice he allowed that charismatic authority might trump apostolic authority.

It is usually stated that Tertullian "became" a Montanist in the first decade of the third century. Although he did return to Carthage and did associate with the Montanists there, it is not accurate to describe this move as in any way leaving the Church or converting to something new. The Montanists did not consider themselves a separate movement, and while there was some debate within the mainstream Church over whether Montanists should be considered heretics, the Montanist movement did not (yet) constitute a schism.[30] Tertullian never thought of himself as leaving the Church; rather, he saw himself as joining a charismatic reform movement that would critique the Church from within.[31]

Nevertheless, Tertullian is usually considered a Montanist

after about 207–08, though we cannot precisely date his move away from Rome (both literally and figuratively).[32] His ethical treatises reflect a stricter (Montanist) morality, sometimes critical of the bishops who were more lenient than Tertullian would like when it came to the forgiveness of sins and the reconciliation of sinners.[33] But his theological writings were thoroughly orthodox, and in fact they helped define orthodoxy, both for Tertullian's time and for the future.[34] Tertullian takes the theology of Irenaeus to the next level by building on the concept of the one essence of divinity and describing the Trinity in terms that would become standard for the Western, Latin-speaking Church. In fact, it may have been the Montanist influence that brought Tertullian to clarify the full divine personhood of the Holy Spirit, in addition to the Father and Son.[35] Although Tertullian supported the idea of ongoing prophecy and charismatic authority, his writings are at every turn grounded in scripture and prior tradition. For him, scripture was still the primary authority, and the inspiration of the Holy Spirit would help interpret scripture and tradition but would never contradict it.[36]

Unlike the apologists, Tertullian was a true theologian, making a distinction between theology and philosophy. He was outwardly very critical of philosophy, though he could not help but be influenced by it, as anyone who had received a classical education would have been.[37] But as a Christian he came to believe (like Irenaeus) that heresy comes from a misuse of philosophy. He famously said, "What indeed has Athens to do with Jerusalem? What concord is there between the Academy and the Church?"[38] For Tertullian, philosophy leads to paganism (that is, polytheism), or in the context of the Church, docetism and gnosticism. In fact, he criticized polytheism as illogical, saying that the existence of multiple gods necessarily implies that those gods cannot be omnipotent or omnipresent if they have to make room for one another and leave certain spheres of influence to other gods. Thus the very definition of divinity (assuming omnipotence and omnipresence) requires monotheism.

Tertullian was a prolific writer, and it would be impossible within the scope of this book to cover all of his writings; however, there are three that are most important for the understanding of the development of the Church and its doctrine.

The Prescription Against the Heretics

Possibly written while still at Rome, this is a standard internal apology. It is interesting for our purposes, however, because of what Tertullian says about heresy in general, and how this illuminates the way the early Christians of the mainstream Church saw their counterparts on the fringes.[39] According to Tertullian, heresy is the minority, while orthodoxy is the majority.[40] Just as there were followers of Jesus who left him (John 6), heresy is the innovation that deviates from the established tradition.[41] While orthodoxy is based on a solid foundation of apostolic succession, heresy seeks but never finds.[42] While orthodoxy interprets scripture correctly, heresy takes scripture out of context and uses it to "prooftext" its own philosophical assumptions or speculations.[43] Yet heresy is necessary, because it becomes the occasion for orthodoxy to be clarified.[44] Still, this does not mean that heresy precedes orthodoxy; on the contrary, heresy is new (and therefore not trustworthy).[45] In the end, heresy is dangerous because it is divisive, and maintaining orthodoxy is an urgent necessity for the sake of the unity of the Church.[46] In contrast to heresy, Tertullian included a version of an early creed to clarify the "rule of faith," the definition of orthodoxy such as it was at the turn of the third century.[47]

Apology

Following in the footsteps of Justin Martyr and Athenagoras, Tertullian wrote an apology for the faith. The occasion of its writing may have been the edict of Septimius Severus in 202 CE, which, according to tradition, was the year in which Tertullian's hero Irenaeus was martyred.[48] In addition to demonstrating that the Christian faith was not a threat to the empire, Tertullian also argued that there were now so many Christians in the empire that it would actually be bad for the empire to get rid of the Church.[49]

Tertullian's *Apology* contains many of the same elements and arguments as the second-century apologies. Belief in the Christian God is older, and therefore more reliable, than philosophy or paganism.[50] Pagan idols are inanimate objects made by humans, and in fact the ones made of precious metals need to be guarded.[51] In the old myths the gods behaved badly, and so even the philosophers criticized the myths.[52] By contrast, Christians are held to a higher moral standard. They don't share their wives, seek revenge, or kill other humans (including abortion, exposure of infants, and capital punishment).[53] According to Tertullian, Christians don't even cheat on their taxes![54] Other than that, he says, *We are just like you.*[55] The implication is that, far from being a threat, the Church is good for the empire.

In addition to the standard defense, Tertullian advanced the cause with some new points. He argued that polytheism is not logical since if there are many gods, one cannot know about them all, let alone worship them all, and yet any gods not worshiped will be offended. If one is not afraid of the consequences of offending countless unknown gods, then those gods must have no real power.[56] In truth, the gods of the pagan pantheon are not gods, but rather demons.[57] Tertullian complained that the live-and-let-live attitude of pagan cults toward one another was not extended to the Church. Everyone else in the empire enjoyed religious freedom; why not the Christians?[58] Instead, he said, the Christians were being condemned without investigation. This is because if they were investigated, no crime would be found, and those who did the investigation would convert.[59] Are Christians accused of cannibalism? They don't even shed blood, let alone eat human flesh. Why not test them by offering them some human flesh to eat, rather than by trying to force them to make pagan sacrifices?[60] Are Christians accused of incest? There is more of a chance that those who expose their children will unknowingly marry a relative.[61] And why are Christians tortured in an attempt to get them to *deny* their "crime," when at any other time, one tortures suspects to get them to confess?[62]

Tertullian further argued that it would be detrimental to the imperial economy to persecute Christians.[63] While it is true that they do not buy frankincense to be used as incense for pagan sacrifices, they do buy it for their funerals. And while it is true that they don't support the temple treasuries, they do give to the poor.[64] Finally, although it is true that Christians don't support the theaters, circuses, or athletic games in the arenas, they do wrestle with God in prayer for the peace of the empire.[65] In fact, Tertullian argued that in spite of the growing trend of blaming natural disasters on the presence of the Church, there were actually fewer disasters since the Christians started praying for the empire.[66] Therefore, it is not in the empire's best interest to kill Christians. Tertullian made a point to refer to the emperor Trajan's letter to Pliny, which forbade seeking out Christians.[67] He also quoted a story that the emperor Tiberius wanted to put a statue of Jesus Christ up in the Pantheon in Rome.[68] The point he was trying to make was that good emperors (like Tiberius) do not persecute the Church, but bad emperors (like the universally hated Nero) do persecute the Church.[69]

Against Praxeas

Tertullian's most important theological work is the treatise *Against Praxeas*. No one knows who Praxeas was, and in fact it might be a pseudonym. He was apparently a confessor who was critical of the Montanists and, according to Tertullian, was at least partially responsible for the Roman church's rejection of Montanism as an acceptable expression of Christianity.[70] He is also said to be an adherent of *modalism*, a heresy that diminished the distinction between the persons of the Trinity in an attempt to protect monotheism by emphasizing the oneness of God (see chapter 7 below). While Praxeas may have been an early teacher of modalism, it is equally possible that he was just a bit behind the times with regard to trinitarian theology, maintaining a Logos Christology that blurred the distinction between Son and Spirit. This may have been the case with the bishops of Rome whom Hippolytus criticized (see below), and in fact some have suggested that Praxeas might be a pseudonym for one of the bishops of Rome. In any case, we know that Tertullian opposed the bishops of Rome on disciplinary grounds, so it is not inconceivable that he opposed them on theological grounds as well. But the bishops of Rome were not really heretics, and in the end the person of Praxeas is probably more of a straw man than a real man, Tertullian taking the opportunity of using an enemy of Montanism as his foil to explain his understanding of the Trinity.

In *Against Praxeas* Tertullian introduced two Latin terms, apparently from Roman legal usage, that would become the very definition of orthodoxy for describing the Trinity. The word *sub-*

stantia describes a property, and is the Latin version of Irenaeus's concept of a shared essence.[71] The Father, Son, and Holy Spirit are one *substantia*.[72] This can be translated into English as "substance," as long as one keeps in mind that it does not refer to material substance. The substance of the Trinity is divinity itself. The other word is *persona*, meaning an individual entity.[73] This is translated as "person," and it refers to each of the three manifestations or *persons* of the Trinity (Father, Son, and Holy Spirit). Note that the word *persons* is not the equivalent of "people," and we would not speak of three "people" of the Trinity. As it is used here, the word *persons* is a technical term that indicates the distinction between Father, Son, and Holy Spirit, while also maintaining the unity of the one God. Therefore, God exists as one divine substance shared by three divine persons.[74] The term *substance* describes the oneness of God, and the term *person* describes the fact that God is also three, providing a way of clarifying the distinction between the Father, Son, and Holy Spirit against modalism.[75]

As Irenaeus had indicated, the generation of the Son from the Father (that the Son is "begotten" from the Father) necessitates that the Son also be the same divine essence, or substance, as the Father.[76] The oneness of God requires it. The fact that the Trinity is one substance is called *consubstantiality*. However, the immutability of the divine also requires that the Father cannot become incarnate, let alone suffer and die. Therefore, some distinction of persons is necessary, even while maintaining the oneness. For Tertullian, the Father alone is the First Cause of all existence and is ultimate transcendence and uncircumscribable. By the same token, only the Son became incarnate, and only his human nature suffered. Tertullian followed Irenaeus in describing the hierarchy of the Trinity as one of Sender and Messenger. The Father is the Sender and the Son is his Messenger. This implies that in some way the Holy Spirit is also the Messenger of the Father and/or the Son. The hierarchy of the Trinity, then, is one of authority, specifically in terms of the internal relationships between the persons, while the oneness of God is maintained by the single substance. Thus Tertullian wrote, "These three (persons) are one, but not one and the same, so that when (Jesus) said, 'I and the Father are one,' he meant a unity of substance, not a numerical singularity."[77]

Tertullian criticized modalism for having a Trinity with too much "monarchy" (unity) and too little "economy" (distinction).[78] Ultimately, this is not really a Trinity at all, but a monad with three names. For the Modalists, the only allowable distinction between the persons of the Trinity was a label that described what God was doing at any given time. When God was the Creator, he was the Father. When God was the Savior, he was the Son, and when God was sustaining the Church, he was the Spirit. To put it another way, God was the Father in the Old Testament, the Son in the gospels, and the Spirit in the Church. Among the many problems with this conception of the Trinity, it gives the appearance that the three persons only exist one at a time. It also gives the impression that the distinction of persons is only by task, or mode of operation (hence the name "modalism"; see chapter 7 for more detail). In fact, the mainstream Church would come to the conclusion that any operation of God is the activity of all three persons of the Trinity, a doctrine called *inseparable operation*.[79] Therefore, popular reformulations of the triune name into formulas such as "Creator, Redeemer, Sustainer" are actually expressions of the heresy of modalism, because they contradict the doctrine of *inseparable operation* and imply a Trinity in which the Father does not save and the Son does not create (cf. John 1:3).

Tertullian also followed Irenaeus in emphasizing that Christ must have both a human and a divine nature in order to be the Savior. Against Marcionite docetism he argued that "what is not assumed is not redeemed," and therefore if Christ did not have a real humanity, he could not be the Savior of humanity. For Tertullian, the birth of Christ demonstrated the two natures. That he had a birth at all proves his humanity against the Docetics and Gnostics who claimed Jesus had no birth or childhood. That his birth was miraculous in nature proves his divinity against the Ebionites. In fact, Tertullian anticipated the conclusion of the fifth-century *Theotokos* controversy when he said that the divine Logos was circumscribed in Mary's womb, so that she was the Mother of the divine nature of Christ, not the human nature only. As the Third Ecumenical Council of Ephesus (431 CE) would later clarify, it is therefore appropriate to call Mary "Mother of God." Tertullian also anticipated the definition of the Fourth Ecumenical

Council of Chalcedon (451 CE) when he said that the two natures are "united but not confused, in one person, Jesus, God and human...the property of each (nature) is preserved."[80]

HIPPOLYTUS

Like Tertullian, Hippolytus was a disciple of Irenaeus, at least as evidenced in his writings. But also like that of Tertullian, Hippolytus's status in the Church is unclear. In fact, the person of Hippolytus is as much of an enigma as the Church has ever produced, to the point that some speculate there were two or even three "Hippolyti" responsible for the writings attributed to him.[81] Acknowledging the debate and the problems associated with ascribing the Hippolytan documents to one person, we will nevertheless treat them as a unit. If they are not from the same pen, they are at least from the same school of thought and represent the next stage in the development of doctrine, bridging the gap from Tertullian to Novatian.

Born around 170 CE, Hippolytus was from the East, and therefore he wrote in Greek. At some point he came to Rome and was an influential presence during the time when Zephyrinus (199–217), Callistus (217–22), and their successors were bishops there. Eusebius says that Hippolytus was also a bishop, but does not know of what city.[82] Hippolytus seems to refer to himself as a bishop in the preface to his *Refutation of All Heresies*. In the year 1551 a statue was found near the church of San Lorenzo, just outside the walls of Rome. The statue appeared to be of a figure seated on a bishop's throne. It had an inscription cataloguing the writings of Hippolytus, along with a list of the dates of Easter attributed to Hippolytus. Many have argued that this was in fact a statue of Hippolytus as a bishop. Pope Pius IV (reigned 1559–65) said that Hippolytus was bishop of the coastal town of Portus, but there is no early evidence for this.[83]

Thus Hippolytus may have been bishop of a smaller town near Rome. On the other hand, he may have been the leader of the Eastern (Greek-speaking) Christians in Rome, functioning as their bishop and even possibly leading a separate catechetical school distinct from the Latin-speaking one headed by the official bishops of Rome.[84] If this was the case, Hippolytus represented a group whose standards of morality and expectations for reconciliation were stricter than the majority, and, like Tertullian, Hippolytus criticized the bishops of Rome, especially for forgiving the sin of "adultery." This probably meant that they allowed second marriages and/or blessed the cohabitation of mixed-class couples who could not be married legally. The bishops of Rome also apparently allowed priests to marry and permitted divorced and remarried men to remain in the priesthood.[85] Hippolytus would complain that they even reconciled some who had been excommunicated by others, possibly even by Hippolytus himself.[86]

Hippolytus also clashed with the bishops of Rome over theology. During the time when Zephyrinus was bishop and Callistus was his deacon (in charge of the catacombs that would later bear his name), a certain Noetus came to Rome from Smyrna. According to Hippolytus, Noetus was so influenced by Eastern monism, he embraced a modalist version of Christianity and came to Rome to teach it.[87] At first, Zephyrinus was tolerant of Noetus teaching in Rome. Even though a modalist faction was developing in the church of Rome, Zephyrinus was apparently advised by Callistus to try to keep the peace with both factions. Hippolytus confronted the bishop and his deacon, and after some debate, Noetus was called before the council of priests.[88] Although at this point he denied that he was teaching modalism, it soon became clear that he was, and so he was summoned before the council a second time. This time he had more support and held his ground. He was excommunicated but continued teaching as the leader of a modalist school.

Callistus became the next bishop of Rome in 217 CE.[89] Hippolytus had not forgotten that Callistus had been conciliatory toward Noetus, and eventually he accused the bishop himself of being a Modalist.[90] For his part, Hippolytus may have overreacted against modalism to the extent that he emphasized the distinction between the Father and Son to the point where Callistus accused him of worshiping two gods.[91] In reality both Callistus and Hippolytus were probably within the realm of orthodoxy. As was the case with earlier bishops of Rome whom Tertullian criticized, Callistus may have retained an aspect of Logos Christology that did not have a clearly defined distinction between the persons of the Trinity, especially the Son and Spirit. This may have looked like modalism to Hippolytus. In addition, Tertullian's concept of consubstantiality, which Hippolytus had not picked up, might also have looked to him like a form of modalism.[92] While Hippolytus appears to accept the idea of a single essence from Irenaeus, he was apparently not comfortable with the way Callistus was expressing it.[93] Callistus also appears to have taught early versions of *circumincessio* (also known as *perichoresis*, or "reciprocity," the mutual interactivity of the three persons of the Trinity) as well as *communicatio idiomatum* (the sharing of properties between the two natures of Christ). Hippolytus rejected the latter because he thought it compromised the immutability of the divine nature.[94] In the end, it is clear that Callistus was not a Modalist, because he excommunicated the modalist teacher Sabellius.[95] Callistus and Hippolytus both agreed that there was a distinction between the Father and Son, in that only the Son was begotten and only the Son suffered and died. Eventually Hippolytus would inadvertently admit that Callistus represented the middle way between the Ebionites (Theodosius) and the Modalists (Sabellius).[96]

Hippolytus continued to be a thorn in the side of two more bishops of Rome, until persecution returned to the city. In the year 235 CE, two prominent leaders of the church in Rome were sent to the mines of Sardinia: the bishop Pontian and Hippolytus. Hippolytus died a martyr in 235 or 236.[97] According to one tradition he was drowned, although he may have died in the mines. He has left a valuable, if confusing, literary legacy. There are several important documents, most of which are the subject of intense debate as to their authenticity and authorship. The most important for the student of the early Church are *Against Noetus* and the *Refutation of All Heresies*.

Against Noetus

Hippolytus admitted that Noetus was motivated by a desire to preserve the oneness of God.[98] Noetus had reasoned that if Christ was God, but not the Father, then that would imply two Gods and compromise the monotheistic basis of Christianity.[99] If extreme dualism (as in docetism) led one to a strict dichotomy between spirit and matter, Noetus's monism led him to the opposite conclusion: that there was no distinction at all between spirit and matter. And if there is no distinction between spirit and matter, then there is no distinction between the divine and human in Christ, and ultimately no distinction among the persons of the Trinity. Thus monism applied to Christianity leads to modalism. Therefore, Noetus taught that the Father became the Son in the incarnation.[100] In other words, the Son is the Father come to earth. He is appropriately called the Father only before the incarnation and the Son only after the incarnation.[101] This is a distinction of mode (time and activity), not a real distinction. Hippolytus responded by labeling Noetus's teaching *Patripassionism*, "the suffering of the Father." In other words, Hippolytus reasoned that if Noetus was right, then the Father died on the cross.[102] Noetus answered the charge by taking a docetic view of the passion: Christ only appeared to suffer because God is immutable.[103]

Hippolytus began *Against Noetus* with a creedal statement of faith.[104] He then went on to defend his understanding of orthodoxy by emphasizing the real distinction between the Father and the Son, against modalist monism.[105] For Hippolytus this distinction did not compromise the oneness of God because God is still one, even though a Trinity (in Greek, *Triados*, a Triad).[106] Following Irenaeus, Hippolytus described the Trinity as one God and one divine power, but with a hierarchy ("economy") of "threefold manifestation."[107] The Father, Son, and the Holy Spirit are all equally worshiped, because together the three are the one God.[108]

Hippolytus also defended the real humanity of Christ against the Modalists' diminished humanity and docetic passion. While Hippolytus made a point of saying that Christ had his own human rational soul, emphasizing his full humanity,[109] his Christology was still partly in the second century. He does not distinguish clearly between the preincarnate Logos and the Holy Spirit.[110] He also follows Theophilus a bit too closely, saying that before the Word was begotten, the Father was alone—though he does try to correct (or redeem) Theophilus by saying that although God was alone, he existed in plurality.[111] The Word was God's reason, wisdom, and counsel, but the Word was not the Son before the incarnation.[112] In fact, Hippolytus understood two processions of the Word.[113] The first procession of the Word was the generation, when the Word was "begotten." At this point, the Word of God was "uttered," or spoken forth to be the agent of creation. When the Word was begotten, he became distinct from the Father, moving from the reason/wisdom *in* God to the Word *with* God.[114] Like all the theologians up to this point, Hippolytus held that the generation of the Word was an event that created the distinction between Father and Son. Before the generation there was no distinction and no distinct personal existence of the Son. At the generation, the Word is extended out from the Father, God from God, power from power, like rays from the sun or water from a spring.[115] The second procession is the incarnation, when the Word becomes the Son because he becomes human.

In addition to clarifying the distinction between the Father and the Son, the distinction between the divine and human natures in the Son was also important. Unlike Tertullian, Hippolytus did not believe that the divine nature could be circumscribed, so for Hippolytus, only the human nature was finite and localized in time and space.[116] The divine nature remained infinite and omnipresent, since (he reasoned) to lack omnipresence is to have a need for movement, and movement is a kind of change, which would seem to compromise divine immutability. Hippolytus would not have agreed with Tertullian on the circumscription of the divine nature in the womb of Mary.

Refutation of All Heresies

Sometimes referred to as *Elenchus* or *Philosophumena*, this document was probably written in the last decade or so of Hippolytus's life, in the late 220s. It is in many ways a less clear version of Irenaeus's *Against Heresies*. Most of the *Refutation* is a catalogue of gnostic beliefs, much of which is taken from Irenaeus and other sources. What is interesting is that by this time the Gnostics seem to have answered Irenaeus's charge that if there was secret knowledge the bishops would know about it. Some apparently responded by saying that the secret knowledge was not given to the apostles but to Jesus' blood relatives, and was handed down through his half brother James.[117] For Hippolytus the danger of gnosticism was that it is a docetic syncretism that ultimately left Christ less than human, and that called the crucifixion and resurrection into question and thereby threatened salvation itself.[118]

Like the other theologians, Hippolytus also criticized philosophy, saying that heresy comes from a syncretism of Christianity with philosophy and/or astrology. Even so, Hippolytus pointed out that while the pagans hold on to the old mythologies, even the philosophers were coming around to various forms of monotheism.[119] He claims that it started with Pythagoras, who got a version of monotheism from the Egyptians.[120] But philosophy could not lead to salvation, since many of the philosophers taught versions of reincarnation, and some even believed in the transmigration of souls across species.[121] Others taught a version of evolution that assumed that matter was eternal and uncreated.[122] This, along with Plato's understanding that the material world was, at best, less real than the spiritual realm, seemed to contradict Genesis on the goodness of God's creation.[123]

The philosophers may have talked about a *logos*, but they often equated this logos with one of the gods of the Greco-Roman pantheon, such as Mercury. They saw the logos as an astrological figure, just one more player in the cosmic drama.[124] Even when the logos of the philosophers was understood as the rational principle behind creation, or a quasi-divine figure who would be judge over the living and the dead, for Hippolytus this was still an inadequate understanding of the Christian Logos as preincarnate Christ.

Nevertheless, it is clear from the *Refutation* that there were certain philosophical concepts that Hippolytus (and the Church) accepted. Christians and pagan philosophers alike shared the definition of deity as that which is eternal and immortal, with no beginning or end.[125] A strict distinction was made between that which is created (and is also therefore finite, corruptible, and perishable) and that which is uncreated (infinite, incorruptible, and imperishable).[126] Deity is assumed to be immutable, since change of any kind compromises perfection and leads to corruptibility. Deity is benevolent; therefore, God is not the creator of evil, but evil comes from the misuse of free will.[127] Finally, deity is simplex, or indivisible.[128] Of course, all of this created a problem for Christians who wanted to maintain both the divinity and the humanity of Christ, since the obvious mutability of the man Jesus seemed to contradict the assumption that divinity must be immutable. The difficulty of interpretation of this paradox led to groups on the extremes rejecting one of the natures in favor of the other. The Ebionites, and later the Adoptionists, denied the divinity in favor of the humanity. The Docetics, Gnostics, and then the Modalists denied the full humanity in favor of the divinity. The mainstream Church had to make a distinction between the divine and human natures in Christ, such that only the divine nature was immutable, and ultimately only God the Father was the First Cause and ultimate Source of all existence.[129]

ORIGEN

Origen Adamantius was born about the year 186 CE in Alexandria, of Christian parents. He was a student of Clement of Alexandria and the philosopher Ammonius Saccas (the founder of neo-Platonism).[130] When he was fifteen or sixteen years old, persecution came to Alexandria and his father was arrested and imprisoned. According to tradition, Origen would have followed his father and confessed his faith to the authorities, but his mother hid his clothes. Choosing modesty over martyrdom, Origen instead wrote a letter to his father in prison encouraging him not to deny the faith on account of his family. His father was eventually beheaded, probably in the year 202 CE. Origen went from riches to rags when the family property was confiscated after the execution of his father. He was supported by a wealthy woman who was a patron of Christian philosophers; however, she also supported a theologian from Antioch named Paul, whom Origen considered a heretic. Origen and Paul debated the faith, but Origen refused to pray with him.

At the age of eighteen, in the year 204, Origen succeeded his teacher Clement as the head of the catechetical school in Alexandria, in part because the persecution left no one else for the job. Since the school itself was a target, Origen only escaped arrest because he moved around from house to house. Eventually he sold all of his secular books for money to support himself, gave up teaching pagan literature, and devoted himself to the school. Origen lived an ascetic lifestyle, sleeping on the floor, refusing to drink wine, wearing no shoes, and limiting his possessions. He fasted to the point of damaging his health. It is said that he also took Matthew 19:12 literally and castrated himself, presumably to avoid scandal if he were to teach women or have female patrons. While some scholars have questioned whether this story is true, Origen's enemies would later use his self-mutilation as a reason to question the validity of his ordination.

Since Christianity was treated as a philosophy in Alexandria, it is possible that students came to the school as an "inquiry," not necessarily intending to be baptized. Many would probably have left before making a commitment to the moral standards of the Church. Still, the school attracted so many students that Origen himself attracted attention. During renewed persecution in Alexandria in the years 215–16 CE, Origen fled to Jerusalem, and then to Caesarea. The bishops of Palestine invited him to teach; however, this got him into trouble with his own bishop, who said that a layperson should not be teaching in the presence of bishops. He was eventually ordained a priest, but in Caesarea, not Alexandria, which only widened the rift between him and his bishop back in Alexandria. But he became so famous as a Christian philosopher that around 225 CE he was summoned by Julia Mamaea, the mother of the emperor Severus Alexander. She sent a military escort to bring Origen to Antioch, where she was staying, so that he could explain Christianity to her. There is also a story that Origen corresponded with the emperor Philip (emperor 244–49).

Origen would eventually be excommunicated by a synod in Alexandria in 231 CE. The synod interpreted Deuteronomy 23:1 as a prohibition against the ordination of anyone who was castrated. But Origen would never return to Alexandria since the persecution caused him constantly to be on the run between Palestine and Asia Minor. He was finally arrested and imprisoned during the Decian persecution (see chapter 7), in about 250. He was tortured and eventually released, but his health was broken and he died soon after his release, probably between 253 and 255.

Origen was a prolific writer, but unfortunately many of his writings are lost or exist only in imperfect forms and fragments. He learned Hebrew so that he could translate and interpret the original language of the Old Testament. He created a parallel text called the *Hexapla*, which included six different versions of the Old Testament: the Hebrew text, the Hebrew transliterated into Greek characters, the Septuagint (the Old Testament translated into Greek), and three other translations, including one used by the Ebionites. At first he limited his text of the Old Testament to the twenty-two books originally written in Hebrew, but later he added the deuterocanonical books. He also participated in a debate about the authenticity of the story of Susannah in the Book of Daniel.

Always the philosopher, Origen wore the philosopher's pallium and interacted with pagan philosophy. As a student of Ammonius, he had known Ammonius's other famous students, Porphyry and Plotinus. He wrote a response to one of the most famous critiques of Christianity in his *Against Celsus*.[131] However, his interaction with philosophy led him into a speculative theology that would later get him into trouble and bring accusations of heresy.

On First Principles

Origen wrote his most famous work while he was still in Alexandria.[132] Unfortunately, most of it only exists in a fourth-century Latin translation by Rufinus, who admitted that he had made changes to Origen's text, especially where Origen seemed heterodox by fourth-century (post-Nicene) standards. In truth, there is still plenty in the text that could be considered heretical, so one wonders what Rufinus took out. Ultimately, *On First Principles* as we have it is an unreliable source for discovering Origen's thought, except where fragments of the original Greek exist. In fact, the elements of the document that are most likely to have come from Origen are those which are the most speculative or heretical. The parts that are sometimes taken as a contribution to Christian theology were most likely edited or inserted after the Council of Nicaea, influenced by Rufinus's own theology, which comes from sources such as Novatian and Athanasius.[133]

In truth, Origen's genius and legacy is not as a theologian so much as a biblical exegete. He wrote many commentaries on scripture, some of which still exist for sections of the Bible, including parts of the gospels of Matthew and John. The commentaries were dictated; Origen composed as he spoke out loud, quoting scripture from memory. The texts were taken down in shorthand, later to be written out by "girls skilled in penmanship" and then duplicated by copyists.[134] Origen is known as the most famous proponent of the allegorical method of interpretation. According to Eusebius, he was not satisfied with the literal meaning, and always looked for a deeper, more spiritual meaning in the text.[135] The philosopher Porphyry, in his *Third Treatise Against the Christians*, gave Origen credit for applying the allegorical method of interpretation to the Old Testament. Porphyry wrote, "While his manner of life was Christian…in his opinions about material things and the Deity, he played the Greek, and introduced Greek ideas into foreign fables."[136] In other words, he applied Greek allegorical interpretation to Jewish writings. His attention to the spiritual meaning often led him to overallegorize, however, and he would be criticized for finding meaning in the text that was never meant to be there.

Problematic Elements in Origen

Origen was condemned as a heretic several times after his death, including at the Fifth Ecumenical Council of Constantinople II in 553 CE. Origen's theology was so intertwined with philosophy and so speculative that it is hard to distinguish what he really believed from what he was only proposing for further thought and debate. He seems to have been the kind of person who "thinks out loud," except that his thoughts were recorded and held against him later. This is especially true of *On First Principles*, which was written while he was still relatively young. In the end, there are several points at which Origen is at odds with the orthodoxy of his own time, not to mention later orthodoxy.

Origen accepted a philosophical understanding of the human soul that assumed that souls preexisted their current bodies, and he probably believed in reincarnation and merit from prelife existence.[137] This was seen as inconsistent with the Christian understanding of the soul as created for one life, after which there was death and resurrection, not reincarnation (Heb 9:27). As applied to the human soul of Christ, Origen implied that his human nature was also preexistent and that the incarnation was simply the coming together of two eternal souls, the Logos and the human soul of Jesus. Although he is sometimes given credit for a doctrine of *eternal generation*, his concept of eternal generation applies not only to the divine nature of Christ in the Logos, but to all human souls.[138] This effectively negates the uniqueness of Christ among humanity. In fact, Origen seems to be saying that both the Logos and the Holy Spirit are created beings.[139] For Origen, the Father and Son are not consubstantial, and he questioned whether Christ should even be worshiped, saying "We may not pray to him who himself prays."[140]

Finally, Origen accepted elements from philosophy that had been rejected by most Christians. He seems to have accepted the possibility of the existence of other gods and speculated that John the Baptist was an angel incarnate.[141] He also believed in a Stoic understanding of the end of the universe as a conflagration, only to be followed by a rebirth in which the universe would start all over again. There were other accusations against Origen, some probably untrue or exaggerated, many leveled at him after his death when he could not defend himself. Nevertheless, it is clear that he may have been too smart for his own good, leaving a legacy tarnished by heresy. Whatever good Origen did would be overshadowed by the ways in which he went to extremes.

NOVATIAN

Born around the turn of the third century, Novatian became a priest in Rome under Bishop Fabian (bishop 236–50 CE).[142] He probably wrote his most important work, *On the Trinity*, during this time. When Fabian was martyred in January of 250, the Roman church was not able to elect a successor, so Novatian's reputation as a theologian earned him the position of acting bishop of Rome. In this role he corresponded with Cyprian, bishop of Carthage, on behalf of the church at Rome. Three of his letters are preserved in the correspondence of Cyprian.

Like Tertullian and Hippolytus before him, Novatian was a moral rigorist, stricter than the majority of the Church, demanding a level of purity that was inevitably unrealistic. When persecution subsided briefly, and those who had denied the faith to save their lives wanted to return to the Church, Novatian recommended excommunication. He became the leader of a rigorist faction that opposed the majority who wanted to allow for the reconciliation of the apostates. When the election for bishop of Rome was finally held in 251, Novatian lost to Cornelius, who represented a middle position between the rigorists and a faction of "laxists" who advocated easy access back into the Church for the fallen. Novatian was subsequently consecrated as a rival bishop of Rome by fellow rigorists, creating a schism that lasted for centuries. Taking the position of a bishop over a scattered flock, Novatian wrote two moral treatises (*On the Benefit of Purity* and *On the Spectacles*) as well as an allegorical treatment of Old Testament dietary laws (*On Jewish Foods*). More will be said about persecution and the schism in chapter 7 below, but for now it is enough to say that while Novatian's ecclesiology would not ultimately be acceptable to the mainstream Church, his theology not only was acceptable to the Church of the mid-third century, but it also took Tertullian's thought to its logical conclusions and helped define orthodoxy for the third century and beyond. This in spite of the fact that Cyprian would write that whatever he taught was irrelevant as long as he was outside the Church.[143]

On the Trinity

Novatian wrote this document as a commentary on the "rule of truth," the Church's definition of trinitarian doctrine. It is an excellent summary of the state of Christian theology up to the mid-third century, and it even anticipates later standards of orthodoxy. Novatian is intentional about charting a course midway between the extremes of modalism on one side and adoptionism (the legacy of the Ebionites) on the other. In fact, he said that Christ was being crucified again "between two thieves," the true Christ in the middle between the extremes. Following Irenaeus and Tertullian, he said that both natures of Christ must be maintained, united in the person of Jesus yet without any confusion that would blur the distinction between them. In his explanation of Christ, Novatian finally took the Church beyond the earlier Logos Christology to a Christology of *kenosis*. The term *kenosis* comes from the phrase "he emptied himself" in Philippians 2:7. The incarnation is thus described as a descent, in which Novatian said the Logos emptied himself of divine power/authority in order to become human.[144] This does not mean, however, that the Son is any less divine during the time of the incarnation, since Novatian made a distinction between divine power, or attributes, and divine substance, or divinity itself. In other words, in the incarnation the Logos maintains full divinity, but he must set aside such divine powers as omnipresence and omnipotence in order to be fully human and truly experience the human condition.

Novatian also follows Irenaeus and Tertullian in the consubstantiality of the persons of the Trinity, balanced with the hierarchy of authority in which the Father and Son are described as being in a relationship of Sender and Messenger. Taking these concepts to their logical conclusions, Novatian clarified that while there is a unity of substance (which was needed to maintain the oneness of the Trinity against adoptionism), there is also a subordination of authority (which was needed to maintain the distinction of persons against modalism). Thus Novatian's Christology is properly expressed as a *dynamic subordination*, in which the subordination of the Son to the Father is not ontological, but is rather a subordination of power that is both relational and voluntary.[145] Therefore, Novatian had clarified the balance of unity and distinction in the Trinity.

Novatian also moves beyond the understanding of the generation of the Word as an event to a true doctrine of *eternal generation*. Unlike previous writers, who conceived of the generation as an event, the point at which the Son becomes distinct from the Father, Novatian knew that there must be an eternal distinction in order to maintain the eternal personhood of the Son and the immutability of the Father. Therefore, the generation of the Son is described as an eternal state of being in which both consubstantiality and distinction of persons is unchanging. In other words, the Son does not go from being *in* the Father to being *with* the Father. The Son is eternally in the Father and eternally with the Father.

Finally, Novatian also advanced the concept of *communicatio idiomatum*, which Callistus may have approached, by describing the ways in which the two natures in Christ were united. In the union the two natures retain their individual integrity, and yet each one "borrows" something from the other. The divine nature received the frailty of humanity, allowing it to experience the human condition, while the human nature received the immortality of divinity, which makes salvation available to the rest of humanity. Therefore, Novatian was the first successfully to strike the balance of unity and distinction, both in the persons of the Trinity and in the two natures of Christ. In this way, he brought theology to a plateau and set the stage for the ecumenical councils and creeds of the fourth century.[146]

CHAPTER 6

The New Testament Canon

The word *canon* means a standard, or rule, by which other things are measured. The canon of scripture is therefore the authoritative handbook for the Christian faith and life. It is the standard by which the doctrines and traditions of the Church are measured and evaluated. Historically, there have been two ways to look at scripture as the authority for the Church. One way is to say that what is not prohibited in scripture is allowed in the Church. In general, the early Christians realized that scripture, while inspired, was not exhaustive, and so they took this approach. The other approach assumes that whatever is not commanded by scripture is not allowed in the Church. This approach was tested in some of the rigorist movements of the early Church, but it is mainly a product of certain branches of the Protestant Reformation and is related to the concept of *sola scriptura*. However, the early Church had no concept of *sola scriptura*. This is partly because the earliest Christians had no specifically Christian Bible. The New Testament itself was developed in the early Church and so is a product of the early Church. In fact, as we will see, the Christians of the early centuries would come to the conclusion that *sola scriptura non satis est* (scripture alone is not enough)—in other words, they would eventually have to go beyond scripture to interpret scripture.

The Bible of the first Christians was, of course, the Old Testament. This meant the Septuagint, the Old Testament in Greek, which included the deuterocanonical (apocryphal) books. It is often abbreviated *LXX* because of a tradition that it was translated from Hebrew by seventy Jewish scholars. From the very beginning, however, Christians interpreted the Old Testament differently from their Jewish counterparts, and so it was inevitable that specifically Christian writings would emerge (in part as commentary on the Hebrew Scriptures) and that some of those writings would become accepted authoritative interpretations of the Old Testament in light of the life and ministry of Jesus. The production of Christian sacred writings naturally led to their addition to the Christian canon, giving the Church its Bible. But this did not happen overnight. The development of the New Testament went through four stages, over a period of almost four centuries.

STAGES OF DEVELOPMENT OF THE NEW TESTAMENT

Stage 1: The Writing of the Apostolic Documents

The first of the Christian documents to be written were the letters of Paul. In the 50s and 60s of the first century, Paul's ministry included writing letters to the Christians in various cities, many of whom were his own converts and students in churches he himself had founded. It is also possible that the Gospel of Mark was written as early as the 50s, combining oral tradition with the testimony of Peter.[1] Some of the other apostolic letters may have been written at this time as well, possibly including Hebrews, James, Jude, and 1 Peter.[2] The two-volume set of Luke and Acts was probably completed by the mid-60s, since Acts ends before the martyrdom of Peter and Paul, though there is significant debate over this.[3] The author of Luke used Mark's Gospel as his primary resource, incorporating other oral tradition as well as possible apostolic testimony. By the time 2 Peter was written the author already has begun to think of Paul's letters as inspired scripture (2 Pet 3:14–16).[4] This indicates that Paul had been martyred by the time 2 Peter was written.

The Gospel of Matthew was probably composed in the 70s or 80s of the first century.[5] According to tradition, it is based on the eyewitness account of Matthew Levi, the former tax collector and disciple of Jesus, though it obviously also made use of Mark and Luke.[6] Some, such as Origen, thought that Matthew was first written in Aramaic or Hebrew, though this may be pure speculation based on the fact that it was written for a Jewish Christian audience.[7] The Johannine literature was probably the last to be written, in the 90s, though it is possible that 2 John and 3 John were written in the early second century.[8]

Stage 2: The Use of the Apostolic Documents

Already in the second half of the first century, apostolic documents were being copied, passed from church to church, and read aloud in worship meetings. The fact that multiple copies of these early documents were made while the originals still existed, combined with the fact that fragments of some very early manuscripts are still extant, lends a confidence of reliability that few other ancient documents share. By the early second century, the letters of Paul (often including Hebrews, the authorship of which was already a matter of debate in the earliest discussions of the canon) were circulating as a collection. One could also obtain a collection of the four gospels, sometimes with the Book of Acts. In fact it is possible that the need to publish these Christian documents was part of the catalyst that led to the development of the codex, or book. Rather than copy documents on scrolls, it became more expedient to cut the scroll into square sections (pages), stack them, and bind them on one side. This made it more convenient to put the material into one package, and it made it easier to find a particular passage in the middle of a document. Rather than unroll a scroll, one only had to turn the pages.

By the middle of the second century, the term *gospels* (in the plural) is used as a category or literary genre.[9] Justin Martyr referred to the gospels as the "memoirs of the apostles," in contrast to the "archives" (the Hebrew Scriptures).[10] Irenaeus commented that there must be four, and only four, gospels.[11] The fact that the documents that would become the New Testament were being read in worship demonstrates that they were already becoming authoritative and coming to be considered inspired scripture on the level of the Hebrew Scriptures.[12]

The first to attempt a standardized list of authoritative Christian documents, as far as we know, was the heretic Marcion. He created a canon, or list of documents that he thought should be included in the Christian scriptures. Since he was a Docetic, however, he edited out anything that made Jesus sound too human, to the point where his canon was limited to edited versions of the Gospel of Luke and Paul's letters. He rejected the Old Testament entirely. In reality, it is likely that various bishops produced many different canonical lists for the Christians in their sees. The first that we know of to come from the mainstream Church is now called the Muratorian Canon, named after its discoverer, Ludovico Antonio Muratori (1672–1750). It may have been written by the Roman priest Caius at the turn of the third century. This particular list did not include some of the writings that are now in our New Testament, specifically Hebrews, 2 Peter, 3 John, and James. Nevertheless, by the end of the second century or the beginning of the third, there was a generally acknowledged group of documents more or less like our New Testament that was considered the scripture of the Church, along with the Old Testament. Clement of Alexandria and Irenaeus had both used the term *New Testament* by the end of the second century.[13]

Criteria for Inclusion

As the Church was debating which documents ought to be included in its New Testament, there were three basic criteria by which the documents were judged. Without a doubt, the most important was authorship. To be considered for inclusion, a document must have been written by an apostle or a close associate of an apostle.[14] Apparently, one degree of separation was the maximum allowable distance from those who knew Jesus personally. If the authorship of a document was called into question, the document itself was suspect. If the authorship was deemed pseudonymous, the document was therefore not "genuine" and was rejected.[15] Of course there was some debate and disagreements over the authorship of certain documents, which led to different lists with different documents included. It is important to note, however, that the gnostic documents (such as the *Gospel of Thomas* and the *Gospel of Peter*) were universally recognized as later pseudonymous/heretical writings and were never considered for inclusion in the canon by the mainstream Church.[16]

The early Christians did understand the issues surrounding the authorship of the first-century (and early second-century?) documents. In fact, the authorship of the Letter to the Hebrews sparked considerable debate in the early Church. Eusebius admitted that the Roman Christians generally did not accept Hebrews as Pauline.[17] The Greek grammar was thought to be too good (and too different from the other letters) to be from Paul's pen.[18] However, Eusebius knew of a tradition going back to Clement of Alexandria that claimed that Paul had written Hebrews in Aramaic as an apologetic (or evangelistic) treatise for Jews, and that it was later translated into Greek by Luke.[19] This would explain the different writing style. Paul's name was then presumably left off the document because his fellow Jews were suspicious of him. Eusebius himself believed that the letter was written by some disciple of Paul who wrote it from notes taken while listening to Paul's teaching. Perhaps this disciple was Luke, perhaps Clement of Rome, perhaps another unknown disciple. In the end, though, Eusebius thinks it would be acceptable to consider the letter Pauline because the content comes from Paul.[20] Eusebius also tells us that the authorship of the Catholic Epistles was disputed.[21] It is interesting to note, however, that no early Church writer ever questioned the Pauline authorship of the Pastoral Epistles or Ephesians, or the traditional authorship of the Synoptic Gospels (Matthew, Mark, and Luke).[22]

The second criterion for inclusion in the canon was the ability to stand the test of time and use in worship. As we have seen, the letters of Paul were originally written to be read in the assembly, and the four gospels quickly gained a place in Christian liturgy. As the apostolic documents were continually read in worship, they took their place alongside the psalms and the prophets as containing a divinely inspired message for the Church. For the most part, if a document was not suitable to be read in worship, it might not be considered acceptable as Christian scripture. But the criterion of apostolic authorship would trump this consideration, so that the Pauline authorship of Philemon and the Johannine authorship of Revelation would keep these documents on the list. In the end, the very fact that these documents were included is a witness to the relatively universal acceptance of their apostolic authorship.[23]

The third criterion was citation by respected theologians. This is a bit of a chicken-and-egg situation, since in order for a document to be quoted by a theologian, it already must have had some measure of authority, or there would be no point in citing it to support an argument. However the citation of a document by the theologians of the late second and third centuries cemented the authoritative status of the documents that would eventually be our New Testament. This brings us to stage three.

Stage 3: The Authority of the Apostolic Documents

Important and influential theologians such as Irenaeus and Tertullian were determined to support their arguments with scripture. They considered Scripture to be divine revelation, which was more reliable than human reason (that is, philosophy).[24] Thus they assumed that the documents they quoted held some weight with their readers. But by quoting them, they gave them even more credibility and authority than they may have already had. The theologians of the late second and third centuries implicitly refined the list of authoritative books by choosing which ones to quote (and not to quote). Irenaeus quoted or referred to every book in our New Testament, except perhaps Philemon and 3 John. Tertullian quoted every book except 2 Peter. By the time of Novatian, these books were included.

Stage 4: Standardization of the Canon

Even though there was general agreement on many, if not most, of the apostolic documents as early as the end of the first century, there was no universal consensus on a precise canonical list of New Testament documents. In fact, the first extant list of authoritative Christian documents that corresponds exactly with our New Testament comes from the year 367 CE. This was Bishop Athanasius of Alexandria's Easter letter of that year. In his letter, he outlined which documents ought to be considered authoritative by the people under his authority. This does not mean that the year 367 saw universal acceptance of Athanasius's list. No doubt it took decades for some measure of standardization to take hold. On the other hand, this also does not mean that the New Testament was born in the fourth century. As we have seen, the process of development goes back to the writing of the documents and includes an assumption of some level of authority from the very beginning. In addition, there may have been lists that match our New Testament from earlier than 367 but are no longer extant. The Codex Sinaiticus, from the mid-fourth century, contains our whole New Testament, along with Barnabas and *The Shepherd* by Hermas.

In the end, some of our New Testament books almost didn't make the cut. For reasons of contested authorship, Hebrews, James, 2 Peter, and 3 John took longer than most to gain acceptance.[25] As we have seen, 3 John and then 2 Peter were the last ones to be universally accepted. In the end, however, it was determined that their authorship was genuine.[26] The Book of Revelation was also questioned as to its suitability for inclusion, although not for reasons of authorship, since almost everyone in the early Church believed it was written by John the apostle.[27] The problem with the Book of Revelation was the way that it was being interpreted and used by the Montanists and other millennialists. As we have seen, even Irenaeus and Tertullian fell into this camp. But most interpreters were convinced that such an interpretation was too literal and was missing the symbolic meaning of the text.[28]

There were, of course, other early documents considered for inclusion in the canon that did not ultimately become part of our Bible. The Didache, 1 Clement, and *The Shepherd* were all early contenders. Irenaeus apparently considered *The Shepherd* to be scripture. But in the end the lack of apostolic authorship, along with the other factors already mentioned in chapter 2, led to their exclusion.

PATRISTIC EXEGESIS

Exegesis is the "drawing out" of meaning from a text. When it comes to scripture, it is never enough to know what the text *says*; one must take the next step and ask what the text *means*.[29] That meaning includes both the original intended meaning of the author and the relevance for the reader. Such is the task of interpretation.[30] Therefore, even when the early Christians could agree on which documents were authoritative, that did not mean they always agreed on their meaning or their message for the Church. The ongoing debates of the early Church are obvious evidence of that fact. However, there were nine assumptions that the early Christians shared when it came to the interpretation of scripture.

Assumption #1: The Sacred Texts, Including the New Testament, Are Divinely Inspired

As we have seen, the author of 2 Peter referred to the letters of Paul as scripture, on the same level of authority as the Hebrew Scriptures (2 Pet 3:14–16). Thus the text of scripture was seen as having been inspired by the same Holy Spirit who inspired the prophets (John 14:26).[31] In fact, Logos Christology affirmed that the text of scripture was a written record of the voice of the divine Logos. To the early Christians, the written word was another incarnation of the living Word. Like the body of Jesus, the text of scripture enfleshes the Word of God. And like Jesus Christ, the written word is both divine and human: divinely inspired, yet written down by humans. The two natures of Christ are paralleled in the dual authorship of scripture. The early Christians did take the aspects of human authorship seriously; however, the ultimate author is God, and therefore every word in the text is there for a reason. As we will see, this conviction will lead some to look for spiritual meaning in even the smallest details of a biblical story. Finally, the same Holy Spirit who inspired the writing of scripture would (with prayer) illuminate its interpretation.[32]

Assumption #2: Revelation Is Progressive

In the early Church, the concept of *progressive revelation* meant that God's intention for the human race gets clearer over time and as the needs of humanity change. Mysteries are revealed with time, so that in the Old Testament God the Father is presented clearly, but God the Son is veiled. In the New Testament, the Son of God is presented clearly, but the Holy Spirit is only partially revealed. Finally, the experience of the Church reveals the Spirit to us. Therefore, as Christians consider and debate the meaning to be discerned from scripture, each generation comes to greater clarity on the doctrines of Christology, soteriology, and even ecclesiology.[33] This is not to say, however, that a new interpretation supersedes an older one. New interpretations can build on and further clarify older ones, but they cannot contradict the conclusions of previous generations. Progressive revelation and apostolic succession were considered interdependent, which meant that the orthodoxy of one's ancestors in the faith was the foundation on which to build the orthodoxy of the present day. Dionysius of Alexandria quoted Deuteronomy 19:14 as relevant on this point.[34] Just as one is not allowed to move the boundary markers set up by one's ancestors, one also does not contradict the accepted doctrines of the previous generations. These accepted doctrines are the very boundary markers of orthodoxy.

It is important to keep in mind that in the ancient world, that which is older is usually assumed to be better than whatever is newer.[35] The older, established interpretation is the tradition, which cannot be changed; it can only be further clarified. The writers of the patristic era would not want to be thought of as innovators. They would not want to be perceived as creating anything new, since what is new is automatically suspect as somehow disconnected from the tradition. The tradition, on the other hand, comes from those who were closest to the Source (Jesus), and it was of the utmost importance to remain consistent with the witness of the apostles.[36]

Assumption #3: There Are Multiple Meanings in Any Given Text

Because the ultimate author of scripture is God, the human author's intended meaning is not the only valid meaning to be gained from a text. Patristic exegesis allows for multiple meanings, and in fact the early Christians believed that God intended multiple meanings so that the scriptures could never be completely mastered or fully understood. The scriptures are a bottomless well, so that no one should think he had drunk his fill of them. Perhaps the best example of this principle would be the way that the gospel writers attribute many of the details of the life of Jesus to the fulfillment of prophecy. It is one thing to say that generally acknowledged messianic prophecies were fulfilled in Jesus. But the apostles went so far as to say that texts in the Hebrew Scriptures that were never thought of as messianic prophecies (such as Isaiah 53, the "suffering servant") were also fulfilled by Jesus. The early Christians therefore reasoned that even though the human author of an Old Testament text had one meaning in mind, God had another meaning in mind for the future Church.[37] Thus the suffering Messiah, an oxymoron to the Jewish mind, is God's mystery revealed in Jesus Christ.

Assumption #4: Paradox Is to Be Embraced, Not Avoided

We have already seen how groups on the fringes of the Church could pick and choose scripture to support their Christologies.[38] The Ebionites rejected texts that affirmed the divinity of Christ (such as Col 2:9), while the Docetics rejected texts that affirmed his humanity (such as Luke 2:40). What the mainstream Church rejected, however, was the presumption of editing scripture. Assuming divine inspiration, even apparently contradictory texts must be held together as true; one cannot be ignored in favor of the other. Once the decision was made that a particular document was to be considered scripture, the question was not *whether* the text is true, but *how* it is true in light of other biblical texts. The heretics were seen as those who took scripture out of context and "prooftexted" their agendas, while the orthodox were those who accepted mystery and embraced the paradox.[39] No doubt this is an idealistic and oversimplified comparison, but it was nevertheless the claim of the extant mainstream bishops.

Assumption #5: Patristic Exegesis Follows the Lead of Apostolic Exegesis

The apologists and theologians of the early Church accepted the methodology of Matthew and Paul when it came to interpreting the Old Testament. Like a Christian *midrash* (commentary), the New Testament interpreted the Old in light of the life and ministry of Jesus. The best interpretation was christocentric. This had the advantage of keeping the Church connected to the Old Testament (not only against docetism, but also to demonstrate that

Christianity is not really something new but the fulfillment of something older than philosophy), even while it allowed the Church to set aside certain aspects of Judaism such as sacrifices and dietary laws.[40]

As we have seen, Logos and kenosis Christology of the second and third centuries affirmed the preincarnation activity of the second person of the Trinity. In other words, Christ appeared in the Old Testament. This was made necessary by the belief that "no one can see God and live" (Exod 33:20), and yet there are times in the Old Testament where people do see a manifestation of the Divine. The early Christians interpreted these theophanies as appearances of the divine Logos in his preexistent state. Hippolytus said that the reason the Messiah is referred to in Daniel 7 as "one *like* a son of man" is because he was not yet the Son of Man, since he was not yet human.[41] In interpreting the Old Testament christologically, the early Christians were not only doing what the apostles had done, they were doing what Jesus had done (Luke 24, John 5).[42]

Assumption #6: Scripture Interprets Scripture

Since God is the author of both the Old and New Testaments, there is an assumed consistency of purpose and ultimate meaning across the two testaments.[43] This is, of course, necessary, not only to affirm that Christ is the fulfillment of the Old Testament, but also for the refutation of Marcionite rejection of the Old Testament. In practice, it means that obscure texts can be interpreted using other (presumably clearer) texts. There is an internal integrity of scripture, regardless of differences in authorship and historical context, that allows the exegete to combine texts from different biblical documents and look for a harmonized meaning.[44]

Assumption #7: In General, Interpretation of the Old Testament Was Nonliteral

Since there were two authors behind any text, God and the human author, most passages had at least two meanings. When it came to the interpretation of the Old Testament, the literal (historical) meaning of the human (that is, Jewish) author was seen as secondary to the spiritual meaning that God had in mind for the Church. The early Christians reasoned that if all one had was the literal meaning, then the Old Testament would be irrelevant for the Church. Therefore, the nonliteral meaning(s) would be held up as the higher, or perhaps the deeper, meaning. The most important meaning is not the one on the surface but the one hidden under the surface, since in the Old Testament Christ is veiled. The true meaning of the Old Testament could not be understood until Christ was revealed in his incarnation.[45] In fact, to interpret the Old Testament literally would come to be criticized as a "Jewish" way of interpretation.[46] To focus on the literal/historical meaning of an Old Testament passage was to fail to take Christ into account. For example, a literal (Jewish) interpretation of 2 Samuel 7:12 would focus on Solomon as the heir to David's throne and the one who would build the Temple in Jerusalem. A spiritual (Christian) interpretation of that passage would focus on Jesus Christ as the descendant of David and the king of an eternal kingdom.

Technically speaking, there were two types of nonliteral interpretation, typology and allegory. Typology, famously attributed to Irenaeus, really goes back to the apostle Paul and even to Jesus himself (for examples, see Matthew 12:40 and 1 Corinthians 15:44–47).[47] Using typology, Old Testament concepts and events are seen as foreshadowing or symbolizing details in the life and ministry of Christ. The Old Testament can then be interpreted as not only predicting Christ but pointing to him. As we have seen, Irenaeus wanted to counteract the Gnostics' rejection of the Old Testament, so he expanded the concept of typology, and the early Church followed his lead in looking for parallels between Old Testament and New Testament elements. The tree of the knowledge of good and evil is a type of the cross; Eve is a type of Mary; the crossing of the Red Sea and the water from the rock are types of baptism; the manna in the desert is a type of the Eucharist.[48] In fact, over time any mention of wood in the Old Testament became a reminder of the cross, and any mention of water became a call to Christian baptism.[49]

Allegory, often attributed to Origen, actually comes from Greek philosophy. In an attempt to maintain the old mythologies in spite of the obvious anthropomorphisms (not to mention immoralities) of the gods, the philosophers advocated interpreting the myths as metaphors that would encourage virtue. In other words, the literal meaning of the myths left one with gods no one should emulate, let alone worship, but the philosophers believed that the myths could be redeemed and reconciled with their own teachings through the use of allegory.[50] Working with Plato's dichotomy between the material and the spiritual, Philo of Alexandria articulated two levels of meaning to be found in a text. The literal meaning was analogous to Plato's material realm, which is not necessarily bad but is certainly inferior to the spiritual. The spiritual meaning was therefore the deeper meaning, more important and indeed *truer* than the literal.[51] And because the spiritual meaning had a divine origin, even the smallest details could be allegorized and interpreted as significant.[52]

With allegorical interpretation, the details of a biblical text can come to represent abstract realities or moral virtues.[53] The point is that in this method of interpretation, the situation of the reader/interpreter is more important than the context of the author of a text.[54] For example, the Church allowed itself to forgo the Hebrew dietary laws by interpreting them allegorically.[55] The unclean animals become metaphors for human vices, so God doesn't really care whether you eat pork, God only cares that you don't act like a pig. The prohibition from eating weasels really means that God does not want us to act like weasels. Weasels are thieves, and so the message from God for the Church is: Don't be a thief.[56] In the restriction to animals with cloven hooves, the two parts of the hoof represent the two testaments.[57] To have one testament only (the Old Testament, like the Jews; or the New Testament, like the Marcionites) would not be adequate. True faith requires two testaments, both the Old and the New.

Another kind of allegory is the so-called "vertical" (or *anagogical*) allegory. This assumes a continuity between what happens on earth and what happens in heaven. Events in the material realm then become lessons about the spiritual realm (for example, see Luke 11:13).

Allegory might be built into the text, such as in a parable, or it might be used to interpret a text with no inherent allegory. Either way, the temptation to find meaning in every detail was sometimes too much for the early Christian exegete to resist. Theoretically, the principle of scripture interpreting scripture was supposed to provide some measure of checks and balances, but in actual practice some of the interpretations were so speculative as to be far-fetched.[58] As we will see, this will result in a backlash against allegorical interpretation in some circles.

In practice, there was not always a clear distinction between typology and allegory. The primary difference between the two is that with typology, there seems to be an acceptance of the historicity of the Old Testament types, because God was at work in human history.[59] With allegory, on the other hand, there is no need for the details to be historical. We can see this in Jesus' parables. It is not necessary for the story of the Good Samaritan to have actually happened for Jesus' point to be made. But when Jesus uses typology and compares the coming tribulation to Old Testament events, he seems to assume the historical reality of those events.

Just as the philosophers saw allegorical interpretation as necessary for holding on to the Greco-Roman myths, the Christians knew that nonliteral interpretation was necessary to redeem the Old Testament from its own anthropomorphisms of God.[60] While the mainstream Christians knew that such anthropomorphisms could not be taken literally, it was precisely the literal interpretation of the Old Testament that led the Docetics and Gnostics to reject it.[61] Nonliteral interpretation was also necessary to interpret certain Old Testament promises as having been fulfilled in Jesus. Finally, a nonliteral interpretation was seen as essential if the Church hoped to attract philosophically minded, educated Romans.

The point for the early Christians was that the Old Testament has a spiritual meaning that is deeper and more important than the literal meaning. The literal meaning might be good enough for the uneducated (or for the Jews), but those who are enlightened and who are serious about their Christian faith and the scriptures will not be satisfied with the literal meaning; they will look for the spiritual meaning. When it came to the Old Testament, then, the Church was left with two choices: either interpret it literally and reject it (as the Marcionites and Gnostics did) as the product of an ignorant people or an untrustworthy demigod, or interpret it nonliterally and accept it (as the mainstream Church did) as a divine mystery that is only revealed in hindsight after the life, death, and resurrection of Jesus Christ.

Assumption #8: In General, Interpretation of the New Testament Was Literal

The Old Testament and the New Testament were considered complimentary, but while the deeper meaning was hidden in the Old Testament, spiritual meaning in the New Testament was thought to be closer to the surface. Therefore, one could read most of the New Testament literally, as recent history, and reserve non-literal methods of interpretation for when it was made necessary by the genre of the text (such as the parables and hyperbole used by Jesus, as well as the apocalyptic sections of the gospels and the Book of Revelation).[62]

As we have seen, the Gnostics interpreted the Old Testament literally and used that as a rationale to reject it and claim that the God of the Old Testament was not the God and Father of Jesus Christ. Ironically, the Gnostics tended to interpret the New Testament nonliterally, especially to discount the human nature of Christ.[63] The mainstream Church and the Gnostics had opposite approaches to scripture. It is no wonder that the Gnostics would eventually separate from the Church and even write their own scriptures. For the mainstream Church, it was not a simple question of literal versus nonliteral; the key was knowing when to use a literal and when to use a nonliteral interpretation.

Assumption #9: Interpretation Is Meant to Be Done in the Context of Prayer

Finally, the early Christian authors agreed that the interpretation of scripture is not an academic exercise but part of a devotional life. Most of the early exegetes were pastors—priests and bishops who interpreted scripture for the Church, not in a vacuum but as part of a community (2 Pet 1:20). In fact, it could be said that interpreting scripture was an act of worship and therefore must be accompanied by prayer. The same Holy Spirit who inspired the writing of the text must be invoked to inspire the reading of the text.[64] As saints Augustine and Anselm came to realize, faith must precede understanding.

THE HISTORY OF PATRISTIC EXEGESIS

While all of the above was true in general, it is difficult to say whether it was all true all at once. Like anything else, the Church's understanding of scripture and its interpretation varied depending on time and place. And just as there were four stages of the development of the canon, there were also four stages of the development of interpretation.

Stage 1: Two Levels of Meaning

Irenaeus and Tertullian in the second and third centuries exemplify the first stage of patristic exegesis. Even though they claimed to reject philosophy, they were still sufficiently influenced by Platonism to assume that there was a spiritual meaning in scripture that was more important than the literal meaning. Therefore, scripture has two levels of meaning, the literal and the spiritual. Even in the New Testament, where they would claim that the spiritual meaning is on the surface, the smallest of details in the narrative could be allegorized to find an even deeper meaning. The spiritual meaning could be interpreted using typology or allegory, but the overall concern is that the interpretation be christological. The basic rule of thumb would be, if the literal interpretation of any text does not lead one to Christ, then one must look for a spiritual meaning.

Stage 2: Three Levels of Meaning

The second stage covers the third through the fifth centuries, though after the third century it is most prevalent in the West and Alexandria. This is traditionally said to be the legacy of Clement of Alexandria and Origen, and the catechetical school of Alexandria is often associated with the methodology of allegorical interpretation.

Other notable examples of stage two include Ambrose of Milan and the early careers of Augustine and Jerome.

In this stage the interpretation of scripture was compared to an ancient understanding of the human person, which was thought to have three parts: body, soul, and spirit (or mind). Thus there were three levels of meaning in scripture. The literal meaning was parallel to the body, grounded in the material world and therefore historical, but less valuable than the spiritual. The spiritual meaning was compared to the spirit or mind. While there may be some value in the literal meaning, the most important meaning for the Church is the spiritual meaning, since that is where the Church gets its doctrine. As before, the spiritual meaning can be derived from typological or allegorical interpretation. But this stage adds a third level of meaning, in between the literal and the spiritual. Corresponding to the soul of the human is the moral meaning of the text. This is the practical relevance for Christian behavior. It is not as important as theology (the spiritual meaning) but it is more important than history (the literal meaning). Therefore, the three levels of meaning can be expressed in this way:

> Literal (Historical)—What Jesus did
> Moral (Ethical)—What we should do
> Spiritual (Theological)—What we should believe

The three levels of meaning were described using an analogy of an egg. Just as an egg has three layers—shell, white, and yolk—so scripture has three layers that need to be peeled back to reveal its deepest meanings. One has to begin with the shell (the literal meaning), but one cannot stop there. In reality, not every text even has a literal meaning (for example, the highly symbolic Book of Revelation). Because of divine inspiration, however, every text has a spiritual meaning.[65] The serious student of scripture cannot be satisfied with the surface meaning but must go on to the deeper meanings. For Origen, spiritual maturity meant seeing the spiritual meaning in scripture. Origen even argued that God might purposely insert historical inaccuracies into the text as clues to tell the reader to look beyond the literal to find the deeper meaning.[66] Thus there may be things in the text that are not historically true but are nevertheless "truthful" in the sense of beneficial.[67]

Stage 3: Reaction against Allegory— Back to Two Levels of Meaning

Stage three covers roughly the fourth and fifth centuries, primarily in the East (Antioch and Asia Minor). It is a reaction against allegorical interpretation (perceived as overallegorizing) and a renewed appreciation for the literal meaning. This methodology is traditionally associated with the church in Antioch and contributes to the (often exaggerated) rivalry between Antioch and Alexandria. It seems to begin officially with Lucian of Antioch (c. 240–312) and his dislike of Origen, though it may go back as far as Theophilus.[68] In his later career, Jerome would also find affinity with this school of thought. If the Alexandrians were influenced by Plato, the Antiochenes were influenced more by Aristotle.[69] They wanted a more concrete interpretation and feared that the allegorical method would lead to excessive speculation, which, in turn, would ultimately lead to heresy.[70] This was, in fact, one of the primary criticisms of Origen. Opponents of allegory argued that it could be used to make the text say anything the interpreter wants it to say. The allegorization of every detail in a biblical story was being used, they feared, to draw out messages that were not really there. In a sense, allegory had disengaged the text from its historical context, and like a ship without an anchor, it was left adrift in a sea of speculation.[71]

While this does not mean that interpretation was no longer going to be christological, the Antiochenes recognized the necessity of taking the historical provenance of a text seriously, to the point of advocating study of the Old Testament on its own terms, apart from the New Testament.[72] Therefore they gravitated toward the literal/historical interpretation as primary because they wanted to understand the intended meaning of the author of a text, before attempting to find a meaning for the Church.[73] In other words, to know what a text *means*, one first has to know what it *meant*.

Proponents of this reactionary movement advocated using the literal sense of the text whenever possible. If there was a moral meaning to be found, it would probably be found in the plain meaning on the surface somewhere in the Bible. They reasoned that if God wants us to behave a certain way, he will tell us plainly. Allegorical interpretation was still a possibility, but was to be used only when absolutely necessary. Even then, the spiritual meaning must always be consistent with the literal and must never contradict the plain meaning of the text anywhere in scripture. Thus this stage moved back toward two levels of meaning (literal/historical and spiritual), with a preference for the literal.

Stage 4: The Middle Way—
Four Levels of Meaning

The final stage of patristic exegesis represents a kind of middle way between extreme allegory and the rejection of allegory. This stage begins in the late fourth and early fifth centuries and continues into the Middle Ages. Its most famous advocate is Augustine of Hippo. Augustine would agree with the Antiochenes that the literal meaning of the scriptures is the foundation for all other meaning, and that the spiritual meaning must be grounded in the historical.[74] Interpretation without a sense of tradition would always lead to heresy.[75] On the other hand, Augustine maintained that the historical meaning of the Old Testament was not always adequate for the Church, and that the Old Testament had to be read through the lens of the New. For Augustine, biblical history was not history for its own sake but served the purpose of prophecy.[76] Therefore, if the literal meaning did not point to Christ, a deeper meaning must be sought.

Augustine's interpretive touchstone was the law of love. Any interpretation of scripture that did not lead one to love God and neighbor was incorrect.[77] Therefore, if the literal meaning did not accomplish this goal, one needed to look for other layers of meaning. Even the allegorization of minor details was fair game if it supported the rule of love.[78] Thus Augustine incorporated what he saw as the best elements of the prior stages and brought the art of interpretation to a certain plateau for the Church. As he understood it, there were four levels of meaning in scripture, one literal and three spiritual.[79] The literal meaning includes not only the historical situation but also the original (human) author's intended meaning. The three levels of spiritual meaning are the analogical (which included both allegory and typology); the moral (what is expected of us, based on what we believe about Christ); and the anagogical (vertical allegory):[80]

Literal (Historical)—What happened
Analogical (Theological)—What we should believe
Moral (Ethical)—How we should behave
Anagogical (Eschatological)—What we hope for

CHAPTER 7

The Church in the Third Century

CHRISTOLOGY AND THEOLOGY IN THE THIRD CENTURY

Modalism (Modalistic Monarchianism)

As I have already indicated, the Marcionites and Gnostics of the second century eventually migrated out of the Church, probably because of a combination of diverging beliefs and pressure from the orthodox bishops. These gnostic movements continued in various forms for centuries, but they cannot properly be called heresies because they were no longer within the Church. They eventually created their own gospels and other writings.[1] Continuing syncretism outside the Church would later result in a version of gnosticism known as Manichaeism.[2] Yet, anyone who leaned toward a hybrid or docetic Christology and who stayed within the Church would probably have migrated toward the group known as *Modalists*, sometimes called "Modalistic Monarchians."[3]

They are referred to as "Monarchians" because they were concerned for the monarchy, or oneness, of God. The Modalists attempted to preserve the oneness of God by an extreme unity between Father and Son that effectively diminished or denied a human nature in Christ. In other words, they rejected the idea of a plurality of persons, arguing instead that there was no distinction at all between the Father and Son. The Father was the Son and the Son was the Father. The Father became incarnate and the personhood of the Son was, in a sense, a "mask" worn by God to appear as Jesus. This Christology (like gnostic Christology before it) effectively negated the humanity of Jesus. The Modalists, however, were not necessarily Docetics, in the sense of believing Jesus had no tangible body. Most probably they believed that he did have a body, but that it was simply God the Father who had put on a suit of flesh.[4]

We have already met Noetus of Smyrna in the writings of Hippolytus. Heavily influenced by philosophical monism, he apparently reasoned that maintaining the oneness of God (monotheism) required the denial of all distinction between Father and Son. Therefore, Noetus taught that the Son was simply a temporary manifestation of the Father.[5] For him, Christ is the Father, who became his own Son in the incarnation.[6] Therefore, God can only truly be called the Father before the incarnation. After the incarnation, God must be called the Son, until the ascension and Pentecost, when God becomes the Holy Spirit. This is a chronology-based distinction between persons, which amounts to a distinction in name only and in which God can only be called by one of the three names at a time.

Therefore, for Noetus, the fact that God is one means that Jesus is not really human. The opponents of Noetus (including Hippolytus) argued that this identification of the Son with the Father leaves God the Father dying on the cross, so they named this Christology *Patripassionism*, the suffering of the Father.[7] Apparently, Noetus countered this accusation by saying that the passion was not real, which confirms the conclusion that modalism solves the problem of monotheism by denying the humanity of Christ.[8]

Noetus was probably the teacher of the more famous Sabellius, who expanded Noetus's teaching in the 220s CE to the point where their opponents began to call the Modalists by the name *Sabellians* and modalism was called *Sabellianism*.[9] Like Noetus, Sabellius taught that "Father," "Son," and "Holy Spirit" were simply three different names for the one God.[10] These three names are only seen as relevant from the human perspective, as they are three manifestations of the Father, or three ways in which the one God reveals himself to humanity. The three names are not, however, true distinctions within God (as a Trinity), nor do they imply relationships within the Godhead. It is as if the one God wears three different masks based on what God is doing or when he is doing it.[11] This means that the three "names" for God become associated with divine activity, such that the "Father" is the name of God when God is Creator, the "Son" is the name of God when God is Savior, and the "Holy Spirit" is the name of God when God is Sanctifier. Therefore, the "threeness" of God only exists as artificial distinctions based on the *mode* of activity by which God is interacting with humanity at any given time.[12] This distinction by labeling the "mode" of activity gave rise to the name modalism, or "modalistic" monarchianism. Therefore, the only distinction between Father and Son that is acceptable to modalism is a distinction of perception, from the human point of view, in which the perceived distinctions are described by function or activity.[13] Also implied is a temporal distinction: that God can be described as Father in the time of the Old Testament, as Son (or Jesus Christ) during the time of his earthly ministry, and as Holy Spirit in the age of the Church. The implication of this is that God can only be described by one name at a time.[14]

The mainstream Church would argue that God must be all three persons at all times, always united in all activity. The most important critique of Modalism, however, was that it assumes a Christ who is not really one of us. In this scheme, Christ is fully divine, but not fully human, since he is one and the same with the immutable and utterly transcendent Father (see Table 4, *Christology and Theology in the Third Century*).

Adoptionism (Dynamic Monarchianism)

The second-century Christology of the Ebionites that saw Jesus as a mere human continued in the third century as a form of adoptionism that is sometimes called "dynamic monarchianism."[15] It is so called because it assumes that divine *power* (*dunamis* in Greek) did not originally belong to Jesus but was received at his baptism—limiting true divine power to the Father alone. This means that Jesus is the recipient of divine power but not a source of divine power. In the early third century, an obscure teacher named Artemon (or Artemas), who is said to have been a student of Theodotus, was the bridge between the Ebionites and the most famous third-century Adoptionist, Paul of Samosata.

Paul (ca. 200–75 CE) was the bishop of Antioch in Syria until he was deposed in 272. In spite of his condemnation, his Christology would influence the Antiochene school of thought for centuries. Paul of Samosata taught that the Logos was the personification of God's will.[16] In this, he was probably influenced by his predecessor in Antioch, Theophilus, and by the idea of the Logos as a thought in the mind of God. Therefore, Paul of Samosata reasoned that Jesus was a mere human who was indwelt by the Logos just as one might say the prophets were inspired by the Holy Spirit. Jesus conquered sin purely by resisting temptation and, as a result, he was rewarded by God with an anointing, which amounted to the "cementing" of a permanent relationship between Jesus the man and the Logos, or the *will* of God. In other words, by conforming his will to the will of God so perfectly and consistently, Jesus was granted an eternal union of wills. This union took place at his baptism, when the Father is heard to call him "son." Jesus was not the Son of God by nature, but as a reward and therefore only by adoption. Before his baptism, it would be inappropriate to call him the Son of God. After his adoption, he can be called the son, as long as it is understood that although he was inspired, indwelt, and anointed, he was not really divine.

Adoptionism does not have an incarnation in the sense of the *descent* of the divine Logos who becomes human. Rather, it is the *ascent* of a mere human who achieves an elevated status as the adopted son of God.[17] His sonship is not ontological but volitional and vocational (cf. Jer 1:1–10). The union between Jesus and God (divinity) is not a necessary union, but only a union of wills, which means it is a union that might not have been. Jesus was the first to be perfect, but anyone might have done it; in fact, Jesus might not have done it. From the perspective of the mainstream Church, the idea that Jesus might have sinned meant that his status as Savior was tenuous. Thus for the orthodox the perfection of Jesus must be an essential element of his nature. But for the Adoptionist, the perfection of Jesus is an achievement of personal discipline and obedience. Therefore, the adoptionist Christ (as that of the Ebionites before) is fully human, but not divine. Divine power may be granted by virtue of his adoption, but it is really no more than the prophets had. Because of this,

Paul of Samosata was outspoken against the worship of Christ, especially the singing of hymns in praise of Jesus.[18]

Paul of Samosata seems to have made a concession to the mainstream in that he did accept the virgin birth. Apparently, the universal acceptance of the birth narratives in the gospels of Matthew and Luke forced him to account for a miraculous birth, which he did by attributing it to divine foreknowledge of Jesus' perfect obedience. In other words, because God knew that Jesus would be the one to achieve perfection, God granted him the gift of a miraculous birth. This gives the impression of a conundrum, precisely because it is an attempt to explain something that is not entirely consistent with adoptionist Christology. In fact, Paul would use the same argument of divine foreknowledge to explain the preexistence of the Logos in John 1:1. He said that by divine foreknowledge the Logos could be *thought of* as preexistent, since God's will has always existed in the mind of God, though he was not actually (that is, substantially) preexistent. Paul would be the last of the Adoptionists to deny a real preexistence of the Logos. Mainstream interpretation of John 1:1 (as well as Phil 2) would force the fourth-century Adoptionists to account for a preexistent Logos that is more than just a personification of God's will.[19]

Paul rejected the interpretation of the incarnation as a Christology of descent (as the orthodox interpreted "the Word became flesh," John 1:14).[20] It was said that he refused to "acknowledge that the Son of God came down from heaven."[21] In fact, this reveals that for the Adoptionists, Christ is not the product of an *incarnation* so much as an *elevation* through the indwelling of the Logos, whom Paul believed to be merely the personification of the will of God (as if to say, "The flesh earned the Word"). In other words, Jesus was filled with the Word of God, in much the same way that the prophets were filled with the Spirit of God. This is, then, a Christology of ascent, in which a mere human earns the adoption by God, resulting in an elevated status. Paul was eventually confronted by one of his own priests, a man named Malchion. He was also accused of Nicolaitanism, that is, keeping a mistress while claiming to be celibate; however, this charge may have been invented to vilify him in the eyes of those who might not understand the intricacies of the theological debate.[22]

143

A synod was held in Antioch in the late 260s at which both Malchion and Gregory Thaumaturgus (Gregory the Wonderworker, a student of Origen) opposed Paul. The council declared Paul of Samosata a heretic, excommunicated him, and replaced him as bishop, but he refused to leave the church at Antioch.[23] Apparently, the controversy caught the attention of the emperor Aurelian, who in 272 finally intervened to keep the peace. Aurelian, a pagan emperor, decreed that the church of Antioch belonged to whoever was in accord with the church of Rome.[24] This is significant because, although Christianity was not yet a legal religion, the emperor acknowledged that it existed throughout the empire and that there was some expectation of connection and consistency from one city to another. Also, the choice of Rome as the city with which others must agree (though for the emperor it was certainly only because Rome was the capital of the empire) contributed to the evolution of the primacy of the bishop of Rome.

From the perspective of his opponents, Paul's adoptionist Christology logically led to a soteriology that lacked sufficient divine intervention. In other words, if the Adoptionists were right, then Jesus first had to earn salvation (adoption) by being perfectly obedient to God's will. Therefore, as "savior," he is only a pioneer who presents us with an example to follow; yet, anyone else would still have to earn his or her adoption by achieving perfect obedience. The emphasis of adoptionist soteriology appeared to be on human effort, based on an optimism about human nature that assumes the possibility of human perfection. The majority of the bishops, by contrast, argued that salvation must be by divine initiative (through the divine nature of Christ), reasoning that if our adoption into the family of God depended on human righteousness we could not hope to have eternal life (see Table 4, *Christology and Theology in the Third Century*).[25]

The Two Dionysii and the Orthodox Middle

Dionysius of Alexandria was the student and successor of Origen.[26] He took over the catechetical school at about the time that Origen was excommunicated in Alexandria, and he became the bishop there in 247 CE. He was exiled in 257 during the persecution of the emperor Valerian but returned to Alexandria a few years later.[27] He died in 264 or 265 CE.

Dionysius of Alexandria saw Sabellian modalism as the Church's greatest threat and so he reacted against it, at first by going to the other extreme. In his attempt to refute modalism's overemphasis on the unity of God, he proposed a distinction of persons in the Trinity that crossed the line into adoptionism. He held that the Son of God was a created being and implied that there was a time when he did not exist.

Dionysius of Rome (bishop 260–68) intervened to correct his Alexandrian namesake. He wrote a document called *Against the Sabellians*, a title sure to catch the attention of Dionysius of Alexandria.[28] However, the treatise is really a warning against going too far in refuting modalism and falling into adoptionism. It is addressed to the church of Alexandria, although it never mentions the Alexandrian Dionysius by name. It does, however, accuse unnamed theologians of opposing one extreme with the other and missing the middle way. Following Irenaeus, Tertullian, and especially Novatian, Dionysius of Rome defended the mainstream against the two extremes of modalism and adoptionism. He argued for the consubstantiality of the persons of the Trinity and the eternal generation of the Son.[29] He clarified that the generation of the Son (that he is begotten) does not imply that he is created, and therefore there was no time when the Son of God did not exist.[30]

Dionysius of Alexandria wrote a response to Dionysius of Rome in which he admitted that he should not have said that the Son was created. He also accepted the orthodoxy of eternal generation and consubstantiality, though he was uncomfortable with the latter because the Greek term used to describe it, *homoousios*, was not to be found in scripture.[31]

This exchange demonstrates that in some ways the concept of orthodoxy was still fluid. On the one hand, the orthodoxy of any given time in the history of the Church is defined as that which is consistent with the orthodoxy of the previous generations, so therefore it is appropriate to speak of orthodoxy at various stages in the development of doctrine. On the other hand, the orthodoxy of one generation cannot be held to the standards of later generations. As we have seen, the early Church's understanding of progressive revelation rejected any deliberate deviation from the conclusions of past generations, but this did not prevent teachers, and even bishops, from testing the boundaries of what the "mainstream" Church could abide. The major heresies, then, are those philosophical and christological extremes that emphasize one aspect of theology by diminishing another. As Hippolytus had complained, the heretics accept one group of biblical passages but reject another, based on their theological agenda.[32] To be fair, scripture itself was a fluid concept, as we have seen; however, the heretics were even choosing between texts by the same author and within the same documents. Ideally, the mainstream Church revered all scripture, accepting paradox and looking for a middle way between the extremes.[33] Novatian had said that the true Christ was to be found in the middle between the heresies, as if he was still being crucified by them, "between two thieves."[34]

Therefore, orthodoxy was, and was perceived as, the middle way between the extreme alternatives. While the Ebionites and Adoptionists emphasized the humanity of Christ but denied his divinity, and the Docetics, Gnostics, and to a certain extent the Modalists emphasized the divinity of Christ and denied his humanity, the mainstream Church refused to choose and accepted both the full humanity and full divinity of Christ (see Table 4, *Christology and Theology in the Third Century*). While adoptionism emphasized the distinction between persons of the Trinity and denied an ontological union between the Father and Son, and modalism emphasized the unity of the Trinity but denied any real distinction of persons beyond functional labels, the mainstream Church embraced the paradox and looked for a balance of unity and distinction (see Chart 2, *Christological Options and Influences*).[35]

It could be said that the history of the Church is like a swinging pendulum. One teacher or group may test the boundaries on one extreme, causing the pendulum to swing wide to one side. Another teacher or group will perceive that this is too far from what can be tolerated and reacts against it, but by going to the opposite extreme. Each generation produces its own version of the previous generation's extremes (and in some ways, this continues to this day). As the boundaries of acceptability are tested, the Church works to find its center of gravity, and so the pendulum swings back

and forth across the decades and centuries, with each new generation supplying teachers and writers who are willing to react to
heresy by going to the opposite extreme and crossing the boundaries of orthodoxy into a heresy of an opposite kind. We will see
this trend continue in the fourth and fifth centuries. Yet in each
generation, "gravity" keeps bringing the pendulum back to the center, as the mainstream Church gains more and more clarity, finds
more precise language to describe its theology, and (with the guid-
ance of the Holy Spirit) comes to the conclusion that orthodoxy
embraces the paradox by finding the place of balance. In other
words, the truth is in the middle.

THE EPISCOPACY AND THE
EMERGING PRIMACY OF ROME

Monoepiscopacy

We have already examined the development of the hierarchy
and the role of the bishop in the second century. We have also seen
how Ignatius of Antioch argued for the limitation of only one
bishop per city (the term *monoepiscopacy* refers to the singular
bishop). The force of Ignatius's argument begs the question, however, since before the third century it is not certain that every city
had only one bishop.

In the early Church, the bishops emerged as the final authority
over two main aspects of the Church: doctrine and discipline. As the
primary teaching office of the Church, the bishop would normally be
in charge of the school of catechesis, and even when there were lay
teachers such as Origen, the bishop held the authority over the content of what was taught.[36] Before the third century, there may have
been more than one catechetical school in some cities, each having
its own overseer. Justin Martyr had his own students in Rome in the
mid-second century. This was not a faction in opposition to the
bishop, though it was probably also not a formal school of catechesis.
Even in the early third century, Hippolytus may have been the leader
of the Greek-speaking Christians in Rome, perhaps with their own
school.[37] But Hippolytus openly criticized the elected bishops of

Rome. Ironically, though, he recognized that more than one disciplinary authority within a city would lead to conflict over excommunication and reconciliation. Already a century before Hippolytus,
Ignatius had realized that having more than one teaching authority
in a city would eventually lead to disagreement and schism. Therefore
he had concluded that the unity of the Church depended on the
authority of a single bishop. In other words, unity of doctrine and
discipline required episcopal monarchy.

In reality, the development of the monoepiscopacy was not uni-
form, so we cannot say with any certainty when it happened. The
bigger the city, and the larger the Christian community there, the
longer it may have taken to consolidate the authority in a single
bishop.[38] If the limit of one bishop per city was not already universally accepted by the middle of the third century, the question would
be called by the schism of Novatian, which we will encounter below.[39]

Cyprian of Carthage (bishop 249–58 CE) would follow
Ignatius on two important and interdependent points. First, there
must be only one bishop in a city.[40] This is because multiple authorities would threaten unity. More than one bishop would ultimately
mean more than one church. As soon as two bishops disagreed on
matters of theology or church discipline, every Christian in that
city would be forced to choose between them. Ultimately, unity is
catholic, but the very definition of heresy is that it is a factioning, a
separation from the majority. Thus, as Ignatius had said, nothing
could be considered valid that was done without the authority of
the elected bishop of the city.[41]

The other point on which Cyprian agreed with Ignatius was
that there could be no salvation outside the Church.[42] These issues
are related because the Church was defined in terms of the sacraments, and the sacraments were under the authority of the bishop.[43]
In any given city, to be *in* the church meant to be in communion
with the bishop.[44] Thus if there were more than one bishop, it
would appear that there was more than one church. In practice, if
one bishop was reconciling those excommunicated by another
bishop, excommunication becomes meaningless (not to mention
ineffective as a deterrent to sin). As we have seen, this was in fact
happening in the time of Hippolytus.

To be excommunicated meant to be excluded from communion, barred from the table of the Eucharist. The Eucharist was, among other things, a symbol of the unity of the Church and the communion of the saints.[45] There is only one Eucharist, and outside the Church there is no valid Eucharist, in fact no valid sacraments at all.[46] If one was not in communion with the bishop, one could not receive the Eucharist, let alone receive a blessing on a marriage or expect a Christian burial in the catacombs or cemeteries near the saints.[47] Therefore, the unity of the Church depended on the unity of its sacraments, and the unity of the sacraments depended on the singular authority of the episcopacy.

By the third century, the bishops also controlled the ordination of priests and the election of their fellow bishops.[48] Whereas originally the priests chose from among the laity who would join their ranks and elected one of their own to represent them as chair of the council, now the bishops had the authority to decide who would be ordained, and *they* chose the new bishops from among the priests.[49] Controlling ordination was the first line of defense in controlling the sacraments and the teaching office of the Church. Thus the only valid sacraments were those performed by the ordained, and the only valid ordinations were those within the chain of apostolic succession.[50]

By the end of the third century, certain cities were emerging as enjoying a level of authority above smaller surrounding cities.[51] These *metropolitans* would eventually have veto power even over ordinations in the other cities under their jurisdiction. The bishops of the metropolitans came to be called "popes."[52] Stephen of Rome was called pope, and at the same time the Christians of North Africa considered Cyprian of Carthage to be their pope.[53] In the fourth century, Eusebius of Caesarea referred to the bishop of Alexandria as pope.[54] In the fifth and sixth centuries, in the West, the term came to be used exclusively for the bishop of Rome.

If the bishop in any given city was the successor of the apostle(s) who founded the church there, the bishop of Rome was considered the successor of Peter. Every bishop was perceived as having been invested with the authority to forgive sin, but Peter was the one with the keys (Matt 16:19).[55] It should come as no surprise, then, that Rome emerged as the primary metropolitan, especially in the West. By the third century, there was a growing consensus that all churches should agree with Rome, at least on matters of doctrine.[56] Tertullian accepted the primacy of Rome and so did Cyprian, although, as we will see, he did not want to submit to Stephen on matters related to the sacraments.[57] While both Stephen and Cyprian accepted the concept of apostolic succession, Cyprian held that it applied only to the teaching office of the Church (doctrine), not to Church discipline.[58] Eventually, however, the metropolitans, and especially Rome, would come to have authority over the other cities on all matters. As we have seen, Dionysius of Rome followed the lead of his predecessor Clement, and took the initiative to write a letter of correction to a fellow bishop. And when Paul of Samosata refused to vacate his see, the emperor Aurelian enforced the authority of Rome and unknowingly increased the power of the episcopacy there.[59] Eventually, the First Ecumenical Council of Nicaea in 325 CE would declare Rome to be the primary metropolitan.

Thus the developing hierarchy, combined with an urgent concern for unity, led to the singular authority of the episcopacy, with the assumption that the authority of the bishop *is* the authority of the church.[60] In fact, the three-level hierarchy of bishop, priest, and deacon was seen as somewhat analogous to the Trinity, with its primary authority, and therefore its unity, invested in and dependent upon the one at the top of the hierarchy, while at the same time maintaining a certain equality, at least between bishop and priest.[61] Therefore, an ontological equality between bishops and priests was understood, even while a hierarchy of authority was acknowledged.[62] In the end, the need for consistency between cities (not just within cities) would drive the Church toward a hierarchy that included "bishops of bishops" (metropolitans) and one singular authority as the primary metropolitan, the bishop of Rome.

Apostolic versus Charismatic Authority: The Case of the Montanists

The concept of apostolic succession assumes that there will be a hierarchy in the Church. This hierarchy, with its developing levels of authority and structure of ordination, naturally leads to an episcopal polity, with the bishops at the top of the pyramid. The point is that it was generally accepted that there was a necessary relationship between hierarchy and unity. The Montanists, on the other hand, practiced a different structure altogether, in which authority is invested based on perceived gifts of the Holy Spirit rather than on the basis of a connection to (or authorization from) previous leaders. This is charismatic authority, as opposed to apostolic authority.

As we have noted briefly above, Montanus was a priest from Phrygia in Asia Minor, who claimed to be a prophet, able to speak with the voice of the Holy Spirit. His daughters, Prisc(ill)a and Maximilla, also claimed to be prophetesses. Together they began a movement characterized by charismatic gifts, ecstatic trances, and possibly speaking in tongues. They called themselves the "New Prophecy," though the movement was also known as Montanism (after its founder) and Cataphrygianism (after its place of origin). The Montanists were morally strict to the point of asceticism. They encouraged celibacy but apparently did not require it, though they prohibited second marriages.[63] Like Hippolytus, they criticized the bishops for forgiving adultery, though this probably means that some bishops were allowing the divorced to remarry and possibly blessing the cohabitation of mixed-class couples who could not legally be married. In fact, the Montanists took a morally superior posture with regard to rest of the Church, calling themselves "spiritual" and the other Christians "carnal."[64] They advocated a dispensationalist/millennialist interpretation of the Book of Revelation, believing that their ability to prophesy was evidence that the second coming of Christ was immanent. They caught the attention of the wider Church in about the year 156 CE.[65]

Montanism is often portrayed as an egalitarian movement in opposition to the developing hierarchy of the mainstream Church. The fact that there were at least two women in prominent leadership roles gives the impression that they rejected a male-only hierarchy. In reality, though, leadership within the New Prophecy was based on gifts of the Spirit, and while they certainly must have believed that the gifts of the Spirit were available to both sexes, only those who could prophesy could be leaders. In the end, it is more likely that having women in leadership of a rigorist group like the Montanists reinforced the development of a male-only clergy, rather than existed as a reaction against it. Having clarified this, it is still true that the Montanist "hierarchy" was relatively flat compared to the mainstream Church. They must have believed that the imma-nent return of Christ made a developed hierarchy unnecessary.

Montanism is also usually characterized as a schismatic move-ment. As we have already seen, however, Tertullian could associate with the New Prophecy without leaving the Catholic Church. We should not assume that the movement had its own congregations or separate meetings.[66] It is more accurate to say that the Montanists were a rigorist, charismatic reform movement within the Church.[67] But inevitably, their emphasis on continuing revelation would come into conflict with both the episcopal structure and the assumption of a finite canon within the mainstream Church.

A synod was held in Rome in 177 to discuss what to do about the New Prophecy. As we have seen, Irenaeus was present at this synod and apparently was able to convince Bishop Eleutherius that the Montanists were not a threat. Eusebius tells us that similar syn-ods had already been held in the East; there, however, the Montanists were declared heretics.[68] The successor of Eleutherius, Bishop Victor, had at first accepted the Montanists until Tertullian's nemesis Praxeas convinced him to change his mind.[69]

Accusations against the Montanists accumulated. Montanus was said to have claimed that he *was* the Holy Spirit, and although this is probably unfounded, a later Montanist leader named Miltiades apparently did claim that Montanus was the Holy Spirit.[70] The opponents of Montanism maintained that it was not the Holy Spirit who spoke through Montanus at all, but that the ecstatic trances of the New Prophecy were evidence of demonic posses-sion.[71] Montanists were accused of giving their own leaders more authority than the scriptures; however, this is not apparent in Tertullian's writings. They were also accused of enticing women to abandon their husbands and then call themselves virgins. They were criticized for wearing expensive jewelry and for prophesying for money.[72] Finally, both Montanus and Maximilla were said to have committed suicide when predictions of Christ's immediate return proved untrue.[73]

Hippolytus accused the Montanists of being Modalists, though this seems impossible (at least in the West) given Tertullian's acceptance of the movement.[74] The Eastern Montanists may have leaned toward modalism; this could explain why they were declared heretics by the Eastern councils when the Roman bishops were reluctant to condemn them.[75] Hippolytus's Eastern connections may have given him information about the Eastern Montanists that he assumed was true of those in the West as well. Although Irenaeus had defended the Montanists, by the time of Hippolytus the Eastern Montanists may have drifted into the modalist heresy. If they did become schismatic in the East, it would have been because they were excommunicated as heretics.[76]

The conflict between the Montanists and the mainstream Church was not really a conflict between an institutionalized, hierarchical, male-dominated organization and an anti-institutional, egalitarian resistance. It was the conflict between apostolic authority and charismatic authority. The Montanists were not antihierarchy per se, but they would have opposed any structure that appeared to suppress the Spirit. Tertullian said that Montanists were followers of the Holy Spirit, not of humans.[77] The majority of the bishops would have argued, however, that anyone can *claim* to speak for the Holy Spirit, but without a centralized authority to oversee the Church's teaching, disagreements would soon lead to division. Thus the primary issue became one of ongoing revelation versus tradition, and these were seen as potentially mutually exclusive since it was only a matter of time before some self-proclaimed prophet claimed the authority of the Holy Spirit to contradict the scriptures or the received tradition.[78] For the mainstream Church, the tradition defined the boundaries of orthodoxy; therefore, any teaching outside the tradition (or outside the succession of bishops) was suspect and probably heresy. But the Montanists were claiming direct access to God without human mediators, and the power that such claims gave to those outside the hierarchy was perceived as dangerous to the unity of the Church.

Tertullian valiantly defended the New Prophecy. He tried to reassure the bishops that "the Paraclete introduces nothing new."[79] The role of continuing revelation was to aid the Church in interpreting scripture, and so the Holy Spirit would never contradict the tradition.[80] Prophecy was meant to fill in the gaps of scripture by providing answers to questions that the apostles never addressed.

In fact, the Montanists believed that one could not correctly interpret scripture without prophecy. And here is precisely the rub. For
the Montanists, interpretation without ongoing prophecy would
leave too many unanswered questions and would leave the interpreter too much room for speculation, thus leading to heresy. For
the bishops, on the other hand, interpretation outside the authority of apostolic succession would lead to heresy, because it would be
too easy for an interpreter to fool himself into thinking that his
own agenda was endorsed by the Holy Spirit. The Montanists
trusted their own discernment of spirits. The rest of the Church
trusted the bishops.

In the third century, therefore, the mainstream (Catholic)
Church was defined as the Church of the bishops. In order to safeguard the teaching office and the disciplinary authority of the episcopacy, and thereby preserve the unity of the Church, it was
implicitly decided that true prophecy had ended with the apostolic
age. Preaching took the place of prophecy in the life of the Church,
and it was reserved for the ordained clergy.[81] Along with the elimi-
nation of prophecy, two related changes took place in the Church:
the separation of a professional clergy from the laity (with the exclusion of the laity from participation in certain aspects of ministry),[82]
and the exclusion of women from leadership roles in the Church.

The Role of Women

Several groups on the fringes of the Church had allowed
women to occupy leadership roles. It was said that Marcion permitted women to baptize. Irenaeus complained that some Gnostics
allowed women to participate in presiding over their eucharistic
liturgy.[83] As we have seen, Montanism also accepted the leadership
of women, provided they had the gift of prophecy. Even Tertullian
did not allow women to teach or administer the sacraments, however;[84] he criticized the apocryphal *Acts of Paul and Thecla*, in which
Thecla baptized herself when Paul refused to baptize her.[85] While
the apocryphal acts of the second and third century had become
popular with women because they often portrayed women as the
protagonists who had a life, and even a ministry, apart from the
authority of a male, they were the product of heterodox groups,

written to promote their agenda of asceticism, rejection of marriage, and rejection of the authority of the bishops in succession from the apostles.

Because of this, the mainstream attitude toward women in leadership was that to allow women to teach, debate, or preside over sacraments is unacceptable, because this is what the heretics do.[86] While the early bishops admitted that Jesus had female disciples, they maintained that Jesus never sent women out as apostles.[87] Therefore, the clerical orders, which were defined by their role in liturgy, were not open to women. Bishops, priests, and deacons had to be men, and the role of women was to learn and pray.[88] In some places, women may possibly have been allowed to instruct the newly initiated, but this would have been limited to women teaching other women.[89] While this was, of course, reinforced by cultural norms that gave authority to men, it was not made necessary by them. There were pagan cults with female priesthoods, and the Church was not afraid to be countercultural in other aspects. But the existence of female priesthoods in the mystery cults only reinforced the Church's aversion to the idea of a woman as presider. Therefore, this was not simply a case of excluding women in order to conform to a patriarchal culture; the issue was that the Church was differentiating itself from pagan culture and from heretical groups.

There were lay orders open to women, specifically that of virgin, widow, and deaconess, though they were not considered clergy because they had no role in liturgy. The one exception to this seems to be the deaconesses, whose responsibility it was to prepare women for baptism by anointing them.[90] Since it would not be appropriate for a male bishop to anoint the body of a woman stripped for baptism, a deaconess would perform the prebaptismal anointing, though the bishop would still pronounce the baptism in the name of the Trinity and anoint the newly baptized woman's head afterward. A deaconess might also visit a sick woman if there were no men in the home to chaperone, or if the visit of a man would cause a scandal.[91]

Widows were supported by the Church from the offerings of those who could afford to give.[92] In return, they made up a kind of order whose ministry it was to pray for the Church and especially for those who had given alms to pay for their support.[93] With the permission of the clergy they might also visit and pray over the sick (probably only women).[94] They were expected to communicate to the clergy when they became aware of any Christian in need and were especially charged with being discreet.[95] The early documents say, however, that they are not to presume to teach others, and if their visitation becomes a distraction, it is better for them to stay at home and pray than become busybodies and gossips.[96] It is unclear whether there was an actual initiation rite for the order of widows, but the stated ideal was that widows should be over fifty years old, so that they would not be tempted to remarry.[97]

The order of virgins seems to be an early version of monasticism, before the emergence of the tradition of living apart from society. There may be some evidence that there were male virgins; however, for the most part, the order of virgins would have been made up of women who chose a celibate life to dedicate themselves fully to God.[98] In doing so, they were a living witness to an eschatology that waited for the immanent return of Christ. They represented the pure bride of the Church waiting for her groom (Matt 25:1–13). There may have been an initiation ceremony that mirrored a wedding, in which the virgins pledged themselves to Christ. The order of virgin provided a viable life alternative for a woman who did not want to marry. With the support of the Church, the virgins could have a sense of security without living under the direct authority of a man. Of course, they were expected to submit to the authority of the bishop, and they probably did not live alone. Eventually, the development of monasticism all but replaced the order of virgin, and some women, such as Melania and Egeria, would have enough money and power to make pilgrimages to the Holy Land and establish whole monastic communities.[99] In this way, some women were able to find their own version of charismatic authority apart from the hierarchy.

PERSECUTION IN THE THIRD CENTURY

By the end of the second century, Christians could be found at all levels of society, in every kind of job, including the military.[100] There had been Christians in some of the imperial households, and even the mistress of Commodus (emperor 180–92) was rumored to have been sympathetic to the Church. At the same time, accusations of antisocial behavior persisted. Pagan Romans feared that if enough people joined the Church and stopped worshiping the traditional gods, these gods would remove their protection, and this could bring about the downfall of the empire. Any natural disaster could be blamed on the Church, and any military defeat could be blamed on the presence of Christians in the legions. As is shown by the martyrs of Lyons and Viennes, at times an angry mob could form and take out their fears and frustrations on their "atheist" neighbors.[101]

We have already seen how emperors such as Marcus Aurelius and Septimius Severus had set the precedent of requiring sacrifice as a sign of loyalty. Christians were now being forced to choose between the self-proclaimed gods of the empire and the Christian God. In fact, the Church demanded loyalty even over family, if that family was not Christian. So the third century begins with a choice: Caesar or Christ? Is the emperor the son of a god, or is Jesus the Son of God? Is the emperor the father (patron) of all, or is God the Father of all?

In the year 212, the emperor Caracalla (emperor 211–17) granted citizenship to all inhabitants of the empire. Until this time, Roman citizenship was a privilege, but now it had become a burden, since taxation was extended and loyalty could be demanded across the empire.[102] Later, Severus Alexander (emperor 222–35) would be tolerant of the Church, and it was his mother, Julia Mamea, who summoned Origen to Antioch to explain Christianity.[103] But this tolerance, along with the possibility of Christians in the imperial household, apparently caused Alexander's successor, Maximinus Thrax (emperor 235–38), to renew persecution. According to Eusebius of Caesarea, Maximinus's hatred for his predecessor led him to order Church leaders put to death.[104] These events set the stage for the persecutions of the mid-third century.

In the year 249 CE, a new emperor would come to the throne who would advocate a revival of traditional Roman religion. His name was Decius (emperor 249–51). Just two years before, Rome had celebrated its millennium.[105] But the empire was plagued by an economic recession in which previous emperors had devalued the coinage to supplement the imperial treasury. In addition, wars in the East had depleted resources and left the borders unstable. Decius himself, as a general, had left an eastern border undefended to come to Rome and claim the throne. The presence of the Christians only added insult to injury in the eyes of the emperor, and as far as he was concerned the Church stood in the way of Rome's return to its glory days. Like Maximinus, he hated the Christians, and he hated the fact that his predecessor was tolerant of the Church. In fact, there was a rumor (probably untrue) that Philip (emperor 244–49) may have even been a Christian.[106] Decius's solution was to call for renewed enthusiasm for the Roman gods, including sacrifices to Jupiter for the benefit of the empire and in honor of the emperor. With this he would kill two birds with one stone: he would bring back the blessing of the gods, and he would force the Christians to give up their superstition. Thus he initiated the first systematic, empire-wide persecution of the Church.

The Decian Persecution

As soon as Decius took the throne, persecution began in the provinces.[107] In late 249, Decius issued an edict commanding all inhabitants of the empire to make a sacrifice on a certain date. The edict was heard by some in the Church as a fulfillment of Jesus' warnings of tribulation in the gospels.[108] Local councils were set up in each city to oversee the sacrifices. This was the first time that such an order was enforced systematically across the empire. Everyone who complied would receive a receipt, called a *libellus* (Latin for "little book," or pamphlet—imagine a sheet of papyrus about the size of an 8.5x11 sheet of paper that would be folded in quarters). A person could be asked to show this *libellus* at any time as proof of compliance, and it could be required to participate in trade (cf. Rev 13:16–17).[109] Failure to sacrifice would be considered an act of treason, punishable by death.

Exactly what was entailed in making a sacrifice depended on where one was in the empire, but it could be as simple as burning some incense on a pagan altar, pouring out a libation offering of wine, or throwing some grain on a fire. It could mean sacrificing an animal (and this may have been Decius's original intention), but with everyone having to sacrifice, it is unlikely that very many cities made their people go through a full animal sacrifice. If an animal was sacrificed, the person would most likely be expected to eat some of the sacrificial meat. A person would also be expected to swear an oath of allegiance to the emperor, and if one was suspected of being a Christian, the Roman official could also require a curse against Christ (cf. 1 Cor 12:3). But even if one admitted to being a Christian, simply renouncing the faith and making the sacrifice would gain one's freedom.[110] Refusal to make the sacrifice could mean imprisonment, torture, exile with confiscation of property (a favorite of those governors who got to keep the property), or execution by decapitation, crucifixion (sometimes upside down), drowning, burning at the stake, or mauling by wild animals in the arena.[111] One could also be condemned to work in the mines, which was not much more than a prolonged death sentence since prisoners were literally forced to work until they dropped dead. Some Romans even took delight in devising especially barbarous methods of execution, such as tying a person to two trees bent over and held by ropes, so that when the ropes were cut, the trees would spring back to their original position, tearing the person in two.[112] Presumably, these more horrific methods of execution were meant to encourage other Christians to decide to make the sacrifice.

The response to Decius's edict was that Christians "ran eagerly to the altars."[113] Many refused to sacrifice on the basis that such a sacrifice was idolatry and, even worse, apostasy. But many others made the required sacrifices, reasoning that they knew in their hearts the pagan gods were not real and therefore it was acceptable to lie to the Romans and pretend to worship by going through the motions of a sacrifice. According to Cyprian, they were motivated as much by a concern to protect their property and businesses as they were concerned for their lives.[114] Some denied they had ever been Christians (which was apparently not required).

Some fled the persecution, and of those captured, many sacrificed after imprisonment or torture. According to Eusebius, even women and children were tortured.[115] Torture could mean starvation, racking, beating, reeds pushed under the fingernails, eyes gouged out or feet hobbled to brand one as a criminal, or slowly pouring boiling tar or molten lead over the delicate parts of a person's body.[116]

Christian women could expect to be raped as a matter of course.[117] The emperor's edict had endorsed the brutalization of Christians across the empire.[118] One can imagine that as more and more Christians died or fled, it became harder and harder for those who remained to stand firm, especially in the absence of their leaders.

In spite of the fact that many people denied their faith to save their lives, many were also martyred, among them Bishop Fabian of Rome, who died in January of 250 CE.[119] Many more were imprisoned, so that the prisons were full of Christians. Even some who *had* denied their faith to save their lives were left to starve to death in prison. Far from destroying the Church, however, Decius had succeeded in giving the Church an opportunity for witness. Across the empire pagans were converted, seeing that Christians would rather die than give up their faith. More documents like the early martyr acts made heroes of the martyrs, recounting their triumph over evil in the arenas. Just as before, these martyrologies contained embellishments, including stories of miraculous submission of the wild animals, which often refused to attack the Christians. The reality of the situation was that many Christians did not deny their faith, or even hide, but in fact reached out to minister to their brothers and sisters in prison, even at the risk of their own lives. This in itself was seen as a form of martyrdom.[120] Between outbreaks of persecution, the Christians continued to minister to the sick and imprisoned, and Romans continued to be moved by this to come into the Church. Decius had to go back to the eastern borders of the empire in 251 CE to repel invading barbarians. He was killed in battle, which many interpreted as God's vindication, and the persecution of Christians briefly subsided.

Novatian, Cyprian, and the Problem of the Lapsed

Thascius Caecilius Cyprianus (Cyprian) was bishop of Carthage in North Africa from 249 CE until his death in 258.[121] He had been ordained and elected bishop within only a few years after his conversion to Christianity. During the Decian persecution, he fled Carthage and attempted to care for his flock from a distance by writing letters, many of which are still extant.[122] Returning to Carthage in the spring of 251, Cyprian came back to a Church that had been broken by the persecution in more ways than one. When Cyprian realized that the very unity of the Church was threatened, he composed the treatise *On the Unity of the Catholic Church*.

In the aftermath of the persecution, two major problems arose. The first concerned the question of what to do about those who had denied the faith to save their lives, known as the *lapsed*. Should they be allowed to return to their churches, or would that be a slap in the face to those who endured torture or whose loved ones had been executed? Some held that mercy should be extended to the apostates. Others said they should be excommunicated. Still others looked for some middle ground between easy reentry and permanent expulsion. Three factions emerged in this debate. The "laxists" advocated allowing the lapsed to come back into the Church with no penalty. This faction was led by one Fortunatus, who also had fled during the persecution.[123] His followers were primarily the lapsed themselves. The "rigorists" advocated excommunication for the lapsed. This group was led by a priest named Novatus in North Africa, and the theologian Novatian in Rome.[124] Cyprian had wanted to excommunicate Novatus, but Novatus fled to Rome to consolidate efforts with the rigorists there.[125] The remaining group was simply everyone else, who couldn't be sure what to do about the problem.

From hiding, Cyprian had counseled patience, saying that as long as the persecution continued, there was still a chance that an apostate might undo his sin through martyrdom.[126] But some priests back in his home see were already reconciling the lapsed and readmitting them to communion.[127] In addition, there were those who had refused to deny the faith and were imprisoned and/or tortured, but who had not been executed. Many Christians attributed to these *confessors* (called this because they had confessed the faith at the risk of their lives) a charismatic authority on the basis of Jesus' words in Matthew 10:17–22. The lapsed were going to the confessors, even visiting them in prison, and begging for their forgiveness. The confessors, some of whom were laypeople, were granting reconciliation without the authority of any bishop. Apparently, lapsed Christians were returning to the churches with letters of reconciliation, or "*libelli* of peace," some of which were written to cover whole families.[128] As with the Montanists, here was

161

a case of a confrontation between charismatic authority and apostolic authority, specifically over Church discipline.[129] Cyprian tried to stop the confessors from granting reconciliation, but he could not directly refute their perceived charismatic authority.[130] He tried to argue that the *libelli* of peace would only be valid if the confessor who granted it was actually martyred, and it should only be honored after the end of the persecution. It should not be a general grant of reconciliation for a group of people, but should be for one person, named in the letter, who must be sincerely repentant.[131] In the end, however, Cyprian was unable to bring the situation under his control as long as he was personally absent from his see.

The second postpersecution problem concerned the episcopacy in Rome. When Fabian was martyred in January of 250, the Roman church was not able to elect a successor. Choosing a bishop at that point would have meant consigning that person to death, since it would not be possible to keep the identity of the bishop of Rome a secret for long. According to one story, the emperor Decius had commented that he would rather encounter a rival for his throne than see a new bishop installed in Rome. When the persecution subsided and the church of Rome was able to hold an election for bishop, Novatian must have expected to be elected. He had been the acting bishop for over a year, and his treatise *On the Trinity* had no doubt earned him a reputation as a first-rate theologian and the spokesman for Roman orthodoxy. However, he was a rigorist. To elect Novatian would have been to submit to the rigorist faction and endorse excommunication for all the lapsed. Therefore, the more pastoral Cornelius was elected instead of the theologian. When Novatian lost the election, Novatus gathered three rigorist bishops from outside Rome and had them consecrate Novatian as bishop of Rome in opposition to Cornelius.[132] Thus Novatian became bishop of the rigorists, claiming to be bishop of Rome. Unless one counts Hippolytus, Novatian is therefore the first true "antipope." A priest named Maximus would eventually become the leader of the rigorists in Carthage and claimed to be bishop there. Fortunatus was set up by the laxist party as their bishop in Carthage. The Church was in schism.

Soon after Cyprian returned to Carthage, he convened a synod. The first Council of Carthage was gathered in April of 251 to address the situation with the rival factions and their bishops. The rigorist and laxist bishops were excommunicated, along with their followers. To counteract the uncontrollable nature of confessor reconciliation, Cyprian said that only God can forgive the sin of apostasy (which of course in this situation included the sin of idolatry).[133] As Cyprian reasoned, this is because no one can judge the servant of another; only that servant's master can judge (Rom 14:4).[134] However, a bishop (and only a bishop) might reconcile the lapsed to the Church, in hopes that God will ratify that decision.[135] But even the reconciliation of a bishop might not be enough without penance, so any who might reconcile the lapsed too easily would not be doing them a favor—in fact might be consigning them to damnation if it meant they would relax their penance.[136] Therefore, anyone who prematurely reconciled someone who had lapsed was threatened with excommunication.[137] The only acceptable exception would be if death was immanent.[138]

To determine a course of action regarding the lapsed, the council identified three categories of lapsed Christians. *Apostates* were those who made the required sacrifices. Any who paid or convinced a sympathetic neighbor to make the sacrifices on their behalf were still considered in this category, on the basis of Matthew 18:6 and parallels. *Libellateci* ("pamphleteers," for lack of a better English translation) were those who bought a *libellus* or bribed a Roman official to obtain a *libellus* without making the sacrifice. *Traitors* were those who surrendered scriptures to be burned or gave up church property to the authorities. Thus the lapsed had to be dealt with individually, on a case by case basis, since the gravity of the sin (and therefore the extent of the penance) depended upon the circumstances, including the intentions of the sinner.[139]

The council decided that apostates could not be reconciled until the point of death. They would remain in a state of excommunication, expected to be in perpetual penance, until death was immanent, and only then would they be reconciled. They might be reconciled earlier if they had sacrificed after being tortured, but only if they actually suffered torture; simply the threat of torture was not enough.[140] The *libellateci* and traitors could be reconciled with penance, but priests or bishops who had lapsed would not be restored to their ministry.[141] No one would be reconciled unless sincere repentance had been demonstrated through penance. Even someone who fell gravely ill and was on the brink of death would not be reconciled if he or she had not shown sufficient repentance before becoming sick.[142]

A similar council was convened in the summer of 251 by Cornelius in Rome and was attended by sixty bishops and even more priests.[143] The Roman synod basically agreed with the conclusions of Carthage. Thus in both Rome and Carthage, the lapsed were not all excommunicated out of hand, but the rigorists were. The immediate result of this was that some of the Roman confessors became followers of Novatian.[144] Apparently, these rigorist confessors were offended that any of the lapsed would be reconciled, and were further scandalized by the fact that Cornelius and the Roman council had reconciled an entire group of apostates, a whole city church and its bishop who had sacrificed together.[145] Cyprian responded by commenting that confessors who separate from the Church should lose that title, and that even martyrdom outside the Church is meaningless and ineffective for salvation.[146]

Novatian sent messengers to Carthage to try to establish himself as the legitimate bishop of Rome, but Cyprian rejected the messengers.[147] He then sent messengers with letters to other bishops across the empire to try to gain support.[148] Apparently he almost convinced Bishop Fabius of Antioch to side with him, until Dionysius of Alexandria wrote to Fabius, who then held a synod in Antioch that excommunicated Novatian.[149] When Cyprian officially took Cornelius's side, the Roman confessors realized they were outside the Church and returned to Cornelius.[150] With the loss of the Roman confessors, Novatus went back to North Africa, and some of Novatian's faction (including Maximus, the rigorist bishop of Carthage), returned to the Catholic Church.[151] Even one of the bishops who had consecrated Novatian as the opposing bishop of Rome returned to the Church. Dionysius of Alexandria wrote to Novatian to try to convince him to come back to the Church and submit to Cornelius. The letter indicates that Novatian may have claimed that he was pushed to separate from the Church by the other rigorists, including Novatus. Dionysius wrote that by excommunicating the lapsed, Novatian "accuses our most compassionate Lord Jesus Christ of being without mercy."[152]

Cornelius sarcastically called Novatian "this master of doctrine," the "champion of the Church's discipline." He called his ordination as a priest into question by suggesting that his baptism was irregular. He further accused Novatian of having refused his duties as a priest to avoid the persecution, and said that now he made his followers swear an oath to him in order to receive the Eucharist.[153] Most of this was probably invented to discredit Novatian and prevent others from following him. Cyprian called Novatian "that wily and subtle man."[154] In about 257, the anonymous *Against Novatian* was written. It compared Novatian to Cain and Judas and quoted to him the scripture, "Do not judge, and you will not be judged..." (Luke 6:37).[155] The author argued that the Church should welcome the lapsed to reconciliation, just as Jesus had forgiven Peter. If Peter, who also denied the faith out of fear, can be reconciled to Christ, so can the lapsed.[156]

Nevertheless, Novatian became the figurehead of the first lasting schism of the Church. Called *Novatianists* in the West and *Purists* (*katharoi*) in the East, the sect grew and continued for centuries, with its own bishops and eventually even its own church buildings. At the First Ecumenical Council of Nicaea in 325 CE, a Novatianist bishop was present and signed the creed. The Novatianists were therefore recognized as orthodox in their theology, even while being schismatics. It would be the first time a group would be formally recognized as Christian, but not Catholic.[157] The canons of the Council of Nicaea declared that Novatianist clergy could retain their ordained status if they returned to the Church. After the persecutions had ended, the Christian emperors allowed the Novatianist churches to keep their property.[158]

A second Council of Carthage was held in May of 252 CE, with a third in 253 and a fourth in 254.[159] In the end, most of the Church followed the lead of Carthage and decided to err on the side of mercy.[160] To excommunicate all the lapsed would decimate the Church and would risk that the excommunicated would give up the faith entirely rather than follow through on their penance. The rigorists were compared to those in the parable of the Good Samaritan who walked by the man on the road and refused to offer him help and healing.[161] In fact, because they were willing to consign the lapsed to possible damnation by denying them reconciliation, they were no better than the thugs who beat the man and left him for dead. As Jesus had said, a good shepherd will leave the ninety-nine safe sheep to find the one that is lost. In the same way, the shepherds (bishops) of the Church should seek out the lost (the lapsed) and bring them back into the fold.[162] Also, since it was becoming clear that persecution would soon be renewed, all the lapsed who were willing to repent were offered amnesty to bring them into the Church to strengthen them for what was to come.[163] Still, this was not a guarantee of salvation. It was meant to prevent the lapsed from giving up hope and help them resist the temptation to sacrifice again, but the only guarantee of the forgiveness of the sin of apostasy was another chance at martyrdom.[164]

Valerian, who became emperor in 253 CE, did not at first actively persecute the Church,[165] but in 257 persecution was renewed and Cyprian was imprisoned. In July of that year Valerian was apparently persuaded to revisit Decius's agenda, and he issued a letter to the senate that, in addition to the usual, forbade Christian assembly, specifically mentioning gatherings outside the city walls (that is, in the cemeteries).[166] Both Novatian and Cyprian were martyred during the persecution of Valerian, in 258 CE. Valerian died in 260, his three-and-a-half-year persecution being compared to the forty-two months of blasphemy in Revelation 13:5.[167] Valerian's successor, Gallienus, ended the persecution with rescripts of his own that discontinued the programs of Decius and Valerian and even restored the cemeteries to the churches.[168]

Penance and Reconciliation

The persecution of the third century, with its subsequent controversy over the lapsed, forced the development of a system of penance. Confession had been a part of the eucharistic liturgy from very early on. It was probably originally a corporate prayer of confession, but the assumption that one should not receive the Eucharist without first confessing one's sins was held from the beginning (cf. 1 Cor 11:27–32).[169] In addition, the possibility of excommunication had always existed in the Church (cf. 1 Cor 5). The bishops were invested with the authority to proclaim the forgiveness of sins based on apostolic succession (from Matt 16:19), and eventually they would confer that authority on the priests as well. But this still left the question of *how* one would be reconciled to communion after being excommunicated, or when one had in effect excommunicated oneself by sinful behavior. The discipline of penance emerged as a way to show the sincerity of one's repentance.[170] Penance was seen as an "outward and visible sign" of an inward reality. By the third century, Christians in different areas were experimenting with penitential systems that would specify certain acts of penance for particular sins. Because of the assumption that not all sins are equal and therefore the penance must fit the level of sin, and because of the need for consistency to avoid priestly favoritism, Celtic priests had devised penitential books that actually set down a standardized list of sins and the corresponding penance.

To be clear, penance was not viewed as a way of earning salvation. Baptism was the sacrament that washed away the stain of original sin.[171] But sins committed after baptism were generally thought to be held against a person. Therefore, confession and penance became the way of dealing with postbaptismal sin.[172] Since a person could lose one's salvation by committing serious sins after baptism, there was a sense in which regular confession and penance helped one retain one's salvation. In this way, confession did contribute to salvation and penance was seen as a kind of merit that made satisfaction for sin and participated in atonement.[173] Penance usually meant fasting and prayer for a specified amount of time, though it could also include almsgiving (Tob 4:10).[174] When the time of penance was complete, a public confession would be made to the assembly, after which a person was granted "peace," or reconciliation, with the laying on of hands by the bishop.[175] The practice of private confession may go back to the confessors, who granted forgiveness on the basis of a visit from someone who had lapsed and who confessed the sin of apostasy to one who was seen as having the charismatic authority to absolve that sin, precisely because he or she had not committed it.

As applied to the lapsed, the Church devised stages of penance that led one from excommunication back into full communion. The penitent began his or her penance as a *weeper*. Weepers were expected to remain outside the worship space, dressed in mourning clothes and begging their brothers and sisters to pray for them. After spending an appropriate amount of time as a weeper, the penitent became a *hearer*. Hearers were allowed to enter the worship space, but just inside the doors, not among the assembly. They may listen to the liturgy, but not participate. Next the penitent became a *kneeler*. Kneelers were admitted into the assembly among the people, but must remain kneeling while the rest would stand. Finally, the last stage was to become a *co-stander*. Co-standers were allowed to stand with the rest and participate in the liturgy, but could not receive communion.[176] Eventually, the co-stander would make his or her public confession and be reconciled. The whole process could take anything from a few weeks to over a decade, depending on the nature of the sin.

Ultimately it was determined that apostasy could be forgiven (but only by a bishop), since all serious sin is a kind of idolatry of one form or another.[177] And if adultery could be forgiven (though the rigorists would have argued it could not), then certainly the *libellateci* and traitors could hope for reconciliation.[178] For the mainstream Church, the only truly unforgivable sin was schism, since by it the schismatic separates himself from the Church and from salvation.[179] Therefore schism is worse than apostasy, and Jesus' words in Matthew 7:22–23 ("I never knew you…") were applied to the schismatics.[180]

THE CONTROVERSY OVER BAPTISM AND REBAPTISM

The persecution and the problem of the lapsed led inevitably to a controversy over the validity of baptism.[181] The issue was not infant baptism (that was universally being done), but the validity of baptisms done by clergy who had lapsed during the persecution or by schismatic clergy.[182] The question was whether someone who had been baptized by a lapsed or schismatic bishop needed to be rebaptized. The standing tradition had been that those coming back into the Church from a heretical group did not need to be rebaptized but only needed reconciliation with the imposition of hands.[183] Cyprian, however, started rebaptizing people, based on a more recent North African practice.[184] Councils held in North Africa in 255 and 256 and presided over by Cyprian confirmed Cyprian's practice.[185]

Cyprian was opposed by Stephen of Rome (bishop 254–57), who wanted to keep the prior tradition of reconciling only.[186] In fact, Stephen wanted to excommunicate anyone who would rebaptize.[187] Eventually, Stephen would even break off communication with Cyprian, which gave the impression that he considered Cyprian excommunicated.[188] In reality, both bishops would agree that it was inappropriate to repeat a valid baptism;[189] they simply disagreed on what constituted a valid baptism.

The North African Understanding of Baptism

At the councils of Carthage it was argued that since baptism affects the remission of sin, only those with the authority to forgive sins can perform a valid baptism.[190] This would mean that any baptism performed by someone outside the succession of bishops, whether because of sin, heresy, or schism, could not be valid.[191] The principle at work here is that one cannot give what one does not have. The grace of forgiveness comes with the conferral of the Holy Spirit, but one who does not have the Holy Spirit cannot grant the Holy Spirit.[192] In this view, the presider is regarded as a conduit of grace from God to the receiver. If the presider has lapsed in his faith by making a pagan sacrifice, or if the presider has broken from the Catholic Church, then he has cut the conduit, and no grace can flow to the one who hopes to be baptized. Therefore, those who had been baptized by Novatian, for example, were not really baptized, and if they wanted to come into the Catholic Church they would need to be baptized.[193] According to Cyprian, he did not in fact rebaptize, because the recipients were never baptized in the first place.[194] For a baptism to be valid, the presider must be beyond reproach.[195]

Cyprian would argue that in fact it would be a disservice not to (re)baptize, since he believed that anyone not baptized could not be saved.[196] Not even martyrdom could save one who died for the wrong Christ.[197] He made no distinction between heretics and schismatics on this point; all risked damnation by removing themselves from the true Church.[198] Moreover, the unity of the Church required that there could be only one baptism.[199] Therefore, to consider a schismatic baptism valid would be the equivalent of saying that the schismatics are also the Church, that they are already in the kingdom of God, and that they are not a schism at all.[200] On the contrary, Cyprian believed that to reconcile without (re)baptism is to commune with the excommunicated, which for him would make a mockery of the discipline of the Church.[201] And after all, he reasoned, didn't the apostles rebaptize those who had been baptized by John the Baptist?[202]

This North African understanding of baptism would continue in the Donatists, who in the fourth century would claim Cyprian as their precedent for the practice of rebaptism. Novatian apparently also shared this view of baptism, since he rebaptized Catholics who came over to his schism.[203] Stephen of Rome would point to Novatian's practice and argue that the North Africans should not rebaptize, since that is what schismatics do.

The Roman Understanding of Baptism

Stephen of Rome, along with the anonymous author of the treatise *On Rebaptism*, was the primary spokesman for the baptismal theology that would become the mainstream (Catholic) understanding. He argued that one should not ask *who* baptized, but only *how* the baptism was performed.[204] The implication is that the spiritual state of the presider does not matter, because it is not the presider who baptizes, it is God who baptizes.[205] There is no conduit of grace from God that leads *through* the presider to the recipient. Grace flows directly from God to the one being baptized. Apostolic succession notwithstanding, a baptism is valid no matter who performs it, as long as one is baptized into Christ. Therefore, to rebaptize is to presume to say that God's work was ineffective in the original baptism; thus, rebaptism is an offense against God.[206]

On principle, Stephen also made no distinction between heretics and schismatics when it came to the validity of baptism.[207] Any baptism was valid as long as it was validly performed. Correct belief was not a requirement, since the disciples themselves had imperfect faith.[208] Even the method of baptism (immersion versus pouring or sprinkling) did not matter; what mattered was that a person was baptized in the name of Christ.[209] Eventually, the North Africans pressed the point, asking whether a person baptized by Marcion would in fact be baptized. In other words, what if someone were baptized into the wrong Christ? Stephen would later clarify that the baptism must be performed in the name of the Trinity (Matt 28:19).[210] Thus even a baptism performed by a heretical bishop would be valid (that is, salvific) as long as the baptism was done in the name of the Father, Son, and Holy Spirit.[211] Of course, this principle applied only if one was within the true Church, so that a schismatic or heretical baptism could not save one if one *remained* outside the Church. The orthodoxy of the presider did not matter because the recipient of the baptism could not be held responsible for the presider's faith; however, the recipient was responsible to remain in the true Church for the baptism to be effective.[212] The point at issue, however, was that if someone were to come over to the Catholic Church from a schism or heresy, that person did not need to be rebaptized, because of the conviction that God was faithful, even when church leaders were not. This Roman understanding of baptism was confirmed at a synod in Rome.

Cyprian admitted that those who come from a heresy and are admitted without rebaptism are not necessarily damned, because it is not their fault if they were converted from paganism into a heretical sect or schism.[213] *Potens est Dominus misericordia sua indulgentiam dare* (It is the Lord's prerogative to grant his mercy). But he did criticize Stephen, who he thought should have known better, for preferring to excommunicate rebaptizers rather than heretics.[214] The more important problem for Cyprian, however, was that he reasoned that by considering a heretical or schismatic baptism valid, the Church would be validating the heresy or schism.[215] Thus by not (re)baptizing, he accused Stephen of creating two baptisms (schismatic and Catholic) where there should be only one (Eph 4:5).

From Stephen's perspective, it appeared as if Cyprian were turning one baptism into two (two consecutive baptisms). For him, rebaptism violates the principle of "one faith, one baptism." But for Cyprian, to validate a heretical or schismatic baptism violates that same principle. Both would argue that the other's baptismal theology actually cheapens Catholic baptism.

For the North Africans, one baptism means *only one*. All other baptisms are excluded because the unity of the Church depends on its purity. The Church is seen as more or less identical with the kingdom (the visible Church *is* the invisible Church), and so it is the duty of the Church to keep itself pure by excluding those who are not also in the kingdom.[216] This is an ecclesiology of *unity through purity*. For the Romans, on the other hand, one baptism means *all is one*. All baptisms are included, as long as they are performed in the name of the Trinity—that is all that is needed to mark them as Christian. For the Romans, the Church on earth is not identical to the kingdom (the visible Church *includes* the invisible Church). This is an ecclesiology of *unity through inclusion*. Thus heretics and schismatics may not be destined for salvation, but this does not prevent God's saving grace from being at work in their baptism, should they later join the true Church. Of course, after the baptism, the believer has a responsibility to remain in the true Church if he or she would hope for salvation, since continuing in a heresy or schism would be to separate oneself from the Church (and God), regardless of the validity of one's baptism.[217] Stephen did admit that although he believed schismatic baptism to be (theoretically) valid based on the operation of God, schismatic confirmation of the baptism could not be valid since the bishop performing the confirmation was outside the succession.[218] Thus the principle that one cannot give what one does not have, which Cyprian applied to baptism, Stephen applied to confirmation.[219]

WHAT, THEN, IS THE CHURCH?

The church of Rome in the middle of the third century had forty-six priests, with seven deacons and seven subdeacons (perhaps based on the fourteen regions of the city, as divided by Augustus—one deacon covered two regions, with a subdeacon as his assistant).[220] There were also forty-two acolytes and fifty-two exorcists, along with other lay offices and over 1,500 widows and others supported by the church.[221] This implies a city church of almost fifty house churches and about ten thousand members. But this begs the question, What constitutes Church membership? Indeed, what *makes one* a Christian? It is easy enough to begin by saying that baptism defines the boundaries of Church membership, but we now know that this does not really answer the question. On the one hand, some who were not yet baptized could consider themselves Christians (for example, Perpetua and other confessor catechumens).[222] On the other hand, some who were baptized might not be considered within the true Church.[223] As it was evolving in the third century, patristic ecclesiology developed along two definable lines.

The question became, Is the Church an enclave of the saved in a world of the damned, or is it a hospital for the soul? The persecution of the third century caused a certain amount of circling of the wagons, and the rigorists emerged from that time determined to honor the martyrs by excommunicating the lapsed. The persecution also caused some to speculate that a presider's status within the Church could affect the validity of the sacraments. Thus there is some affinity between the rigorists and North African baptismal theology, evidenced by the fact that both opposed Rome and its bishops. Hippolytus, Tertullian, and Novatian were some of the best theologians the early Church produced, and yet they were all rigorists. They had very high moral expectations for the baptized, and their followers maintained ever lengthening lists of the sins that could not be forgiven. It seems that for the Montanists, the Novatianists, and the Donatists after them the primary task of the Church is to keep herself chaste, as the bride-to-be of Christ.[224] This would be done by identifying and excluding the unworthy, ultimately protecting the table of the Eucharist, but also ostensibly protecting those who might take the Eucharist unworthily.[225] At the risk of an oversimplification for the sake of convenient categories, we will call this a North African ecclesiology.

For the North African ecclesiology, the Church must be holy (that is, perfect) to be effective. Diluting the purity of the Church might render it unable to save. Tolerance of heresy would inevitably lead to the ordination of heretical priests and the election of heretical bishops, and consequently to invalid sacraments that could not offer salvation. Thus the rigorist ecclesiology is consistent with a sacramental theology that assumes that the faith of the presider affects the validity of the sacrament. This has implications especially for the reliability of not only baptism and the Eucharist, but also penance and reconciliation. How could the average Christian know if the clergy who granted absolution really had the power to grant it, if the Church was not pure? Thus to reconcile the lapsed could ruin the Church for the faithful, so that the only way to help the lapsed was to excommunicate them.

A Roman ecclesiology, on the other hand, believes that the Church is holy because Christ made her holy (Eph 5:25–27). The Church is like the ark of Noah: to be saved from the flood one must be in it, but it contained both clean and unclean animals (cf. 1 Pet 3:20–21).[226] Jesus' parable of the wheat and the weeds (Matt 13) provided an analogy of the Church. The Church on earth (the visible Church) included both true Christians (the wheat) and false ones (the weeds). But it was meant to be that way until the judgment, when the weeds would be pulled up and thrown into the fire. To be fair, even Tertullian and Cyprian used this image for the Church, Cyprian saying it would be prideful to presume to separate the weeds while the Church sojourned on earth.[227] But Tertullian's Montanism and Cyprian's rebaptism reveal the direction in which their ecclesiology leans. Hippolytus had actually criticized Callistus for using this parable to describe the Church.[228]

Roman ecclesiology affirmed that the Church did not have to be perfect to be effective; it only had to be inclusive. The Church was not a cloister of the perfect but a school for the imperfect who hoped to move toward perfection, in which catechesis and liturgy were the lessons. It was understood as a hospital for the soul, in which penance and reconciliation were the medicine.[229] Thus the Church was not identical with the kingdom. The Church on earth (the visible Church) *included* the Church in heaven (the invisible Church) but was not to be equated with it. The heavenly Church is the perfect one, the earthly Church only had to refrain from premature judgment. Therefore, Church membership makes salvation *possible*, but does not guarantee it. Baptism grants forgiveness, but does not guarantee perseverance. For those who held a Roman ecclesiology, the Church was exemplified by the statement, "…whoever is not against you is for you" (Luke 9:50). For the proponents of North African ecclesiology, the Church was exemplified by the statement, "Whoever is not with me is against me, and whoever does not gather with me scatters" (Luke 11:23).[230] Roman ecclesiology is based on the assumption that purity might purify impurity. North African ecclesiology is based on the assumption that impurity defiles purity. In the end, Roman ecclesiology (and indeed Roman sacramental theology) would become the standard in the Church; however, the North African version would continue as long as Christianity itself continued in North Africa. In the controversy between Augustine and the Donatists, Augustine would be the proponent of the Roman ecclesiology.

Both lines of ecclesiological trajectory spring from the conviction that there is no salvation outside the Church. Cyprian famously said that one cannot hope to have God for a Father if one does not have the Church for a mother.[231] Thus true Christianity, and therefore salvation, was limited to those within the bounds of the Church. But it was precisely those bounds which were at issue. In the end, schism was perceived as worse than both heresy and apostasy, and the only truly unforgivable sin was to separate oneself from the Church.[232] To join a schism was to excommunicate oneself, because it was to step out of communication with the bishops in succession from the apostles (Matt 18:17, 2 John 10–11). Eventually, the Catholic Church decided not to permanently excommunicate the lapsed, but it did excommunicate the schismatics.[233]

Therefore, the patristic definition of the Church ultimately rests on the foundation of apostolic succession. Apostolic succession drives both doctrine and discipline. True Christians are those who are connected to the apostles via the succession.[234] They believe the doctrines most consistent with the oldest tradition and accept the authoritative apostolic documents.[235] They receive the sacraments from bishops (and the priests to whom they give authority) in direct line from the apostles.[236] They accept the discipline of their bishops and listen to them as though they are listening to the apostles themselves. Heresy, apostasy, and schism are all divisive, but unity is found in the succession, and the succession is embodied in the bishops.[237] Thus the very unity of the Church was seen to be centered in, and dependent upon, the authority of the bishops. By the middle of the third century, this also meant that there could be only one bishop in each city.[238]

CHAPTER 8

The Church and the Empire

Just at the time that the Church was coming to a certain level of definition of itself, its relationship with the empire changed so drastically that from that time forward the Church and the empire each identified themselves in relation to the other. The early fourth century saw the extremes of the Great Persecution and then arguably the first Christian emperor. More than any other time in the history of the Church, the first quarter of the fourth century could be described as "tribulation."

In the forty years or so from the end of Valerian's persecution to the beginning of the Great Persecution, an atmosphere of mutual toleration filled the empire. The pagans tolerated the Christians, and the Christians even came to trust the pagans to a certain extent, so that being a Christian didn't seem quite so dangerous, and each side felt it was safe to assimilate some practices from the other. At the time, some non-Christians might even have interpreted it as a meeting in the middle as philosophy moved toward a kind of monotheism, and it was thought that the only people who held on to the traditional Greco-Roman mythologies were those invested in government jobs and the less educated folks out in the countryside. In fact, the term *pagan* comes from the Latin *pagani*, meaning "country dwellers."

Although the Church was still technically illegal, in some areas local churches existed as "corporations," possibly even registered with the government as funerary societies.[1] In this way, the churches could own cemeteries and legally bury their dead. In this period, Christians also started to build the first church buildings.[2] What had begun as small groups meeting in people's homes had evolved into converted space, then dedicated space, and now structures built specifically for worship. In Rome, the earliest churches (the so-called *title churches*) were built on land donated by the owners of the original houses used for worship. In some cases, the remains of early Roman houses can be seen in the excavations under the present-day churches.[3] By the end of the third century, some cities in the empire even had a population with a Christian majority. Many non-Christian Romans had come to a kind of resigned comfort with the Christians, and the Christians for their part had let down their guard. They did not see the Great Persecution coming.[4]

THE GREAT PERSECUTION

The emperor Diocletian had come to the throne in 285 CE. Realizing that the empire was too large for one man to govern effectively, he created a *tetrarchy*, or a rule of four, in which the empire was divided in two (East and West) and each half had a senior ruler (called *Augustus*) and a second in command (called *Caesar*). In this way, Diocletian attempted to stabilize the borders on both sides of the empire, since each side would have its Augustus closer at hand. Diocletian retained for himself the highest authority, making himself the Augustus of the East. His second in command in the east was his son-in-law, Galerius. In the West, the Augustus was Maximian, and the Caesar was a general named Constantius (the father of Constantine).

Like Decius before him, Diocletian also tried to bring back the glory days of the empire's golden age through renewed enthusiasm for the old religion. By this time, however, the old religion was coming to be seen as outdated, even by some of the non-Christians who were more philosophically minded. But even more important was the fact that the Christians had become comfortable enough with their place in Roman society that they felt it was safe to openly criticize the emperor's policies. In fact, Diocletian would not have been the first emperor to have Christians in his own household, and it has been suggested that his wife and daughter (Galerius's wife) may have been Christians or at least sympathetic to the Church. They, too, may have been openly disdainful of the old religion. At this point it seems that Galerius, at the beginning of the fourth century, persuaded Diocletian to renew persecution against the Christians.

The so-called Great Persecution began as a test of loyalty in the legions. Some believed that the presence of Christians in the military would negatively affect the ability of the Roman augurs to read the signs that would enable them to predict the best days on which to engage the enemy. Based on prior precedents of pagan sacrifices used as tests of loyalty, it was actually the Romans who asserted that one could not serve both Christ and the emperor. Soldiers who were suspected of being Christians were demoted; some were confronted and eventually martyred.[5]

The first imperial edict of Diocletian against the Church was timed to be issued just before Easter of 303 CE.[6] More edicts came later in 303 and in 304. Christian worship was forbidden. Church buildings were ordered destroyed. Christian scriptures and other writings as well as liturgical items were to be surrendered to the authorities. All Christians were ordered to demonstrate their loyalty to the emperors and to the state by making a pagan sacrifice. Refusal to cooperate meant prison, torture, condemnation to the mines, or execution. The persecution was enforced more in the East, at least in part because Constantius was sympathetic to the Church and did not enforce the persecution in the areas under his control in the West.[7] Many Christian leaders were martyred, however. Others were imprisoned and tortured or condemned to slavery (if they were of the lower classes). The number of apostates was far fewer than in the Decian persecution, to the point where the prisons were filled to capacity.[8] Although in many ways the Church had let down its guard in the decades following the Decian persecution, the problem of the lapsed was still in its collective memory. Some Christians even committed suicide to avoid the possibility of torture and the temptation to make an idolatrous sacrifice.[9] Some were sent to meet the wild beasts in the arena.[10] If the Romans perceived that a whole town was Christian, the town was burned with the people in it.[11] Propaganda became a tool of persecution, as the Romans circulated documents such as the *Acts of Pilate*, an anti-Christian fictional account that made Pontius Pilate the hero of the story, which was made required reading in grammar schools.[12]

Interestingly, Eusebius of Caesarea, in his *Ecclesiastical History*, treats the Great Persecution as if it were divine discipline for moral laxity and internal disputes that arose during the time of relative peace.[13] In this he is following the lead of Old Testament writers who saw the exile into Babylon as God's punishment for idolatry. Just as the Babylonians were to the Jews, the Romans were seen by some Christians as both the instruments of God's chastisement and also the ungodly oppressors who would soon get what was coming to them. This is part of the message of the Book of Revelation.[14] In fact, the untimely death of Galerius would be seen as God's vindication.

Diocletian had retired in 305, leaving Galerius as the Augustus in the east. At the same time, Maximian was forced to step down, leaving Constantius as the Augustus in the West. Persecution continued primarily in the East, under Galerius. It must be kept in mind, however, that an emperor has only so much power to enforce (or prevent) persecution in all the places where the emperor cannot be personally present. In any case, Galerius, seen by the Church as the worst persecutor ever, became gravely ill. From his deathbed in 311 CE Galerius issued the *Edict of Toleration*, in which he admitted that the God of the Christians was indeed God, and promised to end the persecution if the Christians would pray for his recovery.[15] Permission was given to rebuild church buildings and for Christians to gather for worship. All Christian prisoners were to be released. Upon the death of Galerius, however (a horrible death, as some Christian writers were happy to describe), persecution continued under his successor. Christians were barred from visiting the cemeteries, and some were driven out of the cities where they made their homes.[16]

THE FIRST CHRISTIAN EMPEROR

When Constantius died, his son Constantine was proclaimed emperor by his loyal legions. Eusebius compared Constantine to King David, anointed though not yet crowned.[17] Rule over the western half of the empire would come down to civil war between Constantine and Maxentius, the son of Maximian. Their legions met at the river Tiber, on the northern boundary of the city of Rome, in 312 CE. At the time, the Milvian Bridge was just a series of boats joined together to facilitate crossing the river. While there

179

are several versions of the story, the basic tradition includes a dream or a vision in which Constantine saw a Christian symbol emblazoned on the sky. The symbol was probably the *labarum*, the monogram of Christ consisting of the Greek letter *chi* (which looks like an "X") superimposed by the Greek letter *rho* (which looks like a "P"). These are the first two letters in the Greek spelling of *Christos*, or Christ. Other (later) versions of the story say that Constantine saw a cross in the sky.[18] Upon seeing the symbol, Constantine heard the voice of God saying, *In hoc signo vinces* (In this sign you will conquer). Constantine ordered his men to put the sign on their standards, and he and his legions marched into battle under the banner of Christ.

Constantine defeated Maxentius at what would come to be called the Battle at the Milvian Bridge, October 28, 312 CE. Maxentius himself was drowned in the Tiber, and Eusebius would compare his demise to that of the Egyptians who had pursued Moses: "horse and rider thrown into the sea."[19] Constantine was received in Rome as a liberator, and the grateful Romans (who had hated Maxentius and saw him as a tyrant) erected a statue of Constantine, and eventually also a triumphal arch, which still stands near the Colosseum. The inscription on the inside of the arch is a dedication to Constantine that reads, *Liberator Urbis— Fundator Quietis* (Liberator of the City—Founder of Peace).[20]

In 313 CE, Constantine and his coregent Licinius issued the *Edict of Milan*, which legalized Christianity. Although it would only be enforced in the West at first, this is generally seen as the beginning of a Christian empire. It is important to note, however, that the Edict of Milan did not make Christianity the *only* legal religion of the empire. Officially, it simply was meant to end the persecution. In fact, the edict itself was really a letter to the senators granting freedom of worship to all religions.[21] In the edict, Constantine specified that Church property was to be returned at no cost to the Christians. Thus the Church would finally become a legal entity with the right to own property under its own name and receive inheritances. Imperial money was eventually used to build churches, and it is at this time that the typical Roman meeting hall or *basilica* was adapted for Christian use.[22] The edict also exempted clergy and their dependents from taxes and gave bishops the right to use the imperial transportation system. Constantine would also eventually end the use of crucifixion as a form of execution, make Sunday a day of rest from work, and further exempt Christian clergy from civic duties.[23] He began to use some Christian symbolism on his coins, but he did not discontinue the use of pagan symbols.[24]

When Constantine became emperor, he found that the Church was in some ways as divided as the empire. In the West, the Donatist controversy was threatening to split the Church, especially in North Africa. In 314 Constantine convened the Council of Arles, the first council of the Church convened by an emperor. At this council rebaptism was condemned, and therefore the Donatists were considered not only schismatics but also heretics.[25] The Council of Arles also gave Christian bishops the same authority as civil magistrates, so that they could decide disputes between Christians. Constantine himself came to treat bishops as imperial advisors, though he also expected them to return the favor and consult him on ecclesiastical matters.

Constantine would eventually go to battle against Licinius for the sole rule of the entire empire. He defeated Licinius in 324, claiming that God had ordained his rise to power. But as soon as he took power in the East, he realized he had an even bigger problem than the Donatist controversy. The Arian controversy had erupted, which would lead to him convening the first *ecumenical*, or worldwide, council: the Council of Nicaea in 325 CE. Constantine had hoped that the Church would help him unify the empire, but first he had to safeguard the unity of the Church.

Constantine would eventually move the imperial capital out of Rome. The senate was too powerful and too conservative (that is, pagan) for him to make any significant moves toward a Christian empire as long as they were supposed to be his advisors. According to the story, he was told by God in a dream to move his capital to Byzantium, which he renamed Constantinople, which means "Constantine's city." Also called *Nova Roma* (New Rome), the project was begun in 326 and the new Christian city was dedicated in 330. No paganism would be allowed in New Rome. Temples were torn down or converted into churches. New church buildings were built. Pagan statues were destroyed or altered to look like biblical characters or heroes of the faith.[26] One important factor in the move from Rome to Constantinople was that the absence of the emperor in Rome left a void that would eventually be filled by the bishop of Rome. This power vacuum would open the way for the bishop of Rome to become the most important and powerful man in the city of Rome, and would contribute to the evolution of the office of the papacy. Over the centuries, the bishop of Rome would take over some of the programs once run by the government, including feeding the poor and protecting the city from invaders. The people would come to trust in the bishop more than the government for their own security.

Before we move on to the Arian controversy, the question remains of Constantine's faith. Scholars and others have debated the issue, though it seems that for many people, their own agenda determines the outcome of their research. It must be pointed out that much of what is credited to (or blamed on) Constantine did not actually happen until the reign of emperor Theodosius I (379–95 CE). Constantine never ruled as a baptized Christian. Like many men of his time, he postponed baptism until the end of his life, in part so that he would not be held to the moral standards of the Church (and the limit of one postbaptismal sin). Constantine also did not make Christianity the only legal religion. Paganism was not outlawed until the time of Theodosius, when non-Christians were commanded to attend church.[27] Thus Constantine did not invent the connection of church and state. In fact, there had never been such a thing as a "separation of church and state." It had always been assumed that religion and government were interconnected, because religion was traditionally tied to one's nationality. In reality, of course, Constantine did favor Christianity and gave certain privileges to Christian clergy, and financially supported the Church. However all he was doing was changing which religion would be the one favored by the state, while ostensibly allowing freedom of worship for the other religions.

As to his own personal faith, the question usually boils down to whether he was a sincere believer or simply an opportunist who tried to use the Church to his own political advantage. It seems clear that Constantine's mother was a Christian, and his father was at least sympathetic to the Church. His father refused to persecute the Church wherever he ruled, and his mother is the one who would be known to the Church as Saint Helen. According to tradition, she made pilgrimages to the Holy Land as soon as such travel was safe after her son unified the empire. She is said to have found many artifacts and religious relics, some of which she brought back to Rome. She is also said to have found the actual cross of Jesus, as well as the site of his crucifixion and burial. In the end, we will never know whether Constantine grew up believing the faith of his mother, or whether he had a conversion experience on the eve of the Battle at the Milvian Bridge. Either way, however, it seems clear that he reigned as one who believed in Jesus Christ, who believed that the Father of Christ was the God responsible for his rise to power, and who feared that God could take the empire away from him at any time if he proved unworthy. Nevertheless, he ruled with an iron hand and did not hesitate to murder his political enemies, even when they were members of his own family. He looked to the Old Testament more than the New to guide him in running the empire, and he did not hesitate to use the Church to his advantage, especially in an attempt to keep the empire unified.[28]

THE ARIAN CONTROVERSY

Adoptionism came to its most developed form in the early fourth century (see Table 5, *Christology and Theology in the Fourth Century*). The Logos Christology of Theophilus of Antioch, with its lack of an eternally distinct existence of the Word, combined with the Christology of ascent found in the adoptionism of Paul of Samosata to create a Christology in which the Word was not eternal and Jesus was a mere man who earned an adopted divinity.[29] In large part, adoptionism is as much an anthropology as it is a Christology. As an anthropology, adoptionism begins with the optimistic assumption that human perfection is possible. Theophilus and some others of the Antiochene school of thought had rejected the idea of original sin, preferring instead to say that every human was born with a clean slate and with the potential to be perfectly holy. This is consistent with a Stoic understanding of virtue as moral progress. It is also consistent with the Antiochene exegetical methodology that was perceived as being more congruous with

Judaism, in which the essence of religion is following the law. Thus salvation was seen as the result of successfully striving for obedience to God. In other words, eternal life is the reward for an earthly life of righteousness.

In the development of doctrine as we see it in the early Church, Christology and soteriology are interrelated. In other words, the conclusions one reaches regarding Christ and his relationship to God will guide one's conclusions about salvation, or vice versa. With Arianism, it could be argued that an optimistic anthropology leads to a soteriology that emphasizes human effort, which in turn drives an adoptionist Christology.[30] Specifically, if salvation is a reward for obedience, then humans actually save themselves (or not) and the Savior is simply a pioneer, the first one to get it right, and the example to be followed. But Arianism goes beyond the third-century version of adoptionism by allowing a certain level of acquired divinity as part of the Son's reward. Thus Jesus was seen, not as God who became a man, but as a man who became a god, the first one to earn his elevation to a state of adopted divinity. This divinity is a lesser divinity than that of the Father, however, so the Father and Son are not united by consubstantiality but by will (obedience), and therefore the Son is ultimately a created being.[31] The Arians interpreted Colossians 1:15, "firstborn of creation," to mean that Christ was the first created being, created to be the agent of the rest of creation. For them, the fact that Christ was "begotten" (generated) meant that he was created. There was a beginning to his existence and there was a time before this, when he did not yet exist.

In contrast to this, most of the bishops of the Church seem to have assumed an anthropology that, though it did not deny free will, was sufficiently pessimistic to believe that no mere human could ever achieve a level of obedience that would allow him or her to "earn" salvation. Thus Christ as Savior must be far more than an example to follow, and salvation must be more than human effort; it must include divine intervention. Therefore, as we have seen, Catholic Christology was a Christology of descent, in which Christ is God who became human, not the other way around. These two opposite ways of viewing the intersection between anthropology, Christology and soteriology, came face to face in the city of Alexandria.

Arius and Alexander

Arius (ca. 250–336 CE) was a priest of Alexandria under the authority of the bishop there, Alexander of Alexandria. Bishop Alexander was teaching the doctrine of eternal generation as Novatian had understood it.[32] For Arius, however (who apparently would have been more comfortable in the Antiochene school of Theophilus and Paul of Samosata), concepts such as eternal generation and consubstantiality seemed to overemphasize the connection and equality of the Father and the Son. To him these doctrines seemed to be either a form of modalism or a form of ditheism that compromised monotheism by implying two Gods. He reasoned that such an equality of Father and Son would make them no longer Father and Son but "Brothers." Arius reacted by going to the opposite extreme and teaching a modified form of adoptionism. He emphasized the distinction between Father and Son to the point where the Son was not considered divine by nature, but was a created being who acquired divinity. "There was a time when he did not exist," became the shorthand summary of Arius's teaching.

Because of the Church's universal acceptance of John 1:1, Arius could not completely deny the preexistence of Christ, so he admitted that the Logos was preexistent, just not *eternally* preexistent. Following Paul of Samosata, he proposed that the Logos was not the preincarnate Jesus, but simply the personified wisdom of God, a created manifestation of God's mind extended for the purpose of creating the universe. Even the Logos was not eternal, however, but was created just before the rest of creation. Divine foreknowledge of Jesus' perfect obedience led God to prepare the Logos to unite with the human soul of Jesus at his baptism,[33] elevating the man Jesus to a level of quasi-divinity, higher than the rest of humanity but still lower than God.[34] Thus Jesus Christ was an adopted son of God, just as we might become adopted sons and daughters of God.[35] But he was not seen as the unique "natural" Son of God, united with the Father by a shared substance, as the mainstream bishops taught. For Arius, one might call Jesus the son of God after his baptism, but one should not call him the Son of God in an eternal or divine sense.[36] Both Arius and Alexander would agree that Christ was the mediator of God and humanity. For Arius, however, Christ was the mediator because he was *between* God and humanity, while for Alexander and the mainstream Church, Christ is the mediator because he is *both* divine and human.[37]

Arius and Alexander confronted each other in about the year 319. Arius accused his bishop of teaching modalism. Alexander, in turn, accused the priest of dishonoring Christ by demoting him from divine to created. At first the issue seemed to be concentrated on the title "Father" for God. Alexander argued that if there was a time when the Son did not exist, then there was a time when God was not a Father.[38] Paraphrasing Novatian, Alexander's counterslogan became, "Always a Father, always a Son."[39] The implication is that if God changes from not being a Father to being a Father, this would compromise the immutability of God. For Arius, on the other hand, God was only potentially a Father before the creation of the Son. While Arius was also concerned to preserve the immutability of the divine, he believed that the greater threat to divine immutability would be to ascribe a divine nature to one who was born as a baby, grew up and learned things, and eventually died. Thus Arius drew the line of createdness and mutability between the Father and the Son, whereas the Catholics drew that line between the divine and human natures of Christ.[40]

The main differences between Arius, representing the fourth-century version of adoptionism, and Alexander, representing what would be clarified as the orthodox point of view, can be expressed as follows. For Arius, Jesus as *only begotten* son of God means that he is God's favored and adopted son because of his perfect obedience, but ultimately he is created just like the rest of us. The connection between Father and Son is one of cooperating wills, and the distinction between Father and Son is a difference of substance, an ontological subordination in which any divinity that the son has is granted to him and is not his own. For Alexander and the mainstream bishops, on the other hand, Christ as *only begotten* means that he is uniquely and eternally generated.[41] As Novatian had taught, Christ's existence is dependent on the Father, but there was no time when the Son did not exist in reality as a distinct divine being. The Father and the Son are of the same divine substance, and the divinity of the Son is his own, not acquired or bestowed on him by adoption. He is the "natural" Son of God—the Son of God by nature—and

while we may become adopted sons and daughters of God by identification with the natural Son of God, Jesus Christ remains unique
among humanity. His connection with the Father is therefore an
ontological equality and not a connection by will only.

Both sides knew that the human will of Jesus was submissive
to the divine will (Luke 22:42). For the Arians, this submission of
will constituted the only real *unity* between the Father and the Son,
in that the human will of Jesus conformed to the will of God. But
the Christology that would win the day affirmed that this submission of will demonstrated the *distinction* between the Father and
Son, since it showed that the Father and Son are not one and the
same person, even though there is a unity of substance. Therefore,
to summarize, the Arian Christology is a Christology of ascent, in
which Jesus Christ is a man who becomes a god, setting an example of behavior, implying a salvation by will and works. Orthodox
Christology is a Christology of descent, in which Jesus Christ is the
divine Word who became human, who saves by divine intervention.

The Council of Nicaea

The Arian controversy was a source of scandal in the Church,
especially in the East. Both sides had their supporters, and with salvation itself on the line, there was a sense of urgency to come to
some conclusions about what the bishops would endorse. The
emperor Constantine knew that if he hoped to use the Church to
help him keep the empire united, he needed to make sure this issue
did not split the Church. He wrote letters to Arius and Alexander
asking them to reconcile and sort out their differences, but to no
avail, so he ordered all the bishops to attend a council in the city of
Nicaea, southeast of what would later become Constantinople.

The Council of Nicaea, in 325 CE, was the first *ecumenical*
(worldwide) council of the Church. It was attended by hundreds of
bishops from all over the empire (though mostly from the East) as
well as priests and laypeople. The question, as it was posed for
debate, was whether there was a time when the Son did not exist,
or whether he is coeternal with the Father. In other words, was the
Son created, or was he eternally generated? Arius, and those like
him, rejected the concept of eternal generation in favor of saying

what Origen had said, that the Son was the product of the Father's will, not his essence.[42] The majority of bishops believed that the unity of Father and Son went deeper than only a union of will. When it came time to write a statement of faith that would express the belief of the majority, however, the task proved difficult. The council itself had brought to light the existence of a variety of points of view, so that it was not a simple matter of two sides, one Arian and the other Catholic, one heretical and the other orthodox. It is not within the scope of this present book to outline the different factions in detail, but it is important to note that all of them claimed to be able to support their arguments with scripture in one way or another. Thus the task of writing a creed that could be taken by each bishop back to his home area, and that would not only teach the orthodox position but exclude the heretical, turned out to be more than most had bargained for.

The bishops who promoted what would become the orthodox position believed that if they could find a way to describe Christ that would highlight his uniqueness, then Arianism (in all its variations) would be refuted. Whenever biblical language was suggested, however, the Arians found it acceptable, implying that they could interpret it in such a way as to be consistent with their own Christology. Ultimately, it became clear that the creed had to include the doctrine of consubstantiality of the Father and Son. This was finally expressed with the Greek term, *homoousios*, meaning "of the same essence." In other words, the Son is of the same essence (or substance) as the Father. The Arians, of course, could not endorse this term, but the greater problem was that many of the other bishops were also reluctant to endorse it, since it is not found in scripture. For the first time, scripture could not interpret itself. Scripture alone was not enough (*sola scriptura non satis est*), and the bishops had to look outside of scripture to find a term that would interpret scripture in such a way as to provide the orthodox interpretation and rule out the heretical one. Of course, the designation of orthodoxy and heresy as applied to one side of the debate or the other could only be determined at the outcome of the council, but in the end, the word *homoousios* and the doctrine of consubstantiality were determined to be the most consistent with both scripture and tradition (prior orthodoxy). The creed was accepted

188

(though reluctantly by some) and anyone who refused to sign it was excommunicated.

To those who would not sign the creed, the term *homoousios* sounded like modalism, or worse, it sounded gnostic. The fact that the word is not found in scripture did not make bringing the creed home any easier, so many of the bishops who signed it would never use it. In fact, it was not required that every church use the creed. The creed was meant to be a standard by which other creeds would be measured; thus, as long as a bishop could say that the creed used in his area was in agreement with the creed of Nicaea, that was enough. Eventually the creed would also become a tool of catechesis to teach new converts the correct understanding of the person of Christ. By the late fourth century it would become a litmus test for orthodoxy. At the Second Ecumenical Council of Constantinople in 381 CE, the creed was expanded to incorporate the outcome of the debate over the divinity of the Holy Spirit, and the statement of faith that we now know as the "Nicene Creed" was complete.[43] Nicene orthodoxy insisted on a balance of unity and distinction in the relationship of the Father and Son (they are consubstantial, yet not identical) over against the adoptionist emphasis on the ontological difference between Father and Son. To be fair, Arianism also has both unity and distinction in the relationship of Father and Son, but the unity is one of cooperation only, and the distinction is specifically in the assertion that the Father and Son are not consubstantial.

The Arian controversy was not the only topic of discussion at the Council of Nicaea. Among other items on the agenda was the definition of metropolitans, in which Rome was confirmed as primary. It is significant that an Eastern council would acknowledge the authority of the bishop of Rome, not only over other bishops in the surrounding areas, but also over the other metropolitans. Also, the correct calculation for the date of Easter was discussed, and it was decided that all churches must conform to the calculation used in Rome. Although the ruling was not universally accepted or followed, this once again demonstrates that at least in theory the church of Rome held a certain primacy.

Athanasius of Alexandria and Nicene Orthodoxy

After the Council of Nicaea, the Arians and various "semi-Arian" factions did not entirely go away. Throughout the 330s and 340s numerous smaller councils were held, alternately dominated by one party or the other, each one excommunicating its opponents. Sometimes violence broke out, especially in Alexandria. Athanasius (bishop from 328 to 373 CE), who had attended the Council of Nicaea as Alexander's assistant, succeeded him as bishop of Alexandria. Athanasius then became the primary spokesman for Nicene orthodoxy, championing eternal generation and writing such documents as *On the Incarnation of the Word*, *Defense of the Nicene Definition*, and *Against the Arians*.[44] When Athanasius became bishop of Alexandria, Arius himself was bold enough to complain to Constantine, which resulted in an edict of 333 CE that ordered all of Arius's writings to be burned. Consequently, apart from a couple of letters, Arius's writings no longer exist except in fragments quoted by Athanasius and other opponents of Arianism.[45]

Some of the Arian bishops had signed the creed to keep themselves out of trouble, knowing that they could go back to their home areas and ignore it. Others refused to sign the creed. Nevertheless, Arian bishops would be alternately in and out of the good graces of Constantine and his sons over the next few decades. The Arian bishop Eusebius of Nicomedia would even be invited to become the bishop of Constantinople, in direct violation of one of the canons of the Council of Nicaea, which stated that bishops may not move from one see to another. In fact, it would be Eusebius of Nicomedia who would baptize the emperor Constantine at the end of his life. When the Arian bishops were able to gain power, they concentrated their efforts on getting Athanasius removed from his see at Alexandria. In all, he was exiled and reinstated five times. During times of exile, he was protected by the bishop of Rome, who sided with the Nicene bishops against the Arians and semi-Arians. Arius himself was recalled from exile and invited to be reconciled with the Church, but according to tradition, he died the night before he would have received communion. This story is probably unreliable, but it shows how the opponents of Arius saw him as the archheretic whom God would rather kill than reconcile.

It was not until after the Council of Constantinople in 381 CE, when the Greek language used to describe the Trinity could be clarified and enough of the semi-Arians would come over to the Nicene side, that the Arian controversy would subside in the East. It would continue in the West into the fifth century, however, due to the missionizing efforts of the Arian bishops.

UNITY THROUGH STANDARDIZATION

In addition to legalizing Christianity, Constantine had also reunited the two halves of the empire, a move that facilitated greater communication among bishops. He also built basilica churches, some of which would become the city *cathedrals* or the seats of the bishops (from *cathedra*, meaning "throne"). Thus the stage was set for a new attention to standardization within the Church. Whereas the Church had formerly tolerated a greater amount of liturgical and disciplinary diversity, now the Church had the ability to work toward a unity through standardization of practice. In addition, the ease of travel and communication highlighted differences from one city to another, which could sometimes be an embarrassment.[46]

We have several church-order documents, some of which go back to the third century in their original form, that outline church practice and liturgy. When reading these documents, the student of early Christianity should take them as the product of particular communities, and while the leaders of these communities (the writers of the documents) would certainly like to think that all Christians should follow their lead and do as they do, the fact that this was not happening is proven by the very existence of the document. If everyone was practicing their Christian faith the same way across the empire, these documents would not have been necessary. Therefore, we cannot assume that any of the standards proposed by these documents were universally accepted. In addition, these documents were continually updated, so that in their present form they represent an amalgam of material from the third and fourth centuries.

The *Apostolic Tradition*

Traditionally attributed to Hippolytus, this document may in fact have originated in the third century. In its present form, however, it certainly contains layers of later material.[47] It contains instructions for liturgy and ordination, including descriptions of the various church offices, as well as references to an early form of the Liturgy of the Hours and making the Sign of the Cross.[48]

This community expected that new converts would go through a three-year period of catechesis, which included regular exorcisms.[49] The teachers might be clergy, but they could also be laypeople.[50] At the end of the catechumenate, sponsors attested to the candidate's sincerity and morality, at which time the candidate was baptized, a ceremony that also included an exorcism performed by the bishop.[51] An interrogative version of the creed was used as a statement of faith, in which the candidates would respond in the affirmative to the questions, "Do you believe...?"[52] The baptism was sealed with the Sign of the Cross on the forehead, ears, and nose.[53] The children of Christian parents were also baptized, including infants.[54] If a catechumen was martyred before being baptized, the martyrdom would count as a baptism in his or her own blood (cf. Luke 12:50).[55] Just as the "good thief" might hope to be with Jesus in paradise, the sincere believer who died without the chance of baptism was not without that same hope.[56]

A newly baptized Christian's first Eucharist included milk and honey, to symbolize the hope of eternal paradise.[57] The *Apostolic Tradition* contains an early version of a eucharistic prayer, but it also says that the prayers were not static and could be embellished ad lib by the presider, as long as the theology contained in the prayers was orthodox.[58] Members of the community were expected to fast before receiving the Eucharist.[59] In the assembly, men and women were separated and were discouraged from greeting each other with a kiss.[60] The reverence with which the eucharistic elements were handled is consistent with early eucharistic theology that assumed a miraculous transformation had taken place, analogous to the incarnation itself.[61]

With regard to ordination, it is stated that a (male) confessor does not need to be ordained (by the imposition of hands), but can be considered a priest because of the presence of the Holy Spirit.[62] This is an interesting concession to charismatic authority. It has echoes of Cyprian's dilemma of wanting to control the confessors without offending the people who saw them as prophets. The *Apostolic Tradition* also clarified that although a deacon is ordained, he is not counted as a member of the council of priests, and he is not to preside over the sacraments, though deacons did help to distribute the elements.[63] Thus the deacons fall into an in-between area, considered ordained but not authorized to preside over the sacraments. The *Apostolic Tradition* mentions the lay offices of subdeacon, reader, healer, and virgin.[64] What may be one of the earlier layers of tradition is the reference to the consecration of bishops, who are said to be "chosen by all the people."[65] This may refer to a time when laypeople participated in the selection of a bishop, though it may also only mean that the people acknowledged their assent when the new bishop's name was announced in the consecration liturgy.[66]

The *Didascalia Apostolorum*

The *Didascalia Apostolorum*, sometimes called the *Catholic Didascalia*, is written as advice for bishops, claiming to come directly from the twelve apostles, who had gathered in Jerusalem to write it.[67] It mentions Peter and Matthew by name, as if to invoke their authority against heresy.[68] Heresy is defined as blasphemy of the Holy Spirit, because of its inherent rejection of scripture.[69] Specific heresies mentioned are beliefs of the Ebionites, those who reject marriage (possibly Encratites or other ascetic Gnostics), and vegetarians.[70]

There is also a strong antirigorist argument in the *Didascalia*. Bishops are instructed to accept all who repent by showing them mercy.[71] The bishop is described as the physician of the church, so for the bishops to withhold reconciliation would be like a doctor withholding medicine from the sick. To forgive is to follow the example of Christ, but to fail to reconcile a sinner is to commit spiritual murder.[72] Repentant sinners should not be shunned, since that might cause them to give up hope. Rather, they should be sought out like the shepherd who leaves the flock of ninety-nine and goes after the one lost sheep.[73] Even the sin of idolatry can be forgiven, because God wants all to be saved, and God has given the keys of reconciliation to the bishops.[74] To be excommunicated is to be cast out of the kingdom of God; therefore it is to be avoided since if anyone should die in a state of excommunication that person was believed to be damned.[75] Although this document does not specifically say so, it would be assumed that one who died in a state of excommunication could not be buried with the Christian community. The only time a person should be excommunicated is when he or she is unrepentant, or if the sin is repeated after reconciliation.[76]

Of course, heretics and schismatics cannot be reconciled as long as they remain unrepentant, since they effectively excommunicate themselves by separating from the Catholic bishops.[77] In what appears to be a remark directed at Novatian, the document specifically mentions "puritans and sticklers for holiness" who "covet the primacy and dare to make a schism."[78] In fact, anyone who so much as prays with the excommunicated is thereby excommunicated.[79] If heretics or schismatics come back to the Church, however, they are not to be rebaptized, but are only to be reconciled with the imposition of hands.[80] Their prior baptism is considered valid because one baptism is enough, and to be rebaptized would "undo" the baptism.[81] Penance is described in terms of fasting, the *weeper* stage lasting anywhere from two to seven weeks.[82] An interesting connection is also made between fasting and almsgiving, with the recommendation that one might fast and give the money one would have spent on food to the poor.[83] Reconciliation was done by the bishops, who would lay their hands on the penitent sinner, a gesture understood as restoring the Holy Spirit to the person.[84]

In what appears to be an earlier layer of tradition, there is no allowance made for postbaptismal sin.[85] This point seems to contradict the antirigorist argument, since all postbaptismal sin is described as "deadly sin," assuming salvation is thereby lost.[86] To keep oneself holy by refraining from sin was to keep the seal of baptism unbroken.[87] Even so, all sins are cancelled by martyrdom.[88] Thus we seem to have evidence of an early stage in the development of this document, when it was still believed that one could successfully refrain from postbaptismal sin, and a later stage of development from after the controversy over the lapsed, when the goal is reconciliation and rigorism is denounced.

Unlike the community that produced the *Apostolic Tradition*, this community did not have lay teachers; only the clergy were allowed to teach. Laypeople were only allowed to speak "in refutation of idols and concerning the unity of God."[89] Of course, whenever we read of such prohibitions we must always recognize the possibility that laypeople were actually teaching, and that the author(s) of the document wanted that practice to change.

Baptisms could be delegated to priests or even to deacons and deaconesses, but the "seal," or postbaptismal anointing (confirmation), must be performed by a bishop or priest.[90] Once baptized, the believer is encouraged to attend worship regularly, and the author criticizes those who are too busy with the affairs of the world, or who cannot wait to leave the assembly and go to the theater.[91] Men and women sit separately, as in the *Apostolic Tradition*; however, the *Didascalia* further specifies that worshipers face toward the east for prayer.[92] The Eucharist is described as a sacrifice that replaces the sacrifices of the Old Testament, just as baptism replaced circumcision.[93] In addition to the regular church meetings, the Eucharist was also being celebrated in the cemeteries, including Masses for the dead.[94] This refers to more than simply funeral services; it includes celebrations on the anniversaries of the deaths of the martyrs and other beloved dead.[95] This was possible because of the belief that the dead in Christ are not really dead, but live in the presence of God.

The role of the deacon is described in some detail in the *Didascalia*. In this community, the deacons also function as the ushers, or doorkeepers. This means that it is their job to make sure that the people sit in their proper places, according to age or rank of office.[96] They are even charged with questioning visitors to make sure that no one receives the Eucharist unless he or she is a baptized member in good standing with their home church. The deacons also visit the sick, the needy, and the confessors in prison.[97] If possible, they should bribe the guards to gain better treatment of Christian prisoners, and they can use church money to buy the release of slaves.[98] The deacons provide the line of communication between the laypeople and the bishop, keeping the bishop informed of the needs of the people, but also apparently limiting access to the bishop to prevent the office from becoming too focused on administration.[99] Therefore, the number of deacons in a city church should be proportionate to the number of people.[100]

The *Didascalia* specifies that a bishop should be at least fifty years old if possible, and it is desirable (though not required) that he be able to read.[101] A bishop may be married, as long as his wife is a believer.[102] It is expected that a bishop draw a salary from the offerings of the church, but he must share the offerings with the widows, orphans, and any others who need support.[103] The faithful are instructed to give their alms to the bishop, rather than directly to the needy. The bishop will decide who is most in need and will dispense the alms accordingly.[104] In actual practice, the deacons would have distributed the alms, but the bishops retained the authority to determine who would receive support and how much.[105] Finally, the bishop is charged with appointing the other clergy.[106] We can see that by the time this part of the *Didascalia* was written, the selection of church leadership was completely out of the hands of the laity, and even the priests had little or nothing to contribute to the selection of their colleagues. Each bishop chose the priests who would serve under his authority, and together the bishops of a region would select those priests who would be elevated to their level. The *Didascalia* justifies the authority of the monoepiscopacy by saying that in a church the bishop is the head, and the laity are the tail. The tail must obey the head.[107]

The *Apostolic Church Order*

This document is very much like the other two, even combining elements from them with the Didache, except that it is written more like a dialogue, as if the apostles are speaking and their actual words were recorded. It claims to be from the apostles through Clement of Rome, though it is clearly much later. In the list of apostles, it even confuses the two names for Peter (*Peter* from Greek; *Cephas* from Aramaic) and treats the two names as if they refer to two different apostles. The document may contain antignostic elements, since the dialogue style seems similar to some gnostic texts, and it criticizes the practice of women's participation in presiding over the sacraments.[108]

In this document we learn that the office of reader is considered the evangelist of the church.[109] Deacons are not allowed a second marriage.[110] Celibacy is advocated for priests.[111] Bishops might be married, though celibacy is advised as the better path. If a bishop is married, however, he may not be married a second time.[112] As in the *Didascalia*, it is advisable that a bishop should be literate, but even if he is not, he is the ultimate authority over the teaching and discipline of the church.[113]

The *Apostolic Constitutions*

This late fourth-century text rounds out our examination of the church-order documents and the attempts at standardization in the post-Constantinian Church. More than any of the others, it is a compilation of layers of material from different time periods, including portions from the earlier church-order documents. It contains the standard advice that bishops ought to be married only once and be at least fifty years old (though if no one of age can be found suitable, a younger man might be chosen).[114] An important characteristic for a bishop is the ability to read the Old Testament and discern which laws apply to the Church and which do not.[115] The document assumes that bishops have the authority to judge civil cases, and it is implied that bishops have authority even over the aristocracy in their area.[116] As the teaching authority in the Church, the bishop is described as a mediator between God and the faithful (in the context of worship), and as a father to the faithful he is to be honored as God's representative on earth.[117]

The leaders of the Church are compared to the Trinity, though surprisingly, the Father, Son, and Holy Spirit are compared to the bishop, deacon, and deaconess respectively, with the priests compared to the apostles. Ordained bishops, priests, and deacons are expected to remain celibate if they were single when ordained. They may be ordained if married, but only once, and they may not remarry, even if widowed.[118] Here the deaconesses function as liaisons between the clergy and the women of the congregation.[119] Deaconesses are expected to be virgins or widows.[120] The council of priests is compared to the Sanhedrin and the senate, and a relative scheme of payment of officers is outlined, with twice as much going to the priests and deacons as to the widows, readers, cantors, and ushers.[121] Priests and deacons may be ordained by one bishop, but a new bishop must be consecrated by at least two other bishops.[122]

The document includes an interesting description of worship in a Constantinian basilica, in this case the cathedral. The bishop is seated on a throne in the middle of the eastern end, with multiple priests on either side. The deacons stand by, ready to assist in the Eucharist. The laity sit opposite them, men separated from women and children, with the widows and virgins in front. After readings from the Old Testament, a cantor sings one or more psalms, and the people sing a refrain. Then the Book of Acts and/or Pauline epistles are read, after which all the people stand while the gospel is read by a priest or deacon. After the gospel reading there were apparently multiple short homilies by all the priests in attendance and then finally by the bishop. The catechumens and penitents are then excused and the deacons prepare the Eucharist. The faithful exchange the kiss of peace, but only men with men and women with women. Then a deacon leads intercessory prayer, after which the bishop begins the eucharistic prayer. Finally, the elements of the Eucharist are shared while the ushers watch the door so that no one who is an unbeliever, or uninitiated, can come in.[123] Also provided are instructions for an all-night Easter vigil, with the baptism of the catechumens at dawn.[124]

The *Apostolic Constitutions* also contains familiar antirigorist arguments, including the mention of both Peter and Paul as having been forgiven by God for denial and persecution of the faith respectively.[125] In this case, however, excommunication seems to be more of a tool of discipline than a last resort.[126] Rebaptism is condemned as an attempt to crucify the Lord a second time.[127] Infant baptism is encouraged, based on the words of Jesus in Matthew 19:14, "Let the little children come to me, and do not stop them."[128]

In this community believers were expected to pray the Lord's Prayer three times a day and to give one-tenth of their net income to the widows, the poor, and the strangers.[129] Also included are recommended prayers for morning, evening, and mealtime.[130] It is clear that by this time the Church enjoys legal status, and there even appears to be a sense that the Church is starting to experience the phenomenon of nominal Christianity, people joining the Church for reasons other than a faith commitment. This might explain the high expectations for the faithful, even to the point of being unrealistic. In fact, we noted that in the early centuries of the Church, catechism emphasized morality over theology. In the post-Constantinian Church, however, the emphasis shifts to include teaching orthodox theology as preparation (and prerequisite) for baptism.[131]

Finally, it is interesting to note that in the *Apostolic Constitutions*, we have come to the point where *the church* refers to a building.[132]

CHAPTER 9

Ongoing Themes

The early fourth century, with the first Christian emperor and the first ecumenical council, marks a turning point in the history of Christianity. Afterward, the sheer volume of Christian texts makes it impossible to examine them all at the level of detail with which we have looked at the documents of the second and third centuries. When we come to writers such as Augustine of Hippo, for example, the massive volume of their work prevents us from considering their thought as a unit and requires us to talk about the progression of thought throughout their careers. However, certain themes to which we have already been introduced continue the trends begun in the pre-Nicene era and can be traced as we look ahead to the later fathers and doctors of the Church.

While there is an admitted risk of oversimplification as we consider these themes from a bird's-eye view, the present chapter is meant to set the stage for further reading in depth. The following themes continue to be relevant, not only in the medieval Church but into the Renaissance and modern Church as well.

ANTHROPOLOGY

The question of anthropology that was raised by the Arian controversy continued in the Pelagian controversy. In some ways, the issues raised by Pelagius were similar to those raised by Arius. And while Arius had his major opponent in the East, in the person of Athanasius, Pelagius's main opponent was in the West: Augustine, bishop of Hippo Regius in North Africa.

Augustine of Hippo

Aurelius Augustinus (354–430 CE) was born in Thagaste, North Africa (modern Souk Ahras, Algeria), the child of a mixed marriage, a pagan father and a Christian mother. While his parents did not agree on religion, they did agree to give their son the best education possible. He passed through all the ranks of education that North Africa had to offer, eventually going to Carthage and then leaving for Rome to become a professor of rhetoric. He had rejected his mother's Christianity because he thought that the Latin translation of the Bible in use in North Africa was crude; thus he equated a perceived lack of dignity in the writing style with a lack of truth in the content.

Looking for answers elsewhere, Augustine joined the Manichees, a fourth-century version of gnosticism that was in a way the ancient world's equivalent to the Masonic lodge.[1] Manichaeism was an outlawed secret society that claimed to be able to provide the answers to all the questions of the universe. Augustine had hoped to find something to believe in, but he was disappointed when the answers that the Manichees provided turned out to be unsatisfying.[2] The experience taught Augustine that he was approaching the prospect of faith backwards, looking for answers that would then give him something to believe in. After his disappointment with the Manichees, however, he came to conclude that it is not knowledge that leads to faith, but faith that leads to knowledge. In other words, first one has to make a commitment to believe by faith, then one can learn about one's faith. "We believe in order that we may know, we do not know in order that we may believe."[3] This is summarized in the well-known phrase *Credo ut intelligam* ("I believe so that I may understand").

When Augustine left North Africa for Rome, his mother, Monica, followed him. She would also follow him when he left Rome and went to Milan. She is known to the Church as St. Monica, and she has become the patron saint of mothers who pray for the conversion of their sons. In addition, she has a presence in Augustine's autobiography that is a kind of personification of God's grace, which Augustine came to believe was relentless in its pursuit of a person, irresistible and ultimately never thwarted. Augustine was eventually converted to Christianity, in the year 386 CE. His bishop and mentor was the anti-Arian Ambrose of Milan, who would be a significant influence on Augustine's theology, and subsequently Augustine would become the most influential pro-Nicene author in the West. Therefore, when we read Augustine, we must always keep in mind that he wrote to reinforce pro-Nicene orthodoxy, including the consubstantiality, coeternality, and equality of the Son with the Father.

After his conversion, Augustine decided to return to North Africa and form a religious community. Monica died on the way, in the port city of Ostia, happy that she had lived to see her son come to the faith.[4] Upon returning to North Africa, Augustine settled in Hippo Regius (modern Annaba, Algeria), where he was ordained a priest. According to the story, Augustine was ordained against his will. He would have preferred a life of monastic solitude; however, that was not to be. He became the right-hand man to the bishop and eventually succeeded him as bishop of Hippo.

Augustine's most important anti-Arian writing is *On the Trinity*, in which he expands upon the thought of Tertullian and Novatian, emphasizing the equality of the Father and Son against Arianism. Although the creed of Nicaea had only said that the Holy Spirit proceeded from the Father, Augustine proposed that the Holy Spirit proceeded from the Father *and the Son* (in Latin, "and the Son" is one word, *filioque*).[5] This would eventually make its way into the creed in the West and cause friction between East and West; however, the point at this time was to refute Arianism by demonstrating the equal divinity of the Son, emphasizing that he is equally the giver of the Holy Spirit along with the Father. Thus Augustine did for the West what Athanasius had done for the East.

Augustine wrote his autobiography, the *Confessions*, around the turn of the fifth century. The publication of this work was significant since the ancient biography and autobiography were genres of literature in which glorifying the subject was more important than reporting the truth. Thus the fact that Augustine did not refrain from telling his readers of the embarrassing details and the regrets of his life made it both revolutionary and very popular. As Augustine looked back on his life, experiences of peer pressure and (in his own assessment) an inability to control his sexual desire led him to conclude that human perfection was not possible. Ironically, he was critical of himself for his shortcomings and at the same time confident enough to assume that if he couldn't do it right, no one could. Human habits and desires, as well as social pressure, were just too strong to expect that anyone could successfully obey God. If salvation depended on self-control, there was no hope for anyone.

Keeping in mind that his mentor Ambrose was anti-Arian, it could be argued that Augustine's own experience drove him to the extreme opposite of an Arian optimism, leaving him with a pessimism about human nature that could only see it as totally depraved. His disillusionment with Manichaean philosophy only reinforced this pessimistic anthropology, driving him to depart from the classical understanding of virtue as perfectibility. Thus the less he trusted human nature, the more he put all the responsibility for salvation on God's grace, which he came to believe was irresistible. Even when it came to living up to the moral expectations of God, Augustine concluded that if God did not grant the ability to resist temptation, sin was inevitable.

For Augustine, to be happy (or blessed) required confidence in one's eternal destiny. In other words, if our salvation were up to us, we would lose it. The possibility of the loss of salvation would create an uncertainty that would make happiness impossible. This represents a major shift from earlier writers who assumed that salvation could be lost through repeated disobedience. But Augustine reasoned that such a belief would lead to uncertainty and fear. The only alternative to living with this fear was to put all of one's trust in God, as opposed to one's own efforts.

If happiness means having what you desire, then to desire anything other than God would make happiness illusive, since anything other than God can be lost. To desire anything other than God would be to live with the fear of losing (or never acquiring) what we desire. Therefore, the only object of desire (love) that could lead to happiness is God. But Augustine despaired that we cannot keep our love oriented toward God. He reasoned that the only way happiness is possible is if it is God who chooses us, since if it were up to us to choose God, we would ultimately fail. Therefore, Augustine made salvation entirely the work of God's choosing, or *election*, placing the emphasis on divine intervention over human effort.

Pelagius

Pelagius was a British monk who had come to Rome, where he read some of Augustine's writings. He balked at what he perceived as an anthropology that exempted humans from moral responsibility. He reasoned that if the human will is ultimately incapable of obeying God, then how could God blame us when we don't obey? In fact, it would seem that sin itself is really to be blamed on God, since apparently God did not give us the ability to resist it. Before the controversy with Pelagius, the Church fathers seemed to be content with the paradox of some form of original sin (based on Romans 5) with a real human free will.[6] Now Augustine seemed to be taking original sin to an extreme, and so Pelagius reacted by going to the other extreme. He rejected the concept of original sin completely, emphasizing free will to the extent that he seemed to be saying that humans could be good without God's help at all. Whereas Augustine had emphasized the role of God's grace (divine intervention, understood as election) almost to the exclusion of the role of the human will, Pelagius emphasized the role of the will (human effort) and seemed to be diminishing the importance of God's grace.

Although Pelagius was not an Arian, he promoted an optimistic anthropology that was consistent with Arius.[7] After all, he was a monk, and if humans could not obey God through personal discipline and resisting temptation, then what would be the point of the monastic life? If Augustine was right, he reasoned, why even try to be good? One could justify sin simply by pointing out that God had obviously not granted the ability to avoid it. For Pelagius, not only is perfection possible, but it is expected of every believer.

Pelagius was eventually accused of heresy. Specifically, he was charged with having taught that a person does not need God's grace. When confronted at a synod in the East, he was at first able to talk his way out of the accusation by affirming that people do need God's grace. But Augustine knew that he was only able to say this because he was working with a different definition of grace.

Pelagius's definition of grace would be very much like Arius's definition. Grace is the example of Christ, along with his teachings as recorded in the gospels. In other words, Jesus' summary of the Ten Commandments, along with the Beatitudes, constituted everything a Christian needed to be good and obey God. Grace is a gift of God in that it is the example to follow in order to be saved. Ultimately, though, this reduces grace to information. It is external to the human being, and it is *passive*.

For Augustine, grace is *active*; it is a force, one that acts on the human person from the outside but also from the inside. It is the very activity of God, pursuing the believer (as Monica followed Augustine) and giving him or her the power necessary to follow Christ. Without that power, we cannot resist the temptation to satisfy our selfish desires. Sin is a disease that infects the whole human race, and grace is the medicine that will heal our human nature. Although at times (especially toward the beginning of his career) Augustine affirmed the reality of free will, eventually he was pushed by the debate to say that on its own the human will is only free to sin.[8] God's grace frees the human will to do the will of God.[9]

Augustine responded to the challenges of Pelagius with many documents, now considered together as his anti-Pelagian writings. The same skepticism about human nature that made him an anti-Arian also makes him an anti-Pelagian. In *On the Spirit and the Letter*, Augustine makes the connection between Pelagius and Paul's Judaizers, who were in a way the first Adoptionists and precursors to Arius.[10] Augustine says that we have free will only in the sense that we can will (that is, *want*) to do what is right, but we are not actually able to do it without God's help.[11] The only thing one can do by free will is accept God's grace, but even that is really a work of God.[12] For Augustine, humans may have the will to do the right thing, but they do not have the ability. For Pelagius, humans have the ability, though they may not have the will to do the right thing, and may choose to do what is wrong (possibly based on a misunderstanding about what is right).

Other important anti-Pelagian documents include *On Nature and Grace*, *On the Proceedings of Pelagius*, and the *Enchiridion (Handbook) on Faith, Hope, and Love*. The Pelagians had challenged Augustine with the question, If the responsibility for salvation is ultimately on God, and if grace is irresistible, then why are not all people saved? It is clearly God's will that all should be saved (1 Tim 2:4). Augustine's response was his doctrine of election, which emphasized God's choice of who will be saved and who will be damned. Sometimes characterized as a "double predestination," it is an unconditional election whereby God has decided the eternal fate of every human being, before they were born and without the consideration of merit or even faith. Whether someone perseveres in faith is entirely a work of God based on divine election, so that if someone who professes faith should not be saved in the end, that would only mean that the person in question was never really among the elect. This implies that the atonement of Christ must be limited to the elect, or else the cross would be ineffective for some. Against the charge that the predestination of some to damnation seems cruel and unfair, Augustine would reply that all deserve that fate, and the fact that some are elect and predestined to salvation is evidence of God's mercy (cf. Matt 20:1–16).

Pelagius's criticism of Augustine was essentially a criticism of his anthropology. Pelagius understood that Augustine was saying that the sin of Adam (the Fall) had changed human nature, and that it was in a sense broken and in need of repair. But Pelagius argued that human nature was not broken, and it does not need grace to "fix" it. It is possible to avoid sin because the Fall did not damage our human nature. For Pelagius, grace helps those who help themselves. For Augustine, grace helps those who cannot help themselves.

Pelagius was finally condemned as a heretic and excommunicated, though Pelagianism continued as a rigorist faction, not surprisingly gaining the most acceptance in areas that had been open to Arianism. It would take a century before the Church would sort out the teachings of Augustine. At the Council of Orange in 529 CE (ninety-nine years after Augustine's death), the Church chose the middle way and adopted a "semi-Augustinian" approach to anthropology and soteriology. The council accepted Augustine's understanding of original sin but rejected his understanding of election as a form of double predestination that implied a limited atonement. The council accepted the Augustinian definition of grace but allowed that the human will is free to cooperate with grace, as long as it is clear that God's grace takes the initiative in inviting the human will to respond, and the human will could not act without that first invitation of grace.

Although not all aspects of Augustine's teachings were ultimately accepted by the Catholic Church, his thought would influence the Western world toward a skepticism about human nature that led to a spirituality of total dependence on God. By the end of his life he had moved away from the classical optimism that assumed the head could rule the heart. He came to believe that reason could not control the passions, and that the will is not free because it is not free of the strong powers of emotion, desire, habit, and social pressure. The only thing that could subdue these powers was the power of grace. The virtues of the classical world, based on the Stoic notion of moral progress, were gone and were replaced by submission to God's will as the one virtue that mattered. One could argue that Augustine marks the end of the classical world in the West.[13] He certainly contributed to the fifth-century changes that led to the beginning of what are often called the "Dark Ages."[14] In terms of anthropology, Augustine's debate with Pelagius set the stage for the question of original sin, free will, and predestination to be addressed again and again by Thomas Aquinas, Martin Luther, Erasmus, John Calvin, Jacob Arminius, John Wesley, and others.

ECCLESIOLOGY

Just as was the case with anthropology, the ongoing theme of ecclesiology finds Augustine of Hippo at the center of the controversy. In this case, however, his opponents were the Donatists. The Donatists were a rigorist faction in North Africa who held to the North African view of the sacraments (the faith of the presider matters, and a lack of faith can invalidate the sacrament). They claimed Cyprian of Carthage as their spiritual father, since they practiced rebaptism. When Augustine became bishop of Hippo Regius, he was not the only bishop in the city; the Donatists had their own bishop and they were to become a thorn in Augustine's side.

Donatism

Just as the persecution in the third century had led to the emergence of rigorist factions and rebaptizing bishops, the Great Persecution at the beginning of the fourth century brought all of that back to North Africa. In 311 CE, a new bishop of Carthage named Caecilian was elected. After the election it was discovered that he had been consecrated by another bishop named Felix, who had lapsed in the persecution. Felix was not an apostate but was accused of being a *traitor* because he had turned over some church property to the authorities. A rigorist faction rose up and opposed Caecilian on the grounds that his consecration as bishop was invalid. This faction feared, of course, that any sacraments over which he presided would also be invalid.

Although ordination (and consecration) was not technically considered a sacrament yet, the rigorists applied a North African understanding of baptism to the consecration of a bishop, which was understood as a conferral of the Holy Spirit and, with it, the authority of the Church. In other words, a lapsed bishop has forfeited the authority and expelled the Holy Spirit from himself, so therefore he could not confer the Holy Spirit on another, let alone grant authority. The rigorists raised up a rival bishop named Donatus. But the Catholic Christians maintained that Caecilian was still the duly elected bishop and leader of the church in Carthage. From that point on, Carthage, and then North Africa, was split between the Catholics and the Donatists. This split also tended to be along ethnic and class differences. The Catholics were generally Latin-speaking coastal people whose ancestors came to North Africa from elsewhere, while the Donatists were generally inland people who were more indigenous and whose primary language was a Semitic derivative called Berber. The Catholics tended to be in the upper classes, but were consequently the minority.[15] The Donatists tended to be from the lower classes, and so constituted the majority. When Augustine was bishop of Hippo, there were more Donatists there than Catholics.

As we have seen, the emperor Constantine had declared that the Catholics were the true Church, and he had favored them over the Donatists when it came to restoring church property and

208

rebuilding churches after the persecution.[16] The Donatists were condemned at the Council of Arles in 314 CE, and after that time they were the target of discrimination. Donatists evangelizing Catholics were subject to arrest.[17] In spite of this, the Donatists existed side by side with the Catholics in North Africa until the seventh century, when both forms of Christianity were driven out of North Africa by Islamic invasion.

Augustine accepted the Roman understanding of the sacraments and opposed the Donatists for their rigorism and their rebaptism. He wrote a series of anti-Donatist works, including *On Baptism*, *Against the Donatists*, and *The Correction of the Donatists*. Augustine's Roman view of the sacraments, along with his pessimism regarding human nature, inevitably led him to the Roman ecclesiology. In other words, if people cannot be perfect, neither can the Church, so we cannot expect to purify the Church by excluding the impure.[18] If grace is defined as a healing power, then the Church must be more like a hospital, inclusive even of the sick.[19] Therefore, we must be content to include everyone for the Church's time on earth and, as in the parable of the wheat and the weeds, wait until the harvest (judgment) for God to sort out the real Christians from the false ones. Once Christianity was legalized, and especially when it became the only legal religion, the Church had to be inclusive, since all citizens were expected to be baptized members. The Church that had been countercultural (perceived as antisocial) and persecuted had become the authority over the culture.

In the year 410 CE, the city of Rome was sacked by invading Goths. Those who had resisted the move to a Christian empire blamed the fall of Rome on the Church, some claiming that it was the failure to worship the old gods that led to the removal of their protection. Augustine responded by writing *The City of God*. This is really a tale of two cities, one a heavenly city and one an earthly city. A person's citizenship depends on the object of his or her love. If one loves the things of the world, then one is a citizen of the earthly city. But one can never have real security in the earthly city, since the things one loves can always be taken away. If one loves God, on the other hand, then one is a citizen of the city of God and has real security, since in this case the object of love (God) can never be taken away. True security could never be found in the *pax*

Romana, it could only be found in God, since it is God who maintains his hold on his elect. Assuming election, one who is elect could never lose God because the responsibility for perseverance is on God and God's grace. It must be so, or no one would be saved, since humans are incapable of persevering unless it is a work of God.

Theodosius I (reigned 379–95 CE) was the first emperor to attempt to create an empire in which all citizens were baptized Church members. Others would follow him, in effect trying to create the City of God on earth, including Charlemagne and John Calvin. It would generally be understood, however, that as long as it sojourned on earth, the Church would always be an ark of clean and unclean, a field of wheat and weeds.

CHRISTOLOGY

In the second and third centuries, the doctrinal debates had revolved around two primary questions: the relationship of the Father and Son (the balance of unity and distinction of persons in the Trinity) and the relationship of the two natures in Christ (that there is both divinity and humanity in the second person of the Trinity). Each of these questions evolved in the post-Nicene era. The first question was expanded to include the Holy Spirit (that the Holy Spirit is also consubstantial with the Father). The second question applied the categories of the first question to the person of Christ (the balance of unity and distinction of the two natures).

The Cappadocians

Also known as the *Cappadocian fathers*, the term refers to three bishops from the Cappadocia region of Asia Minor: Basil of Caesarea (329–79 CE), his brother Gregory of Nyssa (c. 330–85/86 CE), and their friend Gregory of Nazianzus (325–89 CE). They continued the work begun by Alexander and Athanasius in solidifying the pro-Nicene position in the Church and bringing general acceptance of the creed. They did this by clarifying that consubstantiality (specifically the nonbiblical term *homoousios*) did not imply a form of modalism. As Tertullian and Novatian had made

clear in the first half of the third century in the West, the one substance did not imply that the Father and Son were one and the
same, since the Father and Son maintained a personal distinction.[20]
They also helped settle the question of which Greek terms would
be used as the equivalents of Tertullian's *person* and *substance*.[21] All
of this allowed some of the "semi-Arian" holdouts to come over to
the Nicene side.

The Cappadocians also expanded the Church's understanding
of the Trinity by applying Nicene conclusions about Christ to the
Holy Spirit. In this, they were opposing a group known as *Pneumatomachians* ("Spirit-fighters"), who denied the Holy Spirit's divinity and therefore opposed the worship of the Spirit. Some of these
may have been former Arians or semi-Arians who were willing to
concede consubstantiality to the Son but not to the Spirit. They
apparently applied some of the Arian arguments about Christ to the
Holy Spirit, in effect saying, We may have to accept the divinity of
the Son, but we can't accept the divinity of the Spirit. To them, calling the Holy Spirit "God" would be a form of polytheism.

Basil of Caesarea wrote *On the Holy Spirit* against the Pneumatomachians, affirming the validity of worshiping the Holy Spirit.
The Pneumatomachians responded by claiming that if all three
persons are divine, then that is really a form of tritheism. Gregory
of Nyssa wrote *On Not Three Gods* to counter this accusation, as
well as *On the Holy Trinity*, in which he went further than his
brother had in affirming that the Holy Spirit is consubstantial and
coeternal with the Father. Thus the conclusions of Nicaea about
the Son were applied to the Spirit. Finally, Gregory of Nazianzus,
who would become bishop of Constantinople, wrote the *Theological
Orations*, including the *Fifth Theological Oration on the Holy Spirit*, in
which he said that it is appropriate to call the Holy Spirit God.

The Cappadocians clarified that the Holy Spirit is of the same
divine nature as (consubstantial with) the Father and the Son and is
therefore divine and is worthy of worship. Variations of this had
been affirmed in the West since Tertullian, and in the East at least
since Athanasius; however, the Cappadocians are credited with
effectively ending the debate over the divinity of the Spirit. Their
work led to a revision of the creed at the Council of Constantinople
in 381 CE that expanded the paragraph on the Holy Spirit to what

it is today (with the exception of the Western addition of *filioque*, "and the Son").

Apollinarius of Laodicea (310–90 CE)

With Apollinarius of Laodicea, the pendulum swings to the other extreme from Arius (see Table 5, *Christology and Theology in the Fourth Century*). Apollinarius was a student of Athanasius who reacted against Arius's ontological separation of the Father and Son. He attempted to safeguard the unity and equality of the Son with the Father by emphasizing the divinity of the Son as well as the unity between the divine and human in Christ.[22] In doing this, however, he envisioned a Christ in which the divine nature overshadowed the human nature to the point where the human nature was diminished by the divine nature. From the perspective of the mainstream bishops, Apollinarius seemed to have emphasized the unity between the two natures to the point of creating a kind of christological modalism.

Apollinarius also rejected Arius's anthropological optimism and (like Augustine) reasoned that if Arian soteriology was correct, no one could be obedient enough to be saved. In fact, if Jesus' sonship had depended on human willpower to resist sin, Apollinarius worried that not even Jesus could have been saved. Therefore, he concluded that the only way Jesus could have been without sin would be if there were no human will in him, since it would be the human will that would give in to temptation. He speculated that in the person of Christ, the human rational soul (the human mind) had been replaced by the divine mind, the Logos. So Apollinarius proposed a Christ who had no human will, but into whom the divine Logos was inserted to be the mind of the man Jesus. This was perceived by most bishops as unacceptable, because it seemed to diminish Christ's human nature. Although Apollinarius would have certainly denied it, his Christology seemed to have fewer than two natures, and his Christ seemed to be less than fully human. Apollinarius's Christology was therefore rejected, because of the conviction that a Christ who is not fully human could not represent humanity and be the savior of humanity.

Whereas the orthodox said *the Word became flesh*, and Arianism had said something like *the flesh earned the Word*, Apollinarius seemed to be suggesting that *the Word put on flesh*. The language of "putting on" flesh had been used by the apologists with regard to the incarnation, but in the fourth century it became important to clarify that it was not only a "suit of flesh" that the divine Logos wore, it was a full humanity. The problem is that Apollinarius had reacted against Arius's diminished divinity in Christ by overemphasizing the divinity to the point of diminishing the humanity. The Arians had, in effect, proposed a Christ with only one will (human), but Apollinarius went to the other extreme and ironically also proposed a Christ with only one will (but divine). A Christology of one will only is called *monothelite* (Greek for "one will").[23] The one will of Apollinarius's Christ is divine, so there is no human mind or will, and in fact no free will at all. The majority of bishops would eventually conclude that for Christ to have two natures, he must also have two wills, one divine (the same divine will as the Trinity) and one human.[24]

At the second ecumenical council, the Council of Constantinople in 381 CE, Apollinarius's Christology was condemned as heresy. The conclusions of the Council of Nicaea were reaffirmed and Arianism was also condemned. Orthodoxy was implicitly defined as the middle way between Arianism and Apollinarianism. The creed produced at Nicaea was updated and expanded, including the extended paragraph on the Holy Spirit, which was the result of the Cappadocians' work. What we know as the Nicene Creed today is actually the result of both councils and it is properly called the Nicene-Constantinopolitan Creed. This is the creed still honored and recited in the Church to this day, except that the Western version of the creed has the addition of the *filioque* clause (that the Holy Spirit proceeds from the Father *and the Son*). The *filioque* clause can be traced to Augustine and his own emphasis on the equality of Father and Son against Arianism. It was later added to the creed, first in Spain and then across the West in an effort of standardization under Charlemagne.

Nestorius of Constantinople (Bishop 428–51 CE)

The date of Nestorius's birth is unknown; but he gained a reputation as a proven anti-Arian and became bishop of Constantinople in 428 CE. He seems, however, to have overreacted against Apollinarius (swinging the pendulum once again) to the point where his Christology has some affinity with Arian theology, in the sense that it emphasizes distinction over unity (see Table 6, *Christology and Theology in the Fifth Century*). Understandably uncomfortable with the diminished humanity in Apollinarius's description of Christ, Nestorius attempted to preserve the full humanity of Christ, and at the same time preserve the immutability of the divine nature of Christ, by emphasizing the distinction between the two natures over against the unity of natures. He apparently thought that Apollinarius's emphasis on the unity of natures would inevitably lead to the detriment of both natures, since the humanity would be diminished and the divinity would be mutable. Thus, like the Arians, he apparently rejected any kind of unity other than a unity of wills. Whereas the Arians had said that the unity of Father and Son was a unity of cooperating wills, not a unity of essence, Nestorius would say that the unity of the two natures in Christ was a unity of cooperating wills. In effect, Nestorius was saying the same thing about the two natures within Christ that Arius had said about the Father and Son. Nestorius and his followers were accused of taking this further than he ever really did, to the point where the two natures appeared to be two separate persons, only united as long as the human will in Christ submits to the divine will.[25]

The practical application of Nestorius's Christology was apparent in his rejection of the title "Mother of God" (in Greek, *Theotokos*) as it was being used of Mary. Nestorius held that Mary could appropriately be called "Mother of Christ" (*Christotokos*), but not "Mother of God," since, he argued, this would imply that the divine nature of Christ had a birth and therefore a beginning. It also implied that the divine nature was circumscribed in the womb of the Virgin. Since divinity is eternal and omnipresent, Nestorius did not want to use such a title that, for him, compromised the eternality and immutability of the divine. It seemed to him that this

title for Mary denied the very separation of natures that he was trying to emphasize. If both natures of Christ were circumscribed in
the womb of Mary, that seemed like too much unity of the natures,
and risked the same problems as the Christology of Apollinarius.

Nestorius was opposed by Cyril of Alexandria (bishop 412–44
CE), who argued that Mary was, in fact, the mother of the divine
nature of Christ, and therefore it is appropriate to call her "Mother
of God." For him, the unity of the two natures within the person of
Christ demanded that Mary be the mother of both natures. Cyril
insisted that the union of natures was not simply a union of cooperating wills but a union on the level of Christ's very personhood.
While Nestorius seemed to be suggesting a volitional union, Cyril
emphasized the personal (in Greek, *hypostatic*) union. In the ensuing
debate, Cyril won the support of Celestine, bishop of Rome, who
recognized that the concept of the hypostatic union was consistent
with the Christology of the West, especially that of Tertullian, but, as
we have seen, it was also consistent with Novatian.[26]

The third ecumenical council, the Council of Ephesus, was
convened in 431 CE by the emperor Theodosius II (reigned
408–50 CE). Pope Celestine had given Cyril the authority to preside over the council. Unfortunately for Nestorius, the council met
before his supporters could arrive, so he refused to defend himself,
and it is probably the case that in his absence he was accused of
teaching things that he never really believed or taught.[27] Nestorius
and his supporters held their own separate council, which claimed
to excommunicate Cyril. In any case, Nestorianism (as it was
understood) was condemned as heresy, and the condemnation of
Apollinarius was reconfirmed. Thus the Council of Ephesus
implicitly saw orthodox Christology as the middle way between
Apollinarius and Nestorius. The use of the title "Mother of God"
for Mary was confirmed as appropriate. It is important to keep in
mind that, although "Mother of God" is a title for Mary, the issue
behind it is one of Christology, since the use of the title assumes
that the two natures of Christ are united in such a way that even the
divine nature was circumscribed within the womb of Mary.

Eutyches, Abbot of Constantinople (378–454 CE)

Eutyches was a monk and the abbot of a monastery in Constantinople. He was not a bishop, nor even a theologian. Thinking that he was faithfully reflecting the teachings of Cyril, he overreacted against Nestorius and went even further from the mainstream than Apollinarius had (see Table 6, *Christology and Theology in the Fifth Century*). Whereas Apollinarius had suggested what appeared to be an overlap of the divine nature of Christ over-shadowing the human nature, Eutyches proposed a Christology in which the divine nature completely absorbed the human nature, leaving no human nature after the incarnation. Now it was not simply a matter of only one will in Christ (*monothelite*), it was a Christology of only one nature (*monophysite*). In Eutyches' description of Christ, though he may have theoretically had two natures that came together in the incarnation, he had only one nature after the incarnation, and that nature was divine. This is an extreme unity of natures in the person of Christ that leaves room for no distinction at all and ultimately absorbs and erases the human nature, leaving a Christ who is, at best, less than human and, at worst, docetic. Thus Eutyches described Jesus as consubstantial with God, but not with humanity.

The mainstream Church had been affirming the reality of the two natures of Christ from the very beginning. Adoptionism, and then Arianism, had affirmed one nature only (human), and Apollinarius had responded with a Christology that had more than one, but not quite two natures. Eutyches went even further than Apollinarius in the opposite direction from Arius, with a Christology that once again reduced Christ to one nature, this time divine. But in emphasizing such a unity of natures, it appeared that the one nature that remained after the incarnation was something not consistent with either of the two original natures. Eutyches' Christ was a *tertium quid* (a "third thing") resulting from the amalgam of the two natures, but no longer either one.[28] This implied a change in the divine nature that compromised divine immutability, and from the perspective of the mainstream resulted in a Trinity that was closer to a form of modalism. In any case, the one nature that resulted and remained was divine and had no real connection to humanity. This the mainstream Church could not accept.

Bishop Flavian of Constantinople excommunicated Eutyches at a council in 448 CE. By this time, however, Cyril of Alexandria had died and was succeeded by Dioscorus, who took Eutyches' side, in part for political reasons. The debate now escalated into an argument between bishops, Flavian of Constantinople and Dioscorus of Alexandria. Rome was consulted and Pope Leo I (bishop 440–61) supported Flavian with a letter now known as the *Tome*.[29] In this letter, Leo claimed the authority of apostolic succession, writing as if he spoke for Peter himself. At a synod in Ephesus in 449 CE, with Dioscorus presiding, Leo's Tome was rejected without a hearing (possibly in part because there was no one there who could translate it from Latin into Greek) and both Flavian and Leo were excommunicated. This attempt at asserting the authority of Alexandria over both Rome and Constantinople was ultimately dubbed the "robber synod."[30]

The fourth ecumenical council, the Council of Chalcedon, was convened in 451 CE. Affirming the creed of Nicaea-Constantinople, the bishops of the council resolved not to create a new creed, but only to produce a statement of faith (called the *Chalcedonian Definition*) that would further clarify the christological question. Cyril's description of the hypostatic union was affirmed and Nestorius's condemnation reiterated. In addition, Leo's *Tome* was read and accepted, especially specific language that was taken as sufficient to refute Eutychian monophysitism. As Leo had phrased it (building on language from Tertullian, Novatian, and Augustine), Christ is one person "in both natures."[31] This affirmed a full union of the two natures on the level of Christ's very personhood, while at the same time maintaining a distinction between the two natures that left both natures intact. In other words, with the help of Cyril and Leo, the Church had articulated the balance of unity and distinction between the two natures in the person of Christ to parallel the balance of unity and distinction between the persons of the Trinity. As Tertullian and Novatian had already taught, the Chalcedonian definition further clarified that the two natures of Christ must remain distinct, without change, confusion, or diminishing either nature or creating a third nature.[32] In addition, the human nature of Christ is a full humanity with a rational soul (mind/will). Finally, it was confirmed that it is appropriate to refer to Mary as the Mother of God, since she is also the mother of Christ's divine nature. Thus, just as fourth-century orthodoxy was a middle way between Arianism and Apollinarianism, fifth-century orthodoxy was defined as the middle way between Nestorianism and monophysitism.[33]

With both the Monophysites and the Nestorians condemned as heretics, the Council of Chalcedon had brought the Church to another plateau in the development of doctrine. By defining the doctrine of the Trinity and Christology, the first four ecumenical councils had not only defined orthodoxy, they had defined Christianity itself. But this was done at the expense of unity, since after Chalcedon both extremes refused to submit to the authority of the majority, and so they split from the Church and became separated ecclesial bodies, a division that still exists to this day.[34] Clarifying the boundaries of orthodox Christology naturally led to some being left outside those boundaries, and although the Chalcedonian Christians would have claimed that the non-Chalcedonians were, by definition, not Christian, these groups nevertheless continued their worship of God in Christ according to their own understanding.

From the earliest decades of the Church, the authority of the bishops as successors of the apostles and the development of the hierarchy were meant to preserve the teaching and tradition of the Church and maintain unity. In the post-Chalcedon Church, however, it was no longer as simple as calling those outside the mainstream heretics and therefore unchristian. Now there were those outside the mainstream who had sufficient numbers to survive as separate entities. The Monophysites were centered in Egypt and became the Oriental Orthodox Churches (including the Coptic Church).[35] The Nestorians migrated to Persia and became the Assyrian Church of the East.

Today the Chalcedonian and non-Chalcedonian churches have come to recognize each other and have rescinded their mutual excommunications. Each of the two non-Chalcedonian groups have reconciled with the Roman Catholic Church, to the point of admitting that the other's Christology is not a heresy but is primarily a difference in emphasis. But there is a long way to go before eucharistic unity can be achieved. The Assyrian Church of the East accepts that it is appropriate to call Mary the Mother of God (*Theotokos*), though they reserve the right not to use the title themselves. The Vatican has recognized them as a valid form of Christianity since 1994. The Coptic Church, for its part, does not claim Eutyches as its founder, but instead claims Dioscorus of Alexandria and maintains that it remains faithful to the teachings of Cyril.[36] They prefer to call their Christology *miaphysite*, meaning one composite nature that retains both divinity and a true full humanity.[37] The Coptic Church has been recognized by the Vatican as a valid form of Christianity since 1973, when a joint statement on Christology was issued by Pope Paul VI and Pope Shenouda III of Alexandria. The Greek Orthodox Church has recognized the Coptic Church since 1989, and both signed a joint statement on Christology in 1990.[38] The irony is that, in spite of an officially inclusive ecclesiology, the definition of orthodoxy and the clarification of the boundaries of doctrine ultimately led to exclusion of those who were only perceived as outside the boundaries, not so much because of different beliefs, but because of different ways of expressing their beliefs. In some ways, this was largely due to differences of language or disagreements over the definitions of words. But the authority that was originally meant to safeguard unity finally led to division.

SOTERIOLOGY

The convergence of anthropology and Christology is soteriology, or the doctrine of salvation. As we have already seen, Christology and soteriology are interdependent because what one believes about the Savior will affect what one believes about how salvation works. In addition, what one believes about humanity (anthropology) will determine what the human needs from God in order to be saved. Thus as we have seen with Arianism, an optimistic anthropology leads to an emphasis on human effort and to a soteriology in which all that is needed from Christ is to set a good example. On the other hand, Augustine's pessimistic anthropology leads to an emphasis on divine intervention. The "nuts and bolts" of salvation, then, is the doctrine of the atonement, which answers the question of how the Savior saves.

In the New Testament, atonement is presented in various ways. One of the ways in which the apostle Paul describes atonement is in terms of manumission. Salvation is freedom (from sin, death, fate, superstition) and Christ is our Savior in that he has purchased our freedom through his sacrifice on the cross. This is described as "ransom" (Matt 20:28, 1 Tim 2:6). The mainstream theologians continued this trend, associating the two natures of Christ with two requirements for salvation. The Savior must be human in order to die for humanity (as a representative of humanity), but the Savior must also be divine in order to overcome death and rise in victory, making our resurrection possible.

By the Middle Ages, the "ransom theory" of atonement had become one in which it was speculated that humanity had sold itself into slavery to the devil by committing sin. In order to buy our freedom, Jesus Christ had to pay with his life. Christ was seen as the actual "ransom" itself, the payment that the Father was compelled to give in order to free the human race. This presented a philosophical problem, however. It put the devil in a position of power over God.[39] It would take a group of medieval scholars known as the *Scholastics* to clarify the Church's doctrine of the atonement. With Scholasticism, the philosophy that was abandoned by the theologians finally makes a comeback, with the conviction that both faith and reason are gifts from God and will complement each other. In expanding upon the connection between anthropology, Christology, and soteriology, the Scholastics would become the first systematic theologians.

Anselm of Canterbury (1033/34–1109 CE)

Anselm was influenced primarily by Augustine of Hippo. He took Augustine's *Credo ut intelligam* (I believe so that I may understand), and made it *Fides quaerens intellectum* (faith seeking understanding). In his most famous document, *Cur Deus Homo* (Why the God-Man?), Anselm followed the lead of the early theologians, developing the argument that Christ had to be both divine and human in order to be the Savior of humanity.[40] Anselm begins with a dilemma faced by God. Humans are sinful and therefore deserve eternal separation from God. But God loves humanity and wishes to save humans from the wages of sin. If God were simply to cancel the debt, God's justice would be mocked and an important part of God's nature would be compromised. On the other hand, if God were to condemn all of humanity, God's will to save humanity would go unfulfilled and another important part of God's nature (mercy) would never be realized.[41] The solution to this dilemma must be one in which the debt of justice is paid and humans are given the chance to be free of it.

Cur Deus Homo demonstrates perfectly the connection between Christology and soteriology. Anselm argued that the atonement works because Christ has two natures. The human nature of Christ is required to pay the debt of justice on behalf of humanity (a human must pay the debt that humanity owes), and the divine nature is required because a mere human would have sins of his own and would not be able to pay the debt for himself, let alone the rest of humanity. This has been expressed in more modern times as "Christ paid a debt he did not owe, because we owed a debt we could not pay." The apostle Paul said it this way, that Christ took our curse so that we could have his blessing (Gal 3:13–14). Thus he died in our place as a substitutionary sacrifice, as the Letter to the Hebrews describes it, a once-and-for-all version of the animal sacrifices of the Old Testament. Anselm, however, did not emphasize the sacrificial aspect of Christ's death. For him it was the payment of a debt—it is God's honor that is offended by sin, and that must be repaid.[42] For Anselm, it is not so much the *death* of Christ, but the *life* of Christ that matters. Since his life is the most valuable thing imaginable, it could be given as an overabundant payment for the debt of humanity. Therefore, it has more to do with Christ's giving of himself than with a blood sacrifice. So while Anselm's theory of atonement is sometimes referred to as the *substitution* theory, a better name is the *satisfaction* theory.[43]

According to Anselm, the most we could ever give to God would be our own lives; however, that would be less than we already owed God, even before sin and apart from the debt. But Christ's life is without sin, and therefore it is a surplus payment, the credit of overage being applied to humanity, and so forgiveness is granted. Note, however, that forgiveness is granted to human nature in general, since the problem of sin is a problem of human nature. Like Augustine, Anselm believed that the Fall had damaged human nature. The problem is that we as humans are consubstantial with Adam, and so his sin has corrupted our nature. In Adam, the sin of the individual corrupts the entire human nature. In fact, each person's sin throughout the generations of history contributes to the corruption of human nature, which grows like a snowball rolling downhill, so that sin becomes inevitable.[44] The solution to the problem, then, is that Christ became consubstantial with us, so that in him, the sinlessness of the individual heals the whole human nature.[45] This satisfies both God's justice and God's mercy because it incorporates both divine intervention (the divine nature of Christ) and human representation (the human nature of Christ).

Peter Abelard (1079–1142)

Abelard began with an optimistic anthropology, much like Arius and Pelagius. Therefore he rejected Augustine's understanding of original sin, and he also rejected Anselm's understanding of atonement as substitution/satisfaction. He argued that if grace is a gift of God, no one should have to pay for it, not even Christ. He further maintained that since God had forgiven sin before the coming of Christ, then Christ himself (as a sacrifice) was not needed to forgive sin. In his commentary on the Book of Romans, Abelard refutes what appears to be a caricature of Anselm. He says, in effect, that God *can* save humanity simply by cancelling the debt. In fact, he argued that any other arrangement would have the same philosophical problem as the ransom theory, in that it seems to impose a necessity on God. Therefore, Abelard rejected the idea that Christ's death reconciles humanity to God, saying that if anything, the murder of the Son of God is the worst sin humanity has ever committed and it should make things worse. In this he anticipated some of the contemporary critiques of traditional atonement theories, saying that the very idea of a blood sacrifice seems cruel on the part of God. It seemed to him a great injustice that the innocent (Jesus) would have to die for the guilty. So Abelard proposed that it was not Christ's death that mattered, but his incarnation. On the latter point, he and Anselm would probably agree, but Abelard went so far as to say that the passion of Christ was more of a wake-up call or a motivational object lesson, rather than the satisfaction of a debt or a substitutionary sacrifice.

This claim got Abelard into trouble, however, because he was essentially saying that Christ did not need to die to make salvation possible. In fact, Abelard proposed that those who killed Christ did not actually sin, since they thought they were doing God's will and sincerely intended to do God's will. Apparently taking his cue from some of the teachings of Jesus in the gospels (such as Matt 5:27–28), Abelard made *intention* the criteria for what constituted sin. If one did not intend to sin (but did so inadvertently), the sin would not be held against that person. But if one intended to sin but was unable to carry it out, that person would still be guilty.[46] The point was whether one intended to follow the example of Christ. According to tradition, Abelard's nemesis, Bernard of Clairvaux, responded to this idea with a version of the famous saying, *The road to hell is paved with good intentions.*

Abelard is usually given credit for the *moral influence* theory of atonement, which is often seen as similar to an Arian soteriology in that the Savior is an example to follow, and salvation is by human effort. In other words, it is not Christ's death that saves, but our reaction to it. Christ was the perfect example of self-sacrifice, and his suffering was an act of love for humanity. Does it motivate us to repent and follow the example of Christ as one who loves unselfishly?[47] Like Pelagius, however, Abelard was no Arian. He did not completely reject the idea of salvation as substitution, as he wrote in a letter to his beloved Heloise: "He (Christ) bought you and redeemed you with his own blood." His was not really a salvation by works, but it did emphasize human effort in defining salvation according to whether or not we follow the example of Christ. Nevertheless, he was accused of heresy (by Bernard of Clairvaux) and excommunicated, but was later reconciled to the Church before his death.[48]

Thomas Aquinas (1224/25–74)

Thomas Aquinas is most famous for his unfinished systematic theology, *Summa Theologica*, of which *On Nature and Grace* is a part. Like the other Scholastics, Aquinas affirmed that faith and reason are not contradictory, since both are gifts from God; but he may have found a balance between the two that the others did not. If it could be said that Anselm leaned more toward faith (that is, Augustine), and Abelard leaned more toward reason (that is, philosophy), Aquinas presented the middle way, recognizing that while human rationality is a function of the image of God in the human person, it is nevertheless limited and therefore reason alone will not lead one to God—one also needs divine revelation. On the other hand, revelation requires reason to interpret it, and so each one needs the other. Aquinas combines Augustinian theology with a renewed optimism about human nature that affirmed that people can know and do what is good.

If the pendulum had swung hard to the Augustinian side with Anselm and to the Pelagian side with Abelard, Thomas Aquinas is the center of gravity where the Church would come to rest. Combining the best of the substitution/satisfaction and moral influence theories of atonement, Thomas brought the Church's "semi-Augustinian" anthropology to its logical conclusion and demonstrated how salvation requires divine intervention (God's grace is more than information, it is a power), human representation (Christ's human nature becomes the substitution for humanity), *and* human participation (the will of the individual cooperates with God's grace).[49] This would become the accepted Catholic understanding of atonement. Thomas's thought in general would come to be known as *Thomism*, and while it would be impossible to do justice to Thomas's contribution to the Church in the space available here, it will have to suffice to point out that few Christian writers, before or since, have come close to the legacy of Aquinas. It is also important to note that in the Protestant Reformation, the reformers' reaction against the sale of indulgences led to an aversion to any talk of personal cooperation with grace (that is, works), which made them move back toward Anselm and adopt a modified (more forensic) version of the substitution theory.

Nevertheless, Aquinas had reclaimed the classical optimism about human nature to an extent that set the stage for the Renaissance and even the Enlightenment. For him, as for Augustine, God's grace is a power, the power to change direction in life; however, the human will can accept and respond to grace, which in turn merits more grace, a positive version of the snowball effect.

Soteriology, then, is the question of reconciliation with God and how it is achieved. Can we reach out to God, or must God take the initiative and reach out to us first? The Council of Orange in 529 CE had concluded that although the human will can respond to grace, grace must move first. However, this still begged the question, How much can we contribute to our own salvation (Phil 2:12)? How much does the human will cooperate with grace? What is the balance between grace (what God does) and free will (what we do)? The Church would accept Thomas Aquinas as the best interpreter of the apostle Paul, that to connect with the Divine requires both divine power and willpower. It is not a question of either divine intervention or human effort; it requires the love, mercy, and compassion of a God who takes the initiative to reach out to humanity as well as personal discipline and following the example of Christ. Thus atonement is not one-sided, but is a divine-human dialogue that includes divine initiative (the incarnation, revelation, and the grace of baptism), human response (faith), divine intervention (the grace of healing and forgiveness), and human effort (prayer and good works).

Conclusions

While we have examined the Church of the second and third centuries in some depth, we have only scratched the surface of the proliferation of textual evidence left to us from the post-Nicene Church. Therefore it may seem somewhat hasty to think in terms of conclusions. However, we have been able to point to some important trends that began in the early Church and continued on through to the Middle Ages. Furthermore, these trends can themselves point to certain questions that underlie the debates faced by the Church fathers. It is these questions to which we will now turn, and with which I will leave the reader to explore the Church fathers in greater depth.

What Is Unity, and at What Cost Is It to Be Sought After?

From the beginning it was assumed that the Church must be one. A divided Church was a Church that the gates of hell had overcome (Matt 16:18), and therefore it was desirable, even urgent, that the Church define the boundaries of acceptable teaching and keep everyone inside those boundaries. But at least as early as the writing of the First Letter of John, there were those who would not stay within the boundaries and who "went out from us" (1 John 2:19). Then, from the Marcionites in the second century to the Novatianists in the third century, to the Donatists in the fourth century, to the Nestorians and Monophysites of the fifth century, there were always groups willing to separate from the mainstream Church to maintain their own identity and stand up for their divergent beliefs. How was the Church to balance orthodoxy and unity? How far could the Church go in accepting variations of doctrine before a particular teaching had moved far enough from the "center" that it could no longer be called Christianity?

For that matter, why not just let everyone believe what seemed right to them? The reason this would have been unthinkable was that the Church fathers recognized that theology and Christology always led to a particular soteriology, and they firmly believed that not every soteriology could actually save. Therefore, souls were at stake, and the heretic who insisted on teaching a divergent interpretation was in fact preaching "another gospel," one that would lead innocent people astray and ultimately to their eternal damnation. Hence the need for boundaries.

What Is Authority, and What Are Its Limits?

The need for boundaries immediately begs the question of who has the authority to set the boundaries. As the hierarchy of the Church evolved, authority became concentrated in the bishops, who were the keepers of the Church's doctrine and discipline.

226

Apostolic succession assumes an institutionalization of authority, one that would ultimately be incompatible with charismatic authority. Therefore, limiting the parameters of doctrine required limiting the authority. In the East, ultimate authority was placed in councils, but in the West, authority came to be consolidated in a single point at the top of the hierarchy, the bishop of Rome. Perhaps it is not a coincidence that the West inherited Augustine's pessimism with regard to humanity while the East never did. A pessimistic anthropology might have contributed to the idea that a centralized authority was needed for a people who could not really be trusted. The East, on the other hand, with its more optimistic anthropology and its continuing acceptance of human free will, could allow more participation in authority. In any case, the Council of Nicaea was the last ecumenical council to include participation by anyone other than bishops.

After Constantine legalized Christianity and made travel and communication between bishops more convenient, the Church also had to struggle with the question of standardization. In other words, how much diversity of practice (liturgy, ritual) should the one Church allow, so that she can still call herself one? Thus it was not only doctrinal diversity but also liturgical diversity that caused concern.

What Is the Proper Balance of Unity and Diversity, and How Do We Achieve It?

Just as the Church struggled to find the balance of unity and distinction among the three divine persons of the Trinity, it also had to work toward a balance of unity and diversity among its people. Total unity was not possible, and to force it unnecessarily would create schism, which puts souls at risk no less than heresy does. Therefore, how much diversity should the Church allow for the sake of unity, and at what point must the Church draw the line of definition for the sake of its own integrity? Put another way, conclusions about the relationship of the divine and human in Christ have implications for the body of Christ, in which sincere believers seek a connection with the divine. Of course, we have to be careful not to project our own ideas about "community" on God or make the Trinity some sort of analogy for human relationships, but the point is that what people truly need and want is access to the divine. We want to be one with God, but we do not want to lose our own identity. In the same way, the humanity of Christ is one person with the divine nature, yet retains its distinction. Salvation is nothing more or less than a relationship with God, through Christ, that continues into eternity. But here's the rub: the Church fathers believed that one must have a relationship with the *right* Christ, or it would be ineffective to lead to salvation. A relationship with the Christ of Marcion or Arius would not do it. The true Christ would not be found at the extremes, but would be found in the middle, in the center of gravity, in a place of balance.

The story of the early Church is therefore the story of the Church's struggle to define itself. Often Christians had to describe the Church in reference to its opposition, in other words, clarifying what Christianity *is* by pointing out what it is *not*. Therefore, an orthodox anthropology is not a completely pessimistic understanding of the human as totally depraved, nor is it a completely optimistic understanding of humanity as capable of perfection. Orthodox ecclesiology is not so exclusive as to be purist, but it is also not so inclusive as to be universalist. Orthodoxy Christology is not the extremes of adoptionism or modalism, but affirms both the humanity and divinity of Christ, both the unity and distinction in the Trinity. In fact, the union of human and divine natures in the person of Christ (and consequently the union of the Son with the Father) is the very focal point of the union of humanity with God. Finally, soteriology is not all divine election without human participation, nor is it all human effort without divine intervention. The Church came to believe, and not only believe but wager eternity on this belief, that the truth is in the middle.

Charts and Tables

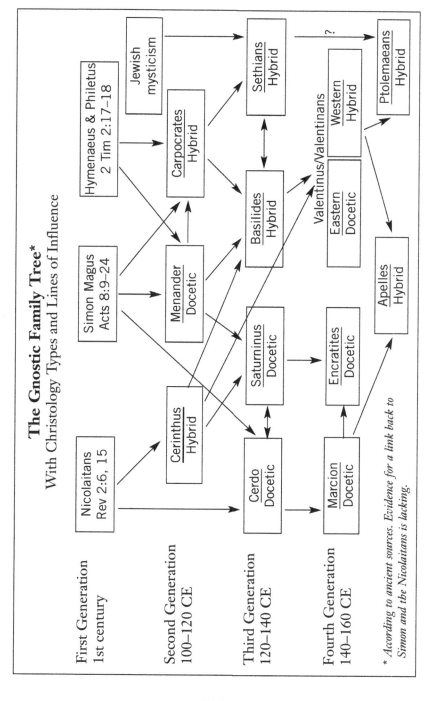

The Gnostic Family Tree*
With Christology Types and Lines of Influence

First Generation
1st century

Second Generation
100–120 CE

Third Generation
120–140 CE

Fourth Generation
140–160 CE

Nicolaitans
Rev 2:6, 15

Simon Magus
Acts 8:9–24

Hymenaeus & Philetus
2 Tim 2:17–18

Jewish mysticism

Cerinthus
Hybrid

Menander
Docetic

Carpocrates
Hybrid

Sethians
Hybrid

Cerdo
Docetic

Saturninus
Docetic

Basilides
Hybrid

Valentinus/Valentinans

Western
Hybrid

Ptolemaeans
Hybrid

?

Marcion
Docetic

Encratites
Docetic

Eastern
Docetic

Apelles
Hybrid

* According to ancient sources. Evidence for a link back to
Simon and the Nicolaitans is lacking.

CHRISTOLOGY AND THEOLOGY IN THE SUBAPOSTOLIC AGE

THE EBIONITES	THE APOLOGISTS & IRENAEUS	DOCETICS & GNOSTICS
Mostly Jewish Christians, they are considered the legacy of the so-called Judaizers of Galatians	Jesus is both fully divine and fully human	Mostly Gentile Christians, retaining elements of their former paganism
Jesus was an anointed prophet, but a mere human	In his divine nature, he is the preexistent agent of creation	Based on extreme dualism: Matter is evil, only the spiritual is good
Jesus was indwelt by the Holy Spirit temporarily	Jesus was fully human, with real flesh (1 John 4:1–3), even after the resurrection	Therefore, Christ could not have real flesh, and Jesus only seemed to be human
The indwelling of the Spirit begins at Jesus' baptism	Jesus was uniquely filled with the Holy Spirit all his life, not just from his baptism	Gnosticism assumes salvation is by secret knowledge
Therefore, he is the recipient of the Spirit, not the giver of the Spirit	The resurrection was a real, bodily resurrection	Some Gnostics believed Jesus had a tangible, but "ethereal" body (hybrid Christology)
Some said the Holy Spirit left Jesus alone on the cross	*Logos Christology:* **Affirms Jesus' Humanity Affirms Jesus' Divinity**	The resurrection was a mystical vision, in which Christ was revealed in his true (nonhuman) nature
The resurrection is a metaphor for eternal life	*Practical responses:* Refusal to ignore any scripture texts, even in the face of paradox or apparent contradiction It is appropriate to worship Jesus Christ Potential balance of devotion & service	*Docetic Christology:* **Denies Jesus' Humanity Affirms Jesus' Divinity**
Ebionite Christology: **Affirms Jesus' Humanity Denies Jesus' Divinity**		*Practical responses:* Worship of angels Lifestyle of extremes—either Asceticism: self-denial, or Libertinism: self-indulgence Emphasis on personal belief, little social responsibility
Practical responses: Require adherence to all Jewish laws Some may have rejected the worship of Jesus Emphasis on following Jesus' example as opposed to a salvation by atonement Possible emphasis on social gospel, less on devotional life	*Note:* Both the Ebionites and the Gnostics envision a Jesus who is not unique among humanity. For the Ebionites, Jesus is not unique because he is not divine—for the Gnostics, Jesus is not unique because we are all divine. The mainstream accepted the paradox of a Jesus who is *both* one of us, *and* unique among us—uniquely filled with the Holy Spirit, and uniquely one with the Father (inseparable operation).	*Objections of opposition:* How can Jesus represent humanity if not human? (What is not assumed is not saved—salvation requires human representation.) Jesus is described as human in the NT (Luke 24:36–43) Jesus ate, even after the resurrection.
Objections of opposition: How could Jesus be a Savior if not divine? (Salvation requires divine intervention) Jesus is described as divine in the NT (Col 2:9) Jesus claimed a unique relationship to God		

232

ASSUMPTIONS OF PATRISTIC EXEGESIS

"...in matters of theology, absolute confidence is possible
for only two classes of people: saints and idiots"
—Origen, *Commentary on Genesis*

1. *The Sacred Texts, Including the New Testament, Are Divinely Inspired* (2 Pet 3:14–16)

     The texts are understood as inspired by the same Holy Spirit who inspired the prophets

     The text of scripture is the recorded voice of the divine Logos

     Therefore, every word is there for a reason (this often leads to allegorizing all the details)

     The written word is another incarnation of the living Word

    > Like the body of Jesus, it enfleshes the Word of God
    > And like Jesus, it is both human and divine

2. *Revelation Is Progressive*

     Things get clearer over time, and the New Testament is clearer than the Old Testament

     New interpretations can build on, but cannot contradict, established ones

     This assumes the authority of the Church through apostolic succession

3. *There Are Multiple Meanings in Any Given Text*

     The human author's intended meaning is not the only valid meaning

     This is because the ultimate author is really God

4. *Paradox Is to Be Embraced, Not Avoided*

     Two apparently contradictory texts can be held in tension, where both are seen as true

     Assuming divine inspiration, one set of texts cannot be ignored in favor of another

     The question then becomes, not *whether* a biblical text is true, but *how* it is true

5. *Patristic Exegesis Follows the Lead of Apostolic Exegesis*

     Interpreting the Old Testament in light of the life and ministry of Jesus: it is always christocentric

     Even Old Testament passages that were never thought of as messianic become prophecies

     Combining texts from different documents, such as the "Suffering Servant" (Isa 53), with messianic prophecies to explain why Jesus as Messiah suffers death

6. *Scripture Interprets Scripture*
   This assumes an internal integrity and consistency of message, even across the testaments
   It is based on the assumption of divine inspiration
   Interpreting one text by the application of other (clearer) texts

7. *In General, Interpretation of the Old Testament Was Nonliteral*
   The most important (that is, christocentric) meaning is hidden under the surface
   The two main types of nonliteral interpretation are typology and allegory

8. *In General, Interpretation of the New Testament Was Literal*
   While the (Christian) meaning was hidden in the Old Testament, it is usually plain in the New Testament
   Some passages, such as parables and apocalyptic, must still be interpreted nonliterally
   The Gnostics tended to interpret the Old Testament literally and the New Testament nonliterally

9. *Interpretation Is Meant to Be Done in the Context of Prayer*
   Interpretation is something done in community (2 Pet 1:20), as part of a devotional life
   Doing theology was not an academic exercise, it was part of the ministry of a pastor
   Interpreting scripture is an act of worship, and must be accompanied by prayer

THE HISTORY OF PATRISTIC EXEGESIS

Stage 1: Two Levels of Meaning

   Roughly the second and third centuries

   Interpretation is literal or nonliteral (spiritual)

   When the literal meaning does not point to Christ, look for a spiritual
   meaning

   Nonliteral (spiritual) interpretation can be typology or allegory

   The higher/deeper meaning is the nonliteral (based on a Platonic assumption that the spiritual is more real)

   The key is Christ, and the best interpretation is always the christocentric
   interpretation

   **LITERAL VS. SPIRITUAL/MYSTICAL (with the assumption that spiritual is
   better)**

Stage 2: Three Levels of Meaning

   Roughly the third through the fifth centuries, especially in the West and
   in Alexandria

   The legacy of Origen and the Alexandrian "school" (that is, methodology)
   of emphasis on allegory

   Based on ancient tripartite anthropology of body, soul, and spirit

   Scripture is like an egg, with a shell, white, and yolk

   To get to the yolk, you have to start with the shell (the literal meaning, on
   the surface)

   However, the serious student of the Bible cannot stop with the shell, but
   must go deeper

   Even more of an insistence that the spiritual (nonliteral) meaning is more
   important

   LITERAL (Historical)—What Jesus did

   MORAL (Ethical)—What we should do

   ALLEGORICAL (Theological)—What we should believe

Reading the Early Church Fathers

Stage 3: Reaction against Allegory—Back to Two Levels of Meaning

Roughly the fourth and fifth centuries, especially in Antioch and the East
Recognizing the problems of overallegorizing every detail
Recognizing that allegory can be used to take the meaning out of an uncomfortable text
A trend to shift away from the nonliteral in favor of the literal meaning
A new appreciation for studying the Old Testament in its Jewish/Hebrew context

LITERAL/HISTORICAL—to be used whenever possible

ALLEGORICAL—to be used only when absolutely necessary, even then it must conform to the literal

Phase 4: Four Levels of Meaning

An attempt at a middle way, or balance of literal and nonliteral
Beginning in the fifth century and evolving into the Middle Ages
Recognizing the necessity of taking the historical context seriously
But also recognizing that the historical interpretation was not always adequate
Also maintaining that the Old Testament had to be read through the lens of the New Testament to be relevant for the Church
The spiritual was to be anchored in the literal/historical

LITERAL/HISTORICAL—What happened

SPIRITUAL (three types):
- Analogical/Theological—What we should believe
- Moral/Ethical—How we should behave
- Anagogical (Vertical Allegory)/Eschatological—What we hope for

CHRISTOLOGY AND THEOLOGY IN THE THIRD CENTURY

ADOPTIONISM	THE THEOLOGIANS	MODALISM
(Dynamic Monarchianism)	Irenaeus Tertullian Hippolytus Novatian	(Modalistic Monarchianism) (a.k.a. Patripassionism, or Sabellianism)
God is one because Jesus is not God		
Jesus Christ is human, but not really divine	**Jesus is God (that is, divine) but Jesus is not the Father**	God is one because Jesus is the Father—the Father and Son are one and the same
Jesus was a mere human, therefore is not preexistent	The Father and Son are *one* (John 10:30), but the Father and Son are not *one and the same* (John 14:28)	**Jesus Christ is divine, but not really human**
He was the first human to achieve perfection	Jesus Christ is the preexistent Logos who became human	The multiple manifestations of God are only the different "masks" that God wears to reveal himself to humanity or to intervene in human history
As a reward for his perfect obedience, God adopted him	**Jesus has his own divine power, but sets it aside for the incarnation**	
The adoption took place at Jesus' baptism	According to Novatian, the incarnation is a voluntary and temporary emptying (*kenosis*) of divine power	The different revelations of God are distinguished by "mode" of activity, or by task/function
Jesus did not have his own divine power (*dunamis*), rather he received power	**THE TRINITY**	The distinctions are more perceived than real
Note the importance of adoption in Roman culture, and in relation to the succession of Roman emperors	Unity of substance/divinity Hierarchy of authority	Note that the implication is that God can only be one manifestation or mode of revelation at a time
	The persons of the Trinity are consubstantial	
Jesus is a son of God, but only by adoption	The three persons of the Trinity cannot be distinguished by function since the unity of substance is also a unity of divine action.	*Objections of opposition:* If Jesus is identical with the Father, then God died on the cross (Patripassionism)
We are also "sons" (heirs) of God by adoption		
Objections of opposition: It appears that Jesus had to be saved by his own obedience Does that imply that for the rest of humanity salvation is also by human effort, that is, by following his example?	The only practical distinction between Son and Father is the incarnation—the Father did not become human	More importantly, the identity of the Son with the Father effectively diminishes the humanity of Christ
	The subordination of the Son is hierarchical, not ontological	
	Jesus as Savior is the embodiment of both divine intervention *and* human representation	

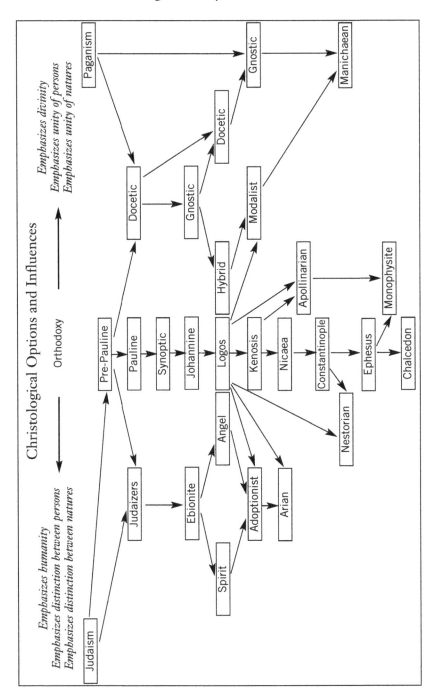

Christological Options and Influences

Emphasizes humanity
Emphasizes distinction between persons
Emphasizes distinction between natures

Orthodoxy

Emphasizes divinity
Emphasizes unity of persons
Emphasizes unity of natures

CHRISTOLOGY AND THEOLOGY IN THE FOURTH CENTURY

ARIANISM	THE COUNCILS OF NICAEA (325 CE) AND CONSTANTINOPLE (381 CE)	APOLLINARIANISM
Arius, priest of Alexandria	Alexander of Alexandria (bishop 313–326 CE)	Apollinarius of Laodicea (over)reacted against Arianism, and against the possibility that Jesus might have sinned
The legacy of adoptionism, however with a qualified (lesser degree of) divinity ascribed to the Son	Athanasius of Alexandria (bishop 326–373 CE)	He emphasized the union of the two natures to the point of "overlap"—the divine Logos replaces the human rational soul (mind/will), to ensure that Jesus would resist temptation
Only the Father is eternal	The Cappadocians	
If the Son were eternal, that would make two Gods	"Begotten" means generated (caused), but not created	
The Logos was preexistent, but not eternally so: "there was a time when he was not"	The Son is eternally generated, coeternal with the Father and has no beginning: "Always a Father, always a Son"	This results in a diminished humanity, since the human nature of Jesus has no human mind or will
Jesus was a mere man who was rewarded for his obedience to God with the indwelling of the Logos	Alexander accused Arius of demoting Christ	It is as if the divine Logos is simply "wearing" a body, along with the soul that animates it, but with no human mind or will
Therefore, "begotten" means created, and "only-begotten" means God's favorite, the "firstborn of all creation" (Col 1:15)	**Orthodoxy is a Christology of descent: Jesus is God (the Word) who became human**	
	Salvation is by divine intervention and human representation	
This is an emphasis on the distinction between the Father and Son, to the point of a separation due to an ontological difference (difference of substance)	Jesus is unlike us in that he needs no salvation	This is an emphasis on the unity of divine and human, but the divine overshadows the human
	He is the only "natural" Son of God—the Son of God by nature, that is, substance	Only one will (divine) in Christ is called "monothelite"
Arius accused Alexander of modalism	We can be adopted by identifying with him	
Arianism is a Christology of Ascent: Jesus is a man who became a god	The Holy Spirit is also divine and worthy of worship	
Jesus as Savior means that he is the pioneer of salvation, the first to save himself and the one who sets the example for the rest of humanity	Note: The equality of substance within the Trinity means that anything that can be said about any of the three persons must also be said about the other two, with only these exceptions:	
Salvation is therefore by human effort, resulting in adoption	The Father is unbegotten	
	The Son is begotten, incarnate	
	The Holy Spirit proceeds	

CHRISTOLOGY AND THEOLOGY IN THE FIFTH CENTURY

NESTORIANISM	THE COUNCILS OF EPHESUS (431 CE) AND CHALCEDON (451 CE)	MONOPHYSITISM
Nestorius (over)reacted against Apollinarius, but it is not clear how far he went; however, his followers seem to have taken his ideas to the extreme	Cyril of Alexandria Leo of Rome The two natures of Christ are unified so that Mary gave birth to both natures, not the human nature only	Eutyches (over)reacted against Nestorius's separation of natures, but went even further than Apollinarius to an extreme union of natures
This is an emphasis on the distinction between the two natures, perceived as a separation of natures	Therefore, it is appropriate to call Mary *Theotokos* (Mother of God)	This is a union of natures to the point of "absorption," in which the divine nature cancels out the human nature
The union of the divine and human in Christ is a union of action only, a moral union, or a cooperation of wills, but not a personal union	The union of the two natures is described as a *hypostatic* (personal) union, a union on the level of Christ's very personhood, and not a mere cooperation of wills	No humanity remains after the incarnation
The two natures are not only distinct, they are separate		Jesus is *homoousios* with the Father, but not with humanity
Therefore, Mary should not be called *Theotokos* (Mother of God), because she could not have been the mother of the divine nature of Christ	Christ is "one person in both natures"	**There is no distinction between the two natures after the union of incarnation**
Nestorius himself had used language of personality to talk about the two natures, making it sound like he thought Christ had a split personality	**The two natures are distinct, but not separate.** The two natures are unified, but not confused	This leaves only one nature (divine) in the person of Christ "Monophysite" = single nature
Later Nestorians pushed the separation of natures to the point where it sounded like they were talking about two separate "persons"	The union of natures does not cause either nature to be diminished or changed	The one nature is perceived as a *tertium quid*, a "third thing," something that is not what either nature was
Christ has: Two natures Two wills	**Christ has: Two natures Two wills**	**Christ has: One nature One will**

IMPORTANT THEOLOGICAL CONCEPTS
AND DOCTRINES

1. Divine Simplicity
   a. God is "simplex," meaning noncomposite: God does not have "parts"
   b. Parts implies corruptibility, that whatever is not simplex could be broken down
   c. Therefore, the three persons of the Trinity are not each one-third of God
   d. Each person of the Trinity is fully God
   e. Not even the mind or will of God are distinct from God's essence
   f. God does not *have* attributes, God simply is what God is
   g. So-called attributes of God are only descriptions of God's essence, or substance

2. Immutability/Impassibility
   a. Immutability is changelessness, the inability to experience change
   b. Impassibility is the inability to suffer (suffering is a form of change)
   c. Divine perfection requires immutability, since change would destroy perfection
   d. Divine omnipresence also requires immutability, since movement is a form of change

3. Inseparable Operation
   a. A function of consubstantiality and divine simplicity
   b. All three persons of the Trinity are unified in all divine activity

4. Appropriation
   a. Also a function of consubstantiality and divine simplicity
   b. What is said of one person of the Trinity must be said of the others (limited exceptions)
   c. What can be said of God/the Trinity can be said of each person

5. *Perichoresis* (Latin: *Circumincessio*) or Reciprocity
   a. A function of divine simplicity, consubstantiality and inseparable operation
   b. The mutual interexistence of the three persons of the Trinity
   c. The interpenetration of the three persons in action (movement toward the unity)
   d. The fact that each divine person exists "in" the other divine persons

241

6. Eternal Generation
   a. "Begotten" does not mean created
   b. What is generated is of the same substance as the Source of generation

7. Consubstantiality (Greek: *homoousios*)
   a. A function of divine simplicity (whatever is not the same substance as God, is not God)
   b. All three persons of the Trinity are the same substance
   c. The result of generation (in the case of the Son) and procession (Spirit)
   d. Describes the unity (oneness) of the Trinity
   e. The Son is also consubstantial with humanity

8. Coeternality
   a. Goes hand in hand with consubstantiality and eternal generation
   b. There is no time lag before begetting or proceeding, no time when the Son did not exist

9. *Communicatio Idiomatum*
   a. As perichoresis is to the Trinity, *communicatio idiomatum* is to the two natures
   b. Properties idiomatic to each nature are communicated to the other nature
   c. For example:
      i. By virtue of the union, the human nature experienced glory and immortality
      ii. By virtue of the union, the divine nature experienced the human condition
      iii. But not to the extent of allowing passibility in the divine nature

10. Circumscribability (Localization)
   a. The ability to be localized in time and space
   b. In the Son, required a *kenosis* of omnipresence
   c. Goes hand in hand with visibility

Appendix

THE PRIMARY SOURCES

Secondary sources have been suggested along the way in the footnotes. For the purposes of this study, however, I have chosen to concentrate more on the primary sources, the documents from the historical Church. It is my hope that this survey of the writings of the early Church will inspire students to read further in the secondary sources on specific topics. For the student who wishes to read the primary sources, the documents mentioned in this book, many are easily accessed on the Internet. For a list of the primary sources Internet links, select the Online Resources tab at www.paulistpress.com, and then select this book's title, *Reading the Early Church Fathers*.

MAP OF THE ROMAN EMPIRE WITH PLACES MENTIONED

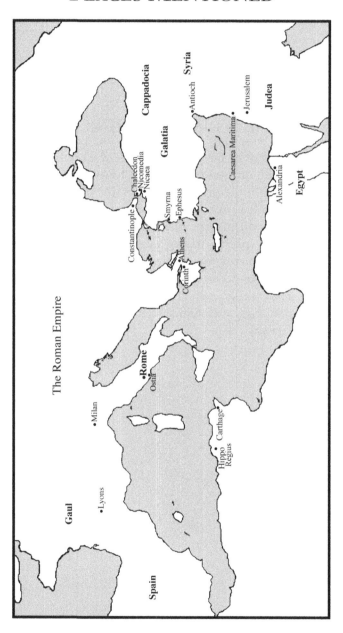

Notes

INTRODUCTION

1. I am indebted to Paul Bradshaw for this insight. See his more specialized list of caveats for reading early liturgical texts, "Ten Principles for Interpreting Early Christian Liturgical Evidence," in Paul F. Bradshaw and Lawrence Hoffman, eds., *The Making of Jewish and Christian Worship* (Notre Dame, IN: University of Notre Dame Press, 1991), 3–21.

2. Theophilus of Antioch, *To Autolycus* 3.29.

3. Irenaeus of Lyons, *Demonstration (or Proof) of the Apostolic Preaching* 74. See also Irenaeus of Lyons, *Against Heresies* 2.22.5–6, where Irenaeus relates a tradition that Jesus' ministry lasted only one year. See also 3.21.3, where Irenaeus says that Jesus' ministry lasted ten years and that he was in his forties when he died, demonstrating that he is in many cases only passing on what he has heard, even if that means including contradictory oral traditions.

CHAPTER 1

1. The earliest use of the word *church* to refer to a place of worship seems to be by Clement of Alexandra, *The Instructor* 3.11, written in the late second century. Even here, however, it does not refer to a church *building*, but to a dedicated worship space, probably a converted home.

2. Early house-church divisions may have been along ethnic (language) lines, socioeconomic lines, or geographic lines in the larger cities.

3. Throughout the present book, the word *Church* is capitalized when it refers to the universal Church, and not capitalized when it refers to a local congregation or city church, that is, the Christians in a particular place.

4. See Justin Martyr, *1 Apology* 16.8.

5. Ignatius of Antioch, *Letter to the Philadelphians* 3.3.

6. Suetonius, *Life of Claudius* 25.4.

7. Athenagoras, *A Plea for the Christians* 3, Theophilus of Antioch, *To Autolycus* 3.4, Tertullian, *To the Nations* (*Ad Nationes*) 1.7.

8. Tacitus, *Annals* 15.44.

9. Suetonius, *Life of Nero* 16.

10. The annexation of Judea to Syria took place in the year 6 CE. It coincided with the appointment of Quirinius as proconsular legate ("governor") of Syria, and resulted in a census, which was apparently the catalyst for the rebellion. The census of 6 CE is mentioned in Acts 5:37. Note that this is not the census described in Luke 2:1–5 (the occasion for Joseph and Mary's journey to Bethlehem). The census of 6 CE cannot be the one mentioned in Luke 2 because the Gospel of Matthew tells us that the birth of Christ took place "in the days of Herod the King" (that is, Herod I, the king in Matthew 2:1–23). This means that the census that forced Joseph and Mary to travel from Galilee to Judea must have taken place before Herod's death, which occurred in 4 BCE. The problem is that Quirinius was not governor of Syria, as Luke 2 is usually interpreted, until 6 CE. To harmonize the gospels it seems that Quirinius would have to be proconsul of Syria at the same time that Herod was king. At that time, however, Quirinius was proconsul in Galatia. In reality, the Greek word *prote* in Luke 2:2 can mean either "first" or "before." In this case, the latter should be used, so that the verse should be translated, "this census was *before* Quirinius was governing Syria." Luke's point would then be to distinguish the census that was taken around the time of Jesus' birth from the more famous one that caused an uprising in 6 CE. The proconsul of Syria at the time of Jesus' birth was Sentius Saturninus. Tertullian mentions a census under Saturninus (*Against Marcion* 4.19), as does Justin Martyr (*1 Apology* 34), but there is no extant Roman record for such a census. In any event, Judea was still a client kingdom and not yet a province under the authority of Syria when Saturninus

was governor. More important, a Roman tax census taken when Judea had become a province, but Galilee was still an autonomous tetrarchy (as in 6 CE), would not be likely to force Joseph and Mary to travel from one realm to another. But when all of Palestine was still united under Herod, people might have been required to register in their hometowns. There was such a census in Egypt in 104 CE. Therefore, the census mentioned in Luke 2:2 must be prior to that of 6 CE.

11. Timothy D. Barnes, "Pagan Perceptions of Christianity," in *Early Christianity*, ed. I. Hazlett (Nashville: Abingdon, 1991), 231. Barnes notes that the fact that Nero could even attempt to blame the fire on the Christians shows that public opinion was already against them. The reader must also keep in mind that the members of the Church were not yet called "Christians." I use the term here strictly for convenience.

12. Note that the Colosseum was not built yet. In fact, the Colosseum now stands in the area that was leveled by the fire. It was built about fifteen years later.

13. According to tradition, Peter was crucified upside down. When he found out that he was to die in the same manner as the Lord, he pleaded that he was not worthy and should die some other way. His executioners mockingly agreed, nailing him to the cross upside down (see John 21:18–19).

14. It is impossible to know to what extent Domitian was personally involved in persecution, especially in the provinces. See Timothy D. Barnes, *Tertullian: A Historical and Literary Study* (Oxford: Clarendon Press, 1971), 150. On the other hand, Tertullian and Eusebius both attest to Domitian as a persecuting emperor. See Tertullian, *Apology* 5, and Eusebius of Caesarea, *Ecclesiastical History* 4.26.9.

15. Cassius Dio 67.14.1–2 refers to the execution of Flavius Clemens and the subsequent exile of his wife, Flavia Domitilla, on a charge of atheism. This may refer to Christianity, but it is not certain. Some argue that it refers to a conversion to Judaism, though there may still have been confusion of the two in the minds of the Romans. Tradition associates the couple with the catacomb of Domitilla in Rome, and also possibly as the former masters of a freedman who would become known as Bishop Clement of Rome.

The later *Acts of Nereus and Achilles* make Domitilla the niece of Clemens, probably in an attempt to present her as a virgin, and this error would find its way into later writers, including Jerome.

16. While there is ongoing debate over the date and authorship of the Book of Revelation, it is this author's conviction that the document was in fact written by the apostle John in the year 95 CE. See James L. Papandrea, *The Wedding of the Lamb: A Historical Approach to the Book of Revelation* (Eugene, OR: Wipf & Stock/ Pickwick Publications, 2011), 16–27.

17. The word *pagan* is used here without the pejorative connotation it might have had in the early Church. The English word comes from the Latin *pagani*, which referred to the country dwellers, those outside of the urban areas. In the time after Christianity was legalized, some claimed that the only people who held on to the Greco-Roman mythologies were the people in the rural areas, since many cities were coming to have a Christian majority. Thus it was used in a derogatory sense, in the way that some today might use the term *redneck*. It is, admittedly, also used somewhat anachronistically when applied in the early centuries of the Church. In the present context, it simply refers to anyone who was not Christian or Jewish, and it assumes that participating in the traditional Greco-Roman worship would be considered a form of idolatry for Jews and Christians.

18. Pliny the Younger, *Epistle* 10.96–97 (to Trajan, with rescript). Pliny implied that he was following an earlier order of Trajan to outlaw Christian assembly; however, there is no extant evidence of such a law. Some have argued that the Christians in Pliny's province were considered guilty of illegal assembly, and not that the name of Christian alone was enough to have them executed. If that were the case, however, then simply making a loyalty sacrifice or denouncing the faith would not suffice to remove the charge.

19. Eusebius of Caesarea, *Ecclesiastical History* 6.5, 8.8.

20. Tertullian, *Apology* 2–4, 10. Tertullian (writing around the turn of the third century) does say that the name of Christian implies the crimes of "sacrilege and treason." This is significant because it makes Christianity, as a form of treason, a capital offense. The apocryphal *Acts of Apollonius* (23–24) mentions a law that stated, "[N]o one at all anywhere shall be called a Christian." The

document may not be reliable on this point and probably reflects the author's perception of public opinion rather than imperial policy. Note that *The Shepherd* by Hermas (9.9, 10.1) says that martyrs suffer "for the sake of the name." It is not clear here whether "the name" means the name of Jesus, or the name Christian, and much depends on the dating of the document to determine whether it would be too early for followers of Jesus even to be called Christians. The important point to note, however, is that by the time of the early second century, believers are called "Christians" (Pliny used the word), and it appears that the name was first used as an insult by the enemies of the Church, which strongly implies that the name Christian emerged at the same time that it was becoming a crime.

21. Tertullian, *Apology* 2, 49. The Romans also tortured the slaves of people suspected of being Christians, to try to get them to accuse their masters (Justin Martyr, *2 Apology* 12).

22. Cf. Timothy D. Barnes, *Early Christianity and the Roman Empire* (London: Variorum, 1984), 40–41.

23. As Barnes correctly points out, we do not know to what extent some emperors endorsed persecution, or for that matter, to what extent their orders were even carried out in the provinces. Therefore, we cannot assume uniformity of enforcement across the empire, even when we have imperial edicts authorizing the persecution of the Church. No doubt many Christians were martyred without the emperors' knowledge and even under emperors who did not endorse persecution. On the other hand, there were also provinces governed by men who did not persecute Christians, even when the emperors encouraged it. A governor's primary goal was to keep the peace, and if the Christians and pagans in his province could coexist peacefully, he had the luxury of looking the other way. In general, the farther from Rome a governor was, the more flexibility he had to deviate from the emperor's current programs. See Barnes, *Tertullian*, 149, 155. It cannot go without mentioning, at this point, that the temple erected in the Roman forum dedicated to the deified Antoninus was later converted into a church.

24. Eusebius of Caesarea, *Ecclesiastical History* 4.13.1–7. Because Christians refused to participate in the sacrifices, some

martyrdoms resulted, though this was an indirect result of the edict.

25. Barnes, *Early Christianity and the Roman Empire*, 44, 49–50.

26. Eusebius of Caesarea, *Ecclesiastical History* 6.41. In the early part of his reign, Severus appeared to be tolerant of the Church. This made some Christian writers reluctant to blame the persecution on him. Tertullian even tried to paint him as a friend of the Church in order to convince the governor of North Africa to discontinue persecution (Tertullian, *To Scapula* 4.3–6).

27. Paul Keresztes, *Imperial Rome and the Christians* (Lanham, MD: University Press of America, 1989), 11–13. The edict is mentioned in Historia Augusta, *Septimius Severus* 17.1, though the reliability of the Historia Augusta has been challenged. See Geoffrey D. Dunn, *Tertullian* (New York: Routledge, 2004), 17. Dunn does not accept the historicity of the edict, based on favorable comments Tertullian makes about Severus in *To Scapula*. However this was an apologetic document and it would not have served Tertullian's purpose to criticize Severus. Note that Eusebius mentions the closing of the catechetical school in Alexandria (*Ecclesiastical History* 6.3). In the end, the change in policy from Trajan's rescript to Pliny (advising that Christians should not be sought out) to the situation in the early third century (when Christians like Perpetua were rounded up) is unexplainable without the edict of 202 CE.

28. Eusebius of Caesarea, *Ecclesiastical History* 6.7. See Papandrea, *The Wedding of the Lamb*, 156–59.

29. Tertullian, *Apology* 7.

30. Enforcement of the edict apparently targeted recent converts, such as Perpetua. See Barnes, *Early Christianity and the Roman Empire*, 40. Perpetua and Felicitas were martyred in Carthage in 203 CE. Even though Perpetua was from the aristocracy, the right of Roman citizens to appeal to the emperor had all but disappeared by this time.

31. *Martyrdom of Polycarp* 2. See also Hermas, *The Shepherd* 24, where it says that the flames of martyrdom purify. This could be a reference to an early belief in purgatory.

32. 2 Clement 20.

33. For an excellent overview of this genre, see Helen Rhee, *Early Christian Literature: Christ and Culture in the Second and Third Centuries* (New York: Routledge, 2005).

34. The lack of crying out in pain was seen as a kind of transfiguration of the martyr (*Martyrdom of Polycarp* 2).

35. Clement of Rome, 1 Clement 6–7, *Martyrdom of Polycarp* 18. Volunteering for martyrdom was frowned upon, however. Since one might risk failing in the end (especially under torture) and losing one's salvation, it was better not to seek martyrdom, but to do as Jesus did, and wait to be arrested. Polycarp was seen as a model, since he neither ran to martyrdom nor ran from it (*Martyrdom of Polycarp* 1, 4).

36. Ignatius of Antioch, *Letter to the Romans* 6.1.

37. *Martyrdom of Polycarp* 18, *Apostolic Constitutions* 6.6 (6.30).

38. There was a saying in the ancient world, "Call no man blessed while he lives." This meant that as long as one was still alive, there was still time for something to go wrong. As we will see, the early Christians believed that one could lose one's salvation by committing serious sins after baptism; therefore, the only way to know for sure if someone had persevered to the end would be to know that the person had died in the manner that was thought to erase all sin.

39. Ignatius of Antioch, *Letter to the Romans* 3.3.

CHAPTER 2

1. On the belief that the grace of baptism could be lost, see Cyprian of Carthage, *Epistle* 54.13, *On the Unity of the Catholic Church* 20–21. Although Cyprian wrote almost two centuries after the Didache, he is expressing what was considered a traditional belief.

2. Didache 2, 16. See also the apocryphal *Apocalypse of Peter* 25.

3. Didache 2.2. See also Juvenal, *Satire IV*. Writing at about the same time as the Didache, Juvenal, a non-Christian Roman writer, criticized the practice of abortion as a convenience of the wealthy class to avoid the "burden" of having children. His motivation for this critique is very different from the Christian critique, but

it does show how prevalent and acceptable abortion was at the time, and even Juvenal called it murder. Apparently, oral drugs could be used to cause a miscarriage. But even if a baby was born, under Roman law it could be legally disposed of, for no other reason than it was unwanted. At times, however, the Roman government tried to encourage the wealthy to have more children, since many couples were opting to limit their children so that their fortunes would not be dispersed. This was seen as a threat to the empire because it resulted in a decrease in population. If the prevailing attitude among Roman aristocracy was that children were a burden, the early Christians responded to this by saying that having children is the very purpose of marriage (Justin Martyr, *1 Apology* 29).

4. Most of the abandoned children were probably girls, since girls were often perceived as a financial burden. Most of the children exposed in this way were probably taken and raised to be slaves (including prostitutes). See *Epistle to Diognetus* 5.6.

5. *Epistle of Barnabas* 19.5, 20.2, Athenagoras, *A Plea for the Christians* 35 (note that Athenagoras also condemns capital punishment), Clement of Alexandria, *The Instructor* 2.10, 3.4 (note that Clement criticized the Romans who, he says, would save an animal but expose a child), Tertullian, *Apology* 9, *Apostolic Church Order* 6. The early Christian writers, exemplified by Tertullian, did not see a difference between abortion and infanticide. See also *Apostolic Constitutions* 7.1 (7.3).

6. Justin Martyr, *1 Apology* 27.

7. 1 Clement 60.4–61.2.

8. 1 Clement 47.6.

9. 1 Clement 44.

10. 1 Clement 3.3. See also 1 Clement 38.2, where the division is described in terms that are reminiscent of 1 Corinthians 12:22–26.

11. 1 Clement 63.3–4.

12. 1 Clement 46.9.

13. 1 Clement 46.9, 47.7.

14. Clement of Alexandria would later remark that Peter is preeminent among the apostles because he is the only apostle for whom Jesus had paid his tax (Matt 17:27). Clement of Alexandria, *Who Is the Rich Man That Shall Be Saved?* 21.

15. On apostolic succession, see Irenaeus of Lyons, *Against Heresies* 2.9.1, 3.1.1, 3.3.1–2, 3.4.1, 4.26.2–4, 4.33.8. See also Tertullian, *The Prescription Against Heretics* 19–21, 23 (an answer to the objection that Peter was rebuked by Paul), 28, 32, 36–37. Note that in chapter 37, Tertullian says that the scriptures do not belong to the heretics, but to those who still hold the "deed" to them, which comes from the "original owners," the apostles. In chapter 28, Tertullian also says that the Holy Spirit guarantees that the Church will not go astray, based on Jesus' promise to Peter in Matthew 16:18–19.

16. Theophilus of Antioch, *To Autolycus* 3.29.

17. 1 Clement 63.2.

18. 1 Clement 42, 44.

19. 1 Clement 25. The phoenix was apparently a popular Christian symbol early on, as evidenced by catacomb paintings and early church apse mosaics.

20. 1 Clement 60.4—61.2.

21. 2 Clement 10, 15. The false teachers in question are Docetics; see chapter 4.

22. 2 Clement 3, 6.

23. 2 Clement 6, cf. Hermas, *The Shepherd* 72.3–4.

24. On the belief that salvation could be lost, see Didache 16, Hermas, *The Shepherd* 74.5, 95.2, Irenaeus of Lyons, *Against Heresies* 5.9.3. Irenaeus says that the Holy Spirit, once received, can be driven out.

25. 2 Clement 2.

26. 2 Clement 4. The second part of this is like Matthew 7:23, but the first part has no biblical parallel.

27. 2 Clement 5.

28. 2 Clement 12. Cf. *Gospel of Thomas* 22. The Gnostics, who produced the *Gospel of Thomas*, were mostly docetic in their Christology, meaning that they denied the real humanity of Jesus Christ.

29. Ignatius of Antioch, *Letter to the Ephesians* 1.3. The belief that the Onesimus of Philemon became bishop of Ephesus provides another possible reason why the Letter to Philemon was included in the New Testament.

30. Ignatius of Antioch, *Letter to the Ephesians* 3.1.

31. Ignatius of Antioch, *Letter to the Trallians* 3.3, 5.2.
32. Ignatius of Antioch, *Letter to the Romans* 4.3.
33. Ignatius of Antioch, *Letter to the Magnesians* 6.2.
34. Ignatius of Antioch, *Letter to the Ephesians* 5.3. See also *Letter to the Magnesians* 6, 13, *Letter to the Trallians* 7, *Letter to the Smyrnaeans* 9.
35. Ignatius of Antioch, *Letter to the Ephesians* 6.1.
36. Ignatius of Antioch, *Letter to the Philadelphians* 4.1.
37. Ignatius of Antioch, *Letter to the Smyrnaeans* 8.
38. On the bishops as recipients of the apostles' authority, specifically the authority of "binding and loosing" granted by Jesus in Matthew 18:18 (interpreted as the authority to absolve sin and excommunicate), see the *Didascalia Apostolorum* 5.
39. For Ignatius, to be outside the authority of the bishop is to be outside of the body of Christ. Ignatius of Antioch, *Letter to the Ephesians* 5, *Letter to the Magnesians* 7, *Letter to the Trallians* 2–3, *Letter to the Philadelphians* 3–4, 7, *Letter to the Smyrnaeans* 8. Ignatius wrote that only bishops have the authority to convene a council, *Letter to Polycarp* 7. Note that Irenaeus also condemned unauthorized meetings, Irenaeus of Lyons, *Against Heresies* 3.2.2.
40. Ignatius of Antioch, *Letter to the Trallians* 3.1.
41. Ignatius of Antioch, *Letter to the Ephesians* 5.3.
42. Ignatius of Antioch, *Letter to the Magnesians* 6.2, 7.1, *Letter to the Trallians* 2.2, *Letter to the Philadelphians* 2.2, 6.2, 7.2, *Letter to the Smyrnaeans* 8.1–2, 9.1.
43. Ignatius of Antioch, *Letter to the Ephesians* 5.2, 20. See also *Letter to the Smyrnaeans* 8, where it is clear that the bishops could delegate the authority to preside over the Eucharist to priests under their authority.
44. Ignatius of Antioch, *Letter to the Ephesians* 20.2, *Letter to the Philadelphians* 4.1, *Letter to the Smyrnaeans* 8.1.
45. Ignatius of Antioch, *Letter to the Romans* 2.1, 4.1, 5.2, 6.3, 7.2.
46. Polycarp of Smyrna, *Letter to the Philippians* 13.2.
47. Irenaeus of Lyons, *Demonstration of the Apostolic Preaching* 3, *Against Heresies* 5.5.1.
48. Eusebius of Caesarea, *Ecclesiastical History* 4.14. The bishop of Rome was Anicetus, bishop from 155 to 166 CE.

49. Polycarp of Smyrna, *Letter to the Philippians* 2.1–2.

50. Polycarp of Smyrna, *Letter to the Philippians* 12.3.

51. Eusebius of Caesarea, *Ecclesiastical History* 3.39.9.

52. That the concept of a day need not be interpreted as a literal day of twenty-four hours, see Irenaeus of Lyons, *Against Heresies* 2.22.2.

53. Assuming the birth of Christ in 5 BCE, if this interpretation had been correct, we all would have been convinced of it in 1995. Early millennialism was probably a reaction against the dualist rejection of matter/creation that is inherent in docetism and gnosticism (see below). In other words, Papias apparently responded to the docetic "false teachers" by affirming that, not only was Jesus Christ a man of real material flesh and blood, but even the material world itself (as God's good creation) is in some sense eternal. It is possibly also a reaction against the philosophical concept of a cosmic cycle of conflagration and re-creation. Papias was followed in this interpretation by the author of the *Epistle of Barnabas* as well as by Justin Martyr, Irenaeus, and Tertullian. See *Epistle of Barnabas* 15, Justin Martyr, *Dialogue with Trypho* 80, and Irenaeus of Lyons, *Against Heresies* 5.28.2–3, 5.35.1–2.

54. Eusebius of Caesarea, *Ecclesiastical History* 3.28, 5.33.4.

55. Barnabas, *Epistle* 16.4.

56. See for example Barnabas, *Epistle* 4.6–8, where the author seems to go much further than Paul on the subject of the rejection of Israel and the validity (or nonvalidity) of the covenant. Also, the emphasis on works suggests a possible adoptionist origin.

57. Hermas, *The Shepherd* 25.1–5.

58. Hermas, *The Shepherd* 13.5.

59. Hermas, *The Shepherd* 83.1.

60. Hermas, *The Shepherd* 33.6.

61. Hermas, *The Shepherd* 25.7.

62. Hermas, *The Shepherd* 12.3, 39.5–7, 98.1.

63. Hermas, *The Shepherd* 34.1–2.

64. Hermas, *The Shepherd* 15.3, 108.1–2. Often in the early Church, a man who hoped to continue an upwardly mobile public career would postpone his baptism until retirement. This was because of the strict moral expectations of the baptized, and the conflict presented when the requirements of a government job

included participation in pagan sacrifice. This created a situation in which there were times and places when the churches were made up of aristocratic women and lower-class men, who had less to lose with regard to their career.

65. Hermas, *The Shepherd* 37.4, 98.3. In *The Shepherd* 14, Hermas also says that those who deny Christ in persecution often do so to protect their property.

66. Hermas, *The Shepherd* 6.8, 96.3. Note that this implies that there were some in the Church who were known to have denied the faith in the last persecution, yet reconciled to the Church. Hermas mentions one by name, a certain Maximus (*The Shepherd* 7.4). This could also argue for a later date than traditionally assigned.

67. Hermas, *The Shepherd* 6.7–8, 103.6. For Hermas, it is a foregone conclusion that there will be more persecution. Given the affinity of the structure of *The Shepherd* to the Book of Revelation, it is clear that Hermas believed Revelation to be predicting greater persecution in the future. See *The Shepherd* 22.1. Of course, he turned out to be right.

68. Hermas, *The Shepherd* 48.3–4.

69. Hermas, *The Shepherd* 65.5.

70. Hermas, *The Shepherd* 50–51.

71. Hermas, *The Shepherd* 17.5, 50.8–9, 51.10.

72. Hermas, *The Shepherd* 69.5.

73. Hermas, *The Shepherd* 65.5.

CHAPTER 3

1. See the introduction to Tertullian's *On the Soul's Testimony*.

2. Justin Martyr, *1 Apology* 10.

3. Justin Martyr, *1 Apology* 9.

4. Theophilus of Antioch, *To Autolycus* 2.3.

5. As proof of this, the apologists will point out that one of the newest additions to the Roman pantheon was Antinous, the young boy whom the emperor Hadrian had seduced. When Antinous drowned in the Nile (possibly a suicide), Hadrian had him

proclaimed a god. See Justin Martyr, *1 Apology* 29, Clement of Alexandria, *Exhortation to the Greeks* 6. Some also said that the gods were in fact demons.

6. Theophilus of Antioch, *To Autolycus* 3.1, 3.4, 3.29.

7. Justin Martyr, *1 Apology* 23, 44, 59, 60, Clement of Alexandria, *Exhortation to the Greeks* 6.

8. Theophilus of Antioch, *To Autolycus* 3.4.

9. Ironically, when Athenagoras argued that Christians were morally superior to the rest of the Romans, he said, in effect, *If you don't believe us, just ask our slaves* (Athenagoras, *A Plea for the Christians* 32). Obviously, one of the ways in which the Church was not critical of Roman society was in its capitulation to the slave culture, though Christians would have argued that they treated their slaves better than the average Roman.

10. Clement of Alexandria, *Exhortation to the Greeks* 10.

11. Eusebius of Caesarea, *Ecclesiastical History* 4.3.

12. Cf. also Theophilus of Antioch, *To Autolycus* 1.5. Theophilus said that when you see a ship sailing into harbor, you assume that there must be a pilot. Therefore, the universe must also have its pilot, who is God.

13. Eusebius of Caesarea, *Ecclesiastical History* 4.9.

14. It has been suggested that the author may be an apologist named Quadratus. A fragment of his apology is preserved in Eusebius of Caesarea, *Ecclesiastical History* 4.3.1–2.

15. *Epistle to Diognetus* 9.

16. *Epistle to Diognetus* 7.7.

17. Justin Martyr, *2 Apology* 12.

18. Justin mentions that Jesus was born 150 years earlier, which, assuming the birth of Jesus at 5 BCE, would put the writing of *1 Apology* at 145 CE. There are other internal clues that point to a slightly later date, however, which shows that either Justin's statement was meant to be approximate, or he already had the current calendar's miscalculation in mind.

19. Justin Martyr, *1 Apology* 2, 45.

20. Justin Martyr, *1 Apology* 45, 68.

21. Justin Martyr, *1 Apology* 31, 36.

22. Justin Martyr, *1 Apology* 12.

23. Justin Martyr, *1 Apology* 45.

24. Justin Martyr, *1 Apology* 67.

25. Interestingly, Justin does not mention singing, though it must be assumed that early Christian worship included singing (or chanting). Pliny's letter to Trajan, written about forty years earlier, does mention the singing of hymns to Christ. It is also interesting to note that in Justin's description of early worship the term he uses for "presider" (sometimes translated "president") is not the New Testament term *presbyter* (priest) but rather the Greek word *proestos*, which means, simply, the leader—the one who stands in front.

26. Justin Martyr, *2 Apology* 3.

27. Justin Martyr, *2 Apology* 7.

28. See also Justin Martyr, *1 Apology* 8, 18, 52.

29. The martyr document does mention the location of Justin's school, "above the baths of Martin."

30. Eusebius of Caesarea, *Ecclesiastical History* 4.29. The accusations against Tatian by later writers are contradictory. Jerome called him the founder of a sect known as the Encratites; however, the Encratites already existed before Tatian left Rome. Eusebius is probably correct in saying that Saturninus was the real founder of the Encratites. Others, including Irenaeus, have accused Tatian of gnosticism, but there is nothing to support this in his extant writings.

31. Tatian, *Address to the Greeks* 5.

32. In spite of the later accusations of gnosticism, Tatian's Christology was more likely an influence on adoptionism and Arianism, both of which saw Christ as a created being who was not eternally coexistent with the Father. See James L. Papandrea, *Novatian of Rome and the Culmination of Pre-Nicene Orthodoxy* (Eugene, OR: Wipf & Stock/Pickwick Publications, 2011).

33. Irenaeus of Lyons, *Against Heresies* 3.11.8. For Irenaeus, the four gospels are the four pillars of the Church, and since there are four winds and four corners of the earth, there also must be four gospels—no more, no less. Irenaeus explains the symbolism of the four gospels: Matthew is the man, emphasizing Jesus' humanity; Mark is the eagle, representing the Holy Spirit and prophecy; Luke is the calf, symbolizing Christ's role as priest and sacrifice; and John is the lion, which represents Christ's royal power. See also Eusebius of Caesarea, *Ecclesiastical History* 6.25.

34. The fragment of Melito's apology is preserved in Eusebius of Caesarea, *Ecclesiastical History* 4.26.

35. Note that Clement of Alexandria wrote that the "new song" of Revelation 5:9 and 14:3 is a reference to the new covenant (*Exhortation to the Greeks* 1). See also James L. Papandrea, *The Wedding of the Lamb: A Historical Approach to the Book of Revelation* (Eugene, OR: Wipf & Stock/Pickwick Publications, 2011), 102–4.

36. Theophilus of Antioch, *To Autolycus* 1.1, 1.12.

37. Theophilus of Antioch, *To Autolycus* 1.2.

38. Theophilus of Antioch, *To Autolycus* 1.5.

39. A note is required on the use of the words *heresy* and *orthodoxy*. It is assumed that the "heresies" were sincere attempts to interpret scripture, many of them motivated by the admirable conviction that no matter how one understands Christ, one cannot compromise monotheism. But it was not long after the writing of the apostolic documents we call the New Testament that the Church started to produce varying (and often mutually exclusive) interpretations of those documents. Often it happened that the position that would come to be confirmed as "orthodox" was not defined until it was forced to be by opposing alternative interpretations. In each generation of the Church's development, the orthodox response was a refutation of the alternatives by an increasingly refined defense of the conclusions of the previous generations. Thus each generation's orthodoxy becomes the foundation for future generations. This does not mean that no one ever challenged the conclusions of a previous generation. But it does mean that when the dust had settled, the Church defined orthodoxy in such a way as to preserve consistency with the previous generations. The Church's tradition, then, is the collective contribution of the early Church to the interpretation of scripture. Put more simply, tradition interprets scripture, and does so in a way that uses the consensus of the previous generations to refute the current alternatives (2 Pet 1:20). Therefore, the history of the Church, specifically the history of the development of doctrine, is the history of the interpretation of scripture.

40. Eusebius said that Clement of Alexandria's name was Titus Flavius Clemens, though there still may be some confusion

with Clement of Rome. See Eusebius of Caesarea, *Ecclesiastical History* 6.13.

41. Clement of Alexandria, *Exhortation to the Greeks* 2. Clement said that "superstition" (or paganism) is the worship of too many gods, but atheism admits to no gods at all. The happy medium between the two dangerous "extremes of ignorance" is monotheism.

42. Clement of Alexandria, *Exhortation to the Greeks* 6.

43. Clement of Alexandria, *Exhortation to the Greeks* 9. The word I have translated as "light" in the second verse is actually the word *beams*. Apparently, a popular analogy for the Trinity in the early Church was the image of the sun, the beams of light from the sun, and the heat from the sun.

44. Clement of Alexandria, *The Instructor* 2.10. See also the *Apostolic Constitutions* 6.5 (6.28). This attitude was at least partially a reaction to the promiscuity and rejection of childbearing in some of the gnostic sects. Since it came to be believed that heretics avoided having children but advocated an orgiastic lifestyle, the Church would promote the opposite view, that sex, even within marriage, was only for the purpose of having children. Cf. also Athenagoras, *A Plea for the Christians* 32–33, in which Athenagoras even worries about the kiss of peace, saying that only one kiss was allowed; a second kiss crossed the line into sin.

45. For example, see Novatian, *On the Benefit of Purity* 7.

46. Clement of Alexandria, *Miscellanies* 1.5. See also *The Instructor* 1.6, 1.11.

CHAPTER 4

1. According to the *Apostolic Church Order* 19, the office of "evangelist" was the person who reads the gospel. Other lists of church officers include "readers." Even though the authority of the teaching office would be reserved for the bishops (and delegated to the priests), it was assumed that the bishop might be illiterate. Therefore, the evangelist was the reader.

2. Didache 11.3.

3. The Greek word *presbyteros* can be translated either "priest" or "elder." In some documents, however, the term seems to have a technical meaning referring specifically to the second generation of Church leaders, the ones whom the apostles chose to succeed them. The letters of 2 John and 3 John are probably by a John "the Elder," not the apostle John but possibly his successor. See Papias 4–7, and Irenaeus of Lyons, *Against Heresies* 2.22.5, 5.5.1. Note that Papias believed that the Book of Revelation was also by John the Elder.

4. Didache 15, 1 Clement 41–42. Note that the bishop and priest are considered equals, with the deacons occupying a lower place on the hierarchy. The word *pastor* simply means shepherd, a concept that seems to go back to Clement of Alexandria, *The Instructor* 1.6, but is clearly based on the concept of Jesus as the Good Shepherd, combined with John 21:15–17.

5. Hermas, *The Shepherd* 3.5.1, 13.1, 102.2. In *The Shepherd*, priests are called teachers. As long as the terms *bishop* and *priest* are interchangeable, the resident pastor was, of course, the teacher of the house-church. Once the office of bishop emerged as an "overseer" of the other priests, the teaching authority would ultimately rest with the bishops, but would be granted to the priests for their churches as long as their teaching was consistent with the bishops'.

6. Note that in the *Martyrdom of Justin*, Justin Martyr tells the Roman authorities that the Christians of Rome do not have a single meeting place because there are too many of them to fit into one space.

7. This was the case in Rome during Clement's time. See also Hermas, *The Shepherd* 8.3. As long as the apostles were alive, they functioned as bishops, as the authority over a region, or over a group of churches, such as the apostle Paul over the churches he founded, or the apostle John over the churches of Asia Minor (mentioned in Revelation 1—2). By the time the apostles were gone, there were likely multiple house-churches in each city, so that the bishop would again have authority over multiple churches, but within a city rather than regionally. Eventually, certain cities would be designated as *metropolitans*, the bishops there having authority over a region, even over the other bishops in that region.

8. Even when the office of bishop came to be an authority over the rest of the priests, it was always assumed that the bishop remained a priest and in that sense was "first among equals." In the third century, Cyprian assumes that bishops are priests, and that bishops and priests are copresiders of the sacraments (Cyprian of Carthage, *Epistle* 51.7, 54.20).

9. 1 Clement 40.5–41.1. It does not appear that church leadership becomes an occupation (with pay) until the late second century. By the time of Tertullian, who wrote at the turn of the third century, he can criticize some heretics because their leaders have to have secular jobs to make a living. The implication is that if their sects were legitimate, they would be able to support their leaders. (Tertullian, *The Prescription Against the Heretics* 41). According to the *Didascalia Apostolorum* 8–9, when bishops do receive pay for leading their churches, they are to consider themselves as sharing the resources of the church with the needy. It appears that offerings were collected and entrusted to the bishop, who distributed money to those in need, keeping some for himself as a salary. The *Didascalia* also includes a schedule of clergy stipends; however, this represents a later development, no earlier than the third or fourth century.

10. Ignatius of Antioch, *Letter to the Ephesians* 3, *Letter to the Magnesians* 3.1, 6.

11. Ignatius of Antioch, *Letter to the Ephesians* 2, 20, *Letter to the Magnesians* 2, 7, *Letter to the Trallians* 2–3, *Letter to the Philadelphians* 4.

12. Ignatius of Antioch, *Letter to the Philadelphians* 4.1, *Letter to the Trallians* 3.1. Note that the word for "bishop" here is singular.

13. Note that in the middle of the second century, Justin Martyr, though not a bishop, was the leader of a philosophical (catechetical?) school in Rome. It appears to be just one of a number of such schools, though we do not know how many, nor do we know whether each school had a different teaching authority over it, or whether the leaders of all the schools would answer to the same bishop.

14. Acts 20:7–12 may point to an early tradition of evening Eucharist, which would be understandable considering the fact that

the Last Supper was in the evening. See Ralph P. Martin, *Worship in the Early Church* (Grand Rapids, MI: Eerdmans, 1964), 33.

15. Justin Martyr, *1 Apology* 67. Note also that in the *Martyrdom of Justin*, it is clear that there are multiple church meetings in Rome.

16. Ignatius of Antioch, *Letter to Polycarp* 5.2.

17. Cyprian of Carthage, *On the Lapsed* 25.

18. *Didascalia Apostolorum* 12. In Rome, however, there was a separate office of doorkeeper.

19. *Didascalia Apostolorum* 16. As the Christian population in a city grew, the deacons could also be charged with communicating with the bishop on behalf of the people, acting as a secretary to the bishop, so that the bishop's time did not become consumed by the needs of individuals.

20. Justin Martyr, *1 Apology* 65, 67. The deacons were to act on behalf of the bishops in visiting the sick and shut-ins. According to the *Didascalia*, they would also bring food to those in prison and were authorized to bribe the guards to treat the Christian prisoners well. They might also use church money to ransom kidnapped Christians or even buy the freedom of Christian slaves or prisoners (*Didascalia Apostolorum* 18–19).

21. *Didascalia Apostolorum* 16. As we will see below, the church of Rome in the third century had seven deacons, which corresponded to the division of the city into regions.

22. See Ignatius of Antioch, preface to the *Letter to the Philadelphians*, and the *Martyrdom of Polycarp* 6. On the restriction of presiding to bishops and priests, see also the *Apostolic Tradition* 8, 28. On the other hand, deacons (and deaconesses) did play a more central role in baptism in some places. See the *Didascalia Apostolorum* 16.

23. *Apostolic Tradition* 14.

24. David Rankin, *Tertullian and the Church* (Cambridge, UK: Cambridge University Press, 1995), 191.

25. Worshiping Christ in the early Church included praying to him (asking for his presence and intervention, cf. Acts 7:59–60 and the prayers of the early martyr acts), calling him "Lord" in confessions of faith that make him the object of faith (cf. Rom 10:9–13, 1 Cor 12:1–3, 15:3–5), conducting sacraments in his name, and

singing hymns in praise of his divinity. See Pliny the Younger, *Letter to Trajan*, where Pliny tells Trajan that the Christians have a habit of singing songs to Christ "as to a god," and Eusebius of Caesarea, *Ecclesiastical History*, 3.33.1–3, 5.28.5–6, where Eusebius says, "All the psalms and hymns which were written by faithful Christians from the beginning sing of the Christ as the Word (*Logos*) of God and treat him as God." See also Martin, *Worship in the Early Church*, 11–12, 19, 24–27, 57–60. The practice of worship in the early Church was based on current Jewish practice and included praise, prayer, and instruction. The experiences of the disciples in the ministry of Jesus, as well as their understanding of his life, death, and resurrection, all resulted in the institution of sacraments, but even these have their Jewish precedents. The concept of worship itself assumes two aspects: service and submission. To worship God (and Christ) means to submit to his will and serve him in the world.

26. Hymn singing in the early church followed the practice of the synagogue (cf. Matt 26:30) and was more like melodic chanting, or singing with a melody of limited range (cf. Tertullian, *Apology* 2.6). Christian hymns probably began as a kind of intoned reading, at a time when it would be hard to distinguish between unison recitation, chanting, and singing.

27. Early Christian melodies probably used a limited number of notes orbiting around a tonic, something close to a Phrygian (pentatonic) scale, and not unlike medieval chant. Their musical intervals were not exactly like ours, so most of their scales would probably sound like minor keys to us, though they may have eventually developed the use of different modes for different liturgical seasons. The Oxyrhynchus hymn, from the third century, is our earliest example of Christian music with notation. It has a range of one octave (see Ralph P. Martin, *A Hymn of Christ* [Downers Grove, IL: InterVarsity Press, 1997], 4, 7). At the beginning, in the house-churches, it seems that anyone might bring a song (1 Cor 14:26), which was then led by the one who composed it. At some times and places, spontaneous hymns may have been seen as a charismatic gift, like a musical version of speaking in tongues; however, this would have gone by the wayside along with prophecy, especially if it became more of a solo rather than including partici-

pation by the congregation. A hymn would usually have been sung as a call and response, possibly based on a psalm or some biblical parallelism, with the leader singing a line alternating with the assembly echoing the same line, or repeating a refrain. See Tertullian, *Apology* 2.6, 39, and Eusebius of Caesarea, *Ecclesiastical History* 2.17.22. See also Martin, *Worship in the Early Church*, 40–41; and *A Hymn of Christ*, 3–4, 6, 13. Possible examples of antiphonal singing in the Bible include Ezra 3:11, Nehemiah 12:24, 31, and Revelation 22:17. Cf. also Didache 10.6 and Justin Martyr, *Dialogue with Trypho* 63.

28. *Odes of Solomon* 14.8, 26.3. See also Revelation 5:8. These songs may have been accompanied by a lyre, though probably not by flutes, horns, or percussion instruments, because those were used in the pagan mystery cults and the Christians did not want to be mistaken for these cults or be perceived as imitating them (Martin, *Worship in the Early Church*, 41). Note that the Essenes also used lyres. The lyre was a sort of cross between a guitar and a small harp. The closest modern equivalent is probably the autoharp. References to harps in the Book of Revelation (14:2, 15:2) probably indicate that lyres were used in Christian worship (cf. also 1 Sam 16:23). But see Clement of Alexandria, *The Instructor* 2.4, where Clement allows the use of the harp but not the playing of songs or tunes that are "secular" (love songs) or that imitate the chromatic melodies of pagan music.

29. This close connection between the incarnation and the Eucharist was typical of the early apologists and theologians. The manna in the wilderness is the bread that came down from heaven, and is interpreted as a foreshadowing of the coming of Christ (John 6). This was the basis for early eucharistic theology, in which authors such as Justin Martyr and Irenaeus connected the incarnation ("the Word *became* flesh," John 1:14) with the Eucharist, using the same language of *becoming* to describe their understanding that the elements of bread and wine *became* the flesh and blood of Christ.

30. *Odes of Solomon* 19, 28, 36. Note also that Clement of Alexandria refers to God as both Father and Mother in *Who Is the Rich Man That Shall Be Saved?* 37.

31. *Odes of Solomon* 33.5ff.

32. *Odes of Solomon* 27, 42.1–2. See also 1 Clement 2.3. The usual prayer position seems to be the so-called "orans" position (*orans* is simply the Latin word for praying). This would be standing with arms out, though not stretched out as in a cruciform position, with head and hands raised (Clement of Alexandria, *Miscellanies* 7.7). Note that Clement says there is some movement of the feet, possibly a swaying back and forth, though he may be saying that at the end of prayer, the true Christian "sets the feet in motion," meaning that prayer leads to action out in the world. According to Tertullian, *Apology* 16, and the *Didascalia Apostolorum* 12, the one who prays should face east.

33. Ordination is a ritual by the time of Tertullian, *The Prescription Against the Heretics* 41.

34. *Apostolic Tradition* 2. In the *Apostolic Tradition*, which contains layers of material that cannot be dated with any certainty, it appears that early on, laypeople participated in the elections. However, this could simply mean that the priests voted and the laity ratified the vote by their assent in liturgy.

35. *Apostolic Church Order* 16. See also *Didascalia Apostolorum* 4.

36. When it came to choosing a bishop, it was preferable if he were unmarried, but if he was married, he must be married only once. If he was married, his wife must also be a believer and be morally above reproach. He should be at least fifty years old, unless the congregation in a particular city is so small that no one over fifty is acceptable; then a younger man might be chosen (*Didascalia Apostolorum* 4).

37. Ignatius of Antioch, *Letter to the Ephesians* 7.2, 8.2, *Letter to the Trallians* 9.1–2, *Letter to the Smyrnaeans* 1.1–2. Aristides, *Apology* 15.

38. Justin Martyr, *1 Apology* 61.

39. In Mark 10, the concepts of "cup" and "baptism" are used symbolically to refer to Jesus' death. We can see in this how the early Christians connected the sacraments to sacrifice.

40. Clement of Alexandria, *Exhortation to the Greeks* 10.

41. Justin Martyr, *1 Apology* 61.

42. 2 Clement 7.6, 8.6, Hermas, *The Shepherd* 11.5, 72.3–4, 93.4. See also 2 Corinthians 1:22, Ephesians 1:13, 4:30, 2 Timothy

2:19. Cf. Romans 4:11, in which Paul refers to circumcision as a seal. Note also that in the Book of Revelation, the mark of the beast is contrasted with the ones who are marked for God. No doubt the concept of being marked for God refers to baptism.

43. Hermas, *The Shepherd* 32.4, 49.2, 60.3–4. Justin Martyr, *1 Apology* 61.

44. For example, see the *Didascalia Apostolorum* 5, 20.

45. Hermas, *The Shepherd* 6.5, 32.4, 33.3, 41, Irenaeus of Lyons, *Demonstration of the Apostolic Preaching* 3, Cyprian of Carthage, *Epistle* 54.13, 75.16, *On the Unity of the Catholic Church* 20-21, and the anonymous *On Rebaptism* 12.

46. Hermas, *The Shepherd* 29.8, 31.6, Clement of Alexandria, *Miscellanies* 2.13, *Who Is the Rich Man That Shall Be Saved?* 39–40.

47. Didache 11.

48. Ignatius of Antioch, *Letter to the Smyrnaeans* 8.2. See also Clement of Alexandria, *The Instructor* 2.1.

49. In the *Apostolic Tradition* 25–27 we can see a separation of the Eucharist (in the morning) from the meal (in the evening). Cyprian would write that even though the Last Supper of Jesus was in the evening, it is appropriate to celebrate the Eucharist in the morning because the resurrection occurred in the morning (Cyprian of Carthage, *Epistle* 62.16). On the other hand, as we have seen, the opposite could be the case. In a city that had too many house-churches for one bishop to cover, the Sunday morning meeting may have gone on without the Eucharist, which waited until all the Christians of the city could gather in one place in the evening. The combination of meal and sacrament probably lasted the longest in the celebrations held at the cemeteries.

50. It was only the Gnostics who interpreted the Eucharist as strictly symbolic. Since they did not believe in the real flesh of Christ, they could hardly see the Eucharist as in any way the real presence of Christ's flesh. The Gnostics interpreted John 6 metaphorically, but most of the Church did not. Even Irenaeus, who is famous for interpretation using typology, did not see the Eucharist as a type or metaphor. For him, the eucharistic bread *becomes* the body of Christ. See Irenaeus of Lyons, *Against Heresies* 5.2.2–3.

51. Justin Martyr, *1 Apology* 66.

52. Irenaeus of Lyons, *Against Heresies* 5.2.2–3.
53. Didache 14.1.
54. 1 Clement 57.2, cf. 1 Cor 5:1–11.
55. Ignatius of Antioch, *Letter to the Philadelphians* 8.1.
56. Clement of Alexandria, *Exhortation to the Greeks* 2.
57. It is a difficult thing to distinguish that element within the universal Church that would come to be called orthodoxy, without relying on anachronisms. While admitting that history is written by the winners of the debates, and terms such as *orthodoxy* and *heresy* can only be defined in hindsight, this treatment takes the approach that, on one hand, what comes to be the orthodox definition of doctrine represents the majority position in any given age of the Church (see Tertullian, *The Prescription Against the Heretics* 1), and at the same time, this treatment accepts by faith the reality of providence and the work of the Holy Spirit in guiding the outcome of doctrinal debates (Matt 16:18). It must be admitted that at some times and places, the orthodox position was not, in fact, the majority, such as was the case in Augustine's North Africa, or the eastern empire of the fourth century under the emperor Constantius. In the bigger picture of worldwide Christianity, however, it was still true that what came to be defined as orthodoxy was the position held by the majority of bishops. Therefore, while admitting the limitations of such usage, I will fall back on the concept of a "mainstream" Church, when that seems to be the most useful designation, to denote the trajectory of orthodox doctrine that ran from the apostles through the ecumenical councils. Furthermore, I maintain that this "mainstream" Church represents a middle way between the extreme (and mutually exclusive) alternative interpretations that emerged in the history of the Church.
58. It is entirely possible that there were more than two groups, and that the different divisions mentioned in 1 Corinthians reflect multiple factions. In fact, there are many theories that attempt to explain the historical situation in Corinth, and what is presented here is just one of them, arguably the simplest, which attempts to place everyone in Corinth into one of two groups. However, theories that propose more than two or three different groups probably overestimate the size of the Corinthian church in the mid-first century. It is clear from 1 Clement 38 that similar

divisions of rich/poor, wise/humble, strong/weak still existed in Corinth even in the early nineties of the first century. Contemporary scholarship on 1 Corinthians also includes theories that suggest that the document we know as 1 Corinthians is actually a composition of fragments from more than one letter. While my interpretation assumes that 1 Corinthians is a single letter, it must be acknowledged that it is probable that the Corinthian correspondence as a whole originally included more than two letters (2 Cor 10:9).

59. I am indebted to my colleague K. K. Yeo for this insight.

60. The philosophical group never would have practiced speaking in tongues, since charismatic worship would violate the Stoic principle that virtue entailed suppression of the passions. The philosophical Christians of Corinth may have complained to Paul about disorder in worship and thus prompted Paul to address the issue. Paul had corrections for both sides of the disputes, however.

61. Hippolytus, *Refutation of All Heresies* 1.16.

62. Philo of Alexandria seems to have taken the concept of dualism further than Plato, and therefore he may be one of the links between Platonic dualism and docetism. The Neo-Pythagoreans also taught an extreme dualism, which may provide part of the explanation for docetism.

63. Hippolytus, *Refutation of All Heresies* 8.3.

64. While early Christian writers tended to trace all docetism back to Simon Magus (Acts 8:9–24) and the Nicolaitans (Rev 2:6, 15), there is no evidence of a direct connection between these New Testament figures and later heretics. It does seem that the Nicolaitans were libertines, but that in itself does not necessarily make them Docetics. Some also connected the Nicolaitans to the deacon Nicolas, mentioned in Acts 6:15, but this is pure speculation based on the similarity of the names. See Irenaeus of Lyons, *Against Heresies* 1.23.1–4, 1.26.3, Hippolytus, *Refutation of All Heresies* 6.14–15, 7.24, and cf. Epiphanius of Salamis, *Panarion* 21, 25.

65. There is probably an intentional triple meaning in this statement of Paul: (1) The human body matters, and what you do with your body does affect your spirit (1 Cor 6:19–20); (2) the Church is the body of Christ, and the philosophical group was disrespecting their brothers and sisters in Christ, fellow members of

the body of Christ; and (3) the body of Christ is in the eucharistic bread.

66. Irenaeus of Lyons, *Against Heresies* 2.14.2.

67. The elements that make up docetism may predate Christianity, as can be seen by the fact that it is present in those who opposed Paul's thinking; within the Church, however, gnosticism emerged as the result of the combination of docetism and syncretism, and then as it evolved, it eventually separated from the Church.

68. Hippolytus, *Refutation of All Heresies* 5.1. For possible references to early gnosticism (called "false knowledge"), see 1 Corinthians 8:1, and 1 Timothy 6:20.

69. Gordon D. Fee, *Pauline Christology: An Exegetical and Theological Study* (Peabody, MA: Hendrickson, 2007), 516–17.

70. For example, see Irenaeus of Lyons, *Against Heresies* 2.22.4, Tertullian, *Against the Valentinians* 26, and Novatian, *On the Trinity* 10.6. See also Larry W. Hurtado, *Lord Jesus Christ: Devotion to Jesus in Earliest Christianity* (Grand Rapids, MI: Eerdmans, 2003), 514.

71. Polycarp of Smyrna, *Letter to the Philippians* 7.1. Polycarp connected the Docetics of his time (the first half of the second century) with the "antichrists" of 1 John 4:2–3. Cf. Epiphanius of Salamis, *Panarion* 41.1.

72. Ignatius of Antioch, *Letter to the Trallians* 10, *Letter to the Smyrnaeans* 4.2.

73. Tertullian, *On the Flesh of Christ*, 16. Tertullian responded that it was the likeness of *sinful* flesh in which Christ came. In other words, he had real flesh, but no real sin.

74. Novatian, *On the Trinity*, 10.9. Novatian responded that Paul was talking about the sins of the flesh, not the human body per se.

75. Eusebius of Caesarea, *Ecclesiastical History* 4.10, 4.11.2. Cf. Epiphanius of Salamis, *Panarion* 41.

76. Eusebius of Caesarea, *Ecclesiastical History* 4.10–11.

77. Eusebius of Caesarea, *Ecclesiastical History* 4.10–11.

78. Irenaeus of Lyons, *Against Heresies* 1.5.4. See also Hurtado, *Lord Jesus Christ*, 257.

79. Hurtado, *Lord Jesus Christ*, 255.

80. Arland J. Hultgren and Steven A. Haggmark, eds., *The Earliest Christian Heretics: Readings from Their Opponents* (Minneapolis: Fortress Press, 1996), 106.

81. Tertullian, *Against Marcion* 1.2.1–3.

82. Hurtado, *Lord Jesus Christ*, 554.

83. Eusebius of Caesarea, *Ecclesiastical History* 4.14.7.

84. We must always be careful when we use a writer's theological opponent(s) as a source for understanding his thought. We cannot assume that the opponents' assessment is completely accurate or fair.

85. Hippolytus, *Refutation of All Heresies* 10.15. Cf. Epiphanius of Salamis, *Panarion* 42.

86. Tertullian, *On the Flesh of Christ* 5; Hippolytus, *Refutation of All Heresies* 8.3. See also Hurtado, *Lord Jesus Christ*, 556–57. While Marcion may well have believed in the crucifixion, he would still have rejected the idea that Jesus suffered, or that his suffering had any atoning significance. Marcion would have interpreted the death of Christ as a demonstration of the true goal of humanity, that of escaping the prison of the flesh.

87. The letters of Paul have an inherent distinction between *flesh* and *body*. For Paul, *flesh* has a negative connotation, not because it belongs to the material world, but because of its connection to sin and temptation. There is no similar negative connotation with the word *body* in Paul, and in fact for Paul the Church is the body of Christ. Marcion would have applied Paul's specific pejorative use of *flesh* to the human body in general.

88. Hurtado, *Lord Jesus Christ*, 551ff.

89. Ignatius of Antioch, *Letter to the Ephesians* 5, 20, *Letter to the Smyrnaeans* 6.1–2. Ignatius presents the issue as though the Docetics rejected the Eucharist, but some probably actually had their own Eucharist in which they rejected the use of wine because they did not believe Jesus had any blood. When Ignatius says they rejected the Eucharist, he means that they separated themselves from the unity of the one legitimate Eucharist of the Church under the authority of the bishop. The use of water instead of wine in the Eucharist is referred to as *aquarianism*. Ignatius is not directly addressing Marcionites (since Marcion did not arrive on the scene until after the time of Ignatius), but Cyprian also confronts the

271

practice of aquarianism. Apparently, those who practiced it claimed that they did not want anyone to smell wine on their breath, which might lead to their condemnation during persecution. But Cyprian considered this an excuse and chastised them for being ashamed of the blood of Christ. Cyprian said that the sacrament must contain wine, not water alone, since Jesus used wine (and even turned water into wine), and Melchizedek used wine. In fact, the Old Testament calls wine the "blood of the grape" (Gen 49:2, Isa 63:2), so no wine means no blood, which means no salvation (Cyprian of Carthage, *Epistle* 62).

90. Eusebius of Caesarea, *Ecclesiastical History* 4.7, 11. See also Hultgren and Haggmark, *The Earliest Christian Heretics*, 112–15. Cf. Epiphanius of Salamis, *Panarion* 42.

91. Irenaeus of Lyons, *Against Heresies* 2.14.1–2. Some have called Marcion a Gnostic; however, Marcion does not seem to have subscribed to the idea of secret knowledge, the hallmark of gnosticism. Therefore, it is more accurate to call Marcion a Docetic, not a Gnostic. By calling gnosticism "a whole new religion" I do not mean to imply that it was a unified or connected organization. It is more appropriate to speak of the many gnostic systems that existed side by side with no uniformity.

92. Since Marcion's belief system did not include this secret knowledge, he cannot be called a Gnostic. Technically speaking, he was a Docetic, but not a Gnostic. Marcionite docetism continued in Marcion's followers and existed alongside gnosticism throughout the second century.

93. Irenaeus of Lyons, *Against Heresies* 1.23.5. See also Hippolytus, *Refutation of All Heresies* 5.2. Hippolytus knew of some Gnostics who said that the secret knowledge was handed down through James, the brother of the Lord. This teaching was probably an answer to Irenaeus's critique that if there was a secret knowledge, the bishops would know it, since they were the successors of the apostles. Cf. Epiphanius of Salamis, *Panarion* 22.

94. Irenaeus of Lyons, *Against Heresies* 1.24.1–2, Hippolytus, *Refutation of All Heresies* 7.16.

95. Eusebius of Caesarea, *Ecclesiastical History*, 4.7, Irenaeus of Lyons, *Against Heresies* 1.25.1. Cf. Epiphanius of Salamis, *Panarion* 27. See also Hippolytus, *Refutation of All Heresies*, 7.20. Hippolytus

believed that there was some interdependence of influence between the Ebionites' *angel Christology* and the Carpocratians. While Hippolytus may be confused about certain aspects of distinction between angel Christology and what Carpocrates taught, one interesting aspect of Carpocratian gnosticism seems to be the belief that the reason Jesus could bring secret knowledge to earth was because he was able to remember his past lives as well as his conversations with God in the time before his journey to earth. Many of the philosophers had believed in reincarnation, and Plato had taught that the reason we make mistakes (sin) in this life is that we cannot remember the lessons learned in our past lives. Plato seemed to believe that if we could only remember the time before this present life, we would not sin. Apparently, Carpocrates picked up on this idea and incorporated it into his Christology.

96. Clement of Alexandria, *Miscellanies* 3.2.5–10. See also Epiphanius of Salamis, *Panarion* 26.42. According to Epiphanius, the Gnostics had a secret handshake so that they could recognize fellow "swingers." It entailed tickling the palm of the other person while shaking hands. Note that these libertine Gnostics practiced orgies but rejected children. They prohibited procreation, believing that sexuality was for pleasure only. The mainstream Church's response to this was to take the opposite position, that sex was for procreation only.

97. Hippolytus, *Refutation of All Heresies* 7.20.

98. Hippolytus, *Refutation of All Heresies* 8.13, Eusebius of Caesarea, *Ecclesiastical History* 4.7. Cf. Epiphanius of Salamis, *Panarion* 23, 47.

99. Hippolytus, *Refutation of All Heresies* 7.16, Eusebius of Caesarea, *Ecclesiastical History* 4.28–29.

100. Irenaeus criticized vegetarianism as a sign of ingratitude toward God for the gift of meat (*Against Heresies* 1.28.1). The asceticism of the Encratites, and in some cases the Ebionites, probably influenced several of the early apocryphal Acts, which present marriage as sinful because it involves sexual intercourse (see Epiphanius of Salamis, *Panarion* 30). These second-century documents often portray the apostles preaching a message of abstinence for all true believers, to the extent that for them following Christ means rejecting marriage. See the *Acts of Thomas* (which has gnostic elements)

and also the *Acts of Paul and Thecla* (which does not seem to be gnostic, though it does advocate celibacy as the only true Christian calling).

101. For their use of water without wine in the Eucharist, see Hippolytus, *Refutation of All Heresies* 8.13, and Epiphanius of Salamis, *Panarion* 47.1.5–7. For the possible use of oil without water in baptism, see the *Acts of Thomas*.

102. Irenaeus of Lyon, *Against Heresies* 3.2.2. Cf. the gnostic *Letter to Flora*. See also John Behr, *The Way to Nicaea: The Formation of Christian Theology, Volume 1* (Crestwood, NY: St. Vladimir's Seminary Press, 2001), 40.

103. See Epiphanius of Salamis, *Panarion* 45.

104. Irenaeus of Lyons, *Against Heresies* 1.6.1, 1.7.2. See also Novatian, *On the Trinity* 10.6.

105. Some Gnostics who held a hybrid Christology (for example, Apelles) did reject the birth of Jesus altogether, saying that Christ simply created for himself a "soulish" or spiritual body. See Irenaeus of Lyons, *Against Heresies* 1.26.1, Tertullian, *On the Flesh of Christ* 10, and Hippolytus, *Refutation of All Heresies* 7.15, 7.21. Irenaeus and Hippolytus knew of some Gnostics (including Cerinthus) who allowed for a kind of resurrection of Christ, though it was only the resurrection of this "soulish" body.

106. This is similar to, but not the same as, the mainstream tendency to assign impassibility to the divine nature of Christ and passibility to his human nature. The mainstream Church did not separate Jesus from the Christ, and of course the human nature of Christ was truly human. The gnostic separation of Jesus from the Christ was specifically meant to avoid attributing any real humanity to him, even the part called "Jesus."

107. Irenaeus of Lyons, *Against Heresies* 1.7.2, Hippolytus, *Refutation of All Heresies* 7.21. See also Hultgren and Haggmark, *The Earliest Christian Heretics*, 34ff. Cf. Epiphanius of Salamis, *Panarion* 28. Although this may sound similar to the Ebionites' Christology (see below), even those Ebionites who admitted to a preexistent Christ maintained that this Christ was a created being, while the gnostic version saw the Christ as a divine being. It is true that in gnostic hybrid Christology the Christ might be described as an angel, but remember that Gnostics regard angels as divine

beings, albeit a lower level of divinity. The closer we look at these alternative Christologies, the more difficult it becomes to distinguish between some of the intricacies of their systems. For example, the difference between the Ebionites' understanding of a created angel and the Gnostics' understanding of a lower order of divine being called angel can be hard to pin down. In the gnostic system, even these lower divinities are often described as born out of some prior procreative act, so that we cannot simply say that ascribing divinity to them means that they are eternal. The main difference seems to be in the difference between creator and created. For the Ebionites (and indeed the mainstream Church), angels are created beings and are not creators. For the Gnostics, even if the divine angels (or *aeons*) have a beginning to their existence, they are the offspring of divine nature, and are therefore the creators of what comes after them. Therefore, the point is not whether Christ is called an angel, but whether he is understood to be divine or created, or some combination of the two.

108. Eusebius of Caesarea, *Ecclesiastical History* 4.7. Cf. Epiphanius of Salamis, *Panarion* 24.

109. Virtually every philosophical concept becomes deified in the gnostic system, and yet these deities are so personified as to be made in the image of humanity, including procreation by coupling. Irenaeus criticized the Gnostics for anthropomorphizing their deities, even while they rejected the God of the Old Testament because of the anthropomorphisms found there (*Against Heresies* 2.13.3).

110. Hippolytus, *Refutation of All Heresies* 7.15.

111. Since salvation is an escape from the body, even those Gnostics who believed in some kind of resurrection of Jesus did not assume that Jesus' resurrection implied a resurrection for humans. The Pauline doctrine of the resurrection of the body (1 Cor 15) is antithetical to gnostic dualism. Cf. Epiphanius of Salamis, *Panarion* 44.1–4.

112. In the *Apocryphon of James*, Jesus says, "I have taught you what to say before the archons." Though it is clear that the secret knowledge must have included some kind of "password" to ascend through the heavenly "tollbooths," there is no extant gnostic document that records any of the gnostic secrets. However, it probably

had to do with knowing and reciting the names of the *aeons* (or *archons*), which are an important feature of Basilidean and Valentinian gnosticism.

113. Irenaeus had criticized the Gnostics on the grounds that they had no apostolic succession. Their response was apparently to claim that they had their own succession of teaching, which originated with Jesus through Matthias (Irenaeus of Lyons, *Against Heresies* 3.3.1–2, Hippolytus, *Refutation of All Heresies* 7.20.1). Other Gnostics taught that the secret knowledge was handed down through James. See Hippolytus, *Refutation of All Heresies* 5.2.

114. Epiphanius of Salamis, *Panarion* 24.5.4–5.

115. Irenaeus of Lyons, *Against Heresies* 1.24.3–7.

116. Irenaeus of Lyons, *Against Heresies* 1.6.2. Hurtado, *Lord Jesus Christ*, 459, 462.

117. Hurtado, *Lord Jesus Christ*, 458, 477. Cf. *Gospel of Thomas* 3.

118. Irenaeus of Lyons, *Against Heresies* 1.29, Hippolytus, *Refutation of All Heresies* 5.9–12. Cf. Epiphanius of Salamis, *Panarion* 39–40.

119. Hurtado, *Lord Jesus Christ*, 634. The second century *Apocryphon of John* and the *Gospel of Judas* are Sethian documents. Note that in the *Gospel of Judas*, Judas is actually an *archon* (demon), so it is not as though he is the hero of the story. See April D. DeConick, *The Thirteenth Apostle: What the Gospel of Judas Really Says* (London: Continuum, 2007).

120. Eusebius of Caesarea, *Ecclesiastical History* 4.11. Cf. Epiphanius of Salamis, *Panarion* 31.

121. Hurtado, *Lord Jesus Christ*, 525.

122. Irenaeus of Lyons, *Against Heresies* 1.6.2. This seems to be based on the ancient anthropology that understood the human as being made up of three parts: the spirit (or rational soul), the soul (or animal soul), and the body. The spirit, or rational soul, was thought to include the mind, while the animal soul was simply the "life force" that drove the instincts, bodily functions, and physical desires of the human.

123. Irenaeus of Lyons, *Against Heresies* 1.25.2, 2.19.3, 2.32.3.

124. Hultgren and Haggmark, *The Earliest Christian Heretics*, 82.

125. It would be impossible to know what the original version of the *Gospel of Truth* was like, since the text that is part of the Nag Hammadi collection is a later, and certainly edited, version. It is important to note that the gnostic gospels were written no earlier than the second century, at a time when the Gnostics were already separating themselves from the mainstream church (1 John 2:19), and so the gnostic gospels were never considered for inclusion in the New Testament canon. Irenaeus called them a deception and a fantasy (*Against Heresies* 1.8.1).

126. Hurtado, *Lord Jesus Christ*, 473, 484.

127. Hurtado, *Lord Jesus Christ*, 587.

128. Irenaeus of Lyons, *Against Heresies* 1.25.2, 2.19.3, 2.32.3.

129. Hippolytus, *Refutation of All Heresies*, 7.26. Cf. Epiphanius of Salamis, *Panarion* 44.

130. Hurtado, *Lord Jesus Christ*, 256.

131. Irenaeus of Lyons, *Against Heresies* 1.7.2.

132. Hippolytus, *Refutation of All Heresies*, 7.26. Cf. Epiphanius of Salamis, *Panarion* 44.

133. Irenaeus of Lyons, *Against Heresies* 1.6.2–4, 2.14.5.

134. See Hultgren and Haggmark, *The Earliest Christian Heretics*, 37–38. See also Hurtado, *Lord Jesus Christ*, 483–84. Cf. Epiphanius of Salamis, *Panarion* 26. The reader must keep in mind, however, that there was great diversity of thought among those we now call Gnostics, and we should not assume that there was one consistent gnostic movement.

135. Hurtado, *Lord Jesus Christ*, 367–68.

136. Irenaeus of Lyons, *Against Heresies* 1.25.2, 2.19.3, 2.32.3.

137. Irenaeus of Lyons, *Against Heresies* 3.11.9. Irenaeus, writing in the late second century, knew that the gnostic gospels (especially the so-called *Gospel of Truth*) were recent productions.

138. *Gospel of Thomas* 13. Thomas actually says to the other disciples, "If I tell you one of the sayings he spoke to me, you will pick up rocks and stone me, and fire will come from the rocks and devour you."

139. Irenaeus of Lyons, *Against Heresies* 3.3.2, 2.11.9.

140. Hurtado, *Lord Jesus Christ*, 166.

141. There are some hints in the Old Testament that the Messiah would be more than human, such as Daniel 7:13, but not until after the life, death, and resurrection of Jesus did these begin to make sense in a Christian context. There were also some hints in extrabiblical Jewish prophetic writings that the Messiah would be more than human, or even superhuman (such as 2 Esdras 13), but these were not universally accepted nor were they consistently interpreted. The average Jewish believer would not have expected the Messiah to be divine, and even the followers of Jesus did not understand his divinity until after the resurrection. This is, in part, why he was killed—he surpassed all expectations and in the end was not the kind of Messiah that the people expected, or even wanted.

142. Behr, *The Way to Nicaea*, 53, 57–59.

143. Hurtado, *Lord Jesus Christ*, 119.

144. Hurtado, *Lord Jesus Christ*, 127.

145. Ignatius of Antioch, *Letter to the Magnesians* 8–10, *Letter to the Philadelphians* 6–9, cf. Epiphanius of Salamis, *Panarion* 30. There was also a group called the Nazareans, mentioned by several early writers. While some have assumed that this was a separate group of Jewish Christians, it is more likely that they are two names for the same group of people (see Jerome, *Epistle* 112). But cf. Epiphanius of Salamis, *Panarion* 29–30. Epiphanius mistakenly thinks the Ebionites are named after a person called Ebion, who was originally a Nazarean, yet he talks about them as if the Ebionites split from the Nazareans making two separate groups. The name *Ebionite* does not derive from a person, so Epiphanius is certainly mistaken. Still, it must be said that the label *Ebionite* as it is used now is an umbrella term for any group that denied the divinity of Christ. We cannot assume that all early Christians who leaned in this direction agreed on all points, nor did they constitute a separate, organized ecclesial body. When there were individual house-churches that leaned in this direction, it would be just as likely to have been because they followed a particular Ebionite, as that they were organized around that Christology.

146. Cf. Epiphanius of Salamis, *Panarion* 30.2.7. Although Epiphanius is mistaken on other points of the Ebionites' origins,

this seems plausible given the connection of the Judaizers to the Jerusalem church. See Hultgren and Haggmark, *The Earliest Christian Heresies*, 116.

147. Some early Church writers thought the name was actually first used as an insult by their opponents, as if it meant that they were intellectually poor, or that they had a poor view of Christ (see Eusebius of Caesarea, *Ecclesiastical History* 3.27). It is more likely, however, that they chose the name for themselves. The belief that Jesus was poor probably comes from his own words in Matthew 8:20, "Foxes have holes, and birds of the air have nests; but the Son of Man has nowhere to lay his head." While this may be an argument for the fact that Jesus was not married, it does not mean that he was homeless. It simply means that he was itinerant. In fact, as the son of a skilled laborer, he came from the working class and would not have been what we would call poor, in the sense of malnourished. Even during his ministry he seems to have lived with Peter's family, and made his headquarters there (Matt 4:13). Note that the Christologies that overemphasize the humanity of Christ also tend to understand salvation in terms of following his example.

148. Eusebius of Caesarea, *Ecclesiastical History* 6.16. There was a general consensus among the orthodox and heretics alike that part of the very definition of divinity included the concept of immutability, the conviction that God does not change. This was based on the assumption that what is divine is also eternal and therefore uncreated. To be uncreated must also mean immutable, since mutability is related to corruptibility. See Theophilus of Antioch, *To Autolycus* 1.4, 2.4.

149. Hippolytus, *Refutation of All Heresies* 7.22–24, 35–36, 10.23–24. According to Hippolytus, Theodotus taught that Jesus had been converted from a life of promiscuity (cf. Epiphanius of Salamis, *Panarion* 54). Epiphanius said that Theodotus had denied Christ to save his life during the persecution, and that he later taught that Christ was not divine as an excuse for his apostasy. Epiphanius implies that Theodotus gained followers because his Christology allowed people to deny Christ in times of persecution, since they believed he was only a man.

150. Eusebius of Caesarea, *Ecclesiastical History* 5.28.6.

151. Hippolytus, *Refutation of All Heresies* 7.24.

152. Aloys Grillmeier, *Christ in Christian Tradition, Volume 1: From the Apostolic Age to Chalcedon (451)* (New York: Oxford University Press, 2004), 78. Other known disciples of Theodotus were Asclepiodotus and Symmachus. Cf. Epiphanius of Salamis, *Panarion* 55.

153. Grillmeier, *Christ in Christian Tradition*, 46. Note that this is not to be confused with the orthodox tendency to interpret Old Testament appearances of the "angel of the Lord" as the preincarnate Christ. The Ebionites' angel Christology denied Christ's preexistence; therefore, he could not be present in the Old Testament. Hermas's *The Shepherd* is one possible example of angel Christology. This second-century document describes Christ as an angel, and salvation is by keeping the law (see Hermas, *The Shepherd* 69.5).

154. Cf. Epiphanius of Salamis, *Panarion* 30.3.7. The so-called *Gospel of the Nazareans* may have been an Aramaic version of Matthew, while the so-called *Gospel of the Hebrews* may have been the edited version of Matthew in Hebrew. Epiphanius refers to a *Gospel of the Ebionites*, though it is not clear whether that is the name of a gospel they used or simply a reference to one of these other gospels no longer extant. On the other hand, Eusebius says that they rejected the Gospel of Matthew altogether, though this probably is a reference to their rejection of the way Matthew connects Jesus to Old Testament messianic prophecies (see Eusebius, *Ecclesiastical History* 6.17).

155. Eusebius of Caesarea, *Ecclesiastical History* 3.27. That the mainstream Church interpreted Isaiah 7:14 as a miraculous conception, see Justin Martyr, *1 Apology* 33, and Irenaeus of Lyons, *Against Heresies* 3.21.6–10. Irenaeus says that since Adam had no father, Jesus (the second Adam) also had no biological father.

156. Eusebius of Caesarea, *Ecclesiastical History* 5.8.

157. Eusebius of Caesarea, *Ecclesiastical History* 6.16.

158. Grillmeier, *Christ in Christian Tradition*, 77.

159. Hippolytus, *Refutation of All Heresies* 7.22. In the case of angel Christology, the spiritual indwelling would be thought to take place at Jesus' conception rather than his baptism, which is why they accepted the idea of a miraculous birth.

160. Martin, *Worship in the Early Church*, 90.

161. Grillmeier, *Christ in Christian Tradition*, 67. Although he was rewarded with an exalted status and adopted sonship, he was not thought to have been made divine at his baptism (see Hippolytus, *Refutation of All Heresies* 7.23). Some Ebionites may have believed that Jesus was rewarded with divine status after the resurrection, perhaps at the ascension. Later, the Arians would extend the exalted status of Jesus to a kind of divinity.

162. Athanasius of Alexandria, *Against the Nations* 46.1.

163. Hippolytus, *Refutation of All Heresies* 7.22–24. Hippolytus says the Ebionites believed that Jesus "received Christ," who descended on him like a dove.

164. Hippolytus, *Refutation of All Heresies* 7.12–13, 22.

165. Irenaeus of Lyons, *Against Heresies* 3.19.1, Hippolytus, *Refutation of All Heresies* 7.22.

166. Hippolytus, *Refutation of All Heresies* 7.22.

167. Irenaeus of Lyons, *Against Heresies* 1.26.2.

168. Irenaeus of Lyons, *Against Heresies* 5.1.3, cf. Hippolytus, *Refutation of Heresies* 8.13.

169. Epiphanius of Salamis, *Panarion* 30. On the apocryphal acts, see Helen Rhee, *Early Christian Literature: Christ and Culture in the Second and Third Centuries* (New York: Routledge, 2005).

170. Tertullian, *On Baptism* 17.

171. See also the *Martyrdom of Perpetua and Felicitas* 7–8.

172. See also the *Apostolic Constitutions* 8.4 (8.29).

173. Clement of Alexandria, *Exhortation to the Greeks* 1, 10.

174. Ignatius of Antioch, *Letter to the Magnesians* 11.1. See also Irenaeus of Lyons, *Against Heresies* 3.19.3.

175. 2 Clement 9.1, Ignatius of Antioch, *Letter to the Smyrnaeans* 12.2.

176. Ignatius of Antioch, *Letter to the Smyrnaeans* 5.2.

177. Irenaeus of Lyons, *Against Heresies* 3.20.3.

178. Clement of Alexandria, *Exhortation to the Greeks* 1, 11.

179. Theophilus of Antioch, *To Autolycus* 2.18.

180. Justin Martyr, *1 Apology* 36, 44, 62, 63. Since God is invisible, anyone in the Old Testament who thinks they are seeing God is really seeing the preincarnate Christ. Also, since the Divine is omnipresent, it was believed that God the Father could not be localized, or *circumscribed*, in one place. Therefore, any time the

"angel of the Lord" appears in a place, and is presented as divine, it was assumed to be the preincarnate Christ (see Theophilus of Antioch, *To Autolycus* 2.22).

181. Clement of Alexandria, *Exhortation to the Greeks* 1, 9, 10.

182. Ignatius of Antioch, *Letter to the Smyrnaeans* 12.2.

183. Clement of Alexandria, *Exhortation to the Greeks* 10–11.

184. Melito of Sardis, *Homily on the Passover* 8. This does not imply that Christ began to be divine at his resurrection; it is simply a poetic way of affirming the two natures of humanity and divinity.

185. For example, see Hermas, *The Shepherd* 78.1.

186. Eusebius also speaks of the tradition of passing down the location of holy sites from one generation to another (*Ecclesiastical History* 7.18–19). Eusebius specifically mentions that the location of the home of the woman with a hemorrhage could be pointed out, and he also knows of statues and paintings of Jesus and the apostles, as well as the location of the "episcopal" throne of James.

187. In the *Martyrdom of Polycarp* 9, the same idea is expressed in Greek. The Greek word for "manly" (*andrizou*) is translated "courageous."

188. 1 Clement 55.

189. See Geoffrey D. Dunn, *Tertullian* (New York: Routledge, 2004), 16–17.

190. On the diary of Perpetua, see Joyce E. Salisbury, *Perpetua's Passion: The Death and Memory of a Young Roman Woman* (New York: Routledge, 1997).

191. Tertullian, *Apology* 50. Here Tertullian famously says that the blood of the martyrs is the seed of the Church.

CHAPTER 5

1. Irenaeus of Lyons, *Against Heresies* 5.31.1. The word *orthodoxy* is from a Greek compound word that literally means "correct praise." As used here, it means the interpretations and teachings that the Church would define as correct, as opposed to the teachings of the heresies. In one sense, the label *orthodoxy* can only be applied after the debate produces a winner; however, it is also true that the orthodoxy of each generation is based on, and

consistent with, the orthodoxy of the previous generations, going back to the apostles.

2. We must keep in mind, of course, that gleaning information about an ancient religious system from the writings of its opponents is difficult, since we cannot take for granted that the orthodox writers were always accurate or fair in their representation of the heresy in question. Nevertheless, much of the information about gnosticism presented above is from Irenaeus's *Against Heresies*.

3. Irenaeus of Lyons, *Against Heresies* 3.3.1–2.

4. Irenaeus of Lyons, *Against Heresies* 2.28.9, 4.6.4.

5. Irenaeus of Lyons, *Against Heresies* 3.22.4, 5.19.1.

6. The gnostic rejection of the material world as evil may have pushed Irenaeus to affirm the goodness of creation by emphasizing the continuity, not only between the Old and New Testaments, but also between the Church age and the "millennium." In other words, it might have made sense to Irenaeus that a literal reign of Christ on the earth affirmed the connection between Christ and creation.

7. Irenaeus of Lyons, *Demonstration of the Apostolic Preaching* 45. See also 30, 43, 51.

8. Irenaeus of Lyons, *Demonstration of the Apostolic Preaching* 12.

9. Irenaeus of Lyons, *Demonstration of the Apostolic Preaching* 49.

10. Irenaeus of Lyons, *Demonstration of the Apostolic Preaching* 5. In this passage, the Holy Spirit is referred to as the wisdom of God, when one might expect that description to be applied to the Logos. This illustrates the fact that thus far in the Church's history there was a concerted effort to understand and describe the relationship between the Father and the Son, but no such attention to the relationship between the Son and the Spirit.

11. Irenaeus of Lyons, *Demonstration of the Apostolic Preaching* 47.

12. Irenaeus of Lyons, *Demonstration of the Apostolic Preaching* 7.

13. Irenaeus of Lyons, *Demonstration of the Apostolic Preaching* 7, *Against Heresies* 5.36.1–2. In actual practice, it was believed that

one could not get to the Father but through the Son, and one could not get to the Son but through the Church.

14. Irenaeus of Lyons, *Demonstration of the Apostolic Preaching* 51.

15. Irenaeus of Lyons, *Demonstration of the Apostolic Preaching* 56.

16. Irenaeus of Lyons, *Demonstration of the Apostolic Preaching* 100.

17. Irenaeus of Lyons, *Demonstration of the Apostolic Preaching* 3.

18. Irenaeus of Lyons, *Demonstration of the Apostolic Preaching* 24.

19. Irenaeus of Lyons, *Demonstration of the Apostolic Preaching* 42. See also Hermas, *The Shepherd* 33.3, 41. Hermas says that the Holy Spirit can be "choked out" of a person who invites evil into his or her life by harboring anger.

20. For a detailed life of Tertullian, see Timothy D. Barnes, *Tertullian: A Historical and Literary Study* (Oxford: Oxford University Press, 1985). Some sources give Tertullian's full name as Quintus Septimius Florens Tertullianus. Note that Barnes thinks he was born a bit later, around 170 CE. See also Geoffrey D. Dunn, *Tertullian* (New York: Routledge, 2004), 3–11.

21. Barnes, *Tertullian*, 246–47.

22. Eusebius of Caesarea, *Ecclesiastical History* 2.2.4.

23. Barnes, *Tertullian*, 24ff.

24. Barnes, *Tertullian*, 11, 58, Dunn, *Tertullian*, 3. See Tertullian, *On Exhortation to Chastity* 7.3, *On Monogamy* 12.2. The tradition that Tertullian was a priest is not attested before Jerome. According to Barnes, there is no evidence that Tertullian was ever in Rome; however, he seems to have at least visited Rome based on comments made in *On the Apparel of Women* 1.7. Note that a priest in Rome at the end of the second century would not necessarily be expected to be celibate.

25. Tertullian, *Against Praxeas* 1.7.

26. It has been argued that Tertullian's *On the Pallium* 3–4 represents anti-Roman sentiment.

27. David Rankin, *Tertullian and the Church* (Cambridge, UK: Cambridge University Press, 1995), 28–29.

28. Tertullian, *On Modesty* 1.2, 10.12. Note that Tertullian rejected *The Shepherd* as scripture because it seemed to advocate forgiveness of adultery. Cf. Cyprian of Carthage, *Epistle* 55.21. See Rankin, *Tertullian and the Church*, 41–42, 46.

29. Rankin, *Tertullian and the Church*, 115, 195–96.

30. Ibid., 29–32.

31. Ibid., 27ff., 41, 44.

32. Ibid., xv, 3, 30. See Tertullian, *On the Soul* 9.4.

33. Barnes, *Tertullian*, 141.

34. Dunn, *Tertullian*, 9.

35. Rankin, *Tertullian and the Church*, 50.

36. Tertullian, *On Monogamy* 3.9.

37. Dunn, *Tertullian*, 31–34.

38. Tertullian, *Prescription Against the Heretics* 7.

39. Even if this document were written later, it is clear that in spite of his association with the Montanists, Tertullian considered himself theologically within the mainstream.

40. Tertullian, *The Prescription Against the Heretics* 1.

41. Tertullian, *The Prescription Against the Heretics* 3, 6.

42. Tertullian, *The Prescription Against the Heretics* 10, 11, 14, 19–21, 28, 32. With the charge that the heretics take delight in being perpetual seekers, avoiding the responsibility of making a commitment to anything, Tertullian is referring primarily to the Gnostics.

43. Tertullian, *The Prescription Against the Heretics* 9, 14, 17.

44. Tertullian, *The Prescription Against the Heretics* 4, 30, 39.

45. Tertullian, *The Prescription Against the Heretics* 29, 31.

46. Tertullian, *The Prescription Against the Heretics* 20.

47. Tertullian, *The Prescription Against the Heretics* 13–14.

48. However, see Dunn, *Tertullian*, 17.

49. Tertullian, *Apology* 1, 37.

50. Tertullian, *Apology* 19, 47. The argument that Christianity is older than Greco-Roman philosophy and religion assumes that Christianity is based on the Old Testament prophets. In fact, the Christian apologists argued that anything worthwhile that the philosophers said was plagiarized from Moses and the prophets.

51. Tertullian, *Apology* 5, 10, 12–13, 16, 25, 29. The contrast is often made between pagan gods, which are made by humans and

need to be guarded by humans, and the actual God who made humans and who guards humans.

52. Tertullian, *Apology* 11–12, 14, 46.

53. Tertullian, *Apology* 6, 9, 37–39, 42, 44–46.

54. Tertullian, *Apology* 42.

55. Tertullian, *Apology* 39, 42.

56. Tertullian, *Apology* 13, 24.

57. Tertullian, *Apology* 22–23, 32.

58. Tertullian, *Apology* 24, 28. This argument comes from Athenagoras. See Athenagoras, *A Plea for the Christians* 1.

59. Tertullian, *Apology* 1–2, 7. Tertullian knows of a story that Pontius Pilate converted to Christianity. See Tertullian, *Apology* 21.

60. Tertullian, *Apology* 9.

61. Tertullian, *Apology* 9.

62. Tertullian, *Apology* 2, 49.

63. Tertullian, *Apology* 44.

64. Tertullian, *Apology* 42.

65. Tertullian, *Apology* 38.

66. Tertullian, *Apology* 40.

67. Tertullian, *Apology* 2.

68. Tertullian, *Apology* 5. Note that the Pantheon that stands in Rome today was not yet built in the time of Tiberius; however, it stands on the site of an earlier one. The current Pantheon was built by Hadrian, but the inscription to Agrippa is an homage to the man responsible for the original.

69. Tertullian, *Apology* 5.

70. Tertullian, *Against Praxeas* 1.

71. For the traditional view, see J. F. Bethune-Baker, *The Meaning of Homoousios in the "Constantinopolitan" Creed* in Text and Studies, ed. J. Armitage Robinson, vol. 7, no. 1 (Cambridge, UK: Cambridge University Press, 1901), 21–23, 65–70. While the strictly legal definition of *substantia* has been rejected as a basis for the theological term, it is still the case that the concept of "property" is a suitable analogy, since property can be nonmaterial, as in the case of intellectual property. See Eric Osborn, *Tertullian: First Theologian of the West* (Cambridge, UK: Cambridge University

Press, 1997), 131–32. Note that Tertullian calls the gospel "the substance of the New Testament" (*Against Praxeas* 31.1).

72. Tertullian, *Against Praxeas* 2.

73. Tertullian, *Against Praxeas* 2. See Bethune-Baker, *The Meaning of Homoousios*, 70–74, and Osborn, *Tertullian*, 132–33, 137.

74. Tertullian, *Against Praxeas* 12, 26.

75. Tertullian, *Against Praxeas* 26.

76. Tertullian, *Against Praxeas* 8.

77. Tertullian, *Against Praxeas* 22, 25.

78. Tertullian, *Against Praxeas* 8–9.

79. Tertullian, *Against Praxeas* 17. See also Ignatius of Antioch, *Letter to the Magnesians* 7.

80. Tertullian, *Against Praxeas* 27. Tertullian actually said, "…the property of each *substance* is preserved." The term *substance* is synonymous with *nature*, since the two natures of Christ are actually two substances, one divine (the same divine substance as the Trinity) and one human.

81. For a treatment of the debate surrounding the authorship of writings attributed to Hippolytus, see Allen Brent, "St. Hippolytus: Biblical Exegete, Roman Bishop and Martyr," in *St. Vladimir's Theological Quarterly* 48:2 (2004), 207–31. For a detailed treatment of Hippolytus, see Allen Brent, *Hippolytus and the Roman Church in the Third Century: Communities in Tension Before the Emergence of a Monarch-Bishop* (Leiden: Brill, 1995). Many scholars do not believe that both *Refutation of All Heresies* and *Against Noetus* could be by the same author; however, I treat them together here in the conviction that they are at least the product of the same school of thought, originating in early third-century Rome. The differences between the two documents can be attributed to the passage of time between writings and to possible differences in audience and agenda (see Brent, *Hippolytus and the Roman Church in the Third Century*, 204–7, 217, 238, 249, 257). Although Brent agrees that the two documents represent the same school of thought, he argues that they are by different authors based on a perceived theological evolution from the *Refutation* to *Against Noetus*: specifically, that on the one hand, *Against Noetus* is more trinitarian because of a more highly developed pneumatology, and on the other hand, it is in some ways a concession to the milder

modalism of Callistus as a tactic to combat the more extreme modalism of Noetus (see Brent, *Hippolytus and the Roman Church in the Third Century*, 208–11, 213–14, 240, 257). However, as I have indicated above, I do not believe that Callistus and the other Roman bishops were Modalists, but that their Christology may have included a holdover from an older form of Logos Christology that blurred the distinction between the preincarnate Logos and the Holy Spirit (see James L. Papandrea, *Novatian of Rome and the Culmination of Pre-Nicene Orthodoxy* [Eugene, OR: Wipf & Stock/Pickwick Publications, 2011]).

82. Eusebius of Caesarea, *Ecclesiastical History* 6.20.

83. Brent, *Hippolytus and the Roman Church in the Third Century*, 234–35.

84. Hippolytus, *Refutation of All Heresies* 9.7. Note that Hippolytus refers to the *school* of Callistus.

85. Hippolytus, *Refutation of All Heresies* 9.7.

86. Hippolytus, *Refutation of All Heresies* 9.7.

87. Hippolytus, *Refutation of All Heresies* 9.2–5.

88. Hippolytus, *Against Noetus* 1. Note that on the charge of heresy, the accused was called before the council of priests, not the bishop alone. This shows that the council still held some authority in the early third century and that the episcopacy was not yet the point of singular authority that it would become.

89. Apparently it was not always necessary to move up through the "ranks" of ordination one at a time, and in rare cases it was possible for a deacon to be elected bishop, on the assumption that he would be ordained priest and consecrated bishop at the same time.

90. Hippolytus, *Refutation of All Heresies* 9.7.

91. Hippolytus, *Refutation of All Heresies* 9.6–7.

92. See Hippolytus, *Refutation of All Heresies* 9.7, 10.13, 10.23.

93. Hippolytus, *Refutation of All Heresies* 10.29. See also Hippolytus, *On the Holy Theophany* 7.

94. Hippolytus, *Refutation of All Heresies* 9.7, 10.23. See also Hippolytus, *Expository Treatise Against the Jews* 4, *On Christ and Antichrist* 4, *Against Beron* 1, 5–6. Hippolytus may have accepted the concept of *circumincessio* (see *Against Noetus* 14). Note that there

is ongoing debate over the authorship of the documents traditionally attributed to Hippolytus.

95. Hippolytus, *Refutation of All Heresies* 9.7.

96. Hippolytus, *Refutation of All Heresies* 9.7. Hippolytus actually accused Callistus of waffling between the two heresies, but in doing so, he betrays that Callistus was looking for the middle way between them.

97. According to one tradition, Hippolytus and Pontian were buried in Rome on the same day. If they were executed together, this would certainly be possible; however, Brent thinks that this tradition was invented to convey the impression that the two were reconciled (see Brent, *Hippolytus and the Roman Church in the Third Century*, 257).

98. Hippolytus, *Against Noetus* 2.

99. Hippolytus, *Against Noetus* 2.

100. Hippolytus, *Against Noetus* 1, 7. This was the modalist interpretation of John 14:8–9, that the Son and the Father were one and the same. See also Hippolytus, *Refutation of All Heresies* 9.5.

101. Hippolytus, *Against Noetus* 1–2. See also Hippolytus, *Refutation of All Heresies* 9.5, 7. Note that Noetus and Callistus could agree on the concept of consubstantiality, which Hippolytus was slow to accept.

102. Hippolytus, *Refutation of All Heresies* 10.23.

103. Hippolytus, *Refutation of All Heresies* 9.5.

104. Hippolytus, *Against Noetus* 1.

105. Hippolytus, *Against Noetus* 10–11.

106. Hippolytus, *Against Noetus* 14.

107. Hippolytus, *Against Noetus* 3, 8, 11, 14.

108. Hippolytus, *Against Noetus* 12.

109. Hippolytus, *Against Noetus* 17. See also Hippolytus, *Against Beron* 8. However, some have argued that certain elements in *Against Noetus* which anticipate later doctrinal controversies may have been added later by editors (see Brent, *Hippolytus and the Roman Church in the Third Century*, 224ff; cf. Irenaeus of Lyons, *Against Heresies* 3.19.3).

110. Hippolytus, *Against Noetus* 16.

111. Hippolytus, *Against Noetus* 10–11.

112. Hippolytus, *Against Noetus* 10–11, 15.

113. Hippolytus, *Against Noetus* 17.

114. Hippolytus, *Refutation of All Heresies* 10.29.

115. Hippolytus, *Against Noetus* 11, 16.

116. See Hippolytus, *Against Beron* 1. However, the authorship of this document is in doubt.

117. Hippolytus, *Refutation of All Heresies* 5.2.

118. Hippolytus, *Refutation of All Heresies* 5.1, 7.15. It is interesting to note that Hippolytus mentions that the Gnostics believed the human spirit to be situated in the brain (see Hippolytus, *Refutation of All Heresies* 4.51).

119. Hippolytus, *Refutation of All Heresies* 1.2.

120. Hippolytus, *Refutation of All Heresies* 1.2, 4.43.

121. Hippolytus, *Refutation of All Heresies* 1.2–3.

122. Hippolytus, *Refutation of All Heresies* 1.5–7, 1.16.

123. Hippolytus, *Refutation of All Heresies* 1.16.

124. Hippolytus, *Refutation of All Heresies* 4.48–49.

125. Hippolytus, *Refutation of All Heresies* 1.1.

126. Hippolytus, *Refutation of All Heresies* 1.16, 4.43.

127. Hippolytus, *Refutation of All Heresies* 1.16. Cf. Plato, *Phaedrus* 100.60. Evil is described by the philosophers as the result of going to extremes. It is a lack of self-control.

128. Hippolytus, *Refutation of All Heresies* 4.43.

129. Hippolytus, *Refutation of All Heresies* 1.18, 10.28–29. See also Hippolytus *Against Noetus* 11.

130. The details of Origen's life, such as we know them, come primarily from Eusebius of Caesarea, *Ecclesiastical History* 6, and Jerome, *Illustrious Men* 54.

131. Among other things, Celsus had objected to the Christian belief in the divinity of Christ on the grounds that it compromised divine immutability (see Aloys Grillmeier, *Christ in Christian Tradition, Volume 1: From the Apostolic Age to Chalcedon (451)* [New York: Oxford University Press, 2004], 105).

132. Eusebius of Caesarea, *Ecclesiastical History* 6.24.

133. Rufinus read Novatian's *On the Trinity*, but thought it was written by Tertullian (see Jerome, *Apology Against Rufinus* 2.19; see also Papandrea, *Novatian of Rome*).

134. Eusebius of Caesarea, *Ecclesiastical History* 6.23.

135. Eusebius of Caesarea, *Ecclesiastical History* 6.2, 6.19.

136. Quoted in Eusebius of Caesarea, *Ecclesiastical History* 6.19.

137. See Origen, *On First Principles* 2.2, 2.10. Origen's predecessor, Clement of Alexandria, had speculated that human souls were preexistent, at least by divine foreknowledge (Clement of Alexandria, *Exhortation to the Greeks* 1). This may have contributed to Origen's philosophical speculation on the human soul.

138. See Origen, *On First Principles* 3.1.13.

139. See Origen, *Commentary on John* 2.6.

140. See Origen, *Commentary on John* 1.23.

141. See Origen, *Commentary on John* 2.4, 2.25.

142. For a more detailed account of the life of Novatian, see Papandrea, *Novatian of Rome*, and James L. Papandrea, *The Trinitarian Theology of Novatian of Rome: A Study in Third-Century Orthodoxy* (New York: The Edwin Mellen Press, 2008).

143. Cyprian of Carthage, *Epistle* 51.24.

144. Cf. Irenaeus of Lyons, *Demonstration of the Apostolic Preaching* 64.

145. Cf. Irenaeus of Lyons, *Demonstration of the Apostolic Preaching* 69.

146. For a more detailed exposition of Novatian's theology, see Papandrea, *Novatian of Rome*.

CHAPTER 6

1. Eusebius of Caesarea, *Ecclesiastical History* 3.3.4. Admittedly, Eusebius is not necessarily a reliable source on this subject, since he is only relating what he has heard, sometimes including contradictory traditions.

2. Eusebius of Caesarea, *Ecclesiastical History* 2.23.25, 3.38.1–3.

3. Eusebius of Caesarea, *Ecclesiastical History* 3.24.5–8.

4. Eusebius of Caesarea, *Ecclesiastical History* 3.3.1. This is not the place to enter into the debate over the authorship or dating of New Testament letters; however, some issues related to authorship and early Christian reception will be dealt with below.

5. Some have speculated that the birth narratives in Luke and Matthew were appended later, after the main parts of the gospels were written. It could be that the miraculous nature of Jesus' birth encouraged a docetic understanding of Christ, which made the mainstream Church worry about the use of the birth narratives. For example, see Tertullian, *Against Marcion* 4.21, and *On the Flesh of Christ* 23. Cf. the *Protevangelion of James*. However, the very fact of a human birth would argue against docetism, so the Docetics (including Marcionites and Gnostics) tended not to talk about Jesus' birth. In any case, such a fear may explain why Mark, the first gospel to be written, has no birth narrative.

6. There is no early evidence for a so-called Q source. Though the early writers, including Eusebius, knew of other written gospel sources from the fringes of the Church, there is no mention of a source that would explain the common elements in Matthew and Luke that are not also in Mark. A better explanation for those common elements is simply that Matthew copied Luke (see Mark Goodacre and Nicholas Perrin, eds., *Questioning Q: A Multidimensional Critique* [Downers Grove, IL: InterVarsity Press, 2004]).

7. Eusebius of Caesarea, *Ecclesiastical History* 6.25.

8. Eusebius of Caesarea, *Ecclesiastical History* 3.24.17. By "Johannine literature" I mean the Fourth Gospel, the three letters attributed to a John, and the Book of Revelation. I personally believe that the gospel, the first letter, and Revelation are by the apostle. Yet, the authorship is not the point as much as the fact that they are the last documents written, in the last decade of the first century (with the possibility that the second and third letters of John were written in the first decade of the second century).

9. Justin Martyr, *1 Apology* 66.3.

10. Justin Martyr, *1 Apology* 67. The use of the term *archives* for the Old Testament goes back to Ignatius of Antioch. The phrase "memoirs of the apostles" may refer to the whole New Testament (gospels and letters), the way that the "archives" would refer to the whole Old Testament (law and prophets).

11. Irenaeus of Lyons, *Against Heresies* 3.11.8.

12. David S. Dockery, *Biblical Interpretation Then and Now: Contemporary Hermeneutics in Light of the Early Church* (Grand Rapids, MI: Baker Book House, 1992), 47.

13. See Clement of Alexandria, *Who Is the Rich Man That Shall Be Saved?* 3, *Miscellanies* 1.5, and Irenaeus of Lyons, *Demonstration of the Apostolic Preaching* 91, *Against Heresies* 4.28.1–2, 4.32.1–2, 5.34.1. Note that in *Against Heresies* 2.27.1–2, Irenaeus refers to the gospels as sacred scripture. See also the *Didascalia Apostolorum* 21.

14. Origen, *Commentary on John* 1.5.

15. E. Earle Ellis, "Pseudonymity and Canonicity of New Testament Documents," in *Worship, Theology and Ministry in the Early Church: Essays in Honor of Ralph P. Martin*, ed. Michael J. Wilkins and Terence Paige, Journal for the Study of the New Testament Supplement Series 87 (Sheffield: JSOT Press, 1993), 217–19. See also Eusebius of Caesarea, *Ecclesiastical History* 6.12, 6.25, and the *Apostolic Constitutions* 6.3 (6.16).

16. See Eusebius of Caesarea, *Ecclesiastical History* 6.12. Note that Eusebius knew that the *Gospel of Peter* had been rejected because it was the product of a docetic community.

17. Eusebius of Caesarea, *Ecclesiastical History* 6.20, 6.25. According to Eusebius, the Roman church claimed that Hebrews was written by Clement of Rome.

18. On the other hand, the reader must keep in mind that normally Paul would have dictated his letters to a scribe. Changing the scribe could theoretically change the style of the letter, especially if Paul dictated in Aramaic and the scribe had to translate Paul's words into Greek.

19. Eusebius of Caesarea, *Ecclesiastical History* 6.13, 6.25.

20. Eusebius of Caesarea, *Ecclesiastical History* 6.25.

21. Eusebius of Caesarea, *Ecclesiastical History* 6.14.

22. For an example of the assumption that Ephesians is apostolic, see Novatian, *On the Trinity* 17.9.

23. By far most early Christians believed that the Book of Revelation was written by John, the disciple of Jesus (see Irenaeus of Lyons, *Against Heresies* 4.21.11, 4.30.4, and Eusebius of Caesarea, *Ecclesiastical History* 6.25). Papias, who claimed to have known John the Elder, is an exception, attributing it to that disciple of the apostle. But the only serious challenge to the Johannine authorship in the early Church came from Dionysius of Alexandria, who was motivated to have the text excluded from the canon

because of what he perceived as the danger of literal interpretation by an Egyptian bishop named Nepos. Dionysius of Alexandria argued that Revelation should not be included in the canon because it was not easily interpreted by the average person and thus lent itself to misinterpretation (see Eusebius of Caesarea, *Ecclesiastical History* 7.24–25). Philip of Side (fifth century) had said that those who say John the Elder wrote Revelation are mistaken, and that Papias and Irenaeus's dispensationalist/millennialist interpretation is also mistaken. George the Sinner (ninth century) also relates what he knew as the traditionally accepted belief, that Revelation was written by John the apostle in the time of Domitian, that the next emperor Nerva had released him, and that he had written his gospel afterward, before being martyred. See Clement of Alexandria, *Who Is the Rich Man That Shall Be Saved?* 42, where Clement says that John was in fact released after Domitian's death and returned to Ephesus. Irenaeus says that John lived into the reign of Trajan, thus at least until 98 CE, and also wrote the Fourth Gospel. (Irenaeus of Lyons, *Against Heresies* 2.22.5, 3.3.4, 3.11.1, 5.18.2). If it seems unlikely that John could have lived to the turn of the second century, note that the Roman dole assumed recipients up to eighty years old, which would have been John's age at about that time (see Eusebius of Caesarea, *Ecclesiastical History* 7.21).

24. For the precedent, see 1 Clement 45, 63.

25. Eusebius of Caesarea, *Ecclesiastical History* 6.25. Eusebius says that 1 Peter is genuine but admits that there was a dispute over the authorship of 2 Peter, 2 John, and 3 John. Jerome wrote that John the Elder wrote 2 John and 3 John (see Jerome, *Illustrious Men* 18). Philip of Side (fifth century) said that the earliest Christians accepted only 1 John as from the apostle, and that the other two Johannine epistles were probably from John the Elder, a disciple of the apostle. That there was also debate over Jude and the other Catholic Epistles, see Eusebius of Caesarea, *Ecclesiastical History* 6.13. Note that Eusebius also mentions Barnabas.

26. Admittedly, it could be argued that the more time went by, the easier it would be to ascribe genuine authorship to a pseudonymous document. However, this is where the second and third criteria would make up for any lingering uncertainty in the first.

27. See note 23 above.

28. Jerome said that it was John the Elder who was responsible for the interpretation of Revelation that we first see in Papias (see Jerome, *Illustrious Men* 18). Note that Jerome calls the literal interpretation of an earthly millennium the "Jewish tradition of the millennium," and he notes that not only Irenaeus (and Tertullian), but also Victorinus of Pettau, Lactantius, and Apollinarius also followed this interpretation. Eusebius criticized Papias's and Irenaeus's interpretation of Revelation, saying that it was a misunderstanding of the apostolic document, which should be understood as symbolic (Eusebius of Caesarea, *Ecclesiastical History* 3.36–39). Photius of Constantinople (ninth century) said that Papias and Irenaeus did not represent the accepted traditional interpretation of Revelation. Finally, Justin Martyr, who himself interpreted the millennium as a literal one-thousand-year reign of Christ in a rebuilt earthly Jerusalem, admitted that many orthodox Christians disagreed with this interpretation (Justin Martyr, *Dialogue with Trypho* 80).

29. Ralph P. Martin, *Worship in the Early Church* (Grand Rapids, MI: Eerdmans, 1964), 87–88.

30. In the early Church, there is no distinction between exegesis and hermeneutics. See Dockery, *Biblical Interpretation Then and Now*, 16.

31. See 1 Clement 45, 63, and Irenaeus of Lyons, *Against Heresies* 2.28.2, 2.30.6, 3.2.1. Irenaeus said that "the Scriptures are indeed perfect, since they were spoken by the Word of God and his Spirit." See also Novatian, *On the Trinity* 18.2, Cyprian of Carthage, *Epistle* 51.6, 19–20, 27, and Augustine of Hippo, *On the Trinity* 15.19.31, *Against the Donatists* 2.4, and *On the Morals of the Catholic Church* 29. Augustine argues that to say Christ's words in scripture are not his is blasphemy.

32. Irenaeus of Lyons, *Against Heresies* 3.21.2.

33. Clement of Alexandria, *Exhortation to the Greeks* 1. Clement says that divine revelation was originally through prophecy (in the Old Testament), but now (in the New Testament) it is revealed plainly. Cyprian implied that the reason revelation is progressive is that the return of Christ is drawing ever nearer (see Cyprian of Carthage, *Epistle* 62.18).

34. Dionysius of Alexandria, *Epistle to Philemon*.

35. Tertullian, *Against Praxeas* 2.

36. On the concept of tradition as an authority alongside scripture, and helping to interpret it, see Irenaeus of Lyons, *Against Heresies* 3.2.2, 4.33.8.

37. Irenaeus of Lyons, *Against Heresies* 4.26.1. Irenaeus maintains that Christ is the hidden treasure in the Old Testament, which means that texts which refer to him could not be properly interpreted before he came.

38. Cyprian of Carthage criticized this in his *Epistle* 51.6, 19–20, 27.

39. Dockery, *Biblical Interpretation Then and Now*, 69.

40. Ibid., 56, 65. The *Didascalia* maintains that there is a primary law in the Old Testament (the Ten Commandments) which is still in effect, but a secondary law (such as the dietary rules) which is no longer in effect since the ministry of Jesus (*Didascalia Apostolorum* 26).

41. Hippolytus, *Against Noetus* 4.

42. Dockery, *Biblical Interpretation Then and Now*, 24–25.

43. Ibid., 94. See Cyprian of Carthage, *Epistle* 51.27.

44. Justin Martyr, *Dialogue with Trypho* 65.2. See also Cyprian of Carthage, *On the Lapsed* 20, where Cyprian says that the gospel cannot be sound in one part and waver in another.

45. Irenaeus of Lyons, *Against Heresies* 4.26.1.

46. Eusebius of Caesarea, *Ecclesiastical History* 7.24–25. This is not entirely true, of course, since there were Jewish exegetes who interpreted the Old Testament nonliterally; however, it nevertheless seems to be a generally held stereotype of the early Christians.

47. Dockery, *Biblical Interpretation Then and Now*, 24, 36, 39.

48. Irenaeus of Lyons, *Against Heresies* 3.22.4, 5.19.1, 5.21.2. Irenaeus also points out that Adam was tempted by food (but failed the test) and Jesus was also tempted by food (but resisted the temptation).

49. Irenaeus of Lyons, *Against Heresies* 4.5.4. See also Justin Martyr, *Dialogue with Trypho* 138, and Clement of Alexandria, *The Instructor* 1.5.

50. Dockery, *Biblical Interpretation Then and Now*, 77.

51. Clement of Alexandria, *Who Is the Rich Man That Shall Be Saved?* 5. Clement wrote, "The Savior teaches nothing in a

merely human way, but teaches all things to his own with divine and mystic wisdom. We must not listen to his utterances carnally, but with due investigation and intelligence must search out and learn the meaning hidden in them." Although Clement is talking here about the New Testament, the quotation demonstrates the point well. Note that Clement interprets "Blessed are the poor in spirit" (Matt 5:3) to mean "the poor are blessed in spirit" (Clement of Alexandria, *Who Is the Rich Man That Shall Be Saved?* 17).

52. Dockery, *Biblical Interpretation Then and Now*, 78.

53. For example, Clement of Alexandria interpreted the cleansing of the Temple (connecting it to 1 Cor 6:19) as a call to self-control (Clement of Alexandria, *Exhortation to the Greeks* 11).

54. Dockery, *Biblical Interpretation Then and Now*, 87.

55. The best example of this is Novatian's *On Jewish Foods*. See also *Barnabas* 10–12, Theophilus of Antioch, *To Autolycus* 2.16, and Irenaeus of Lyons, *Against Heresies* Books 4 and 5.

56. In addition to Novatian, *On Jewish Foods*, see Theophilus of Antioch, *To Autolycus* 2.16, where he says that the prohibited animals ("monsters of the deep, and wild beasts, and birds of prey") represent people ("robbers, and murderers, and godless people") because they prey on those weaker than themselves. See also Clement of Alexandria, *The Instructor* 3.11.

57. Novatian, *On Jewish Foods* 3.10. Alternatively, the double hoof could represent accepting both the Father and the Son, according to the orthodox interpretation of the Trinity (see Irenaeus of Lyons, *Against Heresies* 5.8.4).

58. Some possible examples include Clement of Alexandria, *The Instructor* 2.1, where he says that taking the coin out of the mouth of the fish in Matthew 17:17 represents taking greed out of our lives. Clement also says that Paul's words "when I was a child" in 1 Corinthians 13 should be taken to mean "when I was a Jew" (Clement of Alexandria, *The Instructor* 1.6). Origen even speculated that God might intentionally put historical inaccuracies into the text of the Old Testament, as a red flag to the spiritual interpreter to stop looking at the surface and look for a deeper meaning.

59. Dockery, *Biblical Interpretation Then and Now*, 81.

60. Novatian, *On the Trinity* 6.1, 5. Novatian interprets anthropomorphic elements as attributes of God, thus the feet (and

wings) of God represent omnipresence (cf. Ps 139), and the eyes and ears of God represent omniscience.

61. Irenaeus of Lyons, *Against Heresies* 4.3.1. Sometimes the Gnostics did use allegory for the Old Testament when it suited them (see Irenaeus of Lyons, *Against Heresies* 1.3, 3.2.1). Thus Irenaeus's critique is that the Gnostics interpreted the anthropomorphisms of God literally (rejecting the God of the Old Testament), but in other cases they allegorized the text to make it say whatever they wanted it to.

62. There was some disagreement over the proper method of interpretation for the Book of Revelation. It seems that both Irenaeus and Tertullian followed Papias in a literal interpretation of the millennium and a dispensationalist interpretation of the Book of Revelation as it related to history. However, this does not seem to have been the way the majority of Christians read Revelation (see Eusebius of Caesarea, *Ecclesiastical History* 7.24–25). Interpreting the millennium literally was considered by the mainstream to be a "Jewish" (that is, too literal) way of reading the text. Dionysius of Alexandria wrote against the literal interpretation in a document called *On Promises*, which was apparently a response to another document called *Refutation of the Allegorists* by an Egyptian bishop named Nepos. Dionysius of Alexandria did not claim to understand Revelation but knew that it could not be interpreted literally. He seems to have been motivated to have Revelation excluded from the New Testament canon, and to that end he tried to convince other bishops that Revelation was not written by John the apostle, though he did believe that the apostle had written the Fourth Gospel and the letter of 1 John.

63. Irenaeus of Lyons, *Against Heresies* 3.12.11.

64. Irenaeus of Lyons, *Against Heresies* 3.21.2.

65. Dockery, *Biblical Interpretation Then and Now*, 92. See Origen, *Against Celsus* 4.49.

66. Thus the problems with reconciling a literal interpretation of the creation accounts in Genesis with science (even as Origen knew it) were overcome by claiming that God intentionally put historical inaccuracies into the text as a red flag to alert the spiritually mature reader to stop looking at the literal level and look for the deeper meaning.

67. Dockery, *Biblical Interpretation Then and Now*, 83, 92–93. See Origen, *Against Celsus* 4.71. Note that Origen took this to the extreme, eventually saying that the spiritual meaning was only for a spiritual or intellectual elite. The literal meaning, on the other hand, was there to keep the common people occupied. In this way he comes close to the spiritual caste system of some Gnostics who proposed that the three levels of the human person (body, soul, spirit) applied to three types of people (physical people, "soulish" people, and spiritual people). For these Gnostics, full salvation was available only to the spirituals.

68. Theophilus had attempted to redeem a literal interpretation of the creation accounts in Genesis by saying that God had made the plants before the sun to show that it was not by natural causes that creation happened, but by the will of God (Theophilus of Antioch, *To Autolycus* 2.15). See also Dockery, *Biblical Interpretation Then and Now*, 97, 106, and Aloys Grillmeier, *Christ in Christian Tradition, Volume 1: From the Apostolic Age to Chalcedon (451)* (New York: Oxford University Press, 2004), 167–80.

69. Dockery, *Biblical Interpretation Then and Now*, 115.

70. Ibid., 117.

71. Ibid., 72.

72. Ibid., 107.

73. Ibid., 103–5, 119. There is also the possibility that Jewish influence in Antioch contributed to the Eastern desire to emphasize the literal interpretation. This was certainly the case with Jerome. The characterization of literal interpretation as a Jewish methodology is something of a caricature, however, since Jewish interpreters did use allegory and often saw multiple meanings in a text (see Dockery, *Biblical Interpretation Then and Now*, 27, 32, 76).

74. Dockery, *Biblical Interpretation Then and Now*, 28.

75. Ibid., 71–72.

76. Ibid., 139. See Augustine of Hippo, *City of God* 17.3.

77. Augustine must have realized the danger of using allegory with such a hermeneutical presupposition. It is a short slope from "whatever does not promote love" to "whatever I don't agree with."

78. Dockery, *Biblical Interpretation Then and Now*, 133–34.

79. Ibid., 145, 158–59.

80. The moral interpretation is based on Jewish *midrash*, or commentary/homily. The anagogical interpretation is based on Jewish *pesher*, the interpretation of dreams and prophecy using metaphor. This assumes an apocalyptic promise-fulfillment format. See Dockery, *Biblical Interpretation Then and Now*, 29–31, 38.

CHAPTER 7

1. Contrary to popular myth, the gnostic gospels were never considered for the New Testament canon, since the communities that produced them were already separated from the mainstream Church by the time they were written. In fact, they were written *because* of the separation and the perceived need for the Gnostics to have gospels of their own. Therefore it is not legitimate to refer to them as the "lost books of the Bible."

2. Epiphanius of Salamis, *Panarion* 66. According to tradition, the founder of the Manichaeans was a Persian named Mani, whose father was a Gnostic. Mani was not satisfied with the gnosticism he inherited, however, and he added more syncretistic elements, including Persian Zoroastrianism, to create a new version of gnosticism. Eventually, Mani was exiled from Persia by the Magi (the priests of the Zoroastrian cult) and was forced to travel the world, spreading his ideas. In the late fourth century, Augustine of Hippo would join the Manichaeans for a time before becoming Christian.

3. Note that in the Valentinian gnostic *Gospel of Truth*, the Son is called the "name of the Father" (*Gospel of Truth* 38.7–12, 39.24–26). This demonstrates the similarity between gnosticism and modalism (see Larry W. Hurtado, *Lord Jesus Christ: Devotion to Jesus in Earliest Christianity* [Grand Rapids, MI: Eerdmans, 2003], 544).

4. This was probably at least partly influenced by the imprecise language of some of the apologists who talked of the incarnation as if Christ had "put on" flesh. It may also have been influenced by the hybrid Christology of some Gnostics, who acknowledged a tangible body of Jesus even while they denied a true human nature.

5. Hippolytus, *Refutation of All Heresies* 9.2–5. Cf. Epiphanius of Salamis, *Panarion* 57.

6. Hippolytus, *Against Noetus* 1–2, *Refutation of All Heresies* 9.5.

7. Hippolytus, *Against Noetus* 1–2. See also *Refutation of All Heresies* 10.23.

8. Hippolytus, *Refutation of All Heresies* 9.5.

9. Epiphanius of Salamis, *Panarion* 62.1–2.

10. Epiphanius of Salamis, *Panarion* 62.1.4. Sabellius describes God as "three names in one *hypostasis*," or one person with three names.

11. It is not clear to what extent the proponents of modalism had the concept of the theater mask in mind. In Greek, the words for "person" could have a range of meaning to include the idea of "personality" or even "character." However, it is not as simple as saying that the three names for the Trinity are three "faces" of God, since the point is that in modalism the names refer to God's activity and/or the chronological distinction of Old Testament/New Testament/Church. A better analogy might be to suggest that the three different names for God in modalism are like three different hats that God wears, depending on the task at hand.

12. Sabellius used some of the same analogies for the Trinity that the mainstream writers used, including the analogy of the sun (which Tertullian also used), where the star itself is like the Father, its light is like the Son, and its heat is like the Holy Spirit. However, Sabellius understood this in a way that removed any real distinction between the three, and it is a testimony to the imperfection of analogies that writers on both sides of the debate can use the same analogies to explain their differing Christologies. In fact, what we observe is that it is not the analogy but the explanation of it that becomes the argument in favor of one version of Christology or another.

13. Ironically, this type of distinction is not acceptable to the orthodox, since it violates the principles of inseparable operation and appropriation.

14. The implication of modalism is that God is not a Trinity, since he can only be one "person" at a time, rather like Peter Parker and Spiderman—they cannot both be in the same room at the same time. It is important to see that some analogies that are often used

for the Trinity, such as H_2O (ice, water, steam), are actually analogies of a modalistic "Trinity," not an orthodox one. You cannot have both ice and steam at the same time.

15. John Behr, *The Way to Nicaea: The Formation of Christian Theology, Volume 1* (Crestwood, NY: St. Vladimir's Seminary Press, 2001), 138, see especially note 1.

16. Aloys Grillmeier, *Christ in Christian Tradition, Volume 1: From the Apostolic Age to Chalcedon (451)* (New York: Oxford University Press, 2004), 165. Cf. Epiphanius of Salamis, *Panarion* 65.

17. Eusebius of Caesarea, *Ecclesiastical History* 7.30.

18. Eusebius of Caesarea, *Ecclesiastical History* 7.27–30. See also Malchion, *In the Name of the Synod of Antioch Against Paul of Samosata.*

19. Specifically, for Arius the Logos is a real preexistent entity, though not eternally preexistent, and created, not divine. While Arius is the fourth-century legacy of adoptionism, he modified it to accept a qualified divinity in Christ. For Arius, however, the divinity of Christ was acquired, received as a reward, and it was a lesser degree of divinity than the Father, so that for him the Father and Son were not consubstantial.

20. Eusebius of Caesarea, *Ecclesiastical History* 7.30. See also Malchion, *In the Name of the Synod of Antioch Against Paul of Samosata.*

21. Malchion, *In the Name of the Synod of Antioch Against Paul of Samosata* 3.

22. Eusebius of Caesarea, *Ecclesiastical History* 7.30. See also Malchion, *In the Name of the Synod of Antioch Against Paul of Samosata.*

23. Eusebius of Caesarea, *Ecclesiastical History* 7.30. Eusebius's account includes a possible mention of a church building (*ekklesias oikou*) in Antioch. If this is a reference to a building, it would probably have been a house converted for worship. It is unlikely that there would have been any buildings built specifically as Christian houses of worship at this time; however, there were dedicated worship spaces converted from domestic or other purposes. Before the Church was a legal entity, churches in some cities could own property as social organizations, such as the funerary societies that provided burial for their members. On the other hand, it could be an anachronism in Eusebius's fourth-century text.

24. There was a growing consensus within the Church, based on apostolic succession, that all churches should agree with Rome, at least on matters of doctrine. For example, see Irenaeus of Lyons, *Against Heresies* 3.3.2.

25. Clement of Alexandria, *Who Is the Rich Man That Shall Be Saved?* 8, Irenaeus of Lyons, *Against Heresies* 3.20.3, Novatian, *On the Trinity* 15.7–9.

26. Eusebius of Caesarea, *Ecclesiastical History* 6.29.

27. Eusebius of Caesarea, *Ecclesiastical History* 7.2.6–11.

28. Grillmeier, 154–58. Dionysius of Rome may also have chosen to write the document this way because of accusations that he himself was a follower of Sabellius. While the accusation was unfounded, his own emphasis on the consubstantiality of the persons of the Trinity led some to accuse him of modalism.

29. Lewis Ayres, *Nicaea and Its Legacy: An Approach to Fourth-Century Trinitarian Theology* (New York: Oxford University Press, 2004), 94.

30. Dionysius of Rome, *Against the Sabellians* 2–3.

31. Athanasius of Alexandria, *Defense of Dionysius* 18. Reprinted in J. Stevenson, *A New Eusebius: Documents Illustrating the History of the Church to AD 337* (London: SPCK, 1957, revised edition 1987), 254–55. See also Ayres, 94.

32. Hippolytus, *Against Noetus* 3–4.

33. Cyprian of Carthage, *Epistle* 51.6, 19–20, 27.

34. Novatian, *On the Trinity* 11.5, 11.9, 30.6.

35. For a more detailed treatment of the development of doctrine along these lines, see James L. Papandrea, *Novatian of Rome and the Culmination of Pre-Nicene Orthodoxy* (Eugene, OR: Wipf & Stock/Pickwick Publications, 2011).

36. Tertullian is also an example of a lay teacher, though his relationship to the hierarchy is unclear. On the assumption that teachers (at least in some places) could be lay or clergy, see the *Apostolic Tradition* 19. On the episcopacy as teaching office, see Irenaeus of Lyons, *Against Heresies* 3.3.3. In the early Church, pre-baptism catechesis focused more on morality (how to live as a Christian) than theology (what to believe). Apparently, the early bishops thought it was more important to emphasize the behavioral

commitments that new converts were making, assuming they would learn their theology after baptism.

37. Or, as we have seen, Hippolytus may have been the bishop of a smaller town near Rome.

38. For a detailed treatment of the monoepiscopacy, see Allen Brent, *Hippolytus and the Roman Church in the Third Century: Communities in Tension Before the Emergence of a Monarch-Bishop* (Leiden: Brill, 1995).

39. Eusebius of Caesarea, *Ecclesiastical History* 6.43.

40. Cyprian of Carthage, *Epistle* 40.2, *On the Unity of the Catholic Church* 5. See Ignatius of Antioch, *Letter to the Philadelphians* 2.2, 6.2, *Letter to the Smyrnaeans* 9.1.

41. See also Irenaeus of Lyons, *Against Heresies* 3.2.2, and *Didascalia Apostolorum* 9.

42. Cyprian of Carthage, *Epistle* 72.21, *On the Unity of the Catholic Church* 6. The importance of this question was extended to the sacraments, since the authority to administer the sacraments came from the bishop through ordination (Cyprian of Carthage, *Epistle* 75.3, 8; see also Ignatius of Antioch, *Letter to the Philadelphians* 3.3). In reality, this view was universally held in the early Church. The question was not whether there was the possibility of salvation outside the Church, the question was how to define the Church.

43. Cyprian of Carthage, *On the Unity of the Catholic Church* 7.

44. Ignatius of Antioch, *Letter to the Philadelphians* 8.1. For Ignatius, reconciliation meant returning to the bishop.

45. Cyprian of Carthage, *Epistle* 51.21, 53.2, 54.5.

46. Cyprian of Carthage, *Epistle* 75.3, 8, *On the Unity of the Catholic Church* 13, 17. See Ignatius of Antioch, *Letter to the Ephesians* 5.2, 20.2, *Letter to the Philadelphians* 4.1, *Letter to the Smyrnaeans* 8.1. We will see this same principle applied to baptism in the baptismal controversy.

47. Marriage was not yet considered a sacrament at this time, nor was what is now called the anointing of the sick (formerly Extreme Unction); however; the bishop still controlled these.

48. Cyprian of Carthage, *Epistle* 40.2, 51.8, 54.5–6. See also *Apostolic Tradition* 1.9.6–8.

49. David Rankin, *Tertullian and the Church* (Cambridge, UK: Cambridge University Press, 1995), 191, 195.

50. Cyprian of Carthage, *Epistle* 48.2, 75.3, 8, *On the Unity of the Catholic Church* 10.

51. Tertullian, *On Modesty* 1.7–8. Tertullian mentions "bishops of bishops." Note that Ignatius had said only bishops had the authority to convene a council (*Letter to Polycarp* 7).

52. The English word *pope* is simply one of several possible translations for the Greek and Latin words for "father." Therefore, it is not clear when the term comes to be used exclusively of metropolitans, or if in fact it was used for bishops first, and then the concept of "father" was transferred to the priests along with the authority granted to them by the bishops.

53. Cyprian of Carthage, *Epistle* 73.

54. Eusebius of Caesarea, *Ecclesiastical History* 7.7.

55. Cyprian of Carthage, *Epistle* 26.1. Clement of Alexandria had said that Peter was the preeminent apostle because Jesus had paid his tax for him (Matt 17:27) (Clement of Alexandria, *Who Is the Rich Man That Shall Be Saved?* 21).

56. Irenaeus of Lyons, *Against Heresies* 3.3.2.

57. Tertullian, *The Prescription Against the Heretics* 36. Cyprian of Carthage, *Epistle* 28, 42, 51.6–8, 54.14, 62.1, 70.3, 71.1–3. See also the letter of Firmilian in Cyprian of Carthage, *Epistle* 74.3–6, 24. Cf. Michael M. Sage, *Cyprian*, Patristic Monograph Series, vol. 1 (Cambridge, MA: The Philadelphia Patristic Foundation, 1975), 301.

58. Cyprian of Carthage, *Epistle* 72.13, 73.1–3, 73.9–10, 75.5. See also the letter of Firmilian in Cyprian of Carthage, *Epistle* 74.16–17. Cyprian, like some other bishops, questioned the limits of Rome's authority over other cities. While many would have agreed that all churches should agree with Rome on matters of doctrine, some questioned whether they had to submit to Rome on other matters. Cyprian argued that each bishop is the highest authority in his own area, but is free of the authority of other bishops. Thus the councils of Carthage need not submit to the bishop of Rome. After all, Peter had deferred to Paul on the issue of the Gentiles (see Cyprian of Carthage, *Epistle* 62.1, 70.3, 71.3). Cyprian argued that truth takes precedence over tradition (see

Cyprian of Carthage, *Epistle* 72.13, 73.2–3, 9, and the letter of Firmilian in Cyprian of Carthage, *Epistle* 74.19). Firmilian pointed out that the Romans do not always agree among themselves, so he reasoned that the Roman bishops might err (see the letter of Firmilian in Cyprian of Carthage, *Epistle* 74.3, 6; see also Cyprian of Carthage, *Epistle* 73.1). Therefore, the bishops, even the bishops of Rome, must be teachable and ultimately submit to the consensus of the greater Church (cf. 1 Cor 14:29–30) (see Cyprian of Carthage, *Epistle* 70.3, 73.10). This attitude was confirmed by the seventh Council of Carthage, which criticized Stephen for setting himself up as a "bishop of bishops." Nevertheless, the idea of metropolitans was firmly entrenched. Cf. Tertullian, *On Modesty* 1.7–8. Firmilian summed it up when he wrote as if to Stephen, "...for while you think that all may be excommunicated by you, you have excommunicated yourself alone from all" (see the letter of Firmilian in Cyprian of Carthage, *Epistle* 74.24).

59. Eusebius of Caesarea, *Ecclesiastical History* 7.30.

60. Cyprian of Carthage, *Epistle* 9.1, 3-4, 10.2, 11.2, 26.1, *On the Unity of the Catholic Church* 5.

61. It is interesting to note that in the *Didascalia Apostolorum* 9, the deaconess is compared to the Holy Spirit.

62. Didache 15, 1 Clement 41–42, 44, Cyprian of Carthage, *Epistle* 45.2, 51.7, 54.12, 75.5, *On the Unity of the Catholic Church* 6, 11, 23. See also the anonymous *Against Novatian* 3, 7–8, 12.

63. Rankin, 5, 18.

64. Rankin, 49. Note that this is similar to the Gnostics, who grouped humanity into classes, seeing themselves as the most enlightened.

65. Rankin, 43. Some sources put the year at 172, but that is only five years before the synod in Rome, and so it is unlikely that the controversy would have spread to the West by that time.

66. See Tertullian, *On the Soul* 9.4.

67. Rankin, 41, 44.

68. Eusebius of Caesarea, *Ecclesiastical History* 5.16. Note that these synods are some of the earliest councils of the Church.

69. Tertullian, *Against Praxeas* 1.5.

70. Rankin, 51.

71. Eusebius of Caesarea, *Ecclesiastical History* 5.16–17. The apologist Quadratus is quoted by Eusebius as saying, "The false prophet speaks in ecstasy."

72. Eusebius of Caesarea, *Ecclesiastical History* 5.18. The latter point, that the Montanists were accused of prophesying for money, may actually be evidence of one of the earliest cases of church leaders receiving stipends for their ministry. The accusation may even be the result of sour grapes on the part of mainstream clergy who were jealous that the leaders of the New Prophecy were getting paid in the time before leadership in the mainstream Church was an occupation.

73. Eusebius of Caesarea, *Ecclesiastical History* 5.16. They are compared to Judas, who betrayed Christ and then killed himself. According to Epiphanius of Salamis, Maximilla had claimed that she would be the last prophet (see Epiphanius of Salamis, *Panarion* 48.2).

74. Hippolytus, *Refutation of All Heresies* 8.12, 10.22. See also Eusebius of Caesarea, *Ecclesiastical History* 2.8, and Ayres, 101.

75. On the other hand, the Roman bishops were at first reluctant to condemn Noetus and his followers, and some have accused bishops Zephyrinus and Callistus of being Modalists themselves. In the end, the excommunications of Noetus and Sabellius show that the Roman bishops were not Modalists, and Tertullian's association with the Montanists makes the charge impossible to pin on them as well.

76. Tertullian, *On Monogamy* 1. See Rankin, 38. Note that the so-called "Tertullianists" were fourth-century Montanists in North Africa. However, if they were descendants of Tertullian's followers, it is unlikely that their theology was heterodox.

77. Tertullian, *Against Praxeas* 13.

78. Eusebius of Caesarea, *Ecclesiastical History* 5.16.

79. Tertullian, *On Monogamy* 3.9.

80. Tertullian, *Against Praxeas* 30, *On Monogamy* 3.9. See Rankin, 48.

81. Rankin, 172–74.

82. With regard to the separation of clergy from laity, by the third century, the clergy were spatially segregated from the laity in the assembly. The third century would also see the development of

a paid clergy, which assumed that clergy could be a profession supported by the laity (see the *Didascalia Apostolorum* 9, 12).

83. Irenaeus said that the gnostic liturgy included a magic trick, in which water was poured from a large cup into a smaller cup without spilling. In this ritual, there were said to be women assisting. This probably means that the groups which Irenaeus is criticizing allowed women to function as deacons (see Irenaeus of Lyons, *Against Heresies* 1.13.2).

84. Tertullian, *On Baptism* 17.5, *On the Veiling of Virgins* 9.1. See Rankin, 175.

85. Tertullian, *On Baptism* 17.5. Some have speculated that the *Passion of Perpetua and Felicitas* is a Montanist document (see Timothy D. Barnes, *Tertullian: A Historical and Literary Study* [Oxford: Clarendon Press, 1971], 77ff).

86. Tertullian, *The Prescription Against the Heretics* 41. See also *Didascalia Apostolorum* 15, *Apostolic Church Order* 26. There women are not to stand in the assembly (to preach or to preside) but are expected to remain seated. In the *Apostolic Constitutions* 3.1 (3.9), it is argued that if women were meant to baptize, then Jesus would have been baptized by his mother Mary, rather than by John the Baptist.

87. *Didascalia Apostolorum* 15, *Apostolic Constitutions* 3.1 (3.6).

88. *Apostolic Tradition* 10.

89. *Didascalia Apostolorum* 16. The point being made seems to be that women who have been Christian for a time can help the newly baptized women adapt to the Church's expectations of morality and modesty.

90. *Didascalia Apostolorum* 16.

91. *Didascalia Apostolorum* 16. It is possible that the visitation of the sick might include helping the person bathe or accomplish other personal tasks, which would make it impossible for a man to visit a woman.

92. Justin Martyr, *1 Apology* 67, Clement of Alexandria, *The Instructor* 3.12. See also the letter of Cornelius of Rome in Eusebius of Caesarea, *Ecclesiastical History* 6.43, in which Cornelius writes that in the middle of the third century there were over 1,500 widows and other needy people supported by the church in Rome.

93. *Didascalia Apostolorum* 14–15. The *Didascalia* states that widows should know who gave the money, so that they can pray for that person by name, but they should not divulge the name to anyone.

94. *Didascalia Apostolorum* 15, *Apostolic Church Order* 21.

95. *Apostolic Church Order* 21.

96. *Didascalia Apostolorum* 15.

97. *Didascalia Apostolorum* 14. The *Didascalia* does say that a second marriage is allowed for younger widows (1 Tim 5:14), presumably to relieve some of the burden on the church, since the widows received support from the offerings. However, a younger, remarried widow would not be considered a member of the order of widows.

98. *Apostolic Tradition* 14.

99. For both men and women, after the end of persecution, asceticism and monasticism become the new martyrdom. By the same token, heresy and schism would become the new apostasy.

100. Tertullian, *Apology* 1, 37. Of course, this supports Tertullian's argument and may be an exaggeration (see Michael M. Sage, *Cyprian*, Patristic Monograph Series, vol. 1 [Cambridge, MA: The Philadelphia Patristic Foundation, 1975], 47ff).

101. Tertullian, *Apology* 40.

102. It seems that Caracalla required loyalty sacrifices for all (new) citizens, and while it was not his intention to persecute Christians, some may have been executed at this time for refusing to sacrifice.

103. Eusebius of Caesarea, *Ecclesiastical History* 6.21. See also the Historia Augusta, *Severus Alexander* 22.4, 29.2, 43.6–7, 45.6–7, 49.6, 51.7. The reliability of the Historia Augusta has been questioned; however, even if stories of Alexander's preference for Christianity are exaggerated, his tolerance of the Church is based on historical events. Eusebius says that the emperor Philip (reigned 244–49 CE) was also sympathetic to the Church, and that he actually had once attended an Easter service (see Eusebius of Caesarea, *Ecclesiastical History* 6.19.15, 6.21.3–4, 6.36.3). The story of Philip attending Christian worship is probably apocryphal since it would be unlikely for an unbaptized person to attend worship before the end of the persecutions. However, the anecdote does tell us some-

thing of the precariousness of the Church's status within the empire before the fourth century—at the drop of a hat the Church could go back and forth from pursued to tolerated. It seems that Philip's reign was the calm before the storm.

104. Eusebius of Caesarea, *Ecclesiastical History* 6.28. It was said that Maximinus believed (or claimed) that an earthquake in Asia Minor was a sign from the gods, demonstrating their anger over the many conversions to Christianity. It was under Maximinus that Hippolytus and Bishop Pontian of Rome were sentenced to the mines.

105. The traditional date for the founding of the city of Rome is 753 BCE. Thus the one-thousand-year anniversary was in 247 CE.

106. Eusebius of Caesarea, *Ecclesiastical History* 6.34, 39.

107. Eusebius of Caesarea, *Ecclesiastical History* 6.41.

108. Eusebius of Caesarea, *Ecclesiastical History* 6.41.

109. James L. Papandrea, *The Wedding of the Lamb: A Historical Approach to the Book of Revelation* (Eugene, OR: Wipf & Stock/Pickwick Publications, 2011), 156–59.

110. Eusebius of Caesarea, *Ecclesiastical History* 8.11. Note that Eusebius says that some Marcionites were also the victims of this persecution (see Eusebius of Caesarea, *Ecclesiastical History* 7.12).

111. Eusebius of Caesarea, *Ecclesiastical History* 8.7–8, 8.12.

112. Eusebius of Caesarea, *Ecclesiastical History* 8.9.

113. Eusebius of Caesarea, *Ecclesiastical History* 6.41. See also Cyprian of Carthage, *On the Lapsed* 7–8.

114. Cyprian of Carthage, *On the Lapsed* 6, 10. See also Hermas, *The Shepherd* 14, which may have been in Cyprian's mind.

115. Eusebius of Caesarea, *Ecclesiastical History* 6.41.

116. Eusebius of Caesarea, *Ecclesiastical History* 6.5, 8.7–8, 8.12.

117. Eusebius of Caesarea, *Ecclesiastical History* 8.12.

118. For an account of the persecution in Alexandria, see the letter of Dionysius of Alexandria to Stephen of Rome.

119. Eusebius of Caesarea, *Ecclesiastical History* 6.29. Eusebius records that Fabian was loved by the people of Rome because when he was elected a dove had landed on his head, mir-

roring Jesus' baptism and signifying God's anointing. Cyprian said that the emperor Decius had remarked that he "would rather confront a rival emperor than to see a new bishop installed in the church at Rome" (Cyprian of Carthage, *Epistle* 55.9).

120. Eusebius of Caesarea, *Ecclesiastical History* 7.22.

121. For a thorough treatment of Cyprian and the controversies of the third century, see Michael M. Sage, *Cyprian*, Patristic Monograph Series, vol. 1 (Cambridge, MA: The Philadelphia Patristic Foundation, 1975).

122. Epistles 2 through 39 of Cyprian's correspondence were written from hiding. Later, Cyprian would write that fleeing persecution to avoid the temptation of idolatry was as good as being a confessor (see Cyprian of Carthage, *On the Lapsed* 3). The Montanists, on the other hand, had said that to flee was to be unfaithful.

123. Cyprian of Carthage, *Epistle* 27, 54.9–10.

124. Some of the early sources confuse these two men, as though they were the same person, but they were not. Novatus had been an enemy of Cyprian in North Africa for some time even before the controversy over the lapsed (see Cyprian of Carthage, *Epistle* 42, 48.2). Cyprian accused Novatus of taking Luke 9:59–60 literally and failing in his duty to bury his own father.

125. Cyprian of Carthage, *Epistle* 48.2–3.

126. Cyprian of Carthage, *Epistle* 11.1–3, 13.2, 27.1–3, 51.3–4, 51.7, *On the Unity of the Catholic Church* 19.

127. Cyprian of Carthage, *Epistle* 9.1–2, 11.2.

128. Cyprian of Carthage, *Epistle* 10.1–2, 10.4 (*et cum suis*), 12.1, 13.2, 26.1.

129. Cf. Rankin, 193–94.

130. Cyprian of Carthage, *On the Unity of the Catholic Church* 21.

131. For Cyprian's description of the situation, see Cyprian of Carthage, *On the Lapsed* 6–8, 10.

132. Cyprian of Carthage, *Epistle* 40.1, 48.2.

133. Cyprian of Carthage, *On the Lapsed* 17.

134. Cyprian of Carthage, *Epistle* 51.18.

135. Cyprian of Carthage, *Epistle* 26.1, *On the Lapsed* 17. The granting of the authority to forgive sins in Matthew 16:18–19 was

interpreted as having been given to all the apostles, not just Peter. Thus it was seen as extended to all bishops through apostolic succession. This authority could be granted by a bishop to the priests under his authority (see Cyprian of Carthage, *Epistle* 58.1).

136. Cyprian of Carthage, *Epistle* 53.4, *On the Lapsed* 14–15, 18.

137. Cyprian of Carthage, *Epistle* 27.3, 51.4, 54.4.

138. Cyprian of Carthage, *Epistle* 12.1–2, 51.5.

139. Cyprian of Carthage, *Epistle* 27.3, 51.4, 13, 16, 26. *On the Lapsed* 14, 35. The early Christians did not believe that all sin was equal. Rather, they believed that some sins were worse than others (the worst being apostasy/idolatry and adultery). Therefore the penance must fit the sin.

140. Cyprian of Carthage, *Epistle* 52.2, *On the Lapsed* 13–14.

141. Cyprian of Carthage, *Epistle* 12.1–2, 51.5, 11, 17, *On the Lapsed* 27.

142. Cyprian of Carthage, *Epistle* 51.23.

143. Eusebius of Caesarea, *Ecclesiastical History* 6.42–43.

144. Cyprian of Carthage, *Epistle* 43, 54.9. See also Eusebius of Caesarea, *Ecclesiastical History* 6.43.

145. Cyprian of Carthage, *Epistle* 55.6, 17. See J. Patout Burns, "On Rebaptism: Social Organization in the Third Century Church," *Journal of Early Christian Studies* 1:4 (1993): 374–75, 395.

146. Cyprian of Carthage, *Epistle* 48.1, 51.29, 53.4, Cf. *On the Unity of the Catholic Church* 14.

147. Cyprian of Carthage, *Epistle* 40.1.

148. Cyprian of Carthage, *Epistle* 40.2, 51.3.

149. Eusebius of Caesarea, *Ecclesiastical History* 6.42–46.

150. Cyprian of Carthage, *Epistle* 45.1–3, 51.

151. Cyprian of Carthage, *Epistle* 45.2, 47, 48.2. See also Eusebius of Caesarea, *Ecclesiastical History* 6.43.

152. For Dionysius of Alexandria's letter to Novatian, see Eusebius of Caesarea, *Ecclesiastical History* 6.45, 7.7–8. It is also reprinted in Stevenson, 232–33.

153. For Cornelius's letter, see Eusebius of Caesarea, *Ecclesiastical History* 6.43.

154. Cyprian of Carthage, *Epistle* 45.1.

155. *Against Novatian* 12–14.

156. *Against Novatian* 8.

157. Acknowledging the distinction, Pacian of Barcelona (late fourth century) would later write, "Christian is my name, but Catholic is my surname...by the one I am approved, by the other I am but marked" (Pacian of Barcelona, *Epistle* 1.5–8).

158. See Stevenson, 320. The Novatianists were, however, persecuted by the Catholic bishops of the fourth and fifth centuries. For more detail, see Papandrea, *Novatian of Rome and the Culmination of Pre-Nicene Orthodoxy*.

159. Stevenson, 224.

160. Cyprian of Carthage, *Epistle* 54.16.

161. Cyprian of Carthage, *Epistle* 51.19. See also *Against Novatian* 1.

162. Cyprian of Carthage, *Epistle* 51.15. See also *Against Novatian* 15.

163. Cyprian of Carthage, *Epistle* 53.1-4. See also Burns, 375.

164. Cyprian of Carthage, *On the Unity of the Catholic Church* 19.

165. Eusebius of Caesarea, *Ecclesiastical History* 7.10.

166. Cyprian of Carthage, *Epistle* 80.1. See also Eusebius of Caesarea, *Ecclesiastical History* 7.11. For an excellent overview of where the early Christians were meeting, see Ramsay MacMullen, *The Second Church: Popular Christianity A.D. 200–400* (Atlanta: Society of Biblical Literature, 2009).

167. Eusebius of Caesarea, *Ecclesiastical History* 7.10.

168. Eusebius of Caesarea, *Ecclesiastical History* 7.13.

169. Cyprian of Carthage, *Epistle* 9.2, 10.1, *On the Lapsed* 15, 26.

170. Cyprian of Carthage, *Epistle* 54.13, 58.1. Note that penance here is a verb, to "do penance."

171. Cyprian of Carthage, *Epistle* 75.11. Cf. *On Rebaptism* 10.

172. Cyprian of Carthage, *Epistle* 51.22.

173. *Against Novatian* 10, 14, 18. See also Cyprian of Carthage, *On the Lapsed* 17, 29, and the letter of Firmilian in Cyprian of Carthage, *Epistle* 74.4.

174. Polycarp, *Letter to the Philippians* 10.2, Cyprian of Carthage, *On the Lapsed* 35. See also 2 Clement 16 (quoting 1 Pet 4:8). Note that the *Didascalia* advises that if one cannot afford to

give alms, one should fast and use the money that would have been spent on food to give alms (*Didascalia Apostolorum* 19).

175. Cyprian of Carthage, *Epistle* 9.2, 11.2, 45.2 (the Roman confessors' reconciliation), 58.1, 71.2.

176. Eusebius of Caesarea, *Ecclesiastical History* 6.42.

177. Cyprian of Carthage, *Epistle* 51.27. Although the mainstream Christians did not subscribe to the idea that all sins are equal in the eyes of God, some of the rigorists apparently did, and therefore Cyprian's comment in this letter may be a concession to a rigorist point. However, if the rigorists did hold the conviction that all sin is equal, it led them to create ever-growing lists of sins that could not be forgiven. For the Catholics, admitting that there is some truth to the concept that all sin is a form of idolatry led them to the opposite conclusion, that all sins could be forgiven.

178. Cyprian of Carthage, *Epistle* 51.20–22, 26.

179. 1 Clement 57, Ignatius of Antioch, *Letter to the Philadelphians* 3. In the *Didascalia*, schism is referred to as a coveting of the "primacy" (that is, of the bishop), which may be a reference to Novatian (*Didascalia Apostolorum* 23).

180. Cyprian of Carthage, *Epistle* 72.16, *On the Unity of the Catholic Church* 15, 19, 21. See also *Against Novatian* 8, 10, 14. A century earlier, Irenaeus had written concerning other schismatics, "For no reformation of so great importance can be effected by them, as will compensate for the mischief arising from their schism" (*Against Heresies* 4.33.7).

181. Eusebius of Caesarea, *Ecclesiastical History* 7.2–3.

182. Cyprian of Carthage, *On the Lapsed* 9.

183. Eusebius of Caesarea, *Ecclesiastical History* 7.2–3. Cf. *Didascalia Apostolorum* 10, 24. See also Burns, 377, 398. There may have been some disagreement over whether the imposition of hands constituted reconciliation or a reconfirmation. If Cyprian saw it as confirmation, then it would be the confirmation of an invalid baptism. See Cyprian of Carthage, *Epistle* 75 and the letter of Firmilian in Cyprian of Carthage, *Epistle* 74.

184. Cyprian of Carthage, *Epistle* 71.4, 72.3, 73.3.

185. Cyprian of Carthage, *Epistle* 58.3-6, 71.1, 72.1. See also Stevenson, 224.

186. Cyprian of Carthage, *Epistle* 71.1, 73.1–2. See also Eusebius of Caesarea, *Ecclesiastical History* 7.2–3, 7–9. Note that the church of Alexandria agreed with Rome on this issue.

187. Cyprian of Carthage, *Epistle* 73.8.

188. Burns, 377–78.

189. Cyprian of Carthage, *Epistle* 62.8, 70, 75.12–13. Note that Cyprian admits even a clinical (emergency) baptism is not to be repeated, and the sacrament is not made any less valid by sprinkling or pouring. See also *On Rebaptism* 10.

190. Cyprian of Carthage, *Epistle* 72.7, 75.11. The authority to forgive sins rested with the bishops; however, they could delegate this authority to the priests in their respective areas (see Cyprian of Carthage, *Epistle* 58.1).

191. Cyprian of Carthage, *Epistle* 71.2, 72.6, 24, 73.7, *On the Unity of the Catholic Church* 11, 13, 17. See also the letter of Firmilian in Cyprian of Carthage, *Epistle* 74.26 and *Against Novatian* 3. Note that all schismatic sacraments would be considered invalid. Ordination, though it was not yet considered a sacrament, would also not be valid outside the succession (see Cyprian of Carthage, *Epistle* 48.2, *On the Unity of the Catholic Church* 10).

192. Cyprian of Carthage, *Epistle* 58.2, 62.8. See also the letter of Firmilian in Cyprian of Carthage, *Epistle* 74.8.

193. Cyprian of Carthage, *Epistle* 70.1, 71.1–5, 72.1.

194. Cyprian of Carthage, *Epistle* 70.1. See also the letter of Firmilian in Cyprian of Carthage, *Epistle* 74.22.

195. Cyprian of Carthage, *Epistle* 71.2, 75.12.

196. Cyprian of Carthage, *Epistle* 72.3. See also the letter of Firmilian in Cyprian of Carthage, *Epistle* 74.23.

197. Cyprian of Carthage, *Epistle* 72.16, 21. Cyprian paraphrases Paul in 1 Corinthians 13, that it profits nothing even to give one's body to be burned, if one dies for a heresy. Note that in this interpretation, the love of 1 Corinthians 13 is love for orthodoxy. Cf. *On Rebaptism* 13.

198. Cyprian of Carthage, *Epistle* 72.21, 75.1, 7–9. This was aimed specifically at Novatian. Cyprian acknowledged that his theology was orthodox but said that this did not excuse schism. Note that Montanists are also mentioned in the letter of Firmilian in Cyprian of Carthage, *Epistle* 74.7, 19.

199. Cyprian of Carthage, *On the Unity of the Catholic Church* 11, 13, 17.

200. Cyprian of Carthage, *Epistle* 72.2, 72.6, 24. See also the letter of Firmilian in Cyprian of Carthage, *Epistle* 74.26, and Burns, 393.

201. Cyprian of Carthage, *Epistle* 72.19–20. See also the letter of Firmilian in Cyprian of Carthage, *Epistle* 74.21–23.

202. Cyprian of Carthage, *Epistle* 72.24–25.

203. Cyprian of Carthage, *Epistle* 72.2. See also Eusebius of Caesarea, *Ecclesiastical History* 7.7, where the statement that Novatian, "sets at naught the holy washing" may refer to his practice of rebaptism. In reality, Novatian was probably doing what we would now call, "provisional baptisms," since he probably did not rebaptize those baptized before the schism.

204. Cyprian of Carthage, *Epistle* 72.4.

205. *On Rebaptism* 10.

206. *On Rebaptism* 10. According to the *Didascalia Apostolorum* 26, rebaptism would "undo" the original baptism.

207. Cyprian of Carthage, *Epistle* 73.2.

208. *On Rebaptism* 6, 9.

209. Cyprian of Carthage, *Epistle* 74.18, *On Rebaptism* 10.

210. Cyprian of Carthage, *Epistle* 72.4–5, 12, 18.

211. *On Rebaptism* 10, 12. Any baptism that was not trinitarian would not be considered valid, even by Stephen.

212. *On Rebaptism* 12.

213. Cyprian of Carthage, *Epistle* 72.23.

214. Cyprian of Carthage, *Epistle* 73.8.

215. Cyprian of Carthage, *Epistle* 70.1, 72.12, 20–21, 23–24, 75.3–4. For Cyprian, baptism outside the Church is "adulterous water." See also the letter of Firmilian in Cyprian of Carthage, *Epistle* 74.14, 23.

216. However, Cyprian did apparently make a distinction between the visible Church and the true, or invisible, Church (see Cyprian of Carthage, *Epistle* 48.4, 54.13). Note that there was a belief that the invisible Church was eternal, or at least preexistent (probably connected to the concept of the preexistence of Christ as Logos). It had been created before the sun and moon, but was only revealed in the "last days" (the Church age) for the sake of salvation

(see 2 Clement 14, and Hermas, *The Shepherd* 8.1). This strain of thought, running through Cyprian, may have contributed to Augustine's concept of election.

217. *On Rebaptism* 11–13.

218. Cyprian of Carthage, *Epistle* 75.10. See also the letter of Firmilian in Cyprian of Carthage, *Epistle* 74.8.

219. The reception of the Holy Spirit was associated with the imposition of hands in the confirmation. Baptism and confirmation were thought to be parallel to baptism with water and baptism with the Holy Spirit (and fire) (see Cyprian of Carthage, *Epistle* 71.1, 73.7, and *On Rebaptism* 3, 12, 17). Baptism and confirmation were originally one rite, but by this time they were becoming two separate rites, in part because of the practice of infant baptism (see Cyprian of Carthage, *Epistle* 71.1, 72.21). Baptism could be delegated to priests, but only bishops could confirm (see Cyprian of Carthage, *Epistle* 72.9, and *On Rebaptism* 3).

220. Eusebius of Caesarea, *Ecclesiastical History* 6.43. See also *Apostolic Tradition* 14.

221. Eusebius of Caesarea, *Ecclesiastical History* 6.43. Note that the office of exorcist is also mentioned in the letter of Firmilian in Cyprian of Carthage, *Epistle* 74.10. The office of exorcist seems eventually to have been absorbed by the bishops.

222. *On Rebaptism* 11.

223. Cyprian called baptism the sacrament of unity (*Epistle* 75.6). As we have seen, the question of baptism begs the question of rebaptism and baptismal validity. It was, of course, believed that in general baptism defined Church membership (see the letter of Firmilian in Cyprian of Carthage, *Epistle* 74.14, 17). However, a catechumen could be considered a Christian, as in the case of Perpetua. The term *hearer* described the catechumens, and the term *believer* seems to have been reserved for the baptized, except that a confessor was considered a believer, even if not yet baptized (see *On Rebaptism* 11).

224. Rankin, 114.

225. Those who might take the Eucharist unworthily included the uninitiated, who were to be protected from the Eucharist for their own good. It was believed by some that the unbaptized would risk damnation by taking the Eucharist, even out

of ignorance (see the *Apostolic Constitutions* 7.2 [7.25]). In general, however, to receive the Eucharist without confession would be considered unworthy. By the third century, this included penance and reconciliation (Cyprian of Carthage, *Epistle* 9.2, 10.1, *On the Lapsed* 15, 26). For the concept that the Eucharist would be ineffective if one held malice against another (Matt 5:23–24), see the *Didascalia Apostolorum* 11.

226. *Against Novatian* 2, 5. See also Cyprian of Carthage, *Epistle* 73.11–12, 75.2, *On the Unity of the Catholic Church* 6. For Cyprian, the Church is the ark, and the persecution is the flood.

227. Tertullian, *The Prescription Against the Heretics* 31, 33, Cyprian of Carthage, *Epistle* 50.3, 51.13, 25. Cyprian was, of course, not a rigorist and his argument here is aimed at the Novatianists. Cyprian said that rigorism came from a "too rigid philosophy" (Cyprian of Carthage, *Epistle* 51.16).

228. Hippolytus, *Refutation of All Heresies* 9.7.

229. Cyprian of Carthage, *Epistle* 53.13, *On the Lapsed* 15.

230. Cyprian of Carthage, *Epistle* 75.1. I am careful to distinguish what I am calling North African ecclesiology from the North Africans in general, since Cyprian would agree with significant elements of what I am calling the Roman ecclesiology. However, these categories, simplified though they may be, are proven useful by the ongoing controversy between the Donatists of North Africa and Augustine, who though he was North African, held to more of a Roman ecclesiology.

231. Cyprian of Carthage, *Epistle* 72.21, *On the Unity of the Catholic Church* 6. See also the letter of Firmilian in Cyprian of Carthage, *Epistle* 74.18. This was confirmed in the canons of the seventh Council of Carthage. On the Church as mother, see Cyprian of Carthage, *Epistle* 9.3, 10.2, 40.2, 42, *On the Lapsed* 9.

232. Cyprian of Carthage, *Epistle* 54.21, 75.1, 9, *On the Unity of the Catholic Church* 19, 21. See also the letter of Dionysius of Alexandria to Novatian in Eusebius of Caesarea, *Ecclesiastical History* 6.45. Schism was compared to the split between the northern and southern kingdoms in the Old Testament (2 Kgs 17:20–21).

233. Eusebius of Caesarea, *Ecclesiastical History* 6.43.

234. Tertullian, *The Prescription Against the Heretics* 20–21, 28, 32.

235. Tertullian had said that the Holy Spirit would prevent the true Church from going astray (see Tertullian, *The Prescription Against the Heretics* 28). In a sense, the Holy Spirit guarantees apostolic authority. This may be the earliest hint of what would become the doctrine of papal infallibility, since the infallibility of the bishop of Rome is essentially the infallibility of the Church, based on Matthew 16:18, "the gates of Hades will not prevail against it."

236. Cyprian of Carthage, *Epistle* 51.21, 53.2, 54.5. Both baptism and Eucharist are considered sacraments of unity, and the Eucharist especially is described by Cyprian as the safeguard of unity. This is partly because the presider stands in the place of Christ himself. Thus the unity of the Church is connected to the unity of the eucharistic table, which in turn is connected to the unity (and authority) of the episcopacy.

237. Cyprian of Carthage, *Epistle* 9.1, 3–4, 10.2, 11.2, 26.1, *On the Unity of the Catholic Church* 5, 7. See also Tertullian, *The Prescription Against the Heretics* 20.

238. Cyprian of Carthage, *Epistle* 40.2, *On the Unity of the Catholic Church* 5. See also Eusebius of Caesarea, *Ecclesiastical History* 6.43. Cornelius, speaking sarcastically about Novatian, wrote, "[T]his vindicator, then, of the gospel did not know that there should be one bishop in a Catholic church."

CHAPTER 8

1. Eusebius of Caesarea, *Ecclesiastical History* 10.1, 5.

2. Eusebius of Caesarea, *Ecclesiastical History* 8.1. The *Didascalia* describes the arrangement of worshipers within a basilica church (in this case the cathedral). The bishop's throne was at the eastern end, with the priests around the bishop. The laymen were situated closest to the priests, with the laywomen in the back. The deacons functioned as ushers or "doorkeepers," and visitors were questioned before being allowed to join the assembly (*Didascalia Apostolorum* 12). For more detail on the early basilica churches, see Ramsay MacMullen, *The Second Church: Popular Christianity AD 200–400* (Atlanta: Society of Biblical Literature, 2009).

3. This may be the case with the churches of San Clemente and Santa Cecilia in Rome. Beneath the present church of Santa Cecilia are the remains of a Roman house that date from the third century. According to tradition, the house was owned by the family of the martyr Cecilia, and after her death the land was dedicated for perpetual use by the Church. See James L. Papandrea, *Romesick: Making Your Pilgrimage to the Eternal City a Spiritual Homecoming* (Eugene, OR: Wipf & Stock/Cascade Books, 2012).

4. Eusebius of Caesarea, *Ecclesiastical History* 7.23.

5. Eusebius of Caesarea, *Ecclesiastical History* 8.4.

6. Eusebius of Caesarea, *Ecclesiastical History* 8.2.

7. Eusebius of Caesarea, *Ecclesiastical History* 8.13. The reader should keep in mind Eusebius's agenda of supporting the dynasty of Constantine, so favorable assessments of Constantine's family must be taken with a grain of salt.

8. Eusebius of Caesarea, *Ecclesiastical History* 8.6. In the Roman world, prison was not meant to be a long-term sentence, but rather a holding place where one awaited either release or execution or some other sentence such as condemnation to the mines. Therefore, the prisons were not large and did not hold a lot of people.

9. Eusebius of Caesarea, *Ecclesiastical History* 8.12.

10. Eusebius of Caesarea, *Ecclesiastical History* 8.7.

11. Eusebius of Caesarea, *Ecclesiastical History* 8.11.

12. Eusebius of Caesarea, *Ecclesiastical History* 9.5.

13. Eusebius of Caesarea, *Ecclesiastical History* 8.1, 10.4.

14. See James L. Papandrea, *The Wedding of the Lamb: A Historical Approach to the Book of Revelation* (Eugene, OR: Wipf & Stock/Pickwick Publications, 2011).

15. Eusebius of Caesarea, *Ecclesiastical History* 8.16–17, 9.1–3.

16. Eusebius of Caesarea, *Ecclesiastical History* 9.7.

17. Eusebius of Caesarea, *Ecclesiastical History* 8.13.

18. Since the cross was still being used as a method of execution (it would be Constantine himself who would end this practice), the Church was not yet using the cross as a symbol; therefore it is unlikely that the original version of the story would include a cross. The earliest extant image of the cross is a carving on the

wooden doors of the Church of Santa Sabina in Rome. The doors date back to the fifth century. On the other hand, Tertullian does mention the cross as an object of adoration in his *Apology* 16. This was written in response to a pagan mockery of the crucifixion of Christ, which entailed a donkey on a cross as an object of worship by Christians.

19. Eusebius of Caesarea, *Ecclesiastical History* 9.8–9.

20. It is probable that Constantine himself composed the inscription.

21. Eusebius of Caesarea, *Ecclesiastical History* 9.9, 10.5.

22. Eusebius of Caesarea, *Ecclesiastical History* 10.4. Constantine built several basilica-style churches in and around Rome, some on the sites of earliest Christian worship there (see Ramsay MacMullen, *The Second Church: Popular Christianity AD 200–400*).

23. On Sunday as a day of rest, see the *Apostolic Constitutions* 8.4 (8.33).

24. It is not clear how much an emperor would be personally involved in the design and minting of coins. Many of the city mints had stopped making their own coins since the recession of the third century. This may have consolidated more influence in the emperor, although the continuance of pagan imagery on coins minted during Constantine's reign does not necessarily tell us anything about his personal beliefs.

25. Constantine did not persecute the Novatianists. Although they also practiced rebaptism, at least at first, they were apparently not considered heretics by the official councils (see J. Stevenson, *A New Eusebius: Documents Illustrating the History of the Church to AD 337* [London: SPCK, 1957, revised edition 1987], 320).

26. There is a statue of Constantine's mother, St. Helen, in St. Peter's Basilica in Rome. Most scholars believe that the statue was once a statue of a pagan goddess, but that it was altered and a cross was added to honor St. Helen and the tradition that she found the true cross of Jesus.

27. Thus it was Theodosius, not Constantine, who tried to create a true Christian empire in which citizenship was equivalent to Church membership.

28. Constantine knew what Diocletian had known, that the empire was too big for one man to rule; however, he must have hoped that he could do it with the help of the bishops.

29. Aloys Grillmeier, *Christ in Christian Tradition, Volume 1: From the Apostolic Age to Chalcedon (451)* (New York: Oxford University Press, 2004), 110. Another possible way to look at this is that Arius had combined elements of angel Christology inherited from Lucian of Antioch with elements of the spirit Christology of Paul of Samosata to create the fourth-century evolution of adoptionism. Apparently, Arius was heavily influenced by the Antiochenes—Theophilus, Lucian, and Paul—and perhaps also Origen as well.

30. In large part I am indebted to my former professor, Dennis Groh, and his groundbreaking book. See Robert C. Gregg and Dennis E. Groh, *Early Arianism: A View of Salvation* (Philadelphia: Fortress Press, 1981). For a detailed treatment of the Arian controversy, see Lewis Ayres, *Nicaea and Its Legacy: An Approach to Fourth-Century Trinitarian Theology* (Oxford: Oxford University Press, 2004).

31. In the year 260 CE, Dionysius of Rome held a synod that condemned the idea that the Son and Spirit were created (see Grillmeier, *Christ in Christian Tradition*, 156).

32. See James L. Papandrea, *Novatian of Rome and the Culmination of Pre-Nicene Orthodoxy* (Eugene, OR: Wipf & Stock/Pickwick Publications, 2011). Novatian is the first theologian to articulate the doctrine of eternal generation (though he does not call it by that name). Eternal generation was understood to mean that the Son's existence was caused by the Father (and so is contingent and dependent) but the Son is not created (so there is no beginning to his existence). This teaching probably made its way east through Dionysius of Rome and Dionysius of Alexandria.

33. This part of Arius's teaching may be based on certain elements in Origen. The reader should note that most of what we think we know about what Arius taught comes to us as reported by his opponents, so there is some uncertainty as to the accuracy of the report. There is precious little that survives from Arius's own pen.

34. The possibility of degrees of divinity had already been rejected by the mainstream Church, when it was encountered in

gnosticism. Cf. the gnostic (Valentinian) *Letter to Flora* of Ptolemy. This contains the concept of a "lesser" divinity begotten as a different essence from the unbegotten highest God. On the other hand, the precedent for the concept of degrees of divinity may also be found in Philo's *logos*, which could be interpreted as half divine and half created, thus a mediator in between Creator and creation. After the Council of Nicaea, the leader of the so-called Heterousian (or Anomoian) party, Eunomius, taught that there were degrees of createdness, such that the Son of God is created in relation to the Father, but Creator in relation to the rest of creation. The Eunomians were considered more Arian than Arius and argued that the Son was "unlike" the Father, thus nudging those still on the fence to join the pro-Nicene party. For an excellent overview of the history of the Council of Nicaea and its aftermath, see Ayres, *Nicaea and Its Legacy*. Although Ayres does not give Novatian enough credit for his role as a pioneer in orthodox theology, there is no better book for understanding the fourth-century Arian controversy.

35. Note again the influence of the Roman practice of adopting an heir in order to secure the succession of power.

36. The difference in capitalization of the word *son/Son* is for clarity only. It is not meant to imply that Arius would have made this distinction. Such capitalization is a modern convention and was not part of ancient writing.

37. Imagine a dispute between Canada and Mexico. If someone were to be chosen as a mediator, one might seek a mediator who is from the United States, between Canada and Mexico; or one might seek a mediator who has dual citizenship of Canada and Mexico. The former mediator is between Canada and Mexico, but neither Canadian nor Mexican. The latter mediator is both Canadian and Mexican. In the same way, the Arian Jesus is elevated to a state between God and humanity, but is neither God nor (arguably) human, since he has been elevated above humanity. The Nicene Christ is both divine and human.

38. Clement of Alexandria had implied that before creation God was not a Creator, which may have provided Arius with a precedent for saying (or at least being comfortable implying) that

there was a time before God was a Father (see Clement of Alexandria, *The Instructor* 1.9).

39. Novatian, *On the Trinity* 31.3.

40. The assumption on both sides would be that whatever is mutable must be created, and whatever is uncreated (that is, divine) must be immutable. Augustine would later write that whatever is eternal must be immutable (Augustine of Hippo, *On the Trinity* 1.2).

41. For the Catholics, generation begets the same substance. But for Arius and his followers, the ungenerated (the Father) and the generated (the Son) could not be the same substance. For him, unbegotten and begotten were parallel to uncreated and created. For the Nicene bishops, both unbegotten and begotten are uncreated.

42. Ayres, *Nicaea and Its Legacy*, 53.

43. The Nicene Creed is still the standard of orthodoxy for worldwide Christianity, except that the Western churches have an added phrase. Where the Eastern churches affirm that the Holy Spirit proceeds from the Father, the Western churches add the phrase "and the Son" (in Latin, *filioque*), affirming that the Holy Spirit proceeds from the Father and the Son equally. This was added as an attempt to emphasize the equality of the Father and the Son against Arianism.

44. On eternal generation, see Athanasius of Alexandria, *Defense of the Nicene Definition (De Decretis)* 10, 28-32, *Letter to the Clergy of Alexandria* 52. See also Ayres, *Nicaea and Its Legacy*, 143–44. On the other hand, Athanasius's emphasis on the unity of will between Father and Son (by which he means a unity of activity, or inseparable operation) will leave the door open for both Apollinarius and Nestorius. Apollinarius would say that there is only one will between the Father and Son (that the human nature of Christ has no human will, so there is only one will in the person of Christ), and Nestorius would say that while there are two wills, the union between Father and Son is only a cooperation of wills (see Athanasius of Alexandria, *Discourse Against the Arians* 3.25.10, 3.27-28, 3.30.59–67).

45. Some have argued that there is so little that we can be certain is from Arius himself that the very concept of "Arianism" is better understood as a creation of Athanasius. While there is some

merit to this point of view, in the absence of a better way of talking about the controversy, we continue to use the term *Arianism* to describe the teachings of Arius and others who advocated this fourth-century version of adoptionism.

46. According to tradition, Augustine's mother, Monica, remarked to Ambrose of Milan that the eucharistic liturgy was different in Carthage, Rome, and Milan. Ambrose's reply was, "When in Rome, do as the Romans do." It is also the case that after the legalization of the Church, catechesis would shift in emphasis from morality to theology.

47. A good overview of the problem is in J. A. Cerrato, "The Association of the Name Hippolytus with a Church Order Now Known as The Apostolic Tradition," *St. Vladimir's Theological Quarterly* 48, no. 2 (2004): 179–94.

48. *Apostolic Tradition* 41.5–17, 41.13, 42.1. The signing of oneself with the cross probably meant tracing a cross on one's forehead with the thumb of the right hand.

49. *Apostolic Tradition* 17, 20.3.

50. *Apostolic Tradition* 19.1. It would be assumed that even in the case of lay teachers, the bishops held the final authority over the content of the teaching.

51. *Apostolic Tradition* 15, 20.

52. *Apostolic Tradition* 21.

53. *Apostolic Tradition* 20.8. See also Cyprian of Carthage, *On the Unity of the Catholic Church* 18.

54. *Apostolic Tradition* 21.4.

55. *Apostolic Tradition* 19.2. See also *On Rebaptism* 11.

56. Cyprian of Carthage, *Epistle* 72.22.

57. *Apostolic Tradition* 21.27.

58. *Apostolic Tradition* 4 (Eucharistic Prayer), 9.4–5.

59. *Apostolic Tradition* 36.

60. *Apostolic Tradition* 18.

61. *Apostolic Tradition* 37–38.

62. *Apostolic Tradition* 9. As we have seen, this is based on the assumed charismatic authority granted by the presence of the Holy Spirit in the confessor (Matt 10:19–20).

63. *Apostolic Tradition* 8.2–3. See Cyprian of Carthage, *On the Lapsed* 25.

64. *Apostolic Tradition* 11–14.

65. *Apostolic Tradition* 2.

66. See Cyprian of Carthage, *Epistle* 40.2, 51.8, 54.5–6.

67. *Didascalia Apostolorum* 10, 24.

68. *Didascalia Apostolorum* 10, 24.

69. *Didascalia Apostolorum* 25. In reality, as we have seen, the "heretics" also claimed to be faithful to scripture. This was especially true at the Council of Nicaea, when the Arians complained about the addition of the word *homoousios* (which is not found in scripture) to the creed. Thus the *Didascalia* is presenting the perception that orthodoxy is biblical and heresy is not, though it is not really that simple.

70. *Didascalia Apostolorum* 23, 26.

71. *Didascalia Apostolorum* 6–7.

72. *Didascalia Apostolorum* 6. See also *Against Novatian* 1, and Cyprian of Carthage, *Epistle* 51.19.

73. See *Against Novatian* 15, and Cyprian of Carthage, *Epistle* 51.15.

74. *Didascalia Apostolorum* 5, 11.

75. *Didascalia Apostolorum* 11. See also *On Rebaptism* 13.

76. *Didascalia Apostolorum* 10.

77. *Didascalia Apostolorum* 25.

78. *Didascalia Apostolorum* 23.

79. *Didascalia Apostolorum* 15.

80. *Didascalia Apostolorum* 10.

81. *Didascalia Apostolorum* 24, 26.

82. *Didascalia Apostolorum* 6.

83. *Didascalia Apostolorum* 19.

84. *Didascalia Apostolorum* 7, 10.

85. *Didascalia Apostolorum* 5.

86. *Didascalia Apostolorum* 20. See also Cyprian of Carthage, *Epistle* 48.4, 54.13, 75.15, and *On the Unity of the Catholic Church* 20–21. Cf. *On Rebaptism* 12. There may be a pre-Augustinian doctrine of election/perseverance in Cyprian. He quotes Matthew 15:13, saying that if those in the (invisible) Church are planted, they could not be rooted up.

87. *Didascalia Apostolorum* 16.

88. *Didascalia Apostolorum* 20.

89. *Didascalia Apostolorum* 15.

90. *Didascalia Apostolorum* 16. See also Cyprian of Carthage, *Epistle* 72.9, and the *Apostolic Constitutions* 1.2 (1.16, 1.20).

91. *Didascalia Apostolorum* 13.

92. *Didascalia Apostolorum* 12.

93. *Didascalia Apostolorum* 9, 11. See also Cyprian of Carthage, *Epistle* 62.9.

94. *Didascalia Apostolorum* 26.

95. *Apostolic Constitutions* 6.6 (6.30).

96. *Didascalia Apostolorum* 12.

97. *Didascalia Apostolorum* 16, 18–19.

98. *Didascalia Apostolorum* 18–19.

99. *Didascalia Apostolorum* 9, 11, 16.

100. *Didascalia Apostolorum* 16.

101. *Didascalia Apostolorum* 4.

102. *Didascalia Apostolorum* 4.

103. *Didascalia Apostolorum* 8–9. It may be that priests were paid as well.

104. *Didascalia Apostolorum* 9.

105. See the *Apostolic Church Order* 22.

106. *Didascalia Apostolorum* 9.

107. *Didascalia Apostolorum* 6.

108. Here I am indebted to the research of my colleague Stephanie Perdew VanSlyke. I am grateful for her willingness to share some of her research leading to her PhD dissertation.

109. *Apostolic Church Order* 19.

110. *Apostolic Church Order* 20.

111. *Apostolic Church Order* 18.

112. *Apostolic Church Order* 16.

113. *Apostolic Church Order* 12, 16.

114. *Apostolic Constitutions* 2.1 (2.1–2).

115. *Apostolic Constitutions* 2.2 (2.5).

116. *Apostolic Constitutions* 2.3 (2.11).

117. *Apostolic Constitutions* 2.4 (2.26–27).

118. *Apostolic Constitutions* 6.3 (6.17).

119. *Apostolic Constitutions* 2.4 (2.26–27).

120. *Apostolic Constitutions* 6.3 (6.17).

121. *Apostolic Constitutions* 2.4 (2.28).

122. *Apostolic Constitutions* 3.2 (3.20).
123. *Apostolic Constitutions* 2.7 (2.57). See also 7.2 (7.25) for an example of a eucharistic prayer.
124. *Apostolic Constitutions* 5.3 (5.19).
125. *Apostolic Constitutions* 2.3 (2.12, 14, 18, 20, 24).
126. *Apostolic Constitutions* 2.3 (2.16).
127. *Apostolic Constitutions* 6.3 (6.15).
128. *Apostolic Constitutions* 6.3 (6.16).
129. *Apostolic Constitutions* 7.2 (7.24, 29).
130. *Apostolic Constitutions* 7.5 (7.47–49).
131. *Apostolic Constitutions* 7.3 (7.39).
132. *Apostolic Constitutions* 8.4 (8.34).

CHAPTER 9

1. David S. Dockery, *Biblical Interpretation Then and Now: Contemporary Hermeneutics in Light of the Early Church* (Grand Rapids, MI: Baker Book House, 1992), 136. According to Dockery, Augustine joined the Manichees for the same reason that Marcion had gravitated toward docetism: an attempt to find a satisfying answer to the problem of evil.

2. Eusebius criticized the syncretism of the Manichees, saying that their founder, Mani, had "stitched together" various doctrines and heresies (see Eusebius of Caesarea, *Ecclesiastical History* 7.31).

3. Augustine of Hippo, *Tractates on the Gospel of John* 40.9. Although Augustine seems to be referring to Isaiah 7:9, his Latin version is based on the Greek translation in the Septuagint (LXX).

4. Augustine of Hippo, *Confessions* Book 9.

5. Novatian had hinted at this (see Novatian, *On the Trinity* 29.6–11).

6. Justin Martyr, *1 Apology* 43, Tatian, *Address to the Greeks* 7, Theophilus of Antioch, *To Autolycus* 2.27, Irenaeus of Lyons, *Against Heresies* 4.37.1–4. Irenaeus says that humans have free will because we are made in the image of God, and God has free will. Note, however, that angels also have free will (Justin Martyr, *2 Apology* 7, *Dialogue with Trypho* 141, Irenaeus of Lyons, *Against*

Heresies 4.37.1), but animals do not (Justin Martyr, *1 Apology* 43, Theophilus of Antioch, *To Autolycus* 1.6). The consensus among these writers is that if humans did not have free will, then there would be no moral responsibility and evil would be part of creation. That evil is not part of creation, and God as Creator is not responsible for evil, see Justin Martyr, *1 Apology* 44, Tatian, *Address to the Greeks* 11, Theophilus of Antioch, *To Autolycus* 2.17, Clement of Alexandria, *Exhortation to the Greeks* 6, Hippolytus, *Refutation of All Heresies* 1.16. Therefore, whoever is rejected by God is rejected on the basis of God's foreknowledge of the individual's rejection of Christ by his or her own free will, not on the basis of predestination (Justin Martyr, *1 Apology* 44, *Dialogue with Trypho* 141, Irenaeus of Lyons, *Against Heresies* 4.29.2, 4.39.4). As Theophilus had said, "It was not the tree, as some think, but the disobedience, which had death in it" (Theophilus of Antioch, *To Autolycus* 2.25).

7. Arius had combined adoptionism with an Eastern optimism (based on the Stoic concept of virtue as moral progress) which has affinity with the concept of deification, or *theosis*. He had applied these ideas to Christology, which resulted in a soteriology of human effort. In some ways, however, Eastern Christianity was not influenced as much by Augustine and so never lost this classical optimism. Therefore, the East seems to have retained the assumption of free will, resulting in less of an emphasis on original sin.

8. Augustine of Hippo, *On the Spirit and the Letter* 4.

9. Augustine of Hippo, *On the Spirit and the Letter* 52.

10. Augustine of Hippo, *On the Spirit and the Letter* 23.

11. Augustine of Hippo, *On the Spirit and the Letter* 25, 54. By contrast, Pelagius argued (from Plato) that if we know the good, we can do it. For Pelagius, what we need is information, to know what choices to make. For Augustine, what we need is inner healing from God.

12. Augustine of Hippo, *On the Spirit and the Letter* 60.

13. I am indebted to one of my former professors, Dennis E. Groh, for this idea. My understanding of Augustine is shaped in large part by listening to his lectures when I was his teaching assistant. I will always be grateful for his perspective.

14. But see Rodney Stark, *The Victory of Reason: How Christianity Led to Freedom, Capitalism and Western Success* (New

York: Random House, 2006), in which Stark argues that the "Dark Ages" were not really as dark as we've been led to believe. Note that the fifth century also included the fall of the Roman Empire in the West.

15. Though they were the minority in Hippo, and perhaps even in North Africa, in the bigger picture of the worldwide Church, the Catholics were the majority.

16. Eusebius of Caesarea, *Ecclesiastical History* 10.6.

17. Eusebius of Caesarea, *Ecclesiastical History* 10.6.

18. Augustine assumed that the greater affects the lesser, implying that purity purifies the impure (Augustine of Hippo, *On the Trinity* 6.8).

19. Note that the relative uniqueness of Christ is related to ecclesiology as well. If, as the orthodox argued, Christ is unique among humanity, then the Church must be inclusive, since no one can be perfect like Christ. If Arius and Pelagius are right, however, and Christ is more of an example to be followed than a Savior by divine intervention, perfection might be expected of his followers. The less unique Christ is understood to be, the more is expected of believers, so it is arguably the case that for the Arians as well as the rigorists, the Church is meant to be exclusive, only for true believers.

20. Lewis Ayres, *Nicaea and Its Legacy: An Approach to Fourth-Century Trinitarian Theology* (New York: Oxford University Press, 2004), 190, 194, 216.

21. Hilary of Poitiers had written, "Much obscurity is caused by a translation from Greek into Latin, and to be absolutely literal is to be sometimes partly unintelligible" (Hilary of Poitiers, *On the Councils* 9.

22. Aloys Grillmeier, *Christ in Christian Tradition, Volume 1: From the Apostolic Age to Chalcedon (451)* (New York: Oxford University Press, 2004), 334–37.

23. Ibid., 339.

24. Hippolytus, *Against Noetus* 17, *Against Beron* 8. Hippolytus clarified that the full humanity of the Son meant that he did have a human rational soul (mind and will). This means that the person of Christ has two wills, one divine and one human (see Roch Kereszty, *Jesus Christ: Fundamentals of Christology* [New York: Society of St. Paul/Alba House, 2002], 365; cf. Ayres, *Nicaea and Its*

Legacy, 296–97). Note that there is only one will in the Trinity. The three persons of the Trinity do not have one will each for a total of three wills; this is made necessary by the assumption of monotheism, and is demonstrated by the concept of inseparable operation. The will is an attribute of the substance, not a personal property, so that there is one will in the divine substance of the Trinity, and one will in the human substance of the human nature of Christ. Therefore, the will of the divine nature of Christ *is* the will of the Trinity. When Jesus says, "not my will, but yours be done" in the Garden of Gethsemane (Luke 22:42), it is just as accurate to say that the mind/will of the human nature in Christ conforms to the mind/will of the divine nature in Christ, as it is to say that the mind/will of the Son conforms to the mind/will of the Father. The mind/will of the divine nature of the Son *is* the mind/will of the Father (cf. Gregory of Nyssa, *Against Eunomius* 1.34). Origen had also affirmed the human will in Christ, but apparently did not allow that the human nature of Christ had free will. He seems to have feared the same thing as Apollinarius, that a free human will in Jesus might result in sin, and then he would be disqualified as Savior. Whereas Origen had simply implied that the human will of Christ was not free, Apollinarius speculated that Christ had no human will.

    25. Nestorius's term for the two natures was *prosopon*, the same word others were using to talk about the whole person of Christ. Because of this, Nestorianism is often characterized as dividing Christ into "two persons." But this is a good example of how a debate can be exacerbated by the fact that some people were using the same Greek word to mean different things, or in other cases, different words to mean the same thing.

    26. It is also consistent with the doctrine of *communicatio idiomatum* as we saw it in Novatian (see Novatian, *On the Trinity* 13.5, 18.5, 22.9, 24.8–10).

    27. In a document known as the *Bazaar of Heraclides*, it is said that Nestorius agreed with Leo's *Tome* and the Chalcedonian Definition.

    28. Tertullian, *Against Praxeas* 27. See also Eric Osborn, *Tertullian: First Theologian of the West* (Cambridge, UK: Cambridge University Press, 1997), 140.

    29. Leo of Rome, *Epistle* 28.

30. Leo of Rome, *Epistle* 95.

31. Leo of Rome, *Epistle* 28. Cf. Novatian, *On the Trinity* 13.3. The account of the acceptance of Leo's *Tome* changes depending on who is telling the story. Official reports record that the *Tome* was accepted unanimously, with shouts of "Leo speaks for Peter!" Other accounts claim that the bishops were pressured to accept it by the emperor as part of an attempt to secure the supremacy of Rome (see Matthias F. Wahba, *Monophysitism Reconsidered* [Sacramento, CA: St. Mary Coptic Orthodox Church, n.d.], 8–10).

32. Tertullian, *Against Praxeas* 27.11, *On the Flesh of Christ* 13, Novatian, *On the Trinity* 24.9. Cf. Hippolytus, *On Christ and Antichrist* 4, *Against Beron* 1–2.

33. There is some continuing legacy of traditional schools of thought in Alexandria and Antioch that contributes to the differences in perspective. As Wahba points out, "While Antioch formulated its christology against Apollinarius and Eutyches, Alexandria did against Arius and Nestorius" (*Monophysitism Reconsidered*, 12). In other words, as authors often attempted to define Christology in reaction to perceived heresy, the Antiochenes, building on the foundation of Theophilus, reacted against the Alexandrian emphasis on unity and proposed a distinction of natures. Thus, in the realm of theology Antioch tended to lean toward adoptionism and, in the realm of Christology, toward Nestorianism. On the other hand, the Alexandrians reacted against the Antiochene emphasis on distinction (perceived as too much separation) and proposed a unity of natures that confused the natures. Thus, in the realm of theology, Alexandria tended to lean toward modalism and, in the realm of Christology, toward monophysitism. Even Cyril of Alexandria had at one time been a follower of Apollinarius. In the past it was conventional to say that the Eastern Church emphasized distinction while the Western Church emphasized unity. It has now been recognized that this is an oversimplification, if only because there are orthodox in both the East and the West. If one put Alexandria with the West, however, there is still some truth to it.

34. There were some early attempts at reconciliation, most notably by the emperors Justinian and Zeno.

35. The Oriental Orthodox Church includes the Coptic Orthodox Church of Alexandria, as well as the Armenian, Syrian,

Ethiopian, and Malankara Indian churches (Wahba, *Monophysitism Reconsidered*, 3).

36. Wahba, *Monophysitism Reconsidered*, 12–14. The Coptics agree that Eutyches was a heretic.

37. The phrase "in two natures" from Leo's *Tome* is still thought by the Coptics to leave too much room for a separation of natures. They prefer the phrase "from two natures." But this phrase was rejected at Chalcedon because it was perceived as leaving too much room for a confusion of natures after the incarnation.

38. Wahba, *Monophysitism Reconsidered*, 15.

39. Irenaeus of Lyons, *Against Heresies* 2.5.4. Irenaeus wrote that it is inappropriate to say that God is bound by anything.

40. Sometimes the title *Cur Deus Homo?* is translated "Why God Became Man." However, there is no verb in the title, so a better translation is "Why the God-Man?" Ultimately, it is not about the incarnation per se but about the two natures of Christ, the "God-Man."

41. On the balance of mercy and justice in God, see Clement of Alexandria, *The Instructor* 1.8.

42. Anselm was probably influenced by the concept of a debt of honor, or the allegiance that would be owed to a landowner by his tenants in a feudal society.

43. The label *satisfaction theory* is also preferable because it avoids confusion with a later theory of atonement known as *penal substitution*.

44. James L. Papandrea, *Spiritual Blueprint: How We Live, Work, Love, Play, and Pray* (Liguori, MO: Liguori Publications, 2010), 51–53.

45. Note that the issue here is the question of whether Adam's sin affected only his person or his nature. Pelagius would argue that Adam's sin only affected him as an individual, not human nature in general. Anselm, however (and to a certain extent Augustine), would argue that since Adam and Eve constituted the whole of humanity at the time, when they sinned their sin affected all of humanity through the universality of human nature. If Pelagius was right, and Adam's sin affected only his person, then there is no original sin, and Adam (and indeed Christ) influences us only by example. If, however, one applies the concept of consub-

stantiality to human nature, then Adam's sin affects us in a way that can only be counteracted by Christ's consubstantiality with humanity. This arguably demonstrates that Arian and Pelagian salvation is more of an individual salvation, while Augustine's and Anselm's soteriology leans more toward the corporate (see Augustine of Hippo, *On Original Sin* 16, and Anselm of Canterbury, *On the Virgin Conception and Original Sin*).

46. Note that Clement of Alexandria had said that involuntary sin would not be held against a person. In fact, he said there were two types of involuntary sin; sins committed in ignorance, and sins committed through necessity (Clement of Alexandria, *Miscellanies* 2.14).

47. In this sense, Abelard was influenced by Augustine and his emphasis on love as the primary motivation.

48. For the story of Abelard's life in his own words, see his autobiography, *The Story of My Misfortunes* (*Historia Calamitatum*). Abelard's relationship with Heloise is famous and has been the subject of numerous books and films.

49. Note that each christological position assumes a certain anthropology and necessarily implies a certain soteriology. For example, adoptionism assumes an optimism about humanity that allows that humans could progress to perfection and earn their adoption by God. Adoptionist Christology is one in which Christ is the pioneer of self-salvation. The Savior saves by setting the example for those who may follow in his footsteps. Adoptionist Christology is a Christology of ascent and therefore adoptionist soteriology is ultimately a salvation by human effort—it's what *we* do that saves us, not what Christ did. The grace of God is defined as God's gift of the teaching of Jesus and the example that he set for us. Therefore, the mainstream Church reasoned that if the Adoptionists were right, most (if not all) humans have little hope of salvation, and this is what gave the Arian controversy its urgency in the fourth century. It was one thing for theologians to argue whether Christ was coeternal in the past with the Father, but many Christians worried that if salvation required earning God's favor, then all hope is lost. On the other extreme, the soteriology implied by docetism, gnosticism, and modalism is a salvation of divine intervention, but without any human element. In each case, Christ

is not really a human being, so his interaction with humanity is as divine revealer but not as representative of humanity. This is a version of a Christology of descent, but one in which the descent only goes so far. Christ came only to bring secret knowledge, only to a spiritual elite who were predestined to it, or in the case of modalism the Father comes "in disguise," but in neither case does Christ truly experience the human condition. Thus he is of God, but not one of us. In contrast to these extremes, the mainstream Church affirmed that for Christ to save us, he had to be both divine and one of us. And as one of us, he made it clear that God's love and forgiveness are offered to all people, not just to an elite few.

Subject Index

267, 270–71, 274, 317–19, 325, 328
Eutyches, 216–19, 226, 238, 240, 332–33
Exposure of infants, 19, 35, 101, 251–52

Filioque, 202, 212–13, 324
First Cause, 103, 111

Generation, 96, 103, 107–9, 145, 184, 186, 239, 242, 323–24
Grace, 70, 78, 81–82, 169–70, 174, 201, 203–7, 209–10, 222, 224–25, 251, 334

Hierarchy: within the Trinity, 96, 103, 108, 117, 237
Hippolytus, 102, 105–11, 115, 129, 140, 146–48, 151–53, 162, 173–74, 192, 237, 269–81, 287–90, 296, 301, 303–4, 307, 310, 318, 325, 329, 330, 332; questions of authorship, 107, 287, 289
Historia Augusta, 250, 309
Human effort. *See under* Salvation
Human representation. *See under* Salvation
Hybrid Christology. *See under* Christology
Hymns, 45, 54–55, 63, 143, 198, 258, 264–65
Hypostatic (personal) union, 215, 217, 240

Ignatius of Antioch, 4, 13, 17, 24–28, 32, 42, 51–52, 56–57,

61, 63, 147–48, 246, 251, 253–54, 262–63, 266–68, 270–71, 278, 281–82, 287, 292, 304–5, 314; and authorship, 27
Immutability/mutability, 69, 79, 94, 103, 107, 109, 111, 117, 186, 214, 216, 241, 279, 290
Impassibility/passibility, 68, 72, 94–95, 241–42, 274
Incarnation, 8, 55, 57, 63–68, 71, 73, 78–81, 86–88, 94, 96, 104, 108–10, 114–15, 117, 129–30, 140, 142–43, 190, 192, 213–16, 223, 233, 237, 240, 246, 255, 257, 265, 273–74, 280, 292, 300, 333
Incorruptibility. *See* Corruptibility
Inseparable operation, 104, 232, 241, 301, 324, 331

Jerome, 135–36, 248, 258, 278, 284, 290, 294–95, 299
Jerusalem, 8, 11, 35, 41, 44, 64, 78–79, 82, 87, 99, 112, 130, 193, 279, 295
Justin Martyr, 14, 37–42, 46, 50, 52–53, 58, 92, 100, 121, 147, 246, 249, 252, 255–58, 261–63, 265–77, 280–81, 292, 295–96, 308, 328–29

Katharoi, 165. *See also* Novationists
Kenosis, 117, 237, 242; *see also under* Christology

Works by the Author
from Other Publishers

Trinity 101, 2012

Romesick: Making Your Pilgrimage to the Eternal City a Spiritual Homecoming, 2012

Novatian of Rome and the Culmination of Pre-Nicene Orthodoxy, 2011

How to Be a Saint, 2011

The Wedding of the Lamb: A Historical Approach to the Book of Revelation, 2011

Spiritual Blueprint: How We Live, Work, Love, Play, and Pray, 2010

Pray (Not Just Say) the Lord's Prayer, 2010

"Between Two Thieves: Novatian of Rome and Kenosis Christology," in *Studies on Patristic Texts and Archaeology: If These Stones Could Speak…Essays in Honor of Dennis Edward Groh*, George Kalantzis and Thomas F. Martin, eds., 2009

The Trinitarian Theology of Novatian of Rome: A Study in Third-Century Orthodoxy, 2008

For more information about the author, visit
www.JimPapandrea.com